ID0463064

Donovan's Devils

Also by Albert Lulushi

Operation Valuable Fiend:
The CIA's First Paramilitary Strike Against the Iron Curtain

Donovan's Devils

OSS Commandos Behind Enemy Lines—Europe, World War II

ALBERT LULUSHI

Arcade Publishing
New York

First Edition

Arcade Publishing books may be purchased in bulk at special discounts for sales promotion, corporate gifts, fund-raising, or educational purposes. Special editions can also be created to specifications. For details, contact the Special Sales Department, Arcade Publishing, 307 West 36th Street, 11th Floor, New York, NY 10018 or arcade@skyhorsepublishing.com.

Arcade Publishing® is a registered trademark of Skyhorse Publishing, Inc.®, a Delaware corporation.

Visit our website at www.arcadepub.com.
Vist the author's website at www.albertlulushi.com.

10 9 8 7 6 5 4 3 2

Library of Congress Cataloging-in-Publication Data

Names: Lulushi, Albert, author.
Title: Donovan's Devils: OSS commandos behind enemy lines: Europe, World
    War II / Albert Lulushi.
Description: First edition. | New York: Arcade Publishing, 2016. | Includes
    bibliographical references and index.
Identifiers: LCCN 2015037691 | ISBN 9781628725674 (hardcover: alk. paper) |
    ISBN 9781628726220 (Ebook ISBN)
Subjects: LCSH: World War, 1939-1945—Secret service—United States. | World
    War, 1939-1945—Commando operations—Europe. | United States. Office of
    Strategic Services—History. | Donovan, William J. (William Joseph),
    1883-1959. | Holohan, William V.
Classification: LCC D810.S7 L727 2016 | DDC 940.54/8673094—dc23 LC record
    available at http://lccn.loc.gov/2015037691

Cover design by Owen Corrigan

Printed in the United States of America

To Enit, Alex, Anna, and Tereza

We were not afraid to make mistakes because we were not afraid to try things that had not been tried before.

—William J. Donovan, Director of the
Office of Strategic Services, September 28, 1945

OSS was expected, much as we are now, to make sense of a world in turmoil and, where possible, to change it for the better. The methods to accomplish that mission were—and still are—as broad as the mission itself. . . . Whatever the means, the goal was always the same: To reach behind the battle lines, either to learn about the enemy or to attack him directly. To strike in any possible way, by giving our fighting forces the advantage of intelligence or by giving resistance movements the advantages of equipment, training, and—most of all—hope.

—A. B. Krongard, Executive Director of the
Central Intelligence Agency, June 7, 2002

Contents

List of Maps and Documents

Acknowledgments

I am grateful to all those who made it possible for me to write this book. They include: employees at the National Archives in College Park, Maryland, and the US Army Military Institute in Carlisle, Pennsylvania, who helped me track hundreds of documents from their archives; Mr. Charles Pinck, president of the OSS Society, for his efforts in keeping the OSS spirit alive; and family members of OSS and OG personnel who shared memories of their fathers' activities during World War II.

I received tremendous help and encouragement from David Robarge, CIA chief historian, who patiently reviewed manuscript drafts and recommended numerous ways for improving it.

A big thank you goes to my editors at Skyhorse Publishing: Cal Barksdale, who provided great guidance in defining the scope and focus of the book at the beginning and steered it throughout the publishing process; and Maxim Brown, who edited the manuscript meticulously.

Finally, a big thank you to my family for contributing to the creation of this book and related content: Anna and Enit patiently scoured bookstores in France and Italy to collect numerous research materials; Alex provided invaluable contribution to the design of the apps associated with the book; Esmeralda graced the first Fan Club cover page with her image; and "Slim Shady" kept an eye on everyone. I could not have done it without your help!

Introduction

The Office of Strategic Services was a unique experiment in the history of the United States government's agencies and institutions. It came to life thanks to the unwavering efforts of William J. Donovan, its founder and director, who was convinced that the president needed a central organization to collect, coordinate, and analyze intelligence and conduct secret operations or other activities in the interest of the country before and during World War II. In fulfilling Donovan's vision, the OSS became the first central intelligence agency of the United States, the precursor to the CIA, which "has never looked more like its direct ancestor, the OSS, than it does right now," in the words of General Michael Hayden, director of the CIA between 2006 and 2009. But the OSS was much more than an intelligence organization. It engaged in commando-type actions, special and paramilitary operations, psychological warfare, covert propaganda and morale operations, and other activities, which today we associate with the Special Operations forces. Using today's concepts and vocabulary, the OSS of the 1940s pioneered the convergence of intelligence and military operations into one organization that provides full spectrum intelligence activities.

Much has been written over the years about the "Oh, So Secret" OSS—the cloak-and-dagger organization that conducted daring spying and intelligence activities against the Axis powers and their interests in

Europe, North Africa, the Middle East, and Asia. Many authors have focused on the "Oh, So Social" OSS—home to the well-connected elites, Donovan's "PhDs who could win a bar fight," star athletes, and entertainment personalities.

When I set out to write *Donovan's Devils*, I wanted to tell the story of a different OSS, that of ordinary soldiers, first- and second-generation immigrants, who volunteered for dangerous duty behind enemy lines and risked their lives in France, Italy, the Balkans, and elsewhere in Europe. They dropped in enemy territory by air or sea, often blind and in the dead of night, and then proceeded to operate for days, weeks, and even months, hundreds of miles away from the closest Allied troops. They were men of action who created havoc in the enemy's rear, disrupted communication lines, organized the native resistance, and rescued downed flyers, nurses, and escaped prisoners of war. The enemy showed them no mercy and sometime even their closest friends betrayed them, but they carried out their assignments with honor.

As I began sifting through OSS records at the National Archives to gather materials for the book, I quickly realized that it is impossible to provide a full recounting of these missions within the confines of one book. Thousands of personnel planned and carried out hundreds of special operations during World War II. Therefore, I limited the scope first by geography and focused on missions conducted in the Mediterranean and European theaters of operations. Then, I further narrowed the scope to focus primarily on missions conducted by teams of the OSS Operational Groups Command.

The OGs bear a close resemblance in structure and style to the Special Operations teams of today. Like the Navy SEALs or the US Army Delta Force teams, they operated deep in enemy territory—not in disguise as secret agents but in full uniform like regular soldiers—lived off the land for extended periods, and conducted military-like actions against enemy objectives. They distinguished themselves everywhere they fought and yet their story has not received the attention it deserves. I hope *Donovan's Devils* fills the gap by tracing the evolution of the OGs through a handful of missions they conducted in Europe.

I expected the book to be a story of the OSS coming late to the party and having to learn quickly—the Germans and the British after all had conducted special operations and irregular warfare actions for almost four years by the time the first OG teams arrived in North Africa in 1943. I expected it to be a story of zealous neophytes—"the glorious amateurs," Donovan called them affectionately—who had to show what they were worth and earn the respect of the military hierarchy, always skeptical of unorthodox warfare. Moreover, I expected it to be a story of baptism through the fire, sacrifice, determination to succeed, and significant accomplishments. *Donovan's Devils* is all that.

However, I was surprised that the story also became one of crimes committed during war for various reasons—blind obedience to orders, political motives, revenge, and greed. *Donovan's Devils* describes such crimes as well as the attempts after the war to investigate them and bring the perpetrators to justice. The capture and execution of fifteen OGs of the Ginny team in March 1944 was the largest loss of life that the OSS suffered in any of its missions. The trial of German General Anton Dostler in October 1945 for ordering the execution of these men was the first war crimes trial after World War II. It established the legal precedent that obedience to superior orders is not a valid defense against war crime prosecutions, which opened the way to holding accountable other war criminals at the Nuremberg trials and other judicial proceedings that followed. The tragic death in December 1944 of Major William V. Holohan, commander of the OSS mission Mangosteen-Chrysler, led to a twelve-year-long saga in the United States and Italy to bring justice and closure to the case. In the end, it became an example of the importance we place on rule of law and due process, even when sometimes the cost is justice delayed or justice denied.

Investigating and trying these cases raised many questions at the time. How to investigate war crimes when the perpetrators destroy the evidence? How to reconstruct what truly happened when all the witnesses to the crime were also involved in it? How to determine the degree of guilt and decide who to punish and who to let go free? How to render justice in a fair and expedient way? Should military commissions try suspects? Or should they receive the wider protections of military tribunals? What to do if justice cannot be rendered? Should the United States extradite intelligence officers to another country to face justice?

With our military engaged around the world and intelligence operations as strong as ever overseas, questions like these come up today on a regular basis. By showing how the United States approached and answered these questions in the 1940s and 1950s, I hope that *Donovan's Devils* can also help us answer them today.

List of Acronyms

AFHQ	Allied Forces Headquarters
CFLN	*Comité Français de Libération Nationale* or French Committee of National Liberation
CID	Criminal Investigation Division
CLN	*Comitato di Liberazione Nazionale* or National Liberation Committee
CLNAI	*Comitato di Liberazione Nazionale per l'Alta Italia* or National Liberation Committee for Upper Italy
COI	Coordinator of Information
CSDIC	Combined Services Detailed Interrogation Center
EMFFI	*État-Major des Forces Françaises de l'Intérieur* or General Staff of the French Forces of the Interior
FFI	*Forces Françaises de l'Intérieur* or French Forces of the Interior
JAG	Judge Advocate General
JCS	Joint Chiefs of Staff
NCO	Noncommissioned officer

OG   Operational Group

OKW   *Oberkommando der Wehrmacht*, the German Supreme Command of the Armed Forces

OSS   Office of Strategic Services

OVRA *Organizzazione per la Vigilanza e la Repressione dell'Antifascismo* or Organization for Vigilance and Repression of Anti-Fascism.

SAS   Special Air Service

SD   *Sicherheitsdienst* or Security Service, the intelligence organization of the SS and the Nazi Party.

SFHQ Special Forces Headquarters

SHAEF Supreme Headquarters Allied Expeditionary Forces

SI   Secret Intelligence

SIM   *Servizio Informazioni Militare* or Military Intelligence Service of Italy

SO   Special Operations

SOE   Special Operations Executive

SS   *Schutzstaffel* or Protection Squadron, the paramilitary organization of the Nazi Party.

STO   *Service du Travail Obligatoire* or Compulsory Work Service

T/5   Technician Fifth Grade

Donovan's Devils

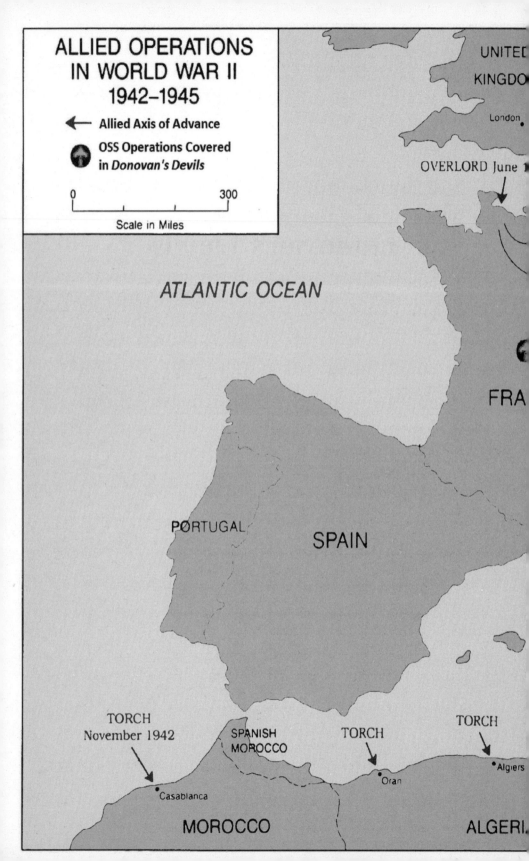

ALLIED OPERATIONS
IN WORLD WAR II
1942–1945

← Allied Axis of Advance

OSS Operations Covered
in *Donovan's Devils*

0   300

Scale in Miles

UNITED
KINGDO

London

OVERLORD June 1

ATLANTIC OCEAN

FRA

PORTUGAL

SPAIN

TORCH
November 1942

SPANISH
MOROCCO

TORCH

TORCH

Oran

Algiers

Casablanca

MOROCCO

ALGERI

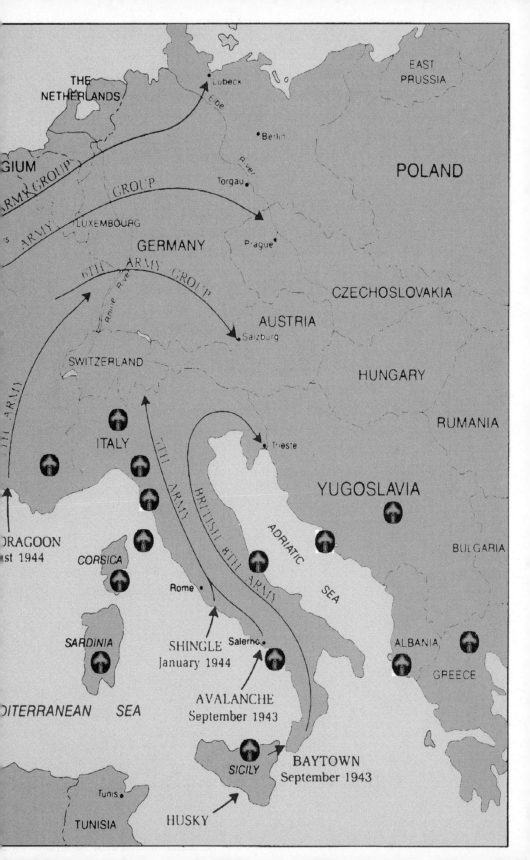

Prologue

In the northeastern coast of Corsica only fifty-six miles from mainland Italy lies Bastia, the island's ancient capital and its largest port. The city is nestled at the base of Cap Corse on a narrow strip of land between the Tyrrhenian Sea to the east and the Sierra di Pignu that rises over three thousand feet above the city to the west. On October 1943, Bastia had been the exit point for German troops and their Fascist allies as they evacuated Sardinia and Corsica. In the afternoon of February 27, 1944, signs of the pitched battle between the retreating Germans and the French resistance forces pursuing them were still very visible in Bastia's streets and on the walls of its medieval citadel. Scars of tracer bullets and craters of artillery shells pockmarked the quays of the commercial port, known as Nouveau Port, and the cobblestone dock of the smaller and older Vieux Port, where local fishermen moored their boats.

In the northernmost dock of the Nouveau Port, in an area cordoned off from the rest of the waterfront, the crews of two American patrol torpedo boats, PT 203 and PT 204, were preparing to put out to sea. Both vessels were seventy-eight-foot PT boats built by Higgins Industries of New Orleans in the second half of 1942 and commissioned on January 20, 1943, at the Municipal Yacht Basin in Lake Pontchartrain. Part of Motor Torpedo Boat Squadron Fifteen, also known as PTRon 15, they had been the first American PT boats to arrive in the Mediterranean at the end of April 1943 and operated as a unit of the British Coastal Forces.[1] Since their arrival, they had participated in actions against the Axis forces across the western Mediterranean, in North Africa, Sicily, the southern Italian coast, and now in the eastern Tyrrhenian Sea along the Tuscan and Ligurian coast.

Patrol torpedo boats were the fastest United States warships afloat at the time. They could take on everything from canoes to battleships and submarines. Enemy tanks and trucks occasionally appeared on their tally sheets, and shooting down enemy planes was one of the most satisfying tasks for the crews. The PT boat could attack the enemy whenever it was within reach, whether on or under the sea, on the land, and in the air.[2] Its hull was constructed of two layers of cross-hatched mahogany wood with a layer of canvas treated with antirot paint installed between the planking. The cabin exterior and interior compartments were plywood and mahogany. By design, the weight of the PT boats was kept to a minimum to maximize range of operations, speed, and maneuverability. In the words of John F. Kennedy, the most famous captain of a PT boat, they were "small, fast, versatile, strongly armed vessels."[3]

A PT boat carried along the port and starboard sides of the fan-tail—the after end of the main deck—two depth charges and four 21" Mark XIII torpedoes. Crewmembers called the torpedoes "fish," but the torpedomen referred to them affectionately as the "lovely ladies."[4] Mounted on the fantail was a 40-millimeter Bofors cannon, which required four men to operate and was equally effective for antiaircraft and surface fire. It was a modified version of the M1 air-cooled cannon originally produced for the United States Army. Its maximum range was 10,750 yards, and the antiaircraft ceiling was 23,500 feet. The fire rate was 120 rounds per minute. The ammunition was loaded from the top in four-round clips. Each round weighed 4.75 pounds, and the projectile it fired weighed almost two pounds.[5]

In the midsection there were two sets of twin Browning .50 cal-iber machine guns mounted on turrets on the port and starboard sides of the cockpit. The twin .50s were as much an icon of a PT boat's image as its torpedoes and could unleash deadly fire against air and surface targets. They were the same version of machine guns mounted on aircraft and could feed ammunition either from the left side or the right using disintegrating link belts. They could fire ball, armor-piercing, incendiary, and tracer ammunition at a rate of 750–850 rounds per minute. The crews preferred to mix one armor-piercing to one tracer round because it combined lethal power with ease of aiming. Their maximum range was 7,200 yards and the effective range about 2,000 yards.[6]

Mounted in the forecastle—the forward area of the boat—was a 20-millimeter Oerlikon antiaircraft gun so powerful that it had earned the name "cannon." A sixty-round drum magazine mounted on the top of the gun housed the ammunition, usually high explosive tracer or incendiary rounds weighing approximately one half pound each. It had a maximum range of 4,800 yards with a ceiling of ten thousand feet, but the effective range was about one thousand yards. A gunner and a loader worked together to replace the quite heavy magazine, cock the gun, fire it, and clear any jams that occurred. They trained until they achieved a rate of fire between 250 and 300 rounds per minute. The best crews practiced with closed eyes so they could perform the same tasks instinctively even in total darkness.[7]

Three 1,500-horsepower Packard W-14 M2500 gasoline engines with twelve cylinders powered the PT boat. Each engine turned a separate propeller shaft, enabling PT boats to reach a maximum speed of forty-one knots or about forty-seven miles per hour. In the midsection of the deck, the PT boats had a mast with a radar mounted on top. The PT boats were the smallest Navy vessels to carry radar, which was indispensable for detecting enemy boats at a distance.[8]

PT boats were painted dark grey and red below the water line for camouflage. PT 203 was a notable exception because it had huge shark jaws painted around its bow. For this reason, it carried the nickname *Shark's Head*. PT 204's nickname was *Aggie Maru*, the Corsican dialect version of Agatha Mary.[9]

As the sun set behind the mountains, Lieutenant Junior Grade Eugene S. A. Clifford, US Naval Reserve, the senior officer in charge that evening, began the predeparture check of each boat. Mishaps happened to PT boats when loose wiring caused navigation lights or even the powerful searchlights to switch on accidentally and expose their position to the enemy.[10] The mission that February night required particular stealth. The PT boats would carry a group of American commandos 120 miles across the Ligurian Sea, drop them at a pinpoint near the port of La Spezia, and wait off the coast to pick them up when they had finished their mission on land. On the way to the pinpoint and back, they would cross the busy shipping lanes between Livorno, La Spezia, and Genoa, which the Germans patrolled regularly and protected with their *Schnellboote*, or S-boats, the PT boats counterparts in the *Kriegsmarine*, or the German navy.

Clifford had finished the inspection of PT 204 when the commando crews arrived in two trucks. There were nineteen of them altogether, four officers and fifteen enlisted men. Clifford knew most of them from prior missions they had conducted together over the past three months. They came from a unit formally known as Unit A, First Contingent, Operational Groups, 2677th Headquarters Company Experimental (Provisional), attached to the Allied Forces Headquarters (AFHQ). Everyone knew them as the Italian OGs. They were first- or second-generation Italian Americans and had all volunteered to join the Operational Group Command of the Office of Strategic Services to conduct sabotage operations and foment guerrilla war in enemy territory deep behind the frontlines.

First Lieutenant Albert R. Materazzi, the executive officer of the OG unit, was in command of the operation that night. He instructed the enlisted men to carry the weapons and equipment from the trucks into the forward cabin below deck of each boat. Then he asked the officers to join him in the charthouse of PT 204 for a final review of the mission objectives. The charthouse was the nerve center of the PT boat from where the captain of the boat, or the skipper, directed its movements. It contained the radar display, radio communications gear, and navigational maps. It had mahogany plywood walls, several rectangular windows looking out in front of the boat, and a thin sheet of airplane cloth atop. Moisture was the enemy of the equipment and maps in the charthouse so the crew took great care to keep it waterproof at all times.

Besides Materazzi and Clifford, the officers gathered in the charthouse included Lieutenant Junior Grade Wittibort, skipper for PT 203, Captain Donald B. Wentzel, who had come along as an observer, and the two officers who would lead the men in the mission ashore, First Lieutenants Vincent J. Russo and Paul J. Trafficante.[11] Materazzi explained that the objective of the mission, code-name Ginny, was to demolish the railroad tunnel entrances and roadbed fill on the La Spezia–Genoa line, roughly five hundred yards southeast of Stazione Framura. This railroad was one of the main supply arteries the Germans used to provision their forces on the Cassino and Anzio frontlines, several hundred miles to the south. It had been very difficult for the Allies to interrupt the flow of trains along this line from the air. The railroad snaked along the Ligurian coast in mountainous terrain with most of the tracks hidden in long tunnels. Materazzi laid out several aerial photographs that American and British reconnaissance planes had taken in the past few days. They showed about a thousand feet of exposed tracks between two tunnels at Stazione Framura. Materazzi explained that the tunnel entrance southeast of Stazione Framura was the weakest point of the railroad because it was the only single-track stretch in the La Spezia–Genoa line.

The plan was to proceed to the pinpoint by PT boat and land thirteen enlisted men and two officers in rubber boats. They were to follow a natural ravine to the target. A security party headed by Lieutenant Trafficante was to go ahead first, neutralize the signal house at the eastern end of the fill, and investigate the tunnel entrance. After they had established security, the working party led by Lieutenant Russo would proceed to the target, and after a complete survey, proceed to demolish it. Materazzi would remain with the boats, maintain communications with the shore parties, and move in to pick them up when they had finished the mission.

Materazzi finished the briefing and everyone moved to his assigned position in each boat. The mooring lines were untied from the forward and aft cleats and the boats got on their way at 1800 hours. They were still inside Bastia Harbor when the radar of PT 204 stopped working. They had to go back and transfer all the personnel and equipment to the standby PT 210. This caused a delay of forty-five minutes, the boats finally clearing the port of Bastia at 1845 hours. A course straight north across the Ligurian Sea would take them from Bastia to the pinpoint for the operation. But on the way, the radar picked up several possible enemy vessels. It was necessary to change course to avoid possible contact. At about 2230 hours, they were four miles off the coast when they observed lights and could discern shore in the dark. From this time onward, the craft proceeded on silent engines. The men came on deck with their equipment and began inflating the rubber boats in preparation for landing. Clifford set course for landfall southeast of Stazione Framura. All he had to go by were his calculations and the instruments in the cockpit. The black light mounted on the cockpit—the only exposed light topside—shone ultraviolet rays and illuminated the phosphorous letters and numbers on the dashboard. Its visibility was limited to only a few feet, which made it ideal for night work. Total darkness enveloped the boat. The night was moonless, the weather rainy, the sky overcast, and the visibility zero.

As the craft moved closer, the men aboard were able to distinguish two mountains to the north, and since it appeared that this might be the pinpoint, the craft headed in that direction. By 0030 hours, it became apparent that they were at the wrong place, so they turned south. A short time later, they saw lights on the shore, which they reckoned to be Stazione Framura. This was confirmed when they spotted a steep cliff three hundred yards south and fifty feet from the shore, which their maps showed to be Scoglia Ciamia. The boats proceeded about five hundred yards southeast of Scoglia Ciamia and stopped. Aboard PT 204, Lieutenant Russo guided the debarking of the engineers, Technicians Fifth Grade (T/5) DiScalfani, Leone, Sirico, Savino, Noia, Lepore, Amoruso, and Sorbello. The men lowered the rubber raft over the side of the boat. Two of them stepped down into the raft and the rest of the crew handed down the packages of explosives and weapons. There was an offshore wind from the northeast, but the sea was calm, which made it easy to hold the raft firmly against the PT boat. When all the equipment and men were aboard the rubber raft, Russo shook hands with Materazzi and climbed into the raft. The crew unfastened the lines that secured the rubber raft to the PT boat and began to row toward the shore. A second raft released from PT 210 followed them at thirty yards' distance. In it were Lieutenant Trafficante and the security party, Technical Sergeant Vieceli, Sergeants Mauro and Aromando, and T/5 Libardi and Squatrito.

Everybody aboard the PT boats was tense. They were already one-and-one-half hours behind schedule, fifteen of their brethren had just disappeared in the darkness headed toward enemy shore, and they could come under fire at any moment. The gunners were in their battle stations ready to open fire if the enemy detected the PT boats or the rubber crafts approaching the shore. At 0145 hours, Materazzi's walkie-talkie radio crackled and Lieutenant Russo reported that he had reached shore but could see only sheer cliffs. Materazzi directed him to row northward until they found the ravine that would lead them to the tunnel entrance. At 0200 hours, Russo reported that they had found a suitable landing spot. At that time, the boat party observed lights on shore just south of Scoglia Ciamia, and they alerted the shore party. Russo made a personal reconnaissance and climbed the mountain in front of him. He heard a train northeast of him, however, and realized that they had landed south of the pinpoint. At 0245 hours, Russo reported that it would take them at least an hour-and-a-half to reach the target and asked for permission to remain ashore and be picked up the following night.

The mission timetable called for departure from the pinpoint at 0330 so that they could put enough distance between the boats and the coast in the cover of darkness. While the boat party was prepared to wait until 0400, Clifford and Materazzi felt that it would take Lieutenant Russo and his men until 0530 hours to reach the target, demolish it, and return to the boats. By that time, it would be daylight and the entire party would be exposed to discovery and attacks by shore batteries, enemy boats, or aircraft. Thus, Materazzi ordered the men to abandon the mission and return to the boat. Russo and Trafficante led their men to the rubber rafts and everyone returned to the PT boats at 0315. The crews helped men, equipment, and rafts aboard and then headed straight south toward Bastia where they arrived at 0730. By mid-morning, the OSS team returned to their base in L'Île-Rousse. Before dismissing them, Materazzi boosted their spirits by reminding them that although they had not been able to demolish the tunnel entrances that night, they had been able to make a good reconnaissance of the target. They were in a great position to succeed the next time around.

A casual observer of the OSS commando operation against the Italian coast that night might have seen its outcome as a setback. But a wider frame of reference would have shown a different picture. Within less than three years, the United States had gone from being a country sitting on the sidelines of the conflict that had engulfed the world to a country that had committed unprecedented human, material, and technical resources to defeating the Axis powers. It was a total war on all fronts, in which millions of Americans from all branches of the military had engaged the enemy in open combat. It was also a war that required new capabilities to spy against the enemy, carry out sabotage activities, and engage the adversary far away from the front lines. The Germans first and then the British in the early years of the war had discovered the great potential of covert warfare to create heavoc in the enemy rear areas and to tie up significant enemy troops that would otherwise be fighting at the front.

The United States had created the Office of Strategic Services to learn from this experience and to develop similar capabilities for the American war effort. The OSS was an organization without precedent in the United States government, but within a short amount of time it had been able to build assets and train personnel to engage in covert opertions like the one attempted on the night of February 27–28, 1944, in Italy.

CHAPTER 1
Office of Strategic Services

In May 1941, almost two years into World War II, the Nazi-Fascist coalition led by Germany, Italy, and Japan was at the zenith of its powers. In Europe, the German troops had just conquered Yugoslavia and Greece in another stunning application of *blitzkrieg*, which added these two Balkan countries to Poland, France, and another half-dozen countries that the German armies had overrun since the beginning of the conflict. In North Africa, Erwin Rommel's Afrika Korps armored troops had pushed the British back into Egypt and rescued the Italian positions in Libya while the collaborationist Vichy government controlled the French colonial territories. In Asia, the Japanese had conquered large swaths of territory in China and positioned troops in Vichy-controlled Indochina. Smart diplomatic maneuvering by both Germany and Japan culminated in neutrality pacts with the Soviet Union, sweetened by secret clauses that had allowed the Soviet Union to annex large swaths of Polish territory after the German invasion in 1939. They ensured that Stalin remained neutral if not friendly toward the continued aggression of the Axis forces in Europe and Asia.

Great Britain and China were the only two countries continuing to put up any meaningful resistance against the Axis powers in May 1941. But China was in the throes of a civil war between the Kuomintang Nationalist Party led by Chiang Kai-shek and the Chinese Communist Party led by Mao Zedong with both factions more interested in fighting one another than the Japanese. And Great Britain faced a critical shortage of war supplies, materials, and manpower, despite the vast resources it could still muster from its colonies. The wild card at the time was the United States.

In May 1941, the Americans were divided over the role that the United States should play in the conflict that had engulfed the world. A strong isolationist sentiment of avoiding involvement in international affairs in general and especially in armed conflicts in Europe and Asia had gained momentum in the aftermath of World War I and during the years of the Great Depression. Most Americans viewed the casualties suffered during the Great War, despite the late entry of the United States in the conflict, as disproportionate to the country's interests. There was a widespread belief that American bankers and arms manufacturers had pushed for US involvement for their own profit.[1]

The isolationists represented an eclectic mix of interest groups, including anti-Roosevelt politicians like Senator Burton K. Wheeler, Democrat of Montana, conservative populists like the aviator Charles A. Lindberg, business leaders like General Robert E. Wood, chairman of Sears, Roebuck & Co., and leftist activists like Norman Thomas, leader of the Socialist Party of America. Their single-minded focus on keeping the country out of the war at any cost prevailed over the disorganized efforts from internationalists to get the Unites States government to counter the Axis's aggressive actions.

In May 1941, twenty months into World War II, the United States remained officially neutral despite the decisive shift of the Roosevelt administration in favor of supporting the nations fighting the Axis nations and of preparing the country for the upcoming conflict.

* * *

A snapshot of New York City life in May 1941 provides a great insight into the divisions in the American public opinion between isolationists and internationalists at the time. On the afternoon of May 18, 1941, New York City celebrated "I Am an American Day," which Congress had proclaimed in 1940 as a nationwide celebration to be held the third Sunday in May to honor men and women born in the United States who reached voting age and persons of foreign birth who attained citizenship in the past year.[2] A crowd of 750,000 gathered at the Mall and the Sheep Meadow in Central Park to attend a mass meeting, which officials designated as the largest patriotic gathering the city had ever seen. Fiorello La Guardia, the flamboyant mayor of New York, presided over the ceremonies, held a speech himself, and introduced guests. At times, he grabbed the baton to conduct a 225-piece band of musicians from the Police, Fire, Sanitation, and Park Departments in Sousa's marches "by shouting, by biting his tongue, by reaching forth and pulling toward himself with straining muscles, by knocking a lock of hair over his forehead, by sweating, and by laughing in tempo with the cymbals."

One of the goals of the meeting was to demonstrate the benefits of citizenship to the three hundred thousand naturalized immigrants and more than two million young Americans who became voters across the country the previous year. To accomplish this, Judge John C. Knox, senior judge of the United States District Court of Southern New York, led the audience in a reaffirmation of the oath of loyalty to the nation. Standing in front of microphones, he asked all present to rise, raise their right hands, and repeat the oath after him. He read it a few words at a time, pausing to allow the participants to repeat after him:

> I solemnly swear—that I will support and defend—the Constitution of the United States—against all enemies, foreign and domestic—and that I will bear true faith and allegiance—to the same.—I further swear that—in the crisis that now confronts my country—and at all other times—I will well and faithfully—discharge my obligations—and duties of my citizenship.
>
> This I shall do—loyally and willingly—and with the determination—that our democracy—must and shall be preserved.—And standing here—beneath the banner of freedom—I pledge allegiance to that flag—and to the country for which it stands—one nation, indivisible—with liberty and justice for all.—I take these obligations—freely and without any mental reservation—or purpose of evasion.—So help me God.

Bishop William T. Manning led the meeting into a prayer: "In this day of world crisis we lift our prayers that the forces of tyranny may be overthrown and that aggression, cruelty and inhumanity may be brought into an end. Stir us in this land to be watchful against subversive and disloyal influences and movements, and firmly to repress such influences by whatever name they may call themselves or under whatever auspices they may seek to propagate their destructive teachings, and stir us to resist with our whole strength all efforts to arouse racial or religious prejudice among our people."

Mayor La Guardia drew great outbursts of applause from the audience when he said, "We have established the lesson for the entire world. We have demonstrated that it is possible for people coming from all lands and climes of the world, or their descendants, to live together as good neighbors, in peace and harmony. If we can do it here, it can be done elsewhere. We have demonstrated that a democracy can be strong. We are demonstrating now that a democracy can be efficient, and let me say to Adolf, Benito and Joe: 'We are not afraid to defend our institutions!'"

The principal speaker of the meeting was Secretary of the Interior Harold L. Ickes who declared, "If we are to retain our own freedom, we must do everything within our power to aid Britain. We must also do everything to restore the conquered peoples their freedom. This means the Germans, too." Ickes attacked directly the isolationists' stance that if Britain were defeated the United States could live along and "defend ourselves single-handed," which Ickes called a "cold-blooded lie." For that to be possible, it was necessary for "the United States to become an armed camp and such a regimen would endanger freedom, democracy and our way of life," he continued. "Perhaps," he said, "such is the America that a certain Senator desires. Perhaps such is the America that a certain aviator, with his contempt for democracy, would prefer. Perhaps such is the America that a certain mail-order executive longs for." Ickes roused the audience's applause when he concluded the speech saying that America must give "everything needed to beat the life out of our common enemy" to friends and allies everywhere in Europe, Asia, Africa, and America.

In addition to the serious speakers who reminded those present of the dangerous times they lived, the meeting included representatives of the lighter side of the American life, singers and comedians "who demonstrated most satisfactorily that to be an American is not merely a matter of grave responsibility but also a lot of fun." Bill "Bojangles" Robinson, the iconic African American tap dancer and star of multiple Broadway and Hollywood musicals,[3] promised, "if Hitler ever started for Harlem, he personally would guarantee that he'd never get past Yankee stadium." Eddie Castor, a country music singer, with his wife Ida standing next to him, told the crowd spread before him that he had not seen that many people "since Ida's relatives came to live with us." Lucy Monroe sang "The Star-Spangled Banner," this being one of the estimated five thousand times over her lifetime in which she would perform the national anthem, including performances for Presidents Roosevelt, Johnson, and Kennedy, at President Truman's inauguration, and at hundreds of other civic and patriotic gatherings.[4] To conclude the program around 5:00 PM, Irvin Berlin led the crowd in the singing of "God Bless America," the "peace song" he had introduced to the public on Armistice Day, 1938,[5] and had since been associated with the internationalists' cause.

"By Nazi standards, the meeting was a flop," declared the *New York Times* the next day, tongue-in-cheek. "Except for a few bands and a few children's groups, nobody marched to it. . . . People walked on the grass. . . . Applause throughout the afternoon was frequent and loud . . . but by any Nazi standards the expressions of approval would have been most inadequate."[6]

* * *

Less than a week later, on May 23, 1941, the American First Committee, the most prominent anti-war organization in the United States at the time, organized a counter-rally at Madison Square Garden.[7] The doors opened at 5:00 PM and by 8:00 PM, the audience had reached the Garden's twenty-two thousand capacity with an estimated eight to fourteen thousand in the streets outside listening to the proceedings in loudspeakers set up on Forty-Ninth Street between Eighth and Ninth Avenues. During a short musical program before the rally, a musician on the podium asked the audience if it wanted to sing "God Bless

America." A chorus of voices responded "NO!" They sang "America" instead, while ushers passed out small American flags in an auditorium itself decorated with flags and white, red, and blue bunting. When the rally opened at 8:40 PM, the audience sang "The Star Spangled Banner" and then recited "The People's Pledge to the Flag," which was done all standing with arms outstretched.

Charles A. Lindbergh and Senator Burton K. Wheeler received an enthusiastic reception from a standing, cheering, and flag-waving crowd when they made their entrance on the platform. In their speeches, they both attacked Roosevelt's foreign policy and demanded that leadership in Washington keep the country out of the war and return to isolationism. They told the audience that America did not have to fear foreign invasion, provided it had the right leadership. Without mentioning the president by name, Lindbergh alluded to him in warning of the loss of democracy at home under the guise of protecting it abroad. If the United States entered the war, Lindbergh continued, our losses are "likely to run into the millions" and "victory itself is doubtful." He asked interventionists to "stop and consider whether democracy, tolerance and our American way of life are likely to survive in such a struggle."

Senator Wheeler in his speech urged the audience to "fight against one-man government in the United States." He expressed fears of the president waging an undeclared war, of the end of constitutional democracy, of inflation or debt repudiation, of trouble from wounded soldiers returning from the war, of post-war economic breakdown and of the establishment of a dictatorship as a result. Wheeler was particularly scornful toward Roosevelt's advisers who were pushing him to wage an undeclared war. He called them "that little coterie who surround him, most of whom have never faced an electorate or met a payroll, or tried a lawsuit and many of whom are impractical dreamers."

Norman Thomas, the Socialist leader, appealed "from the Roosevelt of today to the Roosevelt of yesterday" on the issue of war and peace. He led the audience in the ironic recitation of Roosevelt's pledge during the 1940 campaign that American boys were not going to be sent into any foreign wars. Telegrams read to the audience included anti-war sentiments from novelist Sinclair Lewis, actress

Lillian Gish, and Robert E. Wood of Chicago, chairman of Sears and national chairman of the American First Committee.

The audience responded with loud and repeated outbursts of applause for every isolationist slogan, statement that "America wants to keep out of the war," and for every mention of Lindbergh, Wheeler, and other isolationist leaders. Equally loud boos and hisses filled the hall each time the speakers mentioned President Roosevelt, members of his cabinet, and other persons and organizations who favored all-out aid to Britain or who argued that it was in the interest of the United States to keep Nazi Germany from defeating Britain.

The New York afternoon tabloid newspaper *PM* was an unequivocal critic of the isolationist stance of the American First Committee and its leaders. In the editorial page of the newspaper at the time, its publisher, Ralph Ingersoll, addressed the readers directly with clear warnings that America's fate was tied to the success of the British forces and other nations fighting Germany and Italy. The newspaper's chief political cartoonist, Theodor Seuss Geisel, better known as Dr. Seuss, regularly drew cartoons that reinforced this message featuring his unique characters. In the issue published on the day of the Madison Square Garden rally, the editorial cartoon urged the readers considering attending the rally to "Listen and Think!" A cartoon published a few days later showed Lindbergh on a soapbox delivering his speech while petting a monstrous snake covered in swastika tattoos. "Tis Roosevelt, not Hitler, that the world should really fear," Lindbergh exclaims.

* * *

William J. Donovan was one of the president's advisers who Wheeler and other speakers attacked at the Madison Square Garden rally. At the time, Donovan was one of the most vocal proponents of the idea that the United States needed to prepare for the inevitable conflict and provide all the support possible to Britain in its fight against the Axis forces. As a World War I hero, a Republican politician, and a successful Wall Street lawyer, Donovan embodied the opposite attributes of those who Wheeler called Roosevelt's "little coterie" during his speech.

Donovan earned recognition in World War I at the head of the 165th Infantry Regiment of the 42nd Division of the New York National Guard—the renowned "Fighting 69th" of the Rainbow Division. The legend goes that after the regiment landed in France he ran his men five miles with full packs to "limber them up." As the men were grumbling with exhaustion, Donovan pointed out that he was ten years older and carrying the same fifty-pound pack. One of the men replied, "But we ain't as wild as you, Bill!" There Donovan got his nickname Wild Bill, which stuck with him for the rest of his life.[8] People who knew him well thought of the nickname as affectionate sarcasm because in behavior Donovan was "about as wild as a good baby's nurse, but the nickname has stuck all these years because although inaccurate as an adjective it does somehow fit the drama of his record."[9]

The citations Donovan received in France tell the story of his military service there. On July 28, 1918, a Distinguished Service Cross: "He was in advance of the division for four days, all the while under shell and machine gun fire from the enemy, who were on three sides of him, and he was repeatedly and persistently counterattacked, being wounded twice." Three days later the Distinguished Service Medal: "He displayed conspicuous energy and most efficient leadership in the advance of his battalion across the Ourcq River and the capture of strong enemy positions. . . . His devotion to duty, heroism, and pronounced qualities of a Commander enabled him to successfully accomplish all missions assigned to him in this important operation." And then, for action in combat in the Meuse-Argonne on October 14, the highest of all awards, the Congressional Medal of Honor: "Colonel Donovan personally led the assaulting wave in an attack upon a very strongly organized position, and when our troops were suffering heavy casualties he encouraged all near him by his example, moving among his men in exposed positions, reorganizing decimated platoons and accompanying them forward in attacks. When he was wounded in the leg by a machine gun bullet, he refused to be evacuated and continued with his unit until it withdrew to a less exposed position." "No man ever deserved it more," said General Douglas MacArthur, who witnessed this action as his commander.[10]

Donovan had an innate intuition on how to handle people. In one of his war letters, describing a very bad thirty-six hours at the front, he mentioned dispassionately clipping one man in the jaw because this fellow was destroying the morale of the group, and then later putting his arm around another terrified soldier and coaxing him back to confidence. A veteran of the Old Sixty-Ninth said that the men would follow Donovan anywhere, but they also knew that it was impossible to put one over on him. Reverend Francis P. Duffy, the famous fighting chaplain of the Sixty-Ninth whose monument stands today in Times Square at Broadway and Forty-Sixth Street, said, "His men would have cheerfully gone to hell with him, and as a priest, I mean what I say."[11]

When he returned from France, Donovan put his uniform and medals away and gave his Congressional medal to the regiment. In 1922, he was appointed US attorney in Buffalo, New York. When President Coolidge reorganized the Department of Justice in 1924, he called Donovan to Washington to be assistant to the attorney general, in charge of the Antitrust Division. He was offered the Governor Generalship of the Philippines when President Hoover entered the White House in 1929, but turned it down and went into law practice in New York City. In 1932, he ran for Governor of New York but he was defeated in the Democratic landslide of that year's elections. During this period of corporate law practice, Donovan never lost his interest in world affairs. He visited China and Far East Russia in the early 1920s, and took time off to visit Ethiopia during the 1935 Italian invasion. He was in Spain during its Civil War, carefully observing the Axis efforts to test their new equipment in these foreign adventures.[12]

As World War II engulfed Europe, Donovan became increasingly active in raising awareness of Americans to the dangers ahead. In late 1939 and early 1940, he embraced the cause of the Polish people, raising substantial relief funds in honor of the eighty-year-old Ignace Jan Paderewski, the famous pianist who had served as the president of the first Polish republic after World War I and had gone into exile after the German invasion.[13] As president pro tem of the Paderewski Fund for Polish Relief, Donovan served with Eleanor Roosevelt, enlisted as a vice president of the Fund, which probably brought him for the first time into contact with the inner circle of the president, although surely he was a personality known to Roosevelt.

Donovan, a lifelong Republican, aligned publically with the Democrat president in mid-June 1940, in the midst of the electoral campaign in which Roosevelt was seeking an unprecedented third presidential term. With the Republicans gathered for their nominating convention in Philadelphia, Roosevelt appointed Colonel Henry L. Stimson and Colonel Frank Knox to his cabinet as Secretary of War and Secretary of the Navy, respectively. Both were prominent internationalist Republicans who supported aiding the Allies and were against isolationists. In the face of the initial negative reaction of the convention toward the appointments, Donovan sent a telegram to John D. M. Hamilton, chairman of the Republican National Committee, which was published in newspapers on June 22, 1940. In it, he urged his party to support "without imputation or motive" the commander in chief, who faced the urgent task of preparing the nation for defense. "The immediacy of this problem is measured by days, cannot await the outcome of the election and transcends all other questions," Donovan wrote. "This action does not mean we are prepared to intervene, but only that we are preparing to defend our country. Nor does it preclude us as the opposition party from differing with the President on any other policy, foreign or domestic. A statesmanlike distinction between our right to oppose him as a political leader and our duty to support him as Commander in Chief would strengthen our position before the country," Donovan concluded.[14]

* * *

Knox was confirmed as secretary of the navy and assumed his post on July 11, 1940. Just three days later, Donovan left from La Guardia on the Pan American flying boat *Atlantic Clipper* en route to London on a confidential trip for Secretary Knox and the president. The conflict in Europe was at a critical juncture. The massive German offensive on the western front that had started with the invasion of France, Belgium, Luxembourg, and the Netherlands on May 10 had forced the evacuation of over 340,000 British, French, and Belgian troops from the beaches of Dunkirk in early June and concluded with the surrender of France on June 25. German forces occupied the Channel Islands on

July 1, and the bombing of Britain by the Luftwaffe on July 10 signaled the beginning of the Battle of Britain. An invasion of the British Isles was imminent.

Winston Churchill, who had replaced Neville Chamberlain as prime minister on the same day that the German offensive began, was determined to energize his people for the decisive battles ahead while reaching out for assistance to the United States. Churchill did not paint a rosy picture of the road ahead to his compatriots, having "nothing to offer but blood, toil, tears and sweat" and "many, many long months of struggle and of suffering." But his aim was clear: "It is victory, victory at all costs, victory in spite of all terror, victory, however long and hard the road may be; for without victory, there is no survival."[15] On June 4, one day after the British Expeditionary Force pulled out of Dunkirk, he told the House of Commons:

> "[W]e shall not flag or fail. We shall go on to the end. We shall fight . . . on the seas and oceans, we shall fight with growing confidence and growing strength in the air, we shall defend our island, whatever the cost may be. We shall fight on the beaches, we shall fight on the landing grounds, we shall fight in the fields and in the streets, we shall fight in the hills; we shall never surrender, and even if, which I do not for a moment believe, this island or a large part of it were subjugated and starving, then our Empire beyond the seas, armed and guarded by the British Fleet, would carry on the struggle, until, in God's good time, the new world, with all its power and might, steps forth to the rescue and the liberation of the old."[16]

Churchill's appeal to the United States—the new world expected to come to the rescue of the old—became more direct after the fall of France, leaving no doubt about the stakes at play. In a speech to the House of Commons he warned, "If we can stand up to [Hitler] all Europe may be free, and the life of the world may move forward into broad, sunlit uplands; but if we fail then the whole world, including the United States, and all that we have known and cared for, will sink into the abyss of a new dark age. . . ."[17]

In this context, then, Donovan's mission to Britain was three-fold: assess the ability of the British to withstand the Nazi onslaught, study the formula that had fueled the impressive German conquests, and most importantly look for ways in which the United States could defeat that formula.

Upon his return to the United States, Donovan reported his findings to Knox and Roosevelt in early August and then articulated his views in four articles written in collaboration with Edgar Mowrer, a distinguished foreign correspondent for the *Chicago Daily News* who had won the Pulitzer Prize in 1933 for reporting from Berlin the rise to power of Adolf Hitler. In these articles, Donovan described Hitler's efficient use of subtle as well as covert actions, so called "fifth column" methods, to weaken the resistance of target countries and undermine the morale of their armed forces in advance of lightning strikes by the German air and armored forces. The purpose of the articles was to raise public awareness in the United States to ways in which Nazis had used German nationals and sympathizers to advance their agenda in the victim countries. Donovan outlined the novel ways in which the Nazis had combined overt diplomatic, artistic, business, and propaganda activities, financed to the tune of $200 million annually, with covert espionage and sabotage efforts to soften resistance to the German invasion when it eventually came.[18]

Privately, Donovan brought back a very important message. There was skepticism at that time in some quarters in Washington as to whether the British could effectively carry out Churchill's promise to never surrender. Donovan reported to Roosevelt the British resolve he had seen firsthand. It had a direct influence on American policy, the most immediate effect of which was the agreement to transfer fifty World War I American destroyers in return for leases for military basis in British territories in Newfoundland and the Caribbean.

* * *

At the beginning of December 1940, Donovan undertook a second fact-finding mission overseas on behalf of the president. In fourteen weeks he covered twenty-five thousand miles visiting most of the countries in Northern Africa and the Balkans in addition to Spain, Portugal, Ireland, and England.[19] Upon returning to the United States, Donovan recommended to the president that the United States start preparing immediately for a global war. He particularly stressed the need of a service to wage unorthodox political and psychological warfare, to gather information through every means available, and to centralize its analysis and dissemination, the way the British had begun to do in London. At Roosevelt's direction, Donovan discussed this idea at length with Cabinet members including Secretaries Knox and Stimson, and Attorney General Jackson.[20] Eventually, he molded a role for himself as coordinator of all intelligence information gathered by all government agencies, a role without precedent at the time.

Up to then, the United States government had obtained a wide range of information from scattered agencies acting independently of one another. The State Department had a worldwide system of reporting that yielded volumes of information from those parts of the world where the United States had diplomatic presence. The Army and the Navy each had a highly coordinated intelligence division, which relied on reports from military attachés and observers attached to British units. In addition, trade commissioners and agricultural attachés operating at diplomatic posts sent voluminous reports on economic conditions around the world. The problem that Donovan proposed to solve was looking at all the independent reports from this multitude of sources and analyzing them in relation to each other.

Roosevelt's military order of July 11, 1941, created the position of Coordinator of Information and appointed Donovan to fill it vested "with the authority to collect and analyze all information and data, which may bear upon national security; to correlate such information and data, and to make such information and data available to the President and to such departments and officials of the Government as the President may determine . . ."[21] Donovan reported directly to the president, his role was a civilian one, and his office would not control any of the standing departments or interfere with the existing missions of the various intelligence agencies. Nevertheless, Donovan's

DESIGNATING A COORDINATOR OF INFORMATION

By virtue of the authority vested in me as President
of the United States and as Commander in Chief of the Army
and Navy of the United States, it is ordered as follows:

1. There is hereby established the position of
Coordinator of Information, with authority to collect and
analyze all information and data, which may bear upon
national security; to correlate such information and data,
and to make such information and data available to the
President and to such departments and officials of the
Government as the President may determine; and to carry
out, when requested by the President, such supplementary
activities as may facilitate the securing of information
important for national security not now available to the
Government.

2. The several departments and agencies of the government shall make available to the Coordinator of Information
all and any such information and data relating to national
security as the Coordinator, with the approval of the President, may from time to time request.

3. The Coordinator of Information may appoint such
committees, consisting of appropriate representatives of the
various departments and agencies of the Government, as he
may deem necessary to assist him in the performance of his
functions.

4. Nothing in the duties and responsibilities of
the Coordinator of Information shall in any way interfere with or impair the duties and responsibilities of
the regular military and naval advisers of the President
as Commander in Chief of the Army and Navy.

5. Within the limits of such funds as may be allo-
cated to the Coordinator of Information by the President,
the Coordinator may employ necessary personnel and make
provision for the necessary supplies, facilities, and
services.

6. William J. Donovan is hereby designated as
Coordinator of Information.

(Signed)   Franklin D. Roosevelt

THE WHITE HOUSE

July 11, 1941

*Military order of July 11, 1941, appointed William J. Donovan as Coordinator of
Information.*

THE WHITE HOUSE
WASHINGTON

July 23, 1941

My dear Colonel Donovan:

In your capacity as Coordinator of
Information, which position I established
by Order of July 11, 1941, you will receive
no compensation, but shall be entitled to
actual and necessary transportation, sub-
sistence, and other expenses incidental to
the performance of your duties.

Sincerely yours,

Franklin D Roosevelt

Colonel William J. Donovan
State Department Building
Washington, D. C.

FDR letter to Donovan specifying compensation details as Coordinator of Information.

duties were defined broadly and made sufficiently elastic to allow for
future possibilities "to carry out, when requested by the President,
such supplementary activities as may facilitate the securing of information important for national security not now available to the Government."[22] In his capacity as Coordinator of Information, Donovan
received no compensation but was entitled to transportation, subsis-
tence, and other expenses incidental to the performance of his duties.

All along, Donovan's intentions were to create an all-inclusive
organization that incorporated all the elements of intelligence. First,
it would be a "service of strategic information" for the president. In
Donovan's view, strategy without information was helpless and information collected for no strategic purpose was futile. He aimed for his
organization "to constitute a means by which the President . . . would
have available accurate and complete enemy intelligence reports
upon which military operational decisions could be based."[23] Next,
the organization would conduct psychological warfare that he had
observed the Germans conduct so masterfully to soften their enemies'
defenses. Finally, although not explicitly stated in the military order,
the intent all along had been for the Coordinator of Information to
conduct physical subversion and guerrilla warfare, as well.

The British secret services took a great interest in the newly formed
American spy agency from the beginning. They offered the Americans
access to their operational and training methods and techniques—a
move without precedent among intelligence agencies. In return, they
demanded knowledge of special operations and counterintelligence
activities, which often amounted to complete control. In a memorandum written at the end of June 1941, Lieutenant Commander Ian
Fleming, a British Naval Intelligence officer in 1941—and of James
Bond fame after the war—laid out a series of steps for Donovan to
follow with urgency to set up the new organization in time to meet war
before Christmas. "Unless you make an early attack on the inertia and
opposition which will meet you at every step, there is a serious danger
of your plans being still-born," Fleming wrote. It was a short, three-
page document, which included an outline of the initial structure of
the organization and names of key personnel to staff it. It was striking
for the terse style and direct actions it listed, including:

There is opposition to your appointment, which must not be allowed to organize itself.

Enlist the full help of the State Department and FBI by cajoling or other means. You will have to be (and stay) friends with both.

Dragoon the War and Navy Departments. . . . explain your plans and request their full cooperation. Be prepared to take action quickly if they don't help.

Make an example of someone at an early date for indiscretion and continue to act ruthlessly where lack of security is concerned.[24]

Donovan moved swiftly to develop the elements of the central intelligence service he envisioned. A Foreign Information Service began broadcasting radio messages, issuing pamphlets, and spreading propaganda materials reflecting the American principles and points of view. It also established a number of listening outposts around the world to monitor foreign broadcasts and feed the information back to the United States for the production of intelligence. An Oral Intelligence Unit began interviewing persons recently arrived from abroad and studying foreign nationals to discover what they might reveal concerning the conditions and opinions in their countries of origin. The collection of information by undercover agents also began, but only outside the Western Hemisphere, a territory J. Edgar Hoover had guarded jealously for the FBI.

A Research and Analysis Branch established in August 1941 began to collect and evaluate the basic materials for intelligence reports. A large staff digested and cross-referenced the reports and created summaries for the president and those of his subordinates who were designated to receive them. Very quickly, they realized that no matter how skillfully the analysts condensed and correlated the information, the outcome was piles of new reading materials added to desks already overflowing with other papers that required the attention of the officials. A Visual Presentation Branch began developing techniques for delivering the information to the concerned departments and services in a way that presented all the major facts visually without the need to read the mass of reports behind them.[25]

Seventy years before concepts like data mining, big data, and executive information dashboards became mainstream, Donovan had geographers, historians, economists, military and naval experts, sound and color engineers, and journalists working on making sense of massive amounts of information from a multitude of sources. They looked for ways to present it in an easy-to-grasp form for "[t]he tired mind of the President or another high official, now burdened by a mountain of reports containing this information." One idea reported to be in advanced planning stages in October 1941 was a "huge globe, lighted from within" that would display, plainly marked and in vivid color, information such as the strength and location of all military, air, and naval forces and bases in a given area of the world. It would also show economic consequences of military action in certain areas including what resources had been gained or lost and what ethnic populations were affected. The lighted globe would show the industrial areas of a nation and a simple chart of changes in their productive capacity as determined by air raids or land actions.[26]

* * *

To strengthen the special ties with the British, Donovan placed a branch office of his service in London and the British services established quarters in New York. The cooperation was close especially as Donovan began planning for the eventuality of war even before it came with the Japanese attack at Pearl Harbor on December 7, 1941. Donovan established a section named "Special Activities—K and L Funds" on October 10, 1941, to take charge of espionage, sabotage, subversive activities, and guerrilla units.

There had been no formal authorization for these activities. The president's order of July 11, 1941, merely provided for "such supplementary activities as may facilitate the securing of information important for national security not now available to the Government." But the intent was clear. In September 1941 Donovan sent one of his staff officers, Lieutenant Colonel Robert A. Solborg, to study British practices in close association with the organization and practices of the British Special Operations Executive (SOE). During his visit to England, Solborg received extensive training at all SOE training schools there and studied the entire scope of the SOE organization.[27] The SOE had been formed on July 22, 1940, to conduct warfare by means other than direct military engagement. Its mission was to encourage, facilitate, and conduct espionage, sabotage, and reconnaissance in occupied Europe against the Axis powers, and to aid local resistance movements.

Donovan leveraged SOE to provide training in irregular warfare to his officers. SOE established Special Training School 103 (STS 103), also known as Camp X, on December 6, 1941, between Whitby and Oshawa in Ontario, Canada. The first contingent of American intelligence officers, as well as agents from the FBI, took instructions there in a variety of special techniques including silent killing, sabotage, partisan support and recruitment methods for resistance movements, demolition, map reading, use of various weapons, and Morse code.

With the entry of the United States in World War II, the Special Activities section evolved into a separate Special Operations branch within the COI organization designated as SA/G. In a memorandum to the president on December 22, 1941, Donovan formalized the objectives of SA/G to include "organize and execute morale and physical subversion, including sabotage, fifth column activities and guerrilla warfare." Donovan further defined guerrilla warfare as "(1) The establishment and support of small bands of local origin under definite leaders, and (2) the formation in the United States of guerrilla forces military in nature."[28] Reflecting the wartime conditions at the time, SA/G was oriented from the beginning toward unorthodox warfare in support of military operations under the direction of local area commanders. This was different from other branches of the COI that reported directly to Washington, such as those responsible for collecting intelligence, analyzing it, and preparing reports for dissemination.

Upon his return to Washington from his England trip, Solborg prepared a proposal to create an American Special Operations Service (SOS) in the mold of the British SOE. Submitted to Donovan on January 13, 1942, the proposal captured the objectives and urgency of these operations:

The Axis powers by the enormous extension of territory, which they at present control, and by their brutal behavior against the inhabitants have left themselves open to all sorts of subversive warfare.

Without outside support, however, it is quite impossible for the people concerned to continue such warfare for long owing to the lack of direction, control, communications, materials, etc.

The SOS organization should endeavor to exploit that situation.

The Axis is waging total war and must be answered in the same way. Its fifth column must be out-columned. Information shows that it is vulnerable; that it makes elementary mistakes and its methods are not infallible.

The oppressed people must be encouraged to resist and to assist in Axis defeat, and this can be done by inciting them, by assisting them and by training and organizing them.

We must make up for lost time and we must go to our task with a will. There is so much to be done and so little time in which to do it.[29]

In a wider move reflecting the new realities of the nation engaged in open war, Donovan advocated that the entire organization of the Coordinator of Information be placed under the direction of the Joint Chiefs of Staff. These held their first meeting on February 9, 1942, as they prepared to work with their British counterparts in the Combined Chiefs of Staff. Donovan also floated the idea of establishing an American force like the British Commandos to raid enemy positions in Europe and Asia by land, sea, and air. Through Secretary Knox, Donovan proposed to the president that he himself create and command a unit of five thousand men who would constitute that force. Donovan suggested the new organization be called Special Service Troops and unofficially be known as "Yankee Raiders" or some such term. It would be an independent command reporting to the president through the secretary of the Navy, composed of volunteers from all branches of the Army and the Navy and of specially qualified non-service men. The organization would carry out small independent raids or coups-de-mains and would act in conjunction with larger attacking forces of the Army and the Navy.

President Roosevelt approved the proposal in principle, subject to agreement of the services, who were adamant against it. Ultimately, the Joint Chiefs decided that commando-like units were best suited within the regular military, which lead to the creation of the US Army Rangers, whose first unit was activated in June 1942. Donovan instead was tasked to continue developing within his office forces capable of conducting physical subversion activities and guerrilla warfare deep behind enemy lines that would complement black propaganda and psychological warfare activities.

The president's military order of June 13, 1942, replaced the Office of Coordinator of Information with the Office of Strategic Services, placed it under the jurisdiction of the Joint Chiefs of Staff, and appointed Donovan as director of strategic services. The military order defined the duties of the OSS very broadly and generically:

a.   Collect and analyze such strategic information as may be required by the United States Joint Chiefs of Staff.
b.   Plan and operate such special services as may be directed by the United States Joint Chiefs of Staff.[30]

Although the strategic intent had been simply to roll forward the functions and capabilities of the COI into the new organization and place them under the control of the military, the implementation of the intent was anything but simple. The transfer and operation of a civilian agency, such as the OSS, under military control was without precedent and strained even the most basic bureaucratic processes of the military. Most importantly, military leaders viewed the OSS as encroaching upon the functions of existing organizations within the Joint Chiefs of Staff, the US Army, and the US Navy intelligence organizations, including the Army Intelligence G-2 and the Office of Naval Intelligence. Entanglements in Washington created a stalemate, which put into question the entire existence of the new organization.

Its opponents included none other than General Walter Bedell Smith, the brusque and demanding senior Army officer who at the time served as the secretary of the Joint Chiefs of Staff. Bedell Smith's frustration boiled over at a meeting with officials from the Bureau of the

MILITARY ORDER

By virtue of the authority vested in me as President of
the United States and as Commander-in-Chief of the Army and
Navy of the United States, it is ordered as follows:

1. The office of Coordinator of Information established
by Order of July 11, 1941, exclusive of the foreign information
activities transferred to the Office of War Information by
Executive Order of June 13, 1942, shall hereafter be known as
the Office of Strategic Services, and is hereby transferred to
the jurisdiction of the United States Joint Chiefs of Staff.

2. The Office of Strategic Services shall perform the
following duties:

    a. Collect and analyze such strategic information as
        may be required by the United States Joint Chiefs
        of Staff.

    b. Plan and operate such special services as may be
        directed by the United States Joint Chiefs of Staff.

3. At the head of the Office of Strategic Services shall
be a Director of Strategic Services who shall be appointed by
the President and who shall perform his duties under the direction and supervision of the United States Joint Chiefs of Staff.

4. William J. Donovan is hereby appointed as Director of
Strategic Services.

5. The Order of July 11, 1941 is hereby revoked.

Commander-in-Chief

The White House

    June 13, 1942

Military order creating the Office of Strategic Services.

Budget to discuss the 1943 budget requirements for the new organization, when he learned that Donovan had requested $2 million for the construction of a large presentation building. Smith called the requested building "merely a 'big toy'[with] a good many 'frills,' [which] although it would have value in training officers for future wars, it would have little, if any value, in the present war."[31] Smith said:

> Col. Donovan is still "Wild Bill." He is aggressive and ambitious and very much action-minded. He is a poor administrator and has little organizational sense. His activities might seriously impair the workings of the Joint Chiefs of Staff by placing the Joint Chiefs of Staff on the defensive before the President in explaining why certain suggested strategy plans of Col. Donovan cannot be carried into effect.[32]

Bedell Smith paused for a moment to recognize the value of the intelligence material collected in Latin America and the work of the Research and Analysis Branch before venting his frustration with Donovan's ideas for subversive operations. Smith said:

> Col. Donovan's subversive activities were originally planned to be conducted by civilians of the "burglar type" who would be willing to go to any country of the world and perform any task, either out of patriotism or for sufficient money. If Army or Navy personnel are used on subversive missions, the protection of a uniform and Army and Navy enlistment in time of war will be lost and all parachute troops dropped behind the lines of the enemy would be shot. Col. Donovan, in developing these "subversives" and his attempt to build up a group of "commandos" had been driven by his desire to lead a "personal army." The Marine Corps has been designated as the agency to develop "commandos" and any commando operation requires the closest cooperation between the Army, Navy, and the Air Corps.[33]

Early in November 1942, the JCS assigned two senior military officers to conduct an inquiry into the OSS and provide recommendations on its future functions. They were General Joseph T. McNarney, deputy chief of staff of the Army, and Admiral Frederick J. Horne, vice chief of Naval Operations.[34] They met with Donovan separately, collected a number of memoranda and reports documenting the history and evolution of COI/OSS, and spent time with the staff to see the organization at work. They then spent time reviewing the information and correlating it with data they had collected from military commanders in the field regarding their perceptions of the value that the OSS provided.

* * *

The timing of the review was fortunate for the OSS because a number of its activities at the operational level were beginning to bear fruit. The secret network of agents outside the Western Hemisphere was expanding and the volume of intelligence doubled and trebled each month from agents placed in a number of neutral or Axis-leaning countries, such as Switzerland, Spain, Portugal, or Vichy France. Studies and reports from the Research and Analysis branch and services from the Field Photographic and Presentation branch were receiving wider distribution and higher value recognition. A number of special operations missions launched in 1942 had attracted attention in the highest circles. The first members of Detachment 101 were recruited, trained, and dispatched to Burma to support the military operations in the China-India-Burma Theater. Two professional explorers and OSS operatives, Captain Ilia Tolstoy and Lieutenant Brooke Dolan, scouted across Tibet from India to China in a reconnaissance mission. They carried a letter from President Roosevelt to the Dalai Lama in Lhasa, which was the first such document exchanged between these two heads of state.[35]

However, the recognition of the value that individual components of the OSS provided was not sufficient. The new organization had to demonstrate that it created synergies and provided a greater value by coordinating the contributions of its individual branches in support of military strategy and operations. The test came during the planning and execution of Operation Torch, the US-led Allied landings in French North Africa in November 1942. Since the creation of the COI, Donovan had paid special attention to establishing a presence in the French colonies of North Africa that had remained under the control of the Vichy government. The fact that the United States continued to maintain diplomatic and trade relations with the Vichy government had allowed the placement under diplomatic cover of a number of intelligence operatives who had worked diligently to develop their networks of informants in key cities across North Africa, including Tangier, Algiers, Casablanca, Oran, and Tunis.

In December 1941, Donovan sent Colonel William A. Eddy under the cover of Naval attaché to Tangier to coordinate all the field activities and the reporting to Washington and to the Allied Force Headquarters (AFHQ) established in Gibraltar under the leadership of General Eisenhower. By the time the Torch landings began on November 8, 1942, all the branches of the OSS were actively involved and supporting the operation. They had provided comprehensive reports on the target areas complete with maps, port installation diagrams, beach conditions, order of battle of the French forces, and information about local and tribal leaders.[36] OSS agents who had been in North Africa for more than a year prior to the invasion accompanied the three task forces that landed in Morocco and Algeria. A clandestine intelligence radio network on the ground provided Eisenhower and his staff with fresh intelligence from the main target areas of attack as the task forces approached. OSS had organized cells of resistance among the local Arab tribes as well as French military and civilians disaffected with the collaborationist stance of Vichy. A number of guerrilla activities had been planned to be carried out on the eve of the landings, including seizing airfields and radio stations, cutting telephone lines to the French coastal batteries, and lighting flares on the beaches to indicate the landing spots. In the end, the AFHQ did not provide the green light for most of the actions out of concern that they might cause the French to go on alert prematurely thus robbing the Allies of the element of surprise.[37]

The strong performance of the OSS in the days leading up to and during the execution of Operation Torch and the recognition by Eisenhower and other US field commanders of its strong intelligence collection and reporting capabilities in support of the landings helped break the stalemate within the Joint Chiefs of Staff about the future of the organization. General McNarney and Admiral Horne concluded their inquiry into the OSS operations with findings in its favor. Based on their report, the JCS issued directive 155/4/D on December 23, 1942, which designated OSS as the JCS agency charged outside the Western Hemisphere with "the planning, development, coordination and execution of the military program for psychological warfare," and with "the compilation of such political, psychological, sociological and economic information as may be required by military operations." In the field of intelligence, it placed OSS on a par with the Military Intelligence Service of the Army and the Office of Naval Intelligence. Directive 155/4/D gave OSS the authority to operate in the fields of sabotage, espionage and counter-espionage in enemy-occupied or controlled territory, guerrilla warfare, underground groups on enemy-occupied or controlled territory and foreign nationality groups in the United States.[38]

The directive firmly established OSS by providing it for the first time a definitive charter and eliminating the barriers in its lines of authority to the JCS. In a letter to Donovan sent on the same date that the directive was issued, General George C. Marshall, the US Army chief of staff, wrote, "I regret that after voluntarily coming under the jurisdiction of the Joint Chiefs of Staff your organization has not had smoother sailing. Nevertheless, it has rendered invaluable service, particularly with reference to the North African Campaign. I am hopeful that the new Office of Strategic Services' directive will eliminate most, if not all, of your difficulties."[39]

The immediate effect of the directive was a rapid expansion of OSS, both in personnel and in the operations it carried out. As they began planning irregular warfare activities and special operations, Donovan and his team realized that the OSS was a newcomer in a field where friends and foe had played for years. They quickly set out to study the experience accumulated in the early years of the war and inject it into the new organization.

CHAPTER 2

Irregular Warfare in the Early Years of World War II

The Germans were the first to recognize that irregular warfare could provide a key strategic advantage in their military campaigns in the early years of World War II. In preparation for the invasion of Poland, the *Abwehr*, the German military intelligence organization, created a special force of agents called *Kampfen-Truppen* (combat troops) or *K-Truppen*, to operate independently from regular troops. Some of them, dressed in civilian clothes and carrying only small arms and hand grenades on them, crossed the German-Polish border at the end of August 1939 and traveled deep inside Poland to the vicinity of industrial sites, mines, and others centers of strategic importance to the German war industry. When the invasion began at dawn on September 1, the K-Truppen moved swiftly to capture these objectives and hold them until regular units of the Wehrmacht relieved them. Other K-Truppen groups rode on the armored columns that thrust deep into Polish territory in the first hours of the invasion. They guarded key road junctions and bridges overrun by panzer units and protected them from Polish counter-attacks until the infantry caught up with them. The Abwehr disbanded the K-Truppen at the end of the Polish campaign but their contribution to the success of the blitzkrieg did not go unnoticed.[1] In October 1939, the German Army General Staff approved the creation of a unit of special forces capable of operating unnoticed behind enemy lines and striking where least expected. To maintain its secrecy, the unit went by the name of *Lehr und Bau Kompanie z.b.V. 800* (Special Duty Training and Construction Company No. 800).[2] Its all-volunteer force began training intensively in sabotage, silent killing, and irregular warfare techniques at a camp on the shores of Queenzee, a lake near Brandenburg. For this reason, the unit became known as the Brandenburg Company, and its men as the Brandenburgers.

Borrowing from the K-Truppen experience in Poland, the Brandenburgers' mode of operation was to infiltrate deep into the enemy territory dressed in civilian clothes or even in military uniforms of their opponents. To avoid detection, they recruited people who spoke the language of the target country, knew its customs, and could live among its people without being noticed as foreigners. During the German offensive in the West in spring 1940, the Brandenburgers spearheaded the military strikes against targets in Scandinavia and the Low Countries. On the eve of the attack against Denmark on April 8, Brandenburger units dressed in Danish Army uniforms crossed the border in the dark of night and seized principal road and railway bridges ahead of the Wehrmacht units that invaded in the morning. A month later, Brandenburgers in civilian clothes collaborated with Dutch Nazis to capture the main bridge over the Maas River in the town of Gennep, and secure a key gateway into Holland for the German Sixth Army. In Belgium, Brandenburgers disguised as civilians blended with refugees fleeing the advancing Germans. They penetrated deep behind the lines, captured bridges over the Meuse River, and prevented the Belgians from opening the levees and flooding the low-lying areas through which the German panzer units were advancing on their way to the key port of Antwerp.

On May 14, 1940, Hitler congratulated personally the participants in these operations and ordered the expansion of the force to regiment strength. *Volksdeutchen*, ethnic Germans from Eastern and Central European countries, filled the ranks of the new *Lehr-Regiment Brandenburg*. Throughout the winter of 1940–1941, a number of Brandenburgers disguised as civilians crossed into Hungary, Romania, Bulgaria, and Yugoslavia and took up employment in the local economy in and close to oil fields, railroad junctions, ports on the Danube

River, electrical power stations, and other strategic objects. When the invasion of Greece and Yugoslavia began in April 1941, they moved quickly to occupy these targets and act as guides for the regular troops pouring across the borders.

The Brandenburgers were especially successful on the Russian front where they operated often hundreds of miles behind the Soviet lines dressed in the uniforms of the Red Army or NKVD, the Soviet secret police. One of their preferred tactics was to race ahead of the German troops in captured Soviet trucks and make contact with the Red Army rear guard units. Those Brandenburgers who spoke Russian fluently interacted with the Soviet soldiers; the rest pretended to be wounded and unable to communicate or from non-Russian speaking parts of the Soviet Union. As they retreated with the Red Army units, the Brandenburgers captured bridges and communication arteries and held them until they linked up with advancing German units.

In one of the most daring uses of this tactic, a group of sixty-two Brandenburgers went into action in July 1942 as part of the German Army Group South's drive toward the Caucasus oil fields. Their commanding officer was Baron Adrian von Foelkersam, the grandson of a Russian admiral, who could speak fluent Russian and had proven himself one of the most audacious officers in the Brandenburg regiment. Dressed in NKVD uniforms, the Brandenburgers infiltrated Soviet lines and made their way toward the oil fields in Maikop mingled in a retreating Red Army convoy. At Maikop, they earned the confidence of the unsuspecting NKVD general in charge of the area. For several days, they roamed unchecked and became familiar with the Soviet defensive positions around the city and the oil fields nearby. When the German troops closed in, the Brandenburgers, still in their NKVD disguise, disseminated panic and confusion among the defenders, countermanding genuine orders from the Soviet command and issuing contradicting orders of their own. On the morning of August 9, 1942, advance German troops arriving in Maikop encountered light resistance and found a large part of the oilfield installations intact thanks to the work of the Brandenburgers.

The action in the Caucasus was the zenith of the Brandenburgers' involvement in special operations. After the battle of Stalingrad, the Wehrmacht went into a defensive posture that did not favor the daring raids behind enemy lines for which the Brandenburgers had been distinguished. The German general staff increasingly used the Brandenburger units like regular infantry units to shore up gaps in the Eastern front. Heinrich Himmler, head of the Nazi secret police apparatus, took the banner of special operations in 1943 when he created a new unit under the *Schutzstaffel*, or SS, for such operations. Under the command of Otto Skorzeny, the unit recruited a number of its members from the ranks of the Brandenburgers and borrowed heavily from their playbook. They earned fame in September 1943 when they rescued the deposed Italian dictator Benito Mussolini from a mountaintop resort in Gran Sasso, to the great delight of Hitler. In the initial days of the German offensive in the Ardennes in December 1944, Skorzeny's troops dressed in American uniforms and using American vehicles wreaked havoc in the American rear. They met their end during the Battle of the Bulge that followed, when the Americans hunted them down and shot them summarily for operating out of uniform, in violation of the international laws of warfare.

* * *

The British began thinking about creating irregular warfare units for hit-and-run operations against the Germans as soon as the military campaigns of spring 1940 ended. On the evening of June 4, 1940, as the British Expeditionary Force evacuated the continent from Dunkirk, Lieutenant Colonel Dudley Clarke, an aide to General Sir John Dill, chief of the Imperial General Staff, first captured the idea in a single handwritten page. In it, he described a concept to harass the Germans on the continent, inspired by several precedents in the history of warfare of the past two centuries.[3]

In Napoleonic times, the Spaniards had fought the French occupation for years using small mobile units supported by the local population. They struck the French unexpectedly, fought small skirmishes, called *guerrillas*, or "little wars" in Spanish, and disappeared in the surrounding mountains or forests. Almost a century later,

Afrikaans-speaking settlers in South Africa organized into military units they called *Kommandos* used similar tactics to fight against the British during the Boers Wars. Clarke, who was born in Johannesburg to British settlers there, was caught in the conflict as an infant when his family was trapped for over three months in the town of Ladysmith in the Province of Natal as the Boers laid siege to the British. During the 1936 Arab revolt against the British Mandate in Palestine, Clarke, a military intelligence officer by that time, saw firsthand guerrilla tactics the Arabs were using. They had learned them from the famous T. E. Lawrence—Lawrence of Arabia—some twenty years earlier during the Arab uprising against the Ottoman Empire.

Clarke's concept envisioned the creation of British military units to harass the Germans on the continent in a similar fashion. He called them Commandos, after the Afrikaans term. Clarke submitted his idea to Dill on June 5 who took it to Prime Minister Churchill the same day. The concept of commandos resonated immediately with Churchill who had experienced personally the conflict between the British and the Afrikaners in South Africa. When the Second Boers War started on October 1899, Churchill secured an assignment to South Africa as a war correspondent for the *Morning Post*. He was with British troops when they fell in an ambush organized by Boer Kommandos. Churchill was captured and sent to a prison camp in Pretoria but managed to escape and re-join the British ranks. He witnessed the British attack that broke through the Boer siege of Ladysmith on February 28, 1900, and relieved the British soldiers and civilians trapped there, among whom were an infant Clarke and his family.[4]

As he read Clarke's proposal in 1940, Churchill must have re-lived the speech of General George White, the garrison commander, to the inhabitants of Ladysmith thanking them for the fortitude with which they had endured the dangers and privations of the siege. They had passed through a most trying ordeal, White said, "but, thank God, we kept the flag flying."[5] Launching the commando force was a way for Churchill to keep the flag flying against the German onslaught. In a memo to the War Cabinet the next day, on June 6, 1940, Churchill wrote, "Enterprises must be prepared with specially trained troops of the hunter class who can develop a reign of terror down the enemy coast. . . . I look to the Chiefs of Staff to propose measures for ceaseless offensive against the whole German-occupied coastline, leaving a trail of German corpses behind."[6]

Clarke received the assignment to gather troops and organize a raid across the English Channel as soon as possible. He sent out a call for volunteers and within a few days assembled a force of 115 soldiers. With the French-German armistice due to go into effect in the morning of June 25, 1940, at 0035 hours, Clarke decided to conduct the raid the night before as a gesture to the Germans that the British intended to fight on. Four motorboats carried the raiders to landing points along the French coast south of the port of Boulogne. The objective was to send parties inland to test the German coastal defenses and to capture prisoners for intelligence gathering purposes. The results were far from what Clarke had hoped to achieve. Two of the parties did not engage the enemy. A third one surprised two German sentries and killed them outright without collecting any information of intelligence value. The last party landed on a deserted beach off Boulogne and came under fire from a German patrol on bicycle who happened to be going by. They retreated hastily to the boat, where Clarke, who had gone along as an observer, somehow managed to be hit by a stray bullet that almost sheared his ear off. Each of the boats made their way back to England independently. One of them had a faulty compass and ended up approaching the wrong port. The port authorities left them waiting for hours on anchor while they verified the boat credentials. During that time, the raiders helped themselves to the rum stores of the boat. Once they were allowed ashore, wobbly and disheveled, they were arrested by the military police on suspicion that they were deserters.[7]

Other similar operations attempted in the following months had equally unimpressive outcomes. Traditional military officers, who had criticized the idea of irregular and unconventional warfare from the beginning, tried to squash the commando concept arguing that regular troops could do the same missions and better. But Churchill insisted on developing the capability despite the resentment it had caused. On August 25, 1940, he wrote to Anthony Eden, the secretary of state for war:

I hear that the whole position of the Commandos is being questioned. I thought therefore I might write to let you know how strongly I feel. There will certainly be many opportunities for minor operations, all of which will depend on surprise landings of lightly equipped, nimble forces accustomed to work like packs of hounds instead of being moved about in the ponderous manner which is appropriate to regular formations. For every reason, therefore, we must develop the storm troop, or Commando, idea.[8]

Thus, at Churchill's insistence, by October 1940 the Commandos had grown to two thousand in strength. Everyone volunteered from regular military formations and had basic military training as a minimum, which was complemented by a rigorous training program that included amphibious landings, long marches, survival in the terrain, and close combat. The training paid off during the first successful raid of the Commandos in March 1941 against the Lofoten Islands. They were a group of islands off the coast of Norway about one hundred miles north of the Arctic Circle where several factories processed herring and cod oil into glycerin and vitamin A and B pills for the Wehrmacht's use.[9]

Five hundred Commandos, a detachment of Royal Engineers, and a platoon of fifty-two Norwegian soldiers sailed from their base in Scotland in a convoy protected by five destroyers. After a three-day journey in the North Atlantic, they arrived off the coast of the Lofoten Islands in the early morning of March 4. The only resistance they encountered was from the German trawler *Krebs*, which sailed resolutely against the approaching flotilla and was promptly fired upon and set on fire. The Commandos retrieved a set of spare rotors for a German Enigma coding machine before the ship sank. After the raid, they sent them to Bletchley Park, where they were of great use to the code breakers there. As a civilian coast liner, the *Mira*, came close, the destroyers fired a warning shot across its bow. Most likely not recognizing the warning, the Norwegian skipper failed to stop and the destroyers fired again. *Mira* sank, resulting in the loss of seven civilian lives.

Using small craft, the troops landed on Vest Vaago and Ost Vaago, the two islands where the fish-oil processing factories were located.

The engineers proceeded to destroy all factories on land as well as the nine-thousand-ton *Hamburg*, one of the most modern fish-processing factory ships at the time. They blew up storage tanks containing eight hundred thousand gallons of fuel, which set several small merchant ships on fire. While the engineers went about their business, the Commandos rounded up all the Germans in the islands and their Quisling collaborators. From the telegraph station, Lieutenant Richard L. Wills sent a telegram to one A. Hitler of Berlin: "You said in your last speech German troops would meet the British wherever they landed. Where are your troops?" Equally cheeky was a bus ride taken by Captain Simon Frasier, 15th Lord Lovat, and some of his men to a nearby seaplane base, where they captured several German sailors. The commander of the base later complained about the "unwarlike" behavior of the Commandos and undertook to report accordingly to the Führer.

After six hours on the islands, the raiders returned to the ships and headed for England. It had been an entirely successful operation. The only casualty the British suffered was a wounded officer who accidentally shot himself in the leg with the pistol he was carrying in his pocket. In addition to the destruction of the facilities in the islands, the Commandos brought with them 214 German prisoners and over 300 Norwegians who volunteered to join the free Norwegian forces in Great Britain. The German reaction to the raid was quick. SS troops raided the area and burned several houses as a punishment for the defections. They took over one hundred civilians as hostages and interned them in the first Norwegian concentration camp opened near Oslo. The Wehrmacht began fortifying the islands and moved one hundred thousand additional troops in Norway to protect from future incursions.

* * *

The next stage in the maturity of the Commandos was their ability to conduct ground assaults in coordination with the navy and air support. Given the traditional parochial nature of the individual services, the Commandos needed a leader that not only would inspire the troops but also would entice the services to collaborate. Captain Lord Louis

Mountbatten, a member of the royal family and distinguished navy commander, had the perfect experience and pedigree for the job. At the beginning of October 1941, he was appointed chief of Combined Operations Headquarters and was responsible for coordinating the Commandos' missions with those of the other services. To strengthen Mountbatten's stature with the three services, he held simultaneously the ranks of vice admiral of the Royal Navy, lieutenant general of the army, and air marshal of the air force.[10]

The first coordinated operation came at the end of December 1941 against another target off the Norwegian coast: the islands of Vaagso and Maaloy, which served as an assembly point for German troop convoys headed north around Norway to the fighting front in Finland. It was patterned after the Lofotens raid, except this time the British were certain to encounter significant resistance from the Germans who had installed heavily fortified coastal defense guns in Maaloy and could count on the Luftwaffe's support from nearby air fields.

The task force left the Commando base of operations in Scapa Flow, off the northern coast of Scotland, on Christmas Eve and was in position in front of Maaloy on the morning of December 27, 1941. Starting at 0848 hours, four destroyers and the cruiser HMS *Kenya*, fitted with six-inch guns, rained fire on the small island of Maaloy, less than five hundred yards by two hundred yards, and took out three of the four coastal guns, ammunition stores, oil tanks, and the German barracks located there. Under cover of fire, 105 Commandos approached the shore aboard landing craft. When they were fifty meters from the beach, the naval bombardment stopped. In a perfectly timed action, Hampden bombers appeared overhead and dropped smoke bombs on the beach to cover the landing and initial advance of the Commandos. Despite German resistance, the Commandos overran Maaloy within twenty minutes.

The fighting on Vaagso was heavier, especially in the village of South Vaagso where fifty German crack troops who happened to be vacationing there for Christmas put up a stiff resistance. For several hours, the Commandos fought house-to-house battles and provided cover for the engineers who were mining and destroying the facilities on the island. During this time, the *Kenya* destroyed a German battery four miles southeast of Vaasgo after a prolonged exchange of fire during which the *Kenya* took at least three hits. The destroyers swept the fjords for enemy ships while the British long-range Blenheim and Beaufort fighters strafed nearby airfields and engaged German Messerschmitts that came over to support their troops. The raiding party re-embarked at 1445 hours and the entire task force set sail immediately for Scapa Flow. Over seventy Norwegians took passage back to England. To reduce Nazi reprisals on relatives, each volunteer brought along his entire family. On the trip home to England, in the quarters of the British officers, the men of Vaasgo drank a toast to victory and sang a Norwegian Christmas song.[11]

The Vaasgo raid was a great success in that it demonstrated the British ability to coordinate naval, air, and ground actions to overcome heavily fortified positions and determined resistance from the enemy. Allied losses were seventy Commandos, including seventeen killed, and eight navy casualties, including two killed. In addition, eleven British planes were lost. The engineers demolished all their assigned objectives, including the power station, coastal defenses, the local radio station, a canning factory, and a lighthouse. German losses included 150 killed and 98 captured. Four German fighter planes were shot down while the destroyers sank nine merchant ships totaling 15,000 tons. Two armed trawlers that had been escorting the merchant ships were also captured and sank but not before being thoroughly searched by naval intelligence officers attached to the task force who were able to retrieve the Enigma cipher machines and codebooks.[12]

As an additional benefit, the raid provided a great morale boost and propaganda value. Two war photographers accompanied the Commandos taking pictures of the action, which were released upon returning home. *Life* magazine published several pages of "the merry blazes of Vaasgo" at the end of January 1942 and summarized the operation: "The war would not be won by such raid as the Dec. 27 adventure at Vaasgo, but it will be probably won by the kind of daring and surprise typified by the Commandos. . . . The Vaasgo raid had the enormous benefit of cheering up the entire British Army with a little action in Europe. It also depressed the German garrisons isolated along the long coast of Europe and forced the Germans to regroup and reinforce their defenses."[13]

* * *

After the successful raid at Vaasgo, the military establishment no longer questioned the value of commando-style actions in harassing the Germans and forcing them to disperse their forces to protect from attacks that could pop up anywhere. Churchill however set his sights higher. Writing to Mountbatten, he requested a major shift in focus for the Combined Operations Headquarters, whose "main object must be the re-invasion of France. You must create the machine which will make it possible for us to beat Hitler on land. You must devise the appurtenances and appliances which will make the invasion possible."[14]

In early 1942, Mountbatten set up a training center on the grounds of Achnacarry Castle in Scotland designed to create soldiers equipped with the necessary fighting skills to spearhead the upcoming invasions. Lieutenant Colonel Charles Vaughn, a veteran Commando who had been one of the leaders of the Lofotens raid, headed the center. He set up a twelve-week training program specifically designed to prepare the men who volunteered to join the special operations units for the demands of irregular warfare.

The training emphasized the highest standards of initiative, mental alertness and physical fitness, together with the maximum skill at arms. All trainees were pushed to think for themselves, adjust to unexpected circumstances with sound tactical sense, and devise new courses of action in situations that may be entirely different to those that were anticipated. Mentally, they were trained to maintain an offensive spirit at all times. Physically, all men were expected to maintain the highest state of fitness at all times. To graduate, the recruits had to be able to cover seven miles in one hour and fight immediately upon arrival. After covering nine miles in two hours, or twenty-five miles in eight hours, or thirty-five miles in fourteen hours, they were expected to fight after two hours rest. They learned to climb cliffs, mountains, and difficult slopes. Because the sea was regarded as a natural working ground for the Commandos, they were trained to operate in boats and landing craft.

Other skills developed during the training included the ability to live off the land, a highly tuned night sense, compass use, map reading, route memorization, Morse code, and the use of wireless transmitters or semaphores for communication. Special courses taught demolitions and sabotage techniques, handling high explosives, setting up and using Bangalore torpedoes, and laying all types of booby traps. Fighting tactics emphasized street fighting, occupying and setting up defense perimeters around towns, and overcoming all types of obstacles, such as barbed wire, rivers, and high walls. All recruits learned to drive Allied and enemy motorcycles, cars, trucks, and even tracked vehicles, trains, and motor boats. They received first-aid training, learned how to dress gunshot wounds, and practiced carrying the wounded.[15]

The first cohort of trainees arrived at Achnacarry in March 1942. By the time its gates closed in 1946, twenty-five thousand Allied soldiers—British, American, French, Canadian, Dutch, Norwegian, etc.—had completed the training successfully and received the much coveted green beret of the Commandos. Among the first non-British troops to receive training were the men of the US Army Rangers First Battalion, which was activated on June 19, 1942, under the command of Major William O. Darby.[16] Earlier in the year, the US Army chief of staff, General George C. Marshall, had sent Colonel Lucian K. Truscott, Jr., to Mountbatten's Combined Operations Headquarters in London to arrange for American troops to take part in British Commando raids against German-occupied Europe. The American soldiers that would participate in the raids would come from a broad cross section of units and return to those same units after the raids were over. This would ensure that, when American forces landed in Europe, they would have some combat-experienced men.

On May 26, 1942, the day on which Truscott received the promotion to brigadier general, he proposed to Marshall to organize an American unit along the lines of British Commandos. The British would train the men and include them in combat operations under their control. After receiving training and combat exposure, as many men as possible would return to their original organizations and other men would take their places. Truscott thus intended the new unit to be more of a school than a conventional fighting organization. It differed from other schools in that combat would be part of its curriculum. Marshall approved Truscott's proposal right away.

Major General Dwight D. Eisenhower, who was then chief of the Operations Division in the War Department General Staff, told Truscott that if such units were organized, he should name them something other than "Commandos" because that name was so strongly identified with the British. Truscott chose "Rangers," a name that a number of American units had carried before, during, and after the War of Independence. The new unit was thus designated the First Ranger Battalion. Throughout the month of June 1942, Darby, its commanding officer, selected 26 officers and 452 enlisted men among volunteers that came from the US Army Northern Ireland Forces. On June 28, the battalion moved from Northern Ireland to the Achnacarry training center, where it received Commando training until July 31. On August 1, 1942, six officers and forty-five enlisted men of the Rangers were attached to the Numbers 3 and 4 Commandos and the Canadian 2nd Division for the raid on the French port of Dieppe.

* * *

In the Allied military thinking at the time, the initial target of the invasion of Europe would be a port with sufficient facilities to support the considerable logistic requirements of the landing forces. The Dieppe Raid was intended to test the Germans defenses of such facilities, in addition to rehearsing coordinated action between Allied air power, naval forces, and ground assault teams. According to the plan, an Allied fleet of 237 ships and landing craft left ports from southern England in the evening of August 18, 1942. Troops of Number 3 Commando led by Lieutenant Colonel John Durnford-Slater and Number 4 Commando led by Lieutenant Colonel Lord Lovat formed the advance party of the invasion force. Their mission was to neutralize coastal batteries east and west of Dieppe before they could fire on the ships carrying the main landing force composed of the Canadian 2nd Division.

About an hour before they reached the target, 3 Commando ran into German patrol boats. They suffered significant casualties in the ensuing firefight and were dispersed, with only about half of the Commandos able to land on the designated beach. The commanding officer, Lieutenant Wills, the same one who had sent the telegram to Hitler during the raid in the Lofotens Islands, was shot through the neck. The next ranking officer, Lieutenant Edward Loustalot of the US Rangers, took charge and led the Commandos up a narrow lane behind the beach. He was killed there—the first American soldier of World War II to be killed in Europe.[17] The raiding force was reduced to only eighteen men. They were not able to destroy the assigned battery but managed to snipe at the German crews with sufficient precision to prevent them from hitting the approaching vessels.

Things went better for Lord Lovat's 4 Commando, which included four Rangers: Corporal William R. Brady, Staff Sergeant Kenneth Stemson, Sergeant Alex J. Szima, and Corporal Franklin M. Koons. Upon landing on the beach, the Commandos received an order to storm a seventy-five-foot cliff and knock out two pillboxes on top of it. "It looked like a suicide mission but damned if we didn't make it," Corporal Brady said later.[18] In the ensuing firefight, Corporal Koons became the first American ground soldier to kill a German in World War II.[19] Lovat's raiders were able to destroy the six-inch gun batteries relatively quickly and without serious casualties. By 0830 hours, they had re-embarked the landing craft and headed back for England. This was the only unit participating in the Dieppe operation that completed their objective.

The main landing force, five thousand infantry, mostly Canadians, and twenty-seven Churchill tanks, landed at four beaches in front of Dieppe. They were decimated by the alerted Germans who made the best of the strong fortifications they had built to protect the port and its adjacent beaches. Political considerations and a desire to avoid French civilian casualties had taken off the table the option to soften these fortifications through aerial or naval bombardment, although both the Royal Air Force and the navy did their best to support the troops stranded in the beaches. At 1100 hours, six hours after the landings had started, the withdrawal from the beaches began and continued for three hours under heavy fire. Casualties from the raid included 3,367 Canadians and 275 British Commandos killed, wounded, or taken prisoner. The Royal Navy lost one destroyer and thirty-three landing craft, suffering 550 dead and wounded. The RAF lost 106 aircraft to the Luftwaffe's 48. The German army casualties were 591.[20]

The raid was a disaster that has raised controversies ever since. Historians have advanced a number of theories over the years and continue to bring forward new ones to this day to explain it. They range from the possibility that Mountbatten acted without authorization in launching the raid to the hypothesis that the raid was a cover for the true operation led by Ian Fleming in which British military intelligence would steal the Enigma codes from the German naval headquarters in Dieppe.[21] What remains undisputed is that the Allied planners learned a number of lessons from the failure at Dieppe, which were factored into the planning of the Normandy invasion on D-Day.[22]

In the immediate aftermath of the raid, the British point of view prevailed that the best place to open a second front against the Germans was in the Mediterranean. It was a strategy that Churchill defined as a "wide encircling movement in the Mediterranean having for its primary objective the recovery of the command of that vital sea, but also having for its object the exposure of the underbelly of the Axis, especially Italy, to heavy attack."[23] The first step in implementing this strategy was Operation Torch, the American-led invasion of French North Africa. The Rangers, now operating independently of the British Commandos and under full control of the US Army, were among the first units to engage in what was the first in a long string of strikes against German targets for the remainder of the war.

* * *

Another controversy that arose almost immediately after the Dieppe raid revolved around the treatment of prisoners captured during the raid. Rumors circulated after the war that upon retreating from the beaches the Commandos had shot in cold blood German prisoners whom they could not carry back to England. No proof has surfaced to substantiate these rumors and the German authorities themselves did not allege that this occurred. However, almost immediately after the raid, the Germans raised complaints about the shackling of prisoners by the Commandos. A communiqué issued by the German government on September 2, 1942, said that British troops in Dieppe had received orders to tie the hands of captured Germans whenever possible so that the Germans would be unable to destroy their papers. British officers and men taken prisoners in the attack on Dieppe would be kept manacled unless the British government withdrew its order for the binding of German captives within twenty-four hours, the communiqué threatened. In its response, the British War Office declared that none of the German prisoners taken at Dieppe had been tied. It was making inquiries to find out whether such an order was issued and if one was issued it would be canceled.[24]

An incident at the beginning of October 1942 exacerbated the issue. On the night of October 3, a dozen Commandos landed on the small Channel island of Sark, under German control at the time, to gather evidence that the Germans had deported British subjects for forced labor in Germany. They surprised five Germans sleeping in a hotel and decided to take them back to the boat and on to England for interrogation. According to the official report of the action, the Germans had been recalcitrant so the commandos tied their hands to hurry back to the boat to catch the tide. As they were doing this, one of the Germans attacked his guard and tried to raise the alarm. The Commandos killed four of the German prisoners before running to their boat.[25]

The discovery of the dead men with hands tied behind their backs outraged the German leadership at the top of the Nazi and military hierarchies. The repeated Commando raids had so rattled the security along the European coast that Hitler, in a fit of rage, decided they had to stop. Goebbels, on the other hand, saw a great opportunity to create a psychological diversion to distract the attention of the German people from the bad news that was coming from the East. So, for the next several months a bizarre game of charges and countercharges was played out in radio broadcasts and official communiqués issued from Berlin and London regarding the treatment of prisoners of war.

The first international convention for the treatment prisoners of war was drawn up in Geneva in 1864 and focused on providing for the care of wounded prisoners. That convention was amended several times until the version of July 27, 1929, which was in effect during World War II. The convention provided a captured officer or soldier, within necessary limits of restraint on movement, the same treatment as his rank or grade would receive under the army that was holding him prisoner. Enlisted men could be required to do a reasonable amount of work, in return for food, shelter, and clothing similar to those provided for the capturing forces. Prisoner officers were supposed to be paid the same sum of money given to their captor officers of like rank, and from that income must pay their own lodging, board, and other bills. The International Red Cross was the neutral agency designated to monitor the compliance with the convention requirements. Specific articles of the convention protected the prisoners of war from mistreatment, including the following:

> **Article 2.** Prisoners of war are in the power of the hostile Power, but not of the individuals or corps who have captured them. They must at all times be humanely treated and protected, particularly against acts of violence, insults and public curiosity. Measures of reprisal against them are prohibited.
> **Article 3.** Prisoners of war have the right to have their person and their honor respected . . .[26]

Since the beginning of World War II, the Wehrmacht had waged the war in the East with cruel barbarity and with complete disregard of these conventions, justifying the atrocities in their mind with the idea that the Germans were fighting against an inferior race, which they had the God-given mission to liquidate and replace. In the West, however, despite atrocities against civilians, especially Jewish people, including looting, persecution, and shooting of hostages, mistreatment of prisoners of war had been tempered up to that point "by the desire, so strong in the German soul, to appear to the rest of the world correct and proper."[27] The Germans by and large and certainly the Western Allies had respected the rights afforded to the prisoners of war by the Geneva Convention.

However, as the *New York Times* pointed out at the time, "The Geneva Convention, accepted by both Great Britain and Germany, provides for the treatment of prisoners after they were in safe custody but it does not deal with conditions during military action or in other circumstances where it is a question of the captors' lives or those of the captives."[28] Commandos definitely operated in this gray area and were taught simple and expeditious ways to handle prisoners during their missions. The syllabus for a close combat training course provided the following instruction on how to search a prisoner: "Kill him first. If that is inconvenient, make him lay face to the ground, hands out in front of him. Knock him out with rifle butt, side or butt of the pistol, or with your boot. Then search him."[29]

To secure a prisoner who needed to be kept alive for some time for questioning or intelligence collection, the syllabus instructed the students to "knock him out, place him face down on the ground, and [using fifteen feet of cord that all Commandos carried on them] tie his hands behind his back, lead the cord round his throat, back to his wrists, round both ankles, back to his wrists." Once the prisoner was tied up, he would be gagged. "Almost anything would do to stuff his mouth—turf, cloth, a forage cap, etc. For something to tie over his mouth, strips can be torn from the prisoner's clothing."[30] In this context then it is easy to understand how German prisoners captured during the Dieppe raid or at Sark would have been tied up or killed.

On October 8, 1942, the German radio announced that shackles had been placed on British prisoners of war captured at Dieppe, in retaliation for the tying of German soldiers' hands by members of the British raiding party at Sark. The British response over the BBC radio pointed out that taking reprisals against prisoners was expressly forbidden by the Geneva Convention and that an equal number of German prisoners of war would be manacled and chained unless the British prisoners were released from their chains within forty-eight hours. The British Government denied again that prisoners had been tied up or that orders had been issued authorizing such action.

The next day, Canada announced that in reprisal for the shackling by the Nazis of 107 officers and 1,269 noncommissioned officers and men captured in the Dieppe raid, the Canadian authorities had shackled an equivalent number of German prisoners there. One of the difficulties had been to decide how to bind the prisoners. Handcuffs used for dangerous criminals had been ruled out and "jails and courthouses throughout the country had to be ransacked for foot shackles that would permit some liberty of movement."[31]

On October 16, the German High Command took the war of reprisals against prisoners a step further by announcing that any treatment of German war prisoners that was inhumane or against international law, as it was happening in Russia "will from now on be atoned for by the entirety of prisoners taken by Germany without regard to their nationalities."[32] It became clear that Britain could not win the retaliation game against the Nazis. The Germans would counter their next move with yet another move that raised the stakes, further mistreating or even shooting the prisoners. The Allies took the issue off the table in mid-December when Great Britain and Canada announced that they had removed the chains from German prisoners in reply to a proposal from the Swiss government. The German propaganda limited itself to announcing that the German authorities were giving the proposal the "friendliest consideration," according to Berlin radio.[33]

* * *

The world did not know at the time that in his rage against the Commando raids, Hitler had ordered measures the brutality of which made the debate about shackling prisoners of war look like a harmless argument among academics. On October 18, 1942, Hitler issued a direct order, a *Führerbefehl*, which began by stating that the enemies of Germany, in their commando operations, were using methods of warfare outside the scope of the Geneva Conventions. "From captured documents, it has been learned that they have orders not only to bind prisoners but to kill them without hesitation should they become an encumbrance or constitute an obstacle to the completion of their mission. Finally, we have captured orders which advocate putting prisoners to death as a matter of principle."[34] The order announced that Germany was going to resort to the same methods and the German troops would annihilate these groups of saboteurs and their accomplices without mercy wherever they found them. After that introductory recital, the order continued as follows:

3.) Therefore, I order that: From now on all enemy troops encountered by German troops during so-called commando operations in Europe or in Africa, even if they appear to be soldiers in uniform or demolition groups, armed or unarmed, are to be exterminated to the last man, either in combat or in pursuit. It matters not in the least whether they have been landed for their operations by ships or planes or dropped by parachute. If such men appear to be about to surrender, no quarter shall be given them—on general principle. A full report on this point is to be sent to the OKW [*Ober Kommando der Wehrmacht*, High Command of the Armed Forces] in every single case for publication in the Wehrmacht communiqué.

4.) If individual members of such commandos, acting as agents, saboteurs, etc., fall into the hands of the Wehrmacht through different channels (for example, through the police in occupied territories), they are to be handed over without delay to the *Sicherheitsdienst* [Security Service]. It is formally forbidden to keep them, even temporarily, under military supervision (for example in prisoner of war camps, etc.).

5.) These provisions do not apply to enemy soldiers who surrender or are captured in actual combat within the limits of normal combat activities (offensives, large scale seaborne and airborne landing operations). Nor do they apply to enemy troops captured during naval engagements, or to aviators who have bailed out to save their lives during aerial combat.

6.) I will summon before the tribunal of war all leaders and officers who fail to carry out these instructions—either by failure to inform their men or by failing to act in accordance with this order.

Signed, Adolf Hitler[35]

The original order was promulgated in twelve copies to the top echelons of the Wehrmacht and to Himmler, the Reichsführer SS and chief of the German police. On the same date, Hitler issued an explanation of his "sharp order for the annihilation of enemy sabotage troops." In this explanation, Hitler pointed out that commando and sabotage operations by the enemies of Germany had been extraordinarily successful in the disruption of rear communications, intimidation of groups working for Germany, and destruction of important war plants in the occupied areas. Hitler also pointed out that enemy troops engaged in such missions ran no danger of suffering really serious losses, since, should worst come to worst, they could surrender and claim the status of prisoners of war under the Geneva Convention. The explanation continued as follows:

> If now the German war effort is not to suffer the most severe damage through such procedure, then it must be made clear to the enemy that every sabotage troop without exception is mowed down to the last man. That means that the prospect of escaping here with life, is exactly equal to zero. It can therefore not be permitted under any circumstance that explosion, sabotage or terrorist troops merely place themselves and are captured [sic], to be treated according to the rules of the Geneva Convention, but they are to be totally exterminated under all circumstances.
>
> The announcement, which is to appear in the Armed Forces Report ("*Wehrmachtbericht*") will say quite briefly and laconically that sabotage, terror, or destruction troops were surrounded and mowed down to the last man.[36]

After threatening to call to the strictest account all officers who failed to carry out his order "with all energy," Hitler concluded his explanation as follows:

> Should there be a purpose in sparing one or two men for reason of an interrogation, the latter are to be shot immediately after their interrogation.
>
> Signed, Adolf Hitler[37]

A number of German officers followed this Führerbefehl almost immediately after it was issued. General Nikolaus von Falkenhorst, commander of all German forces in Norway, distinguished himself for applying the Führerbefehl energetically in Norway. The first victims of the Führerbefehl were nine members of a British Commando team captured in September 1942 after sabotaging a hydroelectric station in Glomfjord. After the issuance of the Führerbefehl, the German military handed them over to *Sicherheitsdients* (Security Police or SD), which transferred them to the Sachsenhausen concentration camp in extreme secrecy. The British Commandos were executed with a shot in the neck there on October 22, 1942. Fourteen members of an English sabotage team who landed by glider near Egersund, Norway, on November 20, 1942, were captured and shot after interrogation, even though they were all in British uniforms. Three more sabotage units were captured in December in Norway and were executed after interrogation. On March 30, 1943, ten Norwegian navy personnel, who had participated in a raid by cutter, were captured at Toftefjord, Norway. SD applied the Führerbefehl against them and the incident was reported as follows in the Wehrmacht Report of April 6, 1943: "In Northern Norway an enemy sabotage unit was engaged and destroyed on approaching the coast."[38]

However, Hitler's order was not followed blindly everywhere. When Field Marshal Edwin Rommel, commander in chief of the Panzer Army, Africa, received his copy of the order in North Africa, he ordered it burned at once because he felt the order was contrary to a soldier's morals.[39] On February 11, 1943, the Naval War Staff felt it necessary to promulgate another memorandum on the subject to clarify "some misunderstanding" as to the proper interpretation of the Hitler order. The memorandum made it clear that all commanders and officers who neglected their duty concerning the order ran the serious risk of court martial penalties. This memorandum stated that it was Hitler's view that the military sabotage organization in the East and West would have portentous consequences for the entire German war effort and that shooting of uniformed prisoners acting on military orders must be carried out even after they have surrendered without a fight and asked for pardon.[40]

Thus, going into 1943, special operations and commando actions in Europe had proven capable of drawing Hitler's ire with their successful hit-and-run tactics. It is in this tense environment that new players from the Office of Strategic Services entered the battlefield.

CHAPTER 3

The OSS Operational Groups

The successful landing of American-led forces in Morocco and Algeria in November 1942 coincided with the resounding victory of the British-led forces at the second battle of El Alamein. In this Egyptian coastal town sixty miles west of the port city of Alexandria, the British Eighth Army had stopped Rommel's Panzer Army's eastward advance toward the Suez Canal in July 1942. After refitting, resupplying, and building up their forces, the British went on the offensive on October 23, 1942. Under the decisive leadership of newly appointed commanders General Harold Alexander and Lieutenant General Bernard Montgomery, the Allies broke out of El Alamein on November 11 and began a 1,600-mile chase of the remnants of the Axis troops all the way to Tunisia. Pushed on all sides, the German Afrika Korps and their Italian allies in Tunisia surrendered on May 12, 1943.

After the demise of the Axis forces in North Africa, the Allies began preparing for the next campaigns in continental Europe, beginning with the invasion of Sicily and then the Italian mainland. Fomenting native resistance and creating uncertainty in the Axis rear areas was part of the strategy for the new campaigns in which Donovan believed the OSS had a key role to play. As early as December 1941, he had worked on plans for recruiting, training, and inserting guerrilla units in hostile territory. In August 1942, shortly after the establishment of

the OSS, the Joint Chiefs of Staff approved in principle the formation of these guerrilla units. On December 23, 1942, a directive from
the JCS authorized the OSS to "proceed with the organization and
conduct of guerrilla warfare," subject to the approval of the wartime
theater commanders. The official history of the OSS calls this "the
conception of OGs."

From the beginning, Donovan structured the OGs as military
units staffed only with military personnel. Colonel Russell J. Livermore became the first commanding officer and continued as chief of
OG operations throughout the war. A prominent New York lawyer
with a distinguished record in World War I, Livermore tried unsuc-
cessfully to re-enlist shortly after the attack on Pearl Harbor. He was
a close friend of Donovan's, who appointed him as civilian chief of the
New York branch of the COI early in 1942. In June he was commissioned as a major and went to Washington where he devoted his entire
time to evolving the concept of special harassing operations, which
became the OGs.

The existence of military units within the OSS—a civilian organization in itself—caused a lot of consternation in the War Department,
which viewed with deep-seated disapproval the existence of military
forces outside the regular armed forces structures. Nevertheless, by
early 1943 Donovan had convinced General Eisenhower, then commanding officer of the North Africa theater of operations, of the value
that the OGs could bring in the upcoming battles. On February 3,
1943, Eisenhower requested several operational groups in his theater
to be used as organizers, fomenters, and operational nuclei in enemy-held areas.

The initial table of organization called for a complement of 540
officers and men, all Army personnel on detached duty to the OSS.
The OGs would be highly skilled foreign language–speaking soldiers, trained with commando capabilities, who could be parachuted
in small groups into enemy-occupied territory to harass the enemy
and to encourage and support local resistance organizations. In May
1943, OGs were organized under their own branch within the OSS,
which eventually became a separate command reporting directly
to Donovan.[1]

With Sicily and Italy being the next targets of the Allies in the Mediterranean, recruiting for Italian-speaking OGs took priority between April and May 1943. The Army Ground Forces Headquarters authorized the recruitment of officers and men from divisions of the Second and Third Armies. The first recruits came from infantry divisions and engineer units in Fort Belvoir, Virginia, Fort Jackson, South Carolina, Camp Blanding, Florida, and Camp Breckenridge, Kentucky. At each location, OSS recruiters broadcast and posted announcements calling for volunteers willing to perform hazardous duty overseas. Those who came forward filled out a twelve-page application covering in detail their personal history, including biographical information, education, employment history, financial background, skills, religion, and foreign languages. They provided information about family members, including parents, siblings, children, and in-laws, with particular emphasis on "relatives by blood, marriage, or adoption who live abroad, are under the jurisdiction of a foreign power, are not citizens of the Unites States, or are married to non-citizens." They also listed employment references, character references, and names of neighbors and social acquaintances who could provide further information about them.[2]

Livermore and a small group of officers conducted a highly selective process in which they screened the applications and interviewed personally over two thousand men. Without getting into operational details, they explained that the assignments were behind enemy lines and carried unusual and dangerous risks. They chose only men demonstrating a real desire for such duty. They preferred candidates who spoke Italian fluently, but they accepted a number of second-generation Italian Americans who possessed only basic language comprehension skills. Previous training in demolitions, weapons, scouting, or fieldcraft was particularly desirable and exceedingly valuable. The rigorous character of their work demanded that OG personnel satisfy the same physical requirements as men accepted for parachute training in the Army. In addition, candidates were evaluated based on their emotional and mental stability, as well as good judgment, which were considered paramount for the success of operations behind enemy lines.[3]

At the end of the process, seventeen officers and 126 enlisted men were selected from the pool of two thousand candidates. They received orders to report to the OSS headquarters at 2340 E Street in Washington, DC, where administrative staff processed them into the OSS. From there, the candidates went to a training and holding facility in nearby Bethesda, Maryland. Known as Training Area F, it was located on the grounds of the Congressional Country Club, which the OSS had taken over for the duration of the war.

On May 14, 1943, the OGs recruited for Italian operations were formally activated as a unit designated Company Λ, 2677th Regiment (Provisional), OSS. The basic unit of organization was the group, composed of four officers and thirty enlisted men. The commander, or group leader, was a captain and the group itself was composed of two sections, each led by a first lieutenant. The sections in turn were subdivided into four squads, each led by a staff sergeant. At the point of activation, Company A included four operational groups.

While suitable as a holding area, Training Area F had not been prepared as a training facility in time to serve the needs of the Italian OGs. As a result, immediately after its official creation, Company A left for three weeks of advanced training at the Infantry School in Fort Benning, Georgia. Training included a strenuous course on jungle warfare and some preliminary parachute training, as well as intensive instruction in weapons, techniques, and methods of operations appropriate for a small, self-sufficient band of men who might be required to live and fight as guerrillas. Most of the officers who had already received this training attended special OSS courses in demolition, close combat, and silent killing techniques, which were organized in Quantico, Virginia, and at the nearby Prince William Forest, outside Washington, DC.

On June 12, 1943, the unit reassembled at the Congressional Country Club. Because the departure overseas was imminent, the men received an eight-day furlough, which they used to visit their families. Upon return they learned that there had been a delay in transport, so advanced training began. Classes of four officers and thirty-five enlisted men travelled to Quantico for additional demolitions training while the rest of the unit used the wooded area around the Congressional

Country Club to solve small unit problems—cross-country movement, approach and destruction of targets, and withdrawal. Around this time, the men began calling themselves Donovan's Devils, a name that stuck within the OSS and became synonymous with the OGs.[4]

On July 29, the unit moved on trucks from the Congressional Country Club to a holding area in Hagerstown, Maryland, and began preparing for travel overseas. Although morale was very high, the command continued a modified training program to keep the men occupied at all times. The OGs checked all the equipment and fully prepared for the trip. Each man had to settle his accounts and pay any money owed to the military camp authorities for items like property, equipment, mess bills, and personal telephone calls. They were required to pay any debts owed to civilian establishments in the vicinity, as well. The men completed all needed inoculations and immunizations and obtained correct identification tags, military IDs, and passports. They drew the equipment prescribed in their orders and took a final course in the use of their personal weapons, including a test in marksmanship with the arms issued to them. Military counselors advised them to prepare or update their will, power of attorney, allotments from their paycheck, insurance policies, and next of kin information.[5]

The date of departure from the staging area in Hagerstown was set for August 10. On the day prior, Colonel Ellery C. Huntington, in charge of the OSS security office, arrived from Washington for an inspection of the troops. That same evening, a banquet was held for the entire company where the colonel held a speech in Italian. The entire ceremony was very impressive and the morale of the troops remained very high. On August 10, the unit departed from Hagerstown, Maryland, for the staging area at Camp Kilmer, New Jersey, where they stayed until August 20 filling out additional forms, replacing worn equipment, and drawing clothing as needed. Everyone received a final physical examination. On August 20 at 1900 hours the unit boarded the train to Jersey City and from there took the ferry to Staten Island. At 2330 hours, they embarked aboard the troop transport USS *Monticello*.

The USS *Monticello* departed from the United States at 0930 hours on August 21, 1943, for North Africa. Men were allowed on deck four hours each day. The trip was uneventful except for an explosion in the boiler room that killed a sailor but did not affect the journey otherwise. After a twelve-day journey, on September 1, 1943, the unit debarked at Oran, Algeria. After several days of rest at Oran, they boarded a train to their final destination, the OSS headquarters in Algiers, known as Station X. The train trip was a ritual for all the OSS men arriving from the United States to the North Africa theater of operations. The officers travelled in third-class coaches and the men in diminutive boxcars called *Quarante ou Huit* (Forty or Eight) because they were used to transport forty men of the French Foreign Legion or eight horses. An OSS veteran recalled his train ride to Algiers as follows:

> Much of the landscape was more like a moonscape—bleak, rocky, endless, with shimmering heat waves obscuring the horizon, and small, ragged boys materializing from nowhere crying '*Baksheesh!*' Bright oases bloomed here and there in the form of lovely French colonial towns with palm-lined streets, dazzling adobe walls, arched windows, and red tile roofs. They were alive with gaudy soldiers, dark and light in red fezzes and tunics. . . . We took in stride the cold stares of French Legionnaires who had been loyal to the Vichy government, and who fought against the American invaders of Operation Torch.[6]

On September 8, 1943, the unit arrived at Station X, where it set up pup tents in a former private beach community called Club des Pins. The OGs continued training to maintain their fitness while awaiting further combat orders. During the period from September 9 to 27 nearly all officers and enlisted men of the unit underwent parachute training. Although it was not a formal paratrooper course, the OSS had recruited jump-qualified paratroopers from the 82nd and 101st Airborne Divisions to teach it. They had built a high platform with a cable reaching down to the ground at an angle from which the trainees would slide down to practice approaching the ground, manipulating the parachute raisers, and landing safely. There were also mock C-47 fuselages with benches and a mock door, which the men used to practice hooking up the lines and jumping off the aircraft as commanded by the jumpmaster. This stage of the training led to live jumps that began at one thousand feet and continued at lower altitudes until they reached five hundred feet, which was the typical altitude from which paratroopers jumped. Officers and men had to perform at least four jumps to qualify for parachute drops.[7]

* * *

The Italian OGs of Company A served as the trailblazers for the new type of units created within the OSS. Other units quickly followed to bring the operational group capabilities to other areas in Europe where they were suited for action. By August 1944, when the Operational Group Command had reached full strength, it included 1,100 men in its ranks.

In July and August 1943, the OSS recruited French-speaking men to staff Company B and began training for the invasion of France planned for the following year. As part of their tactical training, they took part in combined airborne troop carrier maneuvers in North Carolina in December 1943. They left the United States for the North Africa theater of operations in January 1944 and arrived in Algiers in February. Six additional groups, two Italian and four French, were formed in the winter of 1943 and 1944 and departed in March 1944 to augment Companies A and B. One German group was formed in the spring of 1944 and arrived in North Africa in July, where it was attached to Company A.[8]

With the agreement of officials from the Norwegian government-in-exile, the OSS recruited personnel from the 99th Infantry Battalion, an all-Norwegian US Army unit stationed in Camp Hale, Colorado. Ten officers and sixty-nine enlisted men volunteered and formed the Norwegian Operational Group, activated on July 28, 1943, at Training Area F, just vacated by the Italian OGs. The group conducted five months of intensive specialized training, including mountain climbing in Colorado and amphibious operations at Martha's Vineyard, Massachusetts. The group departed the United States and arrived in Scotland in December 1943 under the Allied Forces Headquarters Scandinavia command. There was more training and exercise at various SOE bases and schools but the unit was not called to action against targets in Norway given British restrictions on operations against that country. In June 1944, the Norwegian OGs were combined with the French OGs and participated in seven parachute missions into France in August and September 1944.[9]

Company C was created in fall 1943 with OGs destined to cover the Balkans. The first OGs for Yugoslavia left the United States at the end of October 1943; others left at the end of January 1944. The island of Vis, off the Dalmatian coast, became their main base of operations. Vis at the time was a major supply base for the Yugoslav partisans, through which flowed thousands of tons of equipment that the Allies shipped from southern Italy. Over two hundred Yugoslavian OGs became part of the Allied garrison at Vis, which included hundreds of British Commandos and Yugoslav partisans. The OGs conducted joint operations to defend the island against German attacks, to harass enemy forces on other Dalmatian islands, and to obtain battle order information for enemy forces on these islands and on the mainland. They operated from the Vis base until July 1944, when the Germans abandoned the area.[10]

A Greek OG unit was formed at the request of the Greek government-in-exile. In the summer of 1943, an OSS recruiting team visited Camp Carson, Colorado, seeking personnel with Greek language qualifications. So many of the 122nd Infantry Battalion volunteered for duty that its commanding officer offered the entire battalion. Transferring an entire battalion to the OSS was an unprecedented step that required careful negotiations with the War Department. The final approval from Washington arrived in September. A total of 18 officers and 172 enlisted men went through the OG training curriculum. In early 1944, they arrived in Cairo ready for action in Greece. The first group of twenty-three OGs landed by boat on the western coast of Greece on April 23, 1944. The rest followed in groups from three to fifteen officers and men between May and September. As in Yugoslavia, the Greek OGs operated in conjunction with British Commandos and local resistance fighters. The majority of their operations aimed at cutting rail lines and highways to disrupt the German withdrawal north toward Albania and Yugoslavia. By the time the Greek OGs withdrew in November 1944, their accomplishments included fourteen trains ambushed, fifteen bridges blown, sixty-one trucks destroyed, six miles of railroad lines blown, 349 confirmed enemy killed, and almost 1,800 estimated killed or wounded.[11]

* * *

When the Italian OGs of Company A were preparing for deployment in the summer of 1943, their training was ad-hoc and done mainly in existing Army training facilities. In the months that followed, the OSS created a robust training program of its own that delivered strong fighting and survival skills to the personnel from the Operational Group and the Special Operations commands. The training was structured in large scale based on the curriculum of the British SOE training schools. The main objective of the training was to provide the officers and enlisted men in the OG and SO teams with the techniques and skills required to execute their unique mission in enemy-occupied territory.

The mission of these teams was different from the mission of the British Commandos or the US Rangers who operated behind the frontlines as well. Initially, Commandos and Rangers focused on hit-and-run or smash-and-grab raids aimed at creating maximum damage and confusion in enemy territory for a short amount of time. Later, they acted as the spear point of invasion forces, charged with taking key objectives and holding them until they were overrun by regular troops.

The OG and SO teams on the other hand were expected to be efficient, mobile, and self-sufficient units capable of infiltrating deep into enemy territory, making contact with local resistance groups, and converting them into guerrilla units. Serving as liaisons between these guerrilla units and the Allied Forces Headquarters, they would supply the native guerrillas with arms, ammunition, demolitions, communication equipment, clothing, food, medical supplies, and money. Under the direction of the theater commander, these teams would assist the guerrillas in planning and execution of attacks against the enemy forces or installations, and sometime engage in their own independent operations. Ancillary responsibilities of the OG and SO teams included

gathering intelligence and rescuing distressed allied airmen and prisoners of war that had escaped captivity. The OSS training program for
the operators in the OG and SO teams aimed at providing them the
skills required to fulfill this unique mission.[12]

The training program developed the physical strength of the operators and prepared them for survival in hostile terrain. Focus areas
included physical conditioning through swimming, toughening exercises, and obstacle course runs; survival in the field, including camouflage, living off the land, and preparation of shelter and food; and
welfare, including personal hygiene, camp sanitation practice, and
providing first aid, especially under combat conditions. The training
honed the operators' skills to move around undetected through map
studies, which included map sketching, map-and-compass problems,
direction-finding using terrain features, and study of aerial photos.
The wooded areas in the Prince William Forest, along the Potomac
River, and in the Catoctin Mountains were used to conduct scouting
and patrolling exercises, including instruction and practice in the use
of physical cover, reconnaissance, signaling, and infiltration. The operators also learned to repair and operate enemy motorcycles, trucks,
automobiles, and other vehicles they might find in the field.

To enable the OG and SO teams to prepare and lead the local
fighters in the field, the training included classroom instruction in
basic maneuvers, tactical principles, and methods of guerrilla warfare.
Outside the classroom, the trainees practiced small-group operations,
day and night problems, planning and execution of airborne raids, and
street and village fighting. Methods of organizing and training civilians and maintaining the correct attitude and behavior toward civilians
were emphasized. Operators attended lectures on enemy military and
political structures, organizations, uniforms, and insignia. The training also covered procedures in interrogating prisoners, methods of
espionage, and counter-espionage.

To sharpen their fighting skills, the OG and SO teams were taught to
plan and execute demolition jobs of all sizes using explosives, incendiaries,
booby traps, delayed action charges, multiple charges, and even charges
manufactured with material found in the field. The weapons training
covered handling, stripping, cleaning, and firing of a variety of weapons

in the Allies' arsenal, including the .32 Colt and .45 pistols, .30 M1 and Browning automatic rifles, Sten and Bren guns, .45 and 9-mm sub-machine guns, grenade launchers, bazookas, 60-mm and 81-mm mortars, and hand grenades. In addition, the operators learned the function and firing of enemy weapons with which they might come into contact.

Pistol training in particular generated a lot of excitement among the trainees, especially the officers among them, who had been conditioned by the regular military training to consider the pistol primarily as a weapon of self-defense to be fired from static positions and with plenty of time to aim. OSS instructors emphasized instead the pistol as a weapon of attack, which the operators could use to kill while moving with extreme speed, shooting from any position and in any sort of light—even in complete darkness. Here is how an instructor helped his trainees visualize the circumstances in which they would most likely fire their weapon:

> Picture in your mind the circumstances under which you might be using the pistol. Take as an example a raid on an enemy occupied house in darkness. Firstly, consider your approach. You will never walk boldly up to the house and stroll in as though you were paying a social call. On the contrary, your approach will be stealthy. You will be keyed up and excited, nervously alert for danger from whichever direction it may come. You will find yourself instinctively crouching; your body balanced on the balls of your feet in a position from which you can move swiftly in any direction. You make your entry into the house and start searching for the enemy moving along passages, perhaps up or down stairs, listening and feeling for any signs of danger. Suddenly, on turning a corner, you come face to face with the enemy. Without a second's hesitation, you must fire and kill him before he has a chance to kill you.
>
> From this picture these facts are clear:
>
> a) You will always fire from the crouch position—you will never be in an upright position.
> b) You have no time to adopt any fancy stance when killing with speed.
> c) You have no time to use the sights.[13]

The instructor would then go on to explain the instinctive point-ing method of firing in which the operator learned to trust natural hand-eye coordination reflexes to hit the target instinctively:

> A natural crouch position, the body balanced on the balls of the feet and pressed forward over the forward foot; shoulders square to the target. The right hand, holding the pistol, is brought into the center of the body and reaches out toward the target until the arm is almost fully extended, in the natural pointing position. The barrel of the pis-tol is always parallel to the ground. In this position the right hand is turned slightly to the right to allow the barrel to point straight down the center of the line of sight.[14]

Most of the time in training was spent in fire practices that devel-oped and tested the individuals' mastery of the instinctive pointing method under a variety of scenarios. They culminated in realistic mis-sions in which students had to enter specially built houses and in almost complete darkness eliminate a number of targets that would pop up at them from unexpected angles. These houses were built with rough timber with realistic partitions to simulate doors, rooms, hallways, staircases, and so on. They were called "houses of horror" because of various "horror" devices such as seesaw flooring, and objects springing from the floor or dropping from ceilings that were installed to put trainees off balance and to strengthen their ability to handle the fire-arm and shoot efficiently under any circumstance.

The man who brought to the OSS the novel way of using weapons with an aggressive mindset aimed at killing in close quarters was Wil-liam E. Fairbairn, a British martial arts instructor who had introduced similar techniques to SOE and Commando training schools in Great Britain and Canada before transferring to the OSS in 1942. Fairbairn had spent his youth in the Shanghai Municipal Police, where he learned Judo, Kung Fu, and Jiu-Jitsu to survive close fights with some of the toughest criminals of the time. Eventually, he created his own close combat fighting style, which he called Defendu, and taught it for years to police officers in Shanghai. It was in a warehouse there that he cre-ated the first house of horror similar to those built years later for the

OSS at the Prince William Forest and Catoctin Park training sites. In 1940, at the age of fifty-five, Fairbairn returned to England, received a commission as a captain in the British Army, and began teaching his special close combat techniques to the first recruits in the Commandos and SOE organizations. Fairbairn contributed to the invention of the commando knife, a lethal knife with a seven-and-a-half-inch-long stiletto blade. The OSS adopted a shorter and thinner version of it as the knife its agents carried in the field. In early 1942, Fairbairn was transferred to the SOE Special Training School 103 in Ontario, Canada, also known as Camp X, before coming to the OSS as a lieutenant colonel in October of 1943.[15]

Fairbairn called what he practiced "gutter fighting" because it was fighting without rules. He made it a point to begin his course on close combat by telling the students that most of them had been taught to wrestle or box following Marquis of Queensberry rules that prohibited attacking certain parts of the opponents. Then, he continued with a statement like this:

> This, however, is WAR, not sport. Your aim is to kill your opponent as quickly as possible. A prisoner is generally a handicap and a source of danger, particularly if you are without weapons. So forget the Queensberry rules; forget the term "foul methods." That may sound cruel but it is still more cruel to take longer than necessary to kill your opponent. Attack your opponent's weakest points. He will attack yours if he gets a chance.[16]

Fairbairn taught a few basic but effective techniques and had his students rehearse them over and over until they were fully proficient in executing them swiftly, without having to stop and think. He emphasized blows with the side of the hand, which when delivered properly could kill, temporarily paralyze, break bones, or badly hurt the opponent. He explained:

> To deliver them effectively the fingers must be together, thumb up, and the whole hand tensed. The blow is struck with the side of the hand, all the force being concentrated in one small area, i.e.

approximately half-way between the base of the little finger and the wrist joint, or where the hand is broadest. If striking sideways, the back of the hand must be uppermost. No force can be obtained if the palm is uppermost. The effect of the blows is obtained by the speed with which they are delivered rather than by the weight behind them. They can be made from any position, whether the striker is on balance or not, and thus can be delivered more quickly than any other blow.[17]

Fairbairn considered the primary job of the instructor to make his students attack-minded, and dangerously so. "Attack first and keep on attacking," he urged his students. "Don't stop just because an opponent is crippled. If you have broken his arm, for instance, that is only of value because it is then easier to kill."[18]

A final element that made the training of the OG and SO operators unique was the special importance that was placed on maintenance of morale, given the extreme hazards of their mission. The instructors made every effort throughout the training period to keep the aggressive spirit and confidence of the personnel at a high level. They kept the men steadily occupied either with training tasks or with organized group recreation. They used all means available to foster intimate friendship, mutual confidence, and team play among members of the group, and a strong feeling of trust between officers and men. The combat experience of the teams in the field showed the benefits of this aspect of the training. Teams composed of operators who had trained and bonded together were usually more effective in accomplishing the assigned mission and successful in surviving the experience behind enemy lines. Teams that came together in the last minute or included personnel who had not gone through team-forming experiences encountered difficulties and in extreme cases paid with their lives for their deficiencies.

The first engagements of SO and OG personnel against the enemy tested not only their skills and abilities but also the quality of their training. These engagements came against targets on French and Italian islands in the Mediterranean in preparation for and as part of the Allied landings in Sicily and mainland Italy in the fall of 1943.

CHAPTER 4

Special Operations
in the Western Mediterranean

In December 1942, the OSS consolidated all its assets in North Africa into a headquarters station in Algiers, known as Station X, under the command of Colonel William Eddy. It operated as an extension of the Allied Forces Headquarters Special Operations Office, or G-3. Between December 1942 and August 1943, Station X mounted several operations in enemy territory to prepare the way for the Allied invasions in Italy. The number and intensity of these operations increased after the invasions began, first in Sicily in August 1943 and then in southern Italy in September 1943.

The first OSS mission inside Axis-occupied Europe was an infiltration of agents in the island of Corsica in mid-December 1942. Corsica had been part of the French territories left under the control of the Vichy government according to the Franco-German armistice of 1940. After the Allied landings in French North Africa, Germany and Italy moved to occupy all of France. Eighty thousand Italian troops occupied Corsica to the deep resentment of the local population, which remained loyal to the French republic, despite its historical ties to the Italian mainland. The purpose of the OSS mission, code-named Pearl Harbor, was to collect intelligence on the Italian forces on the island and organize networks of resistance ready to take up arms against the occupiers when the invasion against Italy began.[1]

The OSS entrusted the mission to Frederic Brown, code-named "Tommy," an Algiers-based asset who had assisted Colonel Eddy in the preparations for Operation Torch.[2] Brown was on friendly terms with the Algiers chiefs of the *Deuxième Bureau* (Second Bureau), the French military intelligence organization, who were also interested in sending their own mission to Corsica at the time. Brown used these connections to identify men for the mission team and mount the operation. The team leader was Roger de Saule, a senior intelligence officer in the French Air Force. Three Algiers-based Frenchmen born in Corsica would assist him as radio operators and liaison agents. They were the cousins Toussaint and Pierre Griffi and Laurent Preziosi. The Deuxième Bureau secured the use of the 1,600-ton *Casabianca*, the most modern submarine in the French Navy, which had arrived in Algiers in mid-November with its commander and full crew aboard after escaping capture from the Germans in Toulon. With three wireless sets, a million French francs, food, supplies, and false documents, the Pearl Harbor team headed for Corsica on December 11, 1942.

There was no reception party to pinpoint the landing site, so when the submarine arrived near the coast on December 13, the captain surfaced to periscope depth and surveyed the littoral in daylight until he found a suitable beach in the bay of Chioni. Then he submerged and kept the vessel on the sea floor until nighttime. At 0100 hours on the night of December 14, the *Casabianca* resurfaced barely out of the water to avoid detection from Italian patrol boats and moved to within one mile offshore. Two French marines rowed a dinghy with the five OSS agents and a radio set ashore. When they returned, the submarine submerged again, planning to stay out of sight for the next twenty-four hours. It would resurface the following night to bring weapons and the rest of the equipment ashore. The OSS agents moved inland and established a few friendly contacts in the villages nearby.

When they returned to the landing spot on the midnight of December 15, Pierre Griffi sent a message in Morse using his flashlight to the *Casablanca*, which was waiting offshore. The sea that night was choppy with large waves kicked up by the Libeccio, the strong wind that sweeps Corsica and Italy from the southwest. Close to the shore, the dinghy capsized, taking with it all the supplies, weapons, and radio equipment. Its three sailors swam to shore and had no way to return to the submarine, so they decided to stay with the Pearl Harbor team. They tried to signal the *Casabianca* but the waves were so high that the captain could not see the flashlight signals from shore. The situation forced Brown to swim for a perilous hour and a half to the submarine and communicate the situation to the skipper.

Over the next few months, the Pearl Harbor team was able to create a number of nets inside the island. It communicated regularly by radio with Algiers sending information about the strength and morale of the Italian troops. On the night of February 6, 1943, the *Casabianca* returned to pick up the three sailors it had left behind and to deliver a cache of 450 submachine guns and 60,000 bullets. It was the first American supply of arms and ammunition to a European resistance movement in World War II. The two principal liaison agents, Toussaint Griffi and Laurent Preziosi, distributed these arms to their contacts and reported in March that they had two thousand people in the organization who were ready to fight.

Their activities had attracted the attention of the Fascist secret police, the infamous *Organizzazione per la Vigilanza e la Repressione dell'Antifascismo* (OVRA), or Organization for Vigilance and Repression of Anti-Fascism. As a security precaution, Toussaint Griffi and Laurent Preziosi returned to Algiers on March 10, 1943, aboard the *Casablanca*. Roger de Saule handed over command of the networks to a newly assigned officer of the Deuxième Bureau, Paul Colona d'Istria, and returned to Algiers at the end of March. Pierre Griffi, the principal radio operator of Pearl Harbor, remained in Corsica and fell into the hands of OVRA on June 11. Although tortured atrociously, he did not reveal any information. The Fascists executed him in Bastia on August 18, 1943, just a few weeks before the liberation of Corsica.

* * *

The invasion of Sicily, known as Operation Husky, signaled the beginning of the Allied campaign in Italy. In the evening of July 9, 1943, eight task forces totaling three thousand ships and carrying 160,000 men—Americans, British, Canadians, and French—together with 14,000 vehicles, 600 tanks, and 1,800 guns began their way toward Sicily from ports in North Africa and Malta.[3] The invasion began in the early hours of July 10 on a tragic note when paratrooper units of the British First Airborne and the American 82nd Airborne divisions suffered heavy casualties, mostly from friendly fire from naval vessels who took them for enemy troops. Nevertheless, bridgeheads were established and held firmly despite German counterattacks mainly in the American landing zone at Gela. During the first two days of the operation, eighty thousand men, seven thousand vehicles, and nine hundred guns came across the beaches in seemingly endless waves. General Eisenhower, observing the men and equipment streaming ashore, wrote to General Marshal, the US Army chief of staff, on July 12, 1943: "I must say that the sight of hundreds of vessels with landing craft everywhere, operating along the shoreline . . . was unforgettable."[4]

Only a few miles away from Eisenhower, the commanding officer of the German troops in Sicily, General Fridolin von Senger und Etterlin, witnessed the same spectacle and found it equally unforgettable, albeit for different reasons.[5] He recognized that the key to the Allies' success was their ability to use their naval and air supremacy to create extremely flexible seaborne attack routes and supply lines. The deep-rooted weakness of the German political and military leaders, von Senger realized, was that they "could think only in terms of land operations, not in the three-dimensional terms of forces of all arms."[6]

Operation Husky was the first opportunity for the OSS to integrate its activities with those of military units in support of an operation. The OSS Italian branch, headed by Vincent Scamporino and Max Corvo, had wished to send missions in advance to collect intelligence about the enemy and to raise the local population in support of the Allies, but the Allied Forces Headquarters had ruled them out for fear that they would alert the enemy of the upcoming invasion. The OSS contingent that would participate in the operation, two officers and eight enlisted men, was assigned to the intelligence staff, G-2, of General George S. Patton's Seventh Army headquarters, where they were met with an attitude that ranged from complete indifference to mild interest. Donovan, who was in the theater at the time, managed to go to Sicily on D-Day, but the OSS team was able to find transport from North Africa only four days later.

Patton's frontline units required short-range tactical or combat intelligence missions for which the OSS men were not suited. The OSS recruited locals who knew the terrain and could cross the lines unnoticed, but without any significant results. The frontline was so fluid that often the agents were overrun by advancing mechanized units before having had the opportunity to return and report their findings. Therefore, most of the OSS efforts in Sicily went to helping Army units with the interrogation of captured Italian soldiers. In the rear, the OSS team supported the Counter-Intelligence Corps and the Allied Military Government in establishing and maintaining order. To help the overstretched personnel, two officers and eight enlisted men from the Italian OGs arrived from the United States.[7]

There was a lot of enthusiasm and desire to show what the OSS was capable of accomplishing at the time, driven from the top by Donovan himself. Combined with the lack of experience for a number of the men, for whom the Sicilian campaign was the first exposure they had to military actions, it lead to amateurish actions and foul-ups. The official history of the OSS edited after the war was not very keen to such efforts: "This kind of heroics in what was a new business, and by men essentially amateurs, may be understandable but is in no way excusable. It is simply not professional behavior."[8]

One such operation involved Lieutenant Colonel Guido Pantaleoni, Special Operations chief, who traveled to Sicily from Washington in late July 1943. Pantaleoni was a forty-three-year-old Harvard-educated lawyer from New York connected to Donovan through the Paderewski Fund, a charity in support of the Polish people that his wife had set up in 1941 and for which Donovan had been one of the biggest fundraisers.[9] Panteleoni did not have any prior military experience and was eager to use the action in Sicily to get some. As he explained to Max Corvo, "he was expected to lead the French show and he needed experience."[10]

Having just come from Washington and holding a senior position within the OSS, Panteleoni knew top-secret information, including, possibly, the fact that the Allies had broken the German Ultra Code and were reading their communications. Exposure in enemy territory, which could lead to his arrest and interrogation by the Abwehr, could compromise this information. Nevertheless, to gain experience he lead a mission, code-named San Fratello, of four enlisted men and two civilians across the frontlines to collect information about German fortifications on Mount Etna that had slowed down the advance of Patton's Seventh Army.

They left Palermo on August 3, 1943, headed toward Messina and reached the no-man's land in the morning of August 7. On the way, they hired two local guides with mules and bought civilian clothes, which they put over the uniforms. They separated into three groups to be less conspicuous to enemy patrols. The first group of two soldiers and a guide crossed the lines without incident. After forty-five minutes the second group of Colonel Panteleoni, Private Anthony Ribarich, Sergeant Serafin Buta, and a guide headed down the trail. They walked for a half hour when Ribarich stepped on a land mine. Somehow, he received only a minor scratch in the back of his neck, so they decided to press ahead. Two hours later, they came across a German patrol, which ordered them to surrender. A firefight ensued, during which the Americans tried to get rid of the civilian clothes they had put over the uniforms. After twenty minutes Buta was gravely wounded with a bullet in his spine and Panteleoni was wounded in the leg. Any further resistance was useless, so Panteleoni decided to surrender. In his post-action report, Ribarich described his actions:

> Disobeying the order, though wounded in several places, I rolled down the hillside chewing part of the communications code that I was carrying. While running away I exploded another land mine, I heard for the last time the colonel's voice as he was saying to the enemy that his group included Sergeant Buta and Sergeant Ribarich, thus promoting me under battle conditions. I had barely time to hide our civilian clothing and money. After about an hour, surrounded by enemy troops, and without possibility of escape, I gave myself up.

The Germans summarily executed the two local guides and took Panteleoni away immediately after his capture. German and Italian army officers interrogated Ribarich first to gather tactical intelligence.

They searched him thoroughly and took away all his personal belongings, including his dog tags. When they found the transmitting key and earpieces of the radio, they turned him over to an Abwehr lieutenant for a more thorough interrogation. In the evening, the Germans began withdrawing towards Randazzo. They left Buta, mortally wounded, on a stretcher by the side of the road for the American troops advancing their way. The Abwehr lieutenant ordered Ribarich in his car. For the next twenty-four hours, the Germans alternately retreated and stopped to mine the road and the trees on the side of the road. At about 2200 hours on Sunday, August 8, the somnolent Abwehr lieutenant sent the driver to find out what was to be done with Ribarich. Ribarich recalled later what happened next:

> When the driver had disappeared and the only thing I could hear was the slight snoring of the lieutenant, I slowly felt for my penknife, and when I was certain, with a rapid movement, I pressed the spring that released the blade and in a moment sliced his throat. I jumped out of the car and fled as fast as my legs would carry me, despite the pain from my wounds, as I knew what would happen to me if they recaptured me.

Ribarich walked back toward the American lines for two days and two nights and was finally able to make contact with US Army units on August 10. His determination, alertness, resolution to find a way out of captivity, and skills had saved him from the fate that other OSS personnel captured behind the lines suffered in the months to come. Citing his example to OSS trainees in the United States, Donovan called Ribarich "a good kind of man to have . . . and unless we had man of that kind there is no use of our being in this business, and it is important for you gentlemen to keep that in mind when you are thinking about a patrol."[11]

* * *

The dismal performance of the Italian troops in the Sicilian campaign brought to an end Mussolini's rule in Italy. In a meeting of the

Grand Council of Fascism on the night of July 24–25, an overwhelming majority of the Fascist hierarchs turned against *Il Duce* and passed a motion of no confidence against him. On the twenty-fifth, Mussolini appeared before King Victor Emanuel III, who did not mince words, "Dear Duce, things don't work anymore. Italy has gone to pieces. . . . In this moment you are the most hated man in Italy. . . . *Il gioco e finito*— the game is over, Mussolini . . . you'll have to go."[12] At the end of the audience with the king, the Carabinieri—the Italian military police— took Mussolini into custody and drove him to a secret location in a Red Cross ambulance. The king entrusted the formation of a non-political government to Marshal Pietro Badoglio, former chief of staff of the Italian armed forces, who tried to assure the Germans by declaring in his first proclamation that the war continued and that Italy would honor its commitments. Yet it was an open secret that Badoglio and King Victor Emmanuel III intended to leave the Axis and seek an armistice with the Allies. "They say they'll fight but that's treachery! We must be quite clear: it is pure treachery!" fumed Hitler.[13]

As the fighting in Sicily drew to a close, it was clear that Italy would be the Allies' next target. The Germans began the evacuation of their troops across the Straits of Messina in early August. By the time the withdrawal was complete on August 17, they had extricated nearly 55,000 battle-hardened troops, almost 10,000 vehicles, over 50 tanks, and 163 guns, all of which they positioned to counter the Allies' next move.[14] Fresh troops poured in from the Alpine passes in the north to reinforce the troops retreating from Sicily and to capture strategic positions around Rome and other key Italian cities.

Taking advantage of the lull in fighting, Badoglio sent General Giuseppe Castellano to Madrid and then to Lisbon to establish contacts with the Allies and to negotiate the surrender of Italy. On August 19, 1943, Major General Walter Bedell Smith, Eisenhower's chief of staff, and British Brigadier Kenneth D. Strong arrived in Lisbon and handed Castellano a list of 121 standard military terms of surrender, including cessation of hostilities, return of Allied prisoners, surrender of the fleet and air force, and the establishment of an Allied military government. They would become known later as the Short Terms of surrender.[15] The Badoglio government mulled over the terms for a couple of weeks without reaching a decision. Their indecision ended in the early morning hours of September 3, when a massive artillery barrage against the coast of Calabria signaled the opening of the Italian campaign. Montgomery's British Eighth Army crossed the Straits of Messina, landed in Taranto, and began its advance north. That same afternoon, Castellano accepted the Short Terms and signed the agreement on behalf of Badoglio at Cassibile, near Siracusa, Sicily.

Bedell Smith signed the agreement for Eisenhower and immediately handed Castellano an additional set of conditions. They became known as the Long Terms and essentially spelled out the unconditional surrender of the Italian government. To maximize the element of surprise for the Germans, the surrender would be announced on September 8, on the eve of General Mark Clark's American Fifth Army landing on the beaches along the Gulf of Salerno, south of Naples. At the same time, the 82nd Airborne Division of Major General Mathew B. Ridgway would parachute outside Rome, link with four Italian divisions, and seize the capital, thus forcing the Germans to retreat to the north.[16]

Eisenhower dispatched Brigadier General Maxwell D. Taylor, 82nd Division's artillery commander, and Colonel William T. Gardiner of the Troop Carrier Command on a secret mission to Rome to make the final arrangements with the Italians for their surrender. They would also evaluate the situation on the ground and determine whether the 82nd would be able to make the airdrop near Rome and secure the Italian capital at the moment of surrender. As soon as they arrived in Rome, Taylor and Gardiner learned that the Italians were wavering again. Taylor informed Marshal Badoglio in the early hours of September 8 that the airdrop and the main invasion would take place the next day and that the Allies expected the Italian government to announce the armistice beforehand. Badoglio reacted by sending a message to General Eisenhower repudiating the surrender. Taylor, in turn, used his radio to flash the code word "innocuous," signaling the cancellation of the airdrop.[17]

Eisenhower's response to Badoglio was an angry and unequivocal warning that if the Italians reneged on the agreement, the consequences would be grave. "No future action of yours," he radioed, "could then restore any confidence whatsoever in your good faith and consequently the dissolution of your government and your nation would ensue." Without waiting for Badoglio's reply, Eisenhower proceeded to broadcast the official Allied announcement of the Italian surrender at 1830 hours on September 8, 1943. The announcement came when the Italian Cabinet was in conference with King Victor Emanuel III on how to respond to Eisenhower's ultimatum. Faced now with the choice of confirming the surrender or having to fight both the Germans and the Allies, the Italians bowed to the inevitable. At 1945 hours, Badoglio announced the surrender of his nation, officially ensuring that Italian forces would not resist the Allied landings at Salerno the following day. He and the king fled that same evening by boat to Brindisi, a city in the Allied-controlled southern Italy.[18]

* * *

One of the operations that preceded Operation Avalanche, the landings at Salerno, was the capture of the island of Ventotene located in the Mediterranean, east of Naples, about thirty miles from the Italian mainland. The Germans operated a powerful radar station on the island, which had the capability to detect the invasion force and alert the coast. In addition, the island was ideally suited for a directional beacon that would guide the aircraft carrying the 82nd Airborne to Rome. The Allied Forces Headquarters assigned the capture of Ventotene to a naval task force commanded by Captain C. L. Andrews, Jr., US Navy. It included the destroyer *Knight* and an assortment of American patrol boats, British motor torpedo boats, submarine chasers, gunboats, and air rescue boats. The bulk of the fighting force was a group of forty-six paratroopers of the 509th Parachute Infantry Regiment, 82nd Airborne, commanded by Captain Charles W. Howland. The task force included a dozen OSS agents of the Italian Secret Intelligence branch, led by Captain Frank J. Tarallo and Lieutenant Henry R. North. Their assignment was to supplement the Navy intelligence staff and serve as interpreters on the island. Also along for the ride was John Steinbeck, who was in the Mediterranean at the time as a war correspondent.[19]

The task force departed Palermo in the afternoon of September 8 headed north for the 180-mile journey across the Tyrrhenian Sea. Around five o'clock in the afternoon, it sighted the Allied invasion armada sailing slowly toward Salerno. At 2100 hours, the task force received a message from the armada that Badoglio's government had signed the armistice with the Allies. There was relief because now they would not have to fight the Italian garrison in Ventotene. Shortly after midnight, the flotilla was two to three miles off the coast of the island. The smaller boats began a deception routine in the darkness simulating the preparations of a large landing force. Using the voice amplifying system of one of the air rescue boats, one of the OSS Italian agents broadcast a message to the island garrison demanding its surrender. "Italians," he said, "you must now surrender. We have come in force. Your German ally has deserted you. You have fifteen minutes to surrender. Display three white lights to surrender. At the end of fifteen minutes, we will open fire. This will be repeated once more."[20] Ten minutes went by, then twelve, then thirteen. As the deadline was about to expire, three white flares went up from the port. Then, for good measure, the Italian garrison launched another three flares.

Andrews, Tarallo, and three OSS men boarded the dinghy and headed for the entrance of the port. It was pitch dark, a thick haze hung low over the water, and it was impossible to distinguish the narrow entrance of the port that the Romans had carved out of the volcanic island. The dinghy struck shore about three hundred yards off the mark. Tarallo and another man jumped on the rocks and directed the dinghy into the port. As the dinghy was preparing to dock, a loud explosion blew up a supply boat nearby. The Germans on the island had decided to scuttle the boat and retreat up the steep hills to the semaphore station west of the port where they set up strong defensive positions. As they retreated, the Germans blew up military and other facilities on the island.

There were some tense moments as the five Americans that had come ashore waited for the group of paratroopers to arrive from the destroyer. When they finally were there, Howland spread them in positions around the port and on rooftops to provide security. Captain Andrews, the commander of the task force, Captain Tarallo of the

OSS, and Captain Howland of the 82nd paratroop detachment met to discuss next steps. Andrews had received orders to take the *Knight* and the bulk of the task force toward the mainland to carry out diversionary actions in support of the landings at Salerno. They decided that the OSS detachment under Tarallo and the paratroopers under Howland would remain on the island, secure the port, hold it against possible attacks from the Germans, and wait for the return of the *Knight* to engage the Germans.

When Andrews left, the OSS men and the paratroopers searched the port, rounded up about eighty Italian military personnel, and confined them to their barracks. From the prisoners, they learned that the German contingent included three officers and eighty-five men, most of them radar specialists responsible for a radar installation that covered the Tyrrhenian coast. The paratroopers set up defensive positions around the port to protect from a surprise attack from the larger German force. PT boats off the coast laid a barrage of rocket fire on the heights where the Germans had set up their positions to keep them pinned down.

At dawn Tarallo, North, and Howland conferred again and Tarallo proposed to go uphill and bluff the Germans into surrendering. North and four members of the OSS detachment remained at the port guarding the Italian prisoners. Howland and his paratroopers took positions, ready to go into action if needed. Tarallo, two OSS men, and two freed Italian political prisoners headed toward the semaphore station where the Germans had their command post. One of the Italians led the way carrying a flag of truce, a white bath towel on a stick, while the other, who spoke German, would act as an interpreter. The small group climbed slowly and carefully up a steep stone-walled road that led to the semaphore station watching out for booby traps and explosive devices that the Germans might have led behind. They could see abandoned machine gun nests and ammo boxes on both sides of the road.

When they arrived near the crest of the hill, the flag bearer and the interpreter went forward to the German position. Tarallo and the two men took up position and waited. After a long half-hour wait, the two Italians returned and reported that the German commanding officer was ready to receive them. Tarallo and his party went forward into the command post where they met Lieutenant Eingler, the commanding officer of the Luftwaffe detachment that manned the radar installations on the island. Eingler spoke English and Tarallo told him, "The colonel's compliments sir. I am ordered to demand your surrender. At the end of twenty minutes, the cruisers will move up and open fire unless ordered otherwise following your surrender." The German lieutenant hesitated and Tarallo pressed on. "We've got six hundred men ashore and the cruisers are aching to take a shot at you," he said. "What's the good of it? You'd kill some of us and we'd kill all of you. Why don't you just stack your arms and come in?" The German asked what kind of treatment they would get. "Prisoners of war under the Convention of The Hague," said Tarallo.[21] After further hesitation, the German said, "It is no dishonor to surrender to superior forces." Then, he signed the following document:

> I, the undersigned, Commanding Officer of the Axis Armed Forces on the Islands of Ventotene and San Stefano, do hereby surrender unconditionally all men, arms, equipment, and possession of said Islands of Ventotene and San Stefano to the Allied Forces, acting herein by and through Frank J. Tarallo, Captain AUS, and Henry R. North, LT (j.g.) USNR, under direction of Commander Task Group 80.4, Captain C. L. Andrews, Jr., USN on order of Commander Western Naval Task Force and of General D. D. Eisenhower, Commander in Chief of Allied Forces, North African Theater of Operations.[22]

As soon as Eingler signed the agreement, Tarallo instructed the Germans to pile up all their weapons in a clearing. One by one, eighty-seven of them deposited their rifles, machine guns, and even their pistols and began marching down the path to the port. Howland had observed the whole scene with his binoculars from the bottom of the hill. He ordered thirty paratroopers to move up and secure the road the Germans were using to come to the port. Because there were not enough paratroopers to cover the entire way, Howland had them secure the first part of the road and, as the prisoner column marched by them, move downhill and take their place at the end of the line, and so on until the Germans were brought into the city hall. There, the Germans were confined in three large cells with the officers put in a fourth. Howland posted guards with tommy guns at the doors of the cells.[23]

Soon, the situation became tense. The German officers could see from the barred windows of their cell the deserted streets of the town and the port below. Lieutenant Eingler demanded to see the colonel in command but got only Captain Howland. With a harsh and disappointed voice he said, "I don't think you have more than six hundred men. I think you have only a few more than thirty men." Howland said, "We've mined the building. If there is any trouble—any trouble at all—we'll blow the whole mess of you to hell."[24] In the meanwhile, Tarallo radioed Captain Andrews who was off the coast of Salerno aboard the *Knight* protecting the southern flank of the landing craft. The *Knight* returned at full speed to Ventotene and in the morning of September 10, 1943, all the Germans were secured and moved off the island. They were the first German unit to surrender to the Allied forces and became the first prisoners of war of Operation Avalanche.

* * *

With the armistice an accomplished fact, the Germans moved swiftly to seize and disarm the Italians to avoid having to fight them. In Italy proper, in France, Russia, and the Balkans, the Germans took into custody over six hundred thousand Italians and shipped them to internment camps in Germany. Thousands who resisted, especially officers, were shot. Thousands more escaped, determined to join the fight against the Germans, either under the Allies or as partisans. The Germans failed to get their hands on the Italian Navy. Complying with the Short Terms of surrender, columns of battleships, cruisers, destroyers, and smaller craft steamed from their bases on Italy's west and east coasts toward Allied ports at Malta and in North Africa.[25]

On the other hand, the Germans managed to rescue Mussolini from captivity on September 12 in the daring commando operation led by SS officer Otto Skorzeny at Gran Sasso. Installed in power to administer the German-occupied Italy, Mussolini declared the puppet state *Repubblica Sociale Italiana* (Italian Social Republic) supported by the most fervent Fascists organized in blackshirt units that terrorized the civilian population. Thus, the Allied divisions that landed in Salerno and Taranto confronted not neutralized Italian troops but hardened Germans and hardcore Fascists determined to defend every inch of terrain. Under these conditions, the Allied commanders could not spare combat troops to capture and secure the other two major islands in the western Mediterranean, Sardinia and Corsica. The OSS stepped in to fill the void.

After withdrawing from Sicily, the Germans moved a portion of their troops to Sardinia and Corsica to shore up the Italian garrisons on these islands. With the Italians out of the war, the German High Command decided it did not have sufficient troops to commit to their defense. They sent General Frido von Senger, fresh from his experience in Sicily, to organize evacuation to the mainland in a methodical and organized way to minimize losses in personnel and equipment. Von Senger did not fit the mold of the typical German general of World War II. While most of the German corps of general officers were Nazi supporters or tied to the Prussian military tradition, von Senger came from a Catholic family from Baden, in southwest Germany. He was born in 1891 and studied in England between 1912 and 1914 as a Rhodes Scholar, which gave him an affinity for the English language, customs, and culture that he maintained throughout his life. He fought in the trenches in World War I as an infantry reserve officer and received a commission as a cavalry officer in the German army after the war. At the outset of World War II, he took command of a panzer brigade and supported Rommel's drive through France in 1940. After the collapse of France, he spent two years in Italy as the German liaison officer in the Franco-Italian Armistice Commission. In fall 1942, already a two-star general, he took command of the 17th Panzer Division on the Russian front. At the beginning of December 1942, he began a desperate sixty-mile drive to break through Soviet-held territory and relieve the Sixth Army of Friedrich von Paulus encircled in Stalingrad. In face of the fierce Russian resistance and temperatures 20 degrees Fahrenheit below zero, he called off the push on Christmas

Day, 1942, twenty-five miles from this objective. In June 1943, he returned to Italy as chief German liaison officer with the Italian army in Sicily. It was in this capacity that he had a front-row look at the massive power that the Allies unleashed upon the island when the Sicily invasion began.[26]

Upon receiving command of the German forces in Sardinia and Corsica, von Senger immediately decided to evacuate Sardinia and then gradually move the forces up the eastern Corsican coast to the port of Bastia and from there to Italy. The fact that the Germans planned to conduct an organized withdrawal from the islands simplified the task of occupying them for the Allied command, which had no troops to spare. But still hundreds of thousands of Italian troops in Sardinia and Corsica needed to be controlled and disarmed. No one was sure of their allegiance and whether they would surrender peacefully or throw their lot in with their former allies and the resurgent Fascist puppet regime.

The mission of convincing the Italian garrison in Sardinia to lay down their arms was entrusted to Lieutenant Colonel Serge Obolensky of the OSS Special Operations division in Algiers. The OSS gave the mission the code name Bathtub. Obolensky, a former Russian prince and Czarist officer, was a prominent figure in New York social circles. He was born in 1890 in Saint Petersburg, married the daughter of Czar Alexander II, and fought in World War I in the First Cavalry Regiment of the Czar's Imperial Guard. He left Russia after the Bolshevik Revolution and settled in the United States, where he was married a second time, albeit briefly, to an heiress of the Astor family. He described himself a "confirmed bachelor," and others described him as "a natural-born hand shaker"[27] and as someone who "could charm the birds off the trees."[28]

At the age of fifty, he tried to join the Army, but was told it was not considering volunteers of his age. So, he joined the Seventeenth Regiment of the New York National Guard as a private instead. He rose rapidly in rank and was a major by the time he volunteered to join the OSS in 1942. Obolensky took the British Commando course, during which he earned his paratrooper wings by completing the rigorous training program and the required five jumps within the same day. He set up the training program for the OSS Schools and Training Division and in 1943 moved to the OSS Algiers headquarters where he continued to conduct field training of OSS personnel assigned there.

Together with Obolensky, the Bathtub team included Lieutenant Michael Formichelli of the Italian OGs, who would serve as an interpreter, and two radio operators, James Russell of the OSS and William Sherwood of the British Army.[29] The team's mission was to land by parachute in Sardinia and establish liaison between the commander of armed forces of Sardinia, General Antonio Basso, and General Badoglio's staff at the Allied headquarters. Obolensky carried a letter from General Eisenhower introducing him as "the bearer of a special message from his Majesty, the King of Italy, and Marshal Badoglio to the Commanding General of Troops in Sardinia." He also carried a personal letter from General Giuseppe Castellano to General Basso urging him to side with the Allies.

The team left Algiers in a Halifax bomber at 2100 hours on September 13, 1943, and parachuted fifteen miles from Cagliari, the island's capital, at about 2330 hours. Obolensky would later say this about his drop, "It was a beautiful moonlight night in September. We jumped into the middle of a valley. The idea was to avoid the Germans and contact the Italians. We hit the spot just five hours after the Germans moved out, a very lucky coincidence."[30] "It was the best of all six jumps I've made," he would say proudly after the war.[31] Once on the ground, Obolensky and Formichelli asked the radio operators to stay hidden in the foothills with their equipment until they sent for them. Then, the two officers set on foot for Cagliari with help from friendly inhabitants and soldiers they encountered on the way.

By 0900 hours of the fourteenth, they arrived at the airbase of Decimomannu, outside Cagliari, where they contacted officers of the Italian Air Force who immediately notified General Basso of the Americans' arrival. Basso's headquarters were in Bordigali in the central part of the island about one hundred miles north. The roads were not safe and there was a good chance they might run into German rearguard units, so Obolensky travelled under the escort of a platoon of Carabinieri on trucks with mounted machine guns. He arrived at Basso's headquarters at 1700 hours the same day. The officer on duty received him with great courtesy and took him immediately to see the general.

Obolensky presented to Basso General Castellano's letter and explained that the Allied Headquarters expected him to press the Germans relentlessly and destroy them in the process of their evacuation from Sardinia. Obolensky offered special units to help fight the retreating Germans. Basso said that he was doing all he could to push the Germans out of Sardinia and that his troops had been given orders to exert pressure wherever they could. He objected to American troops being sent in. Obolensky ascertained later that except for one or two small skirmishes, the Italian troops never really fought the Germans but just moved up when the Germans had evacuated a place. Basso was not certain of the loyalties of some of his units and had turned down the offer of American troops for fear of possible clashes between Italian and Allied soldiers.

After the meeting with Basso, Obolensky spent what he described as "a few very trying hours" waiting for Formichelli, whom he had sent to the drop zone near Cagliari to contact the radio operators and bring them to Bordigali. The roads were not safe and straggling German patrols still drove through the area. "I will never forget the happy moments of our reunion," he said. They established the first contact with the Algiers base station the next morning, after which they sent regular reports about the order of battle of the Italian divisions in Sardinia, the progress of the German retreat to the north of the island, and their evacuation to Corsica across the Bonifaccio straits.

When Brigadier General Theodore Roosevelt, Jr., arrived on September 18 as the official head of the Allied Military Mission to Sardinia, Obolensky provided detailed information he had collected about morale of troops and population, condition of airfields, and condition of ports and unloading facilities available to the Allies. Roosevelt appointed him as his executive officer on the spot. Roosevelt brought with him two OG officers, First Lieutenants Rocco J. Benedetto and Joseph J. Benucci. They worked as interpreters and contributed immensely to establishing goodwill with the officers and men of the Italian Army. They also collected valuable information from both military and civilian sources that they passed on to the Allied mission.

An emotional reunion took place between the recently arrived OSS personnel and five OSS men whom the Italians had held captive since the end of June 1943. They were members of the first special operations mission launched by the OSS against Fascist Italy. Anthony Camboni, a scale salesman from Chicago, and John De Montis, a Detroit grocer, were born in the village of Ozieri in the north-central part of the island. Despite having lived in the United States for years, they knew the local dialect perfectly and had many friends and relatives in the area. Two privates, Joseph Puleo and Vincent Pavia, supported the team. Lieutenant Charles Taquay was the radio communications officer. Their mission had been to set up an intelligence network in eastern Sardinia and to build up an armed resistance group.

The men infiltrated by PT boats on the eastern shores of Sardinia on the night of June 29, 1943. All five were in regular US Army uniform. Almost immediately after landing, they ran into an Italian patrol. Having never seen American troops before, the Italians did not recognize the uniforms and the two groups parted amicably after exchanging a few pleasantries in Italian. After a while, the Italians realized that something was amiss, so they went back to search for the OSS team. The OSS men had orders not to engage in a firefight, so a comic negotiation ensued in which an almost apologetic Italian sergeant asked for and received their surrender. Higher headquarters were alerted and a major with one hundred men armed to the teeth arrived to pick up the Americans and take them to Porto Torres for interrogation. The OSS men promptly "confessed" that they were an advance party of a larger US invasion force. They were turned over to the *Servizio Informazioni Militare* (SIM), the Italian military intelligence service, and taken to Sassari, where they were held in individual cells during the initial in-depth interrogations.

The SIM officers decided to use the team as double agents against their base in Algiers, a possibility for which the OSS had prepared. In the first message that Lieutenant Taquay sent on July 31, he transmitted a pre-established danger code to indicate that the team was under enemy control and he was transmitting under duress. OSS played along by continuing to exchange radio messages, which probably saved the life of the team. The SIM kept the members of the team under their custody and did not turn them over to the Germans. When the armistice was announced on September 8, the Italians set the Americans free and dressed them in civilian clothes so they would not be recognized by the Germans who were still in Sassari. When Obolensky showed up at General Basso's headquarters, he inquired about the OSS men and they were brought under the protection of a police escort together with their radio equipment. The reunion coincided with the arrival of General Roosevelt in the island, who personally thanked the men for having volunteered for the difficult mission.[32]

* * *

Immediately after Roosevelt's arrival, he and Obolensky inspected all available airfields and ports of Sardinia, the main population centers, and the economic situation in the island to provide the Allied Headquarters with an accurate picture of the contribution of the island to the war effort and the resources that would be required to govern it.[33] The good graces of Obolensky as "a natural-born hand shaker" matched perfectly with Roosevelt's own natural charm and great knowledge of human nature to create friendly relations with all the Sardinians and to make the Allies welcome. This was very important given that there were about two hundred thousand armed Italian troops in Sardinia at the time and only a small token force of Allied military personnel had been sent to take control of the island. During the tour, the local population was exceedingly friendly, always greeting the Americans with shouts of "*Viva l'America*" and "*Viva la Libertà.*" They met a number of people who had lived in Brooklyn or Chicago or had relatives in the States. Some came a long way to meet them and produced old citizenship papers and dollar bills kept hidden for years for fear of reprisals by the Fascist regime.

Two major problems that Roosevelt's team faced in the initial days of Allied control of Sardinia were feeding the island inhabitants and putting the army to work. A survey of the available resources showed that while people were adequately fed for the time, supplies were running very short and the pinch would be very serious unless shipments were made within fifteen days. Roosevelt provided the Allied Chief of

Staff a list of necessities for the next three months, mostly grain, which he considered essential since it formed the basis of the Sardinian diet. He requested other items, like sugar, tobacco, soap, and coffee, as "luxuries that are not strictly necessary but would make the people happy." With regards to the treatment of the Italian soldiers in the island, Roosevelt arranged for two hundred million lire, about two million dollars, to be sent in small notes to ensure continued payments. He suggested that they be put to work in a number of projects including clearing up the debris in Cagliari, which had been heavily bombed by the Allies and was practically uninhabitable. They could also improve roads and fix runways in the airfields, which the Allies would be soon using against the Germans in mainland Italy.

While in Sardinia, Roosevelt and Obolensky paid special attention to the remnants of the Nembo division, a unit of elite Italian parachutists that had been posted in Sardinia to counter the Allied invasion. Most of the Nembo men were new recruits that had no battle experience, but the nucleus consisted of hardened veterans of the Italian Folgore paratroop division who had fought in Rommel's Panzer Army in Africa and had close affiliation with the Germans. A group of six officers and one hundred men had decided to leave with the Germans after shooting the division chief of staff who tried to stop them. They followed the retreating Germans to Corsica and from there in mainland Italy where they became part of the German Fourth Parachute Division.

Roosevelt reviewed the Nembo and talked personally to a number of officers and men. Obolensky, as a US paratrooper, had many topics in common to discuss with them. He got along particularly well with the commanding officer, General Bruno, only four months older than himself, who was pleased enormously to hear how Obolensky had become a paratrooper in his fifties. The Italian paratroopers proudly described their unique style of jumping, which they called the "angel leap." Rather than jumping feet first in a perfectly vertical position, the Italian paratroopers plunged earthward in a spread-eagle position. Their parachute was attached at the lower back and had a special tulip-like design, which gave the paratroopers a higher rate of descent thus shortening the time they were in the air and vulnerable to ground fire. When he was within seconds of landing, the paratrooper pulled a control rope, which converted the tulip shape of the canopy to the traditional umbrella shape and slowed down the fall. The angel leap often caused the trooper to land on all-fours, so the Italians had developed special leather pads, gauntlets, and a sausage-like helmet visor to protect the paratroopers' knees, knuckles, and nose from the impact. An Italian paratrooper said proudly that while the British, Americans, and Germans jumped like automatons, "the Italians invested even this unnatural act with inspiration and imagination—and a pinch of artistry."[34]

All the officers and men of the Nembo expressed their desire to fight against the Germans. The division was well supplied with submachine guns, heavy mortars, and machine guns. Roosevelt and Obolensky felt that some very good guerrilla units could come out of Nembo. In Obolensky's judgment, they needed parachute and ground training in the American way of jumping, a short course in demolitions and explosives, and about two weeks of tactical training to be ready for deployment. They were included in the Italian Co-Belligerent Army together with other royalist forces and fought on the side of the Allies for the duration of the war.

Obolensky and the other OGs who had joined Roosevelt's staff in Sardinia returned to Algiers within a few weeks when Roosevelt's mission was replaced by the permanent Allied Military Government structures in the island. During the brief duration of their mission, they demonstrated courage and the unique traits that Donovan had envisioned for the OSS personnel engaged in special operations.

* * *

The landing of the Allies in Sicily and the fall of Mussolini raised the hopes of the French patriots for the liberation of Corsica. On September 8, 1943, when the BBC evening news bulletin announced that the Italian government had signed an armistice, the Corsican Liberation Committee headed by Colona d'Istria ordered a general insurrection. A telegram from Colona d'Istria in the evening of September 9 informed the French headquarters in Algiers that the insurgents were masters of the capital, Ajaccio, and needed armed reinforcements.[35]

The Allied Forces Headquarters made it clear that if the French wanted to intervene in Corsica, it would have to be with their own means—all the Allied resources and means of transportation were tied up supporting the beachheads in southern Italy, still in a precarious situation at that time. The French decided to send the First Army Corps, commanded by General Henri Martin, to help the resistance forces using two submarines, the *Casabianca* and the *Aréthuse*, as well as two destroyers and two torpedo boats that were available to them. Operation Vésuve began when 109 French commandos from the First Shock Battalion stacked aboard the *Casabianca*, converted into a troop transport, crossed the Mediterranean, and landed at Ajaccio on the night of September 13. In the next ten days, the bridgehead was reinforced with six thousand troops from French North Africa, four hundred tons of weapons, jeeps, antiaircraft guns, fuel, and food.[36]

General von Senger attempted initially to deploy his forces on the west side of the island to regain control of Ajaccio. He quickly realized that the French insurgents were determined not to let the Germans through and decided to avoid getting bogged down in deadly, uncertain guerrilla warfare. On September 13, von Senger moved to capture Bastia, the main port on the eastern coast of Corsica that held the keys to an orderly withdrawal of the troops and equipment. The Italian garrison initially refused to evacuate Bastia and elements of the Reichsführer SS brigade had to attack and take it by force on the night of September 13. Among the Italian prisoners, there were some two hundred officers.

The next morning, von Senger received an order from his superior officer, Field Marshal Albert Kesselring, who commanded all the German forces in Italy. On Hitler's instructions, von Senger had to shoot all the Italian officers in his custody and report their names that same evening. The basis for the order was a general directive issued by the *Oberkommando der Wehrmacht* (OKW), the German Supreme Command of the Armed Forces. It directed the German military to treat all Italian officers captured fighting after September 10 as guerrillas and shoot them on the spot. Scores of German officers in the Balkans, Italy, Russia, and elsewhere, obeyed this order, leading to thousands of Italian officers and soldiers killed. One notable exception was von Senger, who later wrote:

It was thus obvious that for me the time had come to refuse to obey orders. I at once spoke by radio-telephone with Kesselring, informing him of my decision. He accepted it without comment and agreed to pass it on to the OKW. I arranged for the officer prisoners to be returned immediately to the mainland, where they were at least safe from the gallows. I am grateful of Kesselring because he more or less accepted my decision and left it at that.[37]

Starting on September 17, von Senger concentrated his actions on defending the east coast road network and the port of Bastia long enough to evacuate the units under his command. They consisted of the Reichsführer SS brigade and the 90th Panzer Grenadier division, which had arrived from Sardinia, in total some thirty-two thousand men with heavy equipment, including tanks, artillery guns, materiel, and various vehicles.[38]

Donovan persuaded the French authorities in Algiers to allow a small token force of Americans to accompany the French Expeditionary Force to Corsica. On September 17, 1943, the entire fourth group of the Italian OGs, thirty men and four officers under the command of Captain James Piteri, left the OSS camp in North Africa and sailed to Ajaccio aboard an Italian destroyer.[39] Anthony Scariano, one of the OGs from the group, described the enthusiastic reception the local Corsican population gave them when they landed: "They were shooting pistols and rifles in the air, singing La Marseillaise, yelling and screaming and dancing with joy. They were lighting matches and brandishing flashlights, houses were lighted up, and there was no attempt at a black-out or any other form of antiaircraft security. Obviously the Germans had pulled out and were retreating northward."[40]

Upon arrival, the OGs "borrowed" several Italian trucks and their drivers to move around the island. The drivers were so pleased with the Americans and the rations they received that they did not want to go back to their units. Since no one seemed to care, they stayed with the OGs for quite a long time. The OGs' mission was to harass German vehicles as they retreated along the eastern coast of the island toward Bastia. Generally, they engaged in light skirmishes with rear guard elements. However, on the night of September 24–25, the Germans put up a stiff resistance near Barchetta, at a mountain pass that controlled the main highway approach to Bastia from the west.[41]

The coalition of forces battling the Germans was a rainbow of colors and nationalities, which became the norm for the Italian campaign. Alongside the Americans were Corsican patriots in civilian clothes and North-African *Goumiers*—members of the feared djellaba-wearing crack troops from Berber tribes of the Moroccan Atlas mountains, also known as Goums. Italian gunners provided artillery support. Two nights before the battle, Captain Pitteri and Technician Grade 5 John Tessitore lay all night on their stomachs above a bridge that cut across the mountains and observed German positions a hundred yards below. The next night at 2300 hours, a group of eleven Americans carrying bags full of hand grenades and Molotov cocktails started with a unit of Goums across the mountains to Barchetta, nine and a half kilometers away. A veteran of the operation described the terrain as "fantastically tough, high rocky drops to span and thorny maquis to crawl through." The Americans and Goums reached the heights above Barchetta at dawn and took up positions among the rocks above the German positions.[42]

Then, they charged down the mountainside, weaving though the maquis and throwing grenades at the Germans below, the Goums chanting their blood-curdling death cry. The Germans responded with heavy mortar fire. A German tank rolled toward them. First Lieutenant Thomas L. Gordon, leading the Americans, jumped forward, hurled a grenade, caught the tank in the belly, and disabled it. Then, suddenly, came a German mortar burst, exploding directly in the midst of a group of Americans. Lieutenant Gordon fell and with him, a few yards away, Technical Specialists 5 Rocco Grasso and Sam Maselli. John Tessitore, although wounded, braved the enemy fire to come to the aid of the fallen comrades. The remainder of the men helped hurriedly with first aid and then worked on to better positions. The attack resumed after the men regrouped, but the Germans held and it took another two days of bitter fights to take Barchetta. When the Americans returned to the high mountainside spot where their comrades fell, they found the body of Lieutenant Gordon across that of T/5 Grasso. He had apparently died while trying to give first aid to his wounded comrade. The body of Maselli was never found.[43] In early 1944, the French awarded Gordon the highest decoration in France, the Legion of Honor, Knight Degree. Grasso and Maselli received the War Cross with Bronze Palm, whereas Tessitore received the War Cross with Silver Star.

From Barchetta, the OGs pressed on with the Goums, Corsicans, and Italians toward Bastia. They were divided into three sections, one removing mines from the beaches, the second and the third attacking enemy vehicles on the highways to Bastia and L'Île-Rousse. Lieutenant Victor Giannino led ten OGs on a reconnaissance and tank-destroying mission. They belly-crawled up a mountain totally surrounded by Germans and spend three days and three nights there in a cold, wind-blown rain. Lieutenant Vincent Russo and six men made a three-day forced march in soaking rain to conduct a demolition mission north of Bastia. On the way back, they rescued a number of wounded Goums and Italians encircled in a small cave near a fishing village. The OGs slipped down the cliffside shoulder to shoulder, over slippery rocks where one slip would be the last. They found the wounded and sneaked them out of the encircled village in a fishing boat.

In missions like these, the OGs passed through high mountain villages, which had not seen an American in years. But the villagers had heard of Americans, and wherever the OGs went they were treated to warm receptions. The villagers improvised American flags and hung them out of the windows. At Farina, a tiny town high in the mountains between Saint-Florent and Bastia, the whole town turned out to throw a quick party. One of the OGs described the atmosphere: "There was dancing with the town belles. There were fresh eggs, hot soups. The Americans were enthusiastically kissed, French style, on both cheeks."[44]

At the end of September and during the first three days of October, the Germans sought only to protect their retreat to the port of Bastia and the evacuation of the troops and equipment to the Italian mainland. Their artillery slowed down the advancement of the Allied forces through the final pass before reaching Bastia. The narrow road through the pass wound in five sharp ascending S curves with steep brush and rock-covered inclines on one side of the road and sheer drops on the other. For two bloody days the Allies tried to force their way up the pass and onto Bastia, with gains often measured in inches. Finally, the Germans withdrew from their defensive positions and evacuated the last troops. Bastia was liberated on October 4, but had been devastated by the fighting and Allied bombings. All the bridges leading to the city were blown up, the water mains were broken, and the electricity system was shut down.

The OGs set up headquarters in Bastia with a small auxiliary office in Ajaccio. The enlisted men were settled in L'Île-Rousse. On October 21, 1943, the entire Company A of the Italian OGs moved from Algiers to Corsica, which became their home for the next ten months.[45]

CHAPTER 5

Rescuing Escaped Prisoners of War

After Italy signed the armistice on September 8, 1943, there was a brief period of power vacuum across the country until the Germans and Mussolini's new puppet government moved in and established their control. Many thousands of Allied prisoners of war took advantage of the situation to escape from captivity, go into hiding in the mountains, and look for ways to travel south to Allied territory. The OSS Operational Group Command devised a daring plan to send a contingent of OGs into enemy-held territory to find and direct the escaped POWs to safety. The British were planning a mission along the same lines using elements of the Second Special Air Service (SAS) Regiment. The SAS was a special warfare force in the British Army very similar in structure and mission to the OSS Operational Groups. They were organized in small teams of parachute-trained soldiers who operated behind enemy lines to conduct harassing actions, disrupt supply and communication lines, and collect intelligence.

Given the similarity of the British and American plans, the Allied command approved a joint mission, codename Simcol, to cover a two-thousand-square-mile area in central Italy that stretched from the Adriatic coast to the east to the Apennine Mountains to the west, and between the cities of Ancona to the north and Pescara to the south.[1] Several teams of OG and SAS personnel would parachute by air or land from the sea at different pinpoints in the operational zone, collect escaped POWs, and direct them to rendezvous points along the Adriatic coast where Allied boats would wait to pick them up and take them to safety. Upon completion of the mission, the men would either take the last boat at one of the rendezvous, try to get back through the lines, or hide in the mountains until the Allied armies arrived.

On September 25, 1943, a team of two OG officers, Lieutenants Peter Sauro and Paul Trafficante, and sixteen noncommissioned officers and enlisted men assembled in Algiers to prepare for the mission. They received clothing, equipment, arms, and ammunition. Each man received maps, 15,000 lire ($150) for operational expenses, one 9-mm submachine gun, one .45-caliber automatic pistol, and extra ammunition clips and cartridges. They left Algiers on September 26 and arrived at Bari, in southern Italy, where they reported to Lieutenant Colonel A. G. (Tony) Simonds, the British officer in charge, after whom the operation Simcol was named. Until October 1, they held joint planning conferences involving the OG personnel and all the British components (SAS, air, and navy) that would execute and support the mission. Realizing that the British lacked Italian-speaking personnel, Sauro assigned nine members of the OG team to support the British groups—one man for each of the four groups slated to go by parachute, and the five groups that would operate in boats.

On October 2, at the Bari airfield, the OGs received instructions on how to jump from the plane, an English Albermale. The ground crews loaded the containers with supplies and fitted the OGs with English parachutes. Colonel Simonds provided a final briefing in late afternoon and then Sauro and his team of nine took off in one airplane.

At dusk, they parachuted on their pinpoint near the town of Catignano, twenty miles west of Pescara, in the Abruzzo region. Everyone landed safely and, with the help of friendly local villagers, recovered four equipment containers dropped with them. One equipment chute containing food and an extra radio battery failed to open and the contents were smashed. Sauro ordered the villagers to bury all the chutes and containers, to distribute the food among escaped POWs in the area, and to alert them about their presence.

The first fifteen POWs arrived in the morning. They represented groups of other POWs who had remained in hiding. Sauro told them that until October 10 British boats would arrive to pick up escaped prisoners every other night between 2400 and 0100 hours at a location on the beach south of Pescara. The boats would give light signals every fifteen minutes. The password to get onboard was "Jack London." Sauro asked them to disseminate the information to all other prisoners in the area who they might meet. After this initial meeting, Sauro and the team took off toward their target area in the mountains of Gran Sasso. Sauro thought it best to split into two separate teams to cover more territory, make it easier for the escaped prisoners to approach them, and reduce the chances that the Germans would round up the entire team.

As each team pursued their course, they found prisoners in groups of six or seven, and sometimes as many as thirty or forty. Their attitude was wary when first approached because they could not believe that uniformed Allied soldiers were this far inside enemy territory. Often the prisoners ran for the hills when they saw the OGs, thinking they were Germans. It worked best when the OGs were not out looking for the prisoners but instead remained at a house in the area for a day or two and let the villagers be sure that they were Allied troops. Then the families themselves would go with a mule or horse and bring the prisoners from their hiding places. By the last night of scheduled boat rendezvous on October 10, the two teams had contacted personally four hundred prisoners, and through them more escaped prisoners. Sauro estimated that his men were responsible for directing between eight hundred and two thousand men to boat rendezvous during those few days.

On October 10, the two teams met near Farindola in the foothills of the Apennines, thirty miles west of Pescara and over one hundred miles north of the frontlines. The planned part of their mission was over. They chose not to take the last boat ride back to safety, and now they had to find a way to return to the Allied lines. They would have to make their escape on their own, because they had not been able to establish radio communications with the OSS base in Algiers or with the British base in Bari. Neal M. Panzarella, the team's radio operator, discovered immediately upon landing that the receiver was dead. He tried to fix the broken receiver using his spare kit, changing tubes, and checking wires, to no avail. Nevertheless, he sent out his call sign and transmitted messages of their progress for several days at the times and frequencies agreed upon—once a day at 1500 hours to Algiers and three times a day at 1700, 1900, and 2100 hours to Bari. Now that the mission was complete, the radio equipment was a burden and liability, so they destroyed it and buried the pieces. Lieutenant Sauro ordered a group of five OGs under the command of Technical Sergeant Phillip J. Arengi to begin the trek south immediately. Sauro and the other four OGs remained in the area continuing to look for POWs and directing them toward the Allied lines.

* * *

Sauro and his team remained in Farindola until the end of October when they decided it was time to head toward the frontlines. The Germans had established firm control over the area and had set up strong checkpoints and patrols to capture escaped POWs making their way toward the lines. The Pescara River, the last natural barrier the POWs had to cross before reaching the Allied positions, became impassable due to the autumn rains and the strong security at the few bridges available. On the last day of October, Sauro ordered three of his men, Sergeants Giuli, Salvaggio, and DeLuca, to head west into the mountains for twenty to thirty miles and then to turn south toward the lines to eliminate the need to cross the Pescara River in the area that the Germans patrolled most heavily. The strategy paid off for these three men, who were able to reach the Allied lines after several weeks of difficult hikes.

Sauro and Panzarella were not as successful. They started out to try to cross the lines on the morning of November 1. Like the previous group, they also headed west into the mountains and walked all day until ten thirty that night. They bedded down in a field and started out again early the next morning. They had covered twenty miles since they began the journey, staying undercover for most of the time given the large concentrations of Germans in the area. On the night of November 2, they approached a house and managed to get some sleeping quarters in a barn. The farmer and his wife told them they had helped many POWs who had passed through, but they warned them that it was almost impossible to continue through the mountains because of the cold weather and the snow that had started to set in on the mountains. Both Sauro and Panzarella were in pain by that time from walking and the cold weather.

So on the morning of November 3 they began to make their way back slowly toward Farindola. They were forced to spend a night up in the Gran Sasso Mountains with only one blanket each for cover. It was very cold, and they got very little sleep. The next morning, they ran into three escaped prisoners who had taken refuge in a cave. One was a South African sergeant, and the other two were Free French troops from North Africa. They had taken to the hills because the Germans had raided the area where they were staying. Sauro and Panzarella were too weak to travel farther and needed some rest, so they stayed with the POWs. They saw several houses burning that morning in the town of Farindola. Germans had set them on fire because the people were harboring and feeding escaped prisoners.

They remained in that cave for several days. It was very damp, and several inches of snow covered the ground. They managed to survive on food an Italian family brought them. After a few days—it was the middle of November now—they went down to the valley where they stayed in an unoccupied farmhouse near the river Agri, not too far from the town of Farindola. A local family kept them supplied with food, at great risk to themselves. There was not much to do but lay low and try to pick up information about the enemy movements in the area. Sauro kept in touch with several British officers, all former prisoners of war, and helped them whenever possible with money to buy shoes, clothing, and medicine for the sick prisoners in their area. It was a morale boost for the prisoners to find someone in uniform behind the lines who offered them information and encouragement.

* * *

On January 13, 1944, with about three to four feet of snow on the ground, American planes appeared overhead and began strafing the area. Around 1215 hours, Sauro asked Panzarella and one of the

French soldiers to go to a ridge nearby and find out what they could about the positions that the planes were attacking. They went to the ridge, keeping off the skyline to avoid detection. They could see the planes zooming down and strafing but could not see what they were hitting because of a hill in front of them. While they were focused on the attacking planes, they failed to see a German soldier who sneaked up from behind and surprised them.

Panzarella was quick on his feet and was able to hide behind some rocks but the French soldier was not able to escape. The German asked him where Panzarella was, but the French soldier would not say. At this time, the German was about twenty-five yards from Panzarella's hiding spot but only a few steps from the Frenchman. The German fired three shots at the French soldier, missing him each time. Panzarella looked up from behind the rock where he was hiding and tried to take a shot at the German but he spotted him and immediately fired at Panzarella. The bullet came very close to hitting Panzarella, whose ears were ringing from the report. A few seconds after that, Panzarella saw the French soldier lying in the snow with blood all around him. Panzarella heard the German threatening to kill him outright. Panzarella made another attempt to fire on the German who responded immediately with a shot at Panzarella and one at the French soldier. By this time, the Frenchman's leg was beginning to stiffen up and he was losing a lot of blood. Panzarella thought the best thing to do was to surrender and save the Frenchman's life. He hid his pistol behind the rock and covered it with snow. Then he called out to the German and came out from cover.

Panzarella asked the German for a bandage, patched the Frenchman's wounded leg and then proceeded to carry him on his back through snow that was hip deep. It took them three hours to get to the nearest house where they got some Italian men to help carry the wounded soldier using a ladder as a litter. While they were carrying the Frenchman, Panzarella told one of the Italians to go back and notify Sauro of their mishap and to recover his pistol.

The Germans took them to a guardhouse, gave them something to eat, and dressed the French soldier's wounds. On January 14, the Germans took them by truck about thirty miles south to a place near the frontlines at Manopello. They stayed there overnight and on the night of January 15 were moved again. The Germans dropped off the Frenchman at the hospital in Chieti and took Panzarella to a schoolhouse crammed with several other prisoners, frontline Canadian troops but also escaped POWs who had been recaptured. The Germans interrogated Panzarella several times but he did not disclose any information about his association with the OSS or why he was behind the lines.

In between interrogations, Panzarella, three British soldiers, and a Canadian lieutenant hatched a plan to break out. Panzarella helped pry the screened windows open. He still had a few escape compasses concealed on him, some Italian money, and a map. He distributed the money and the compasses to the rest of the prisoners; the Canadian officer sketched out copies of the map outlining the escape route south. They were waiting for the dark to make their break when the Germans moved them from the schoolhouse, loaded them on trucks, and took them to a prison camp in Aquila, sixty miles west.

Panzarella fell sick while in the camp and was too weak to attempt another escape, although opportunity knocked. On one occasion, he was in a transport train moving prisoners from Aquila to the Laterina POW camp, two hundred miles north. Fifteen prisoners out of the fifty-odd prisoners confined in his boxcar were able to escape but Panzarella could not move. From Laterina, Panzarella was taken to a camp in Germany, Stalag VII-A, where he arrived on March 13, 1944. Stalag VII-A was Germany's largest POW camp, located just north of Mossburg in southern Bavaria. Panzarella spent the rest of the war in this camp until the American Third Army arrived at the camp's gates on April 29, 1945, and freed eighty-thousand Allied soldiers held there.[2]

Lieutenant Sauro managed to hide from the Germans who captured Panzarella on January 19, 1944. He moved from village to village for several months with the help of Italian sympathizers. At some point, he decided to shed his uniform and put on civilian clothes. His luck ran out on April 26, 1944, when he failed a document check at a German roadblock. Although in civilian clothes when caught, he managed to convince the Germans that he was a downed pilot. He received

POW status and spent the rest of the war in captivity, first at Stalag Luft III, a Luftwaffe-run POW camp near the town of Sagan, about one hundred miles southeast of Berlin, and then at Stalag XIII-D in Nuremberg, northern Bavaria.[3]

* * *

The group of five OGs under the command of Technical Sergeant Phillip J. Arengi that split from Sauro and his group on October 10, 1943, proceeded slowly through the mountains because the ground was very muddy from the autumn rains. They were able to move freely in uniform at first. But as they got closer to the frontlines, the German troops were everywhere, even in small towns. It was too dangerous to travel by day, and they could not travel by night because they did not know the terrain. It had been different during the execution of the operation between October 2 and 10, when they had local guides and could travel continuously day and night.

With difficulty, they made their way to the area near Catignano where they had parachuted on October 2. They learned from local farmers that they could use a bridge nearby to get on the other side of the Pescara River. They traveled with caution for ten miles to the town of Rosciano where the bridge was located to check out this information. They found that the Germans had posted sentries on the bridge guarding it at all times. Germans troops had occupied the houses on both sides. The Pescara River was too wide and murky to swim across at that time of the year, so they decided to go back to Catignano. They heard the British Eighth Army was advancing rapidly and figured they should stay in the mountains until the Allied troops reached the area. They waited during the latter part of October until November when they learned that the British had stopped their advance and had settled along the frontlines for the winter.

The group decided to stay in Catignano where they had found shelter at a house that had good security. On Christmas Day, three Germans came to the house. The OGs saw them come from a thousand yards away and immediately took their equipment and hid in a ravine nearby. They were still in uniform. The Germans had just come to eat and left soon after, so the OGs returned to the house with their equipment. Not an hour had gone by when three more Germans came. The owner of the house said they might as well stay in the bedroom. The Germans just wanted to eat and did not bother looking around. But when they left Arengi felt it was best to move to another location. The Germans who were camped nearby were bound to discover them sooner or later.

That same day they moved to another house where they stayed a week. On January 1, 1944, they moved again to another house nearby. They changed into civilian clothes and kept their .45 pistols. The villagers hid their Tommy guns, ammunition, and other military-issued articles, including their uniforms, in haystacks. Their group had doubled in size now to include other escaped prisoners. From the owner of the house they heard in January of a local organization known as the A Force that had established a series of safe houses and was leading prisoners through the lines. It took about a month to contact them. When they met at the beginning of February, the A Force Italian contacts said that the link was not completed and told Arengi to wait for their return. Then, at the beginning of March, three partisans returned and told the team to get ready for the journey to pass through the lines.

The guides had pre-arranged posts where the escapees stopped each night to eat and sleep. One of them, called Peppino, led the way toward the frontlines until just south of the town of Guardiagrele, one half hour's walk from the lines. He handed them to another guide with the nickname "Three Shirts," who would be their guide near the lines. Three Shirts took them to his house to wait until the snow melted because they were too visible against the snow background even during moonless nights. The next night another guide called Umberto took the lead. Other escapees had joined the group of the Americans, including four British POWs and another thirty prisoners of mixed nationalities who all wanted to join the Allied Forces. Among them was a group of Yugoslavs who posted their own guard to make sure they would not be left behind while they slept. The group got on the move at two in the morning and mixed in with the stream of refugees from small towns nearby who were crossing the line as well. They passed by an abandoned machine gun nest and followed a stream to the left of Guardiagrele. At six in the morning, they met a British patrol and were safe in Allied territory.

Thus, with the exception of Sauro and Panzarella, who became POWs, the rest of the OG team that parachuted together on October 2, 1943, managed to return across the lines. Although it took some of them months to complete the journey, they succeeded against the odds. The other nine OGs of mission Simcol who were attached to the British SAS teams were equally successful in fulfilling their initial mission and then making their way back with their lives. The story of Technician Grade 5 Joseph Padula represents well the experience of these nine operators in enemy territory.

* * *

Padula and his group of British parachutists dropped in the evening of October 2 at Porto Recanati on the Adriatic coast. They were the team that deployed the furthest inside German-held areas, over 170 miles northeast of Rome. The Germans went after them the moment they hit the ground, and they had to spend the first twenty-four hours in forced marches to evade capture. Eventually, they broke up into small squads of three men each and covered their assigned territories, returning every two days to the designated assembly area with the POWs they had collected.

Their orders stated emphatically that they should not to engage the enemy until they had completed their primary mission. For the first several weeks, they were careful to evade the Germans and quickly leave the area if they were detected. On occasion, they raided Fascist warehouses, taking food, guns, and ammunition that they distributed to the POWs they encountered. They gave these POWs instructions, a compass, and money to buy shoes, clothes, and other items that would enable them to get back to the Allied lines. By the beginning of November, they felt they had completed their mission, but they continued to look for and assist POWs.

Then, in Padula's words, they "received a 'Royal Rookin' from the Italian people." The Germans offered a reward for every Allied prisoner captured—1,800 lire for a soldier and 3,500 lire for paratroopers, dead or alive. Padula later said that many Italians were set on collecting the money. After several close encounters, they were convinced that they could not trust the Italians and must therefore stick closer to the mountains and caves. They trekked south for eighty miles until they arrived in the mountains of Grand Sasso, where they spent weeks waiting for the British Eighth Army's advance to reach them. They moved frequently from one village to the other, collecting any escaped prisoners they could find and avoiding the Germans.

No word came of the Allied troops' advance, and the pressure from the Germans and the local Fascists became intense. Therefore, they decided to split—every man for himself. Padula established quarters in a small mountain village called Chiciardi. Every night he went out in search of POWs and found quite a few whom he brought back to the village. Whenever he could, he stole rifles and ammunition from the Fascists, and eventually most of the POWs were armed.

On one such outing on March 26, 1944, Padula was picked up by three Fascists who were rounding up all available men in the area to fight in the Fascist blackshirt formations. Padula was in civilian clothes so they did not realize he was an American. They put him in a truck with six or seven other men. There was one guard in the back of the truck in addition to the driver and his companion in front. Padula knew that he would be finished if they took him to the Gestapo offices. He acted fast, wrestled the Fascist guard to the ground, ran away, and returned to the village of Chiciardi where the rest of his friends were.

The following day, Fascist and SS troops surrounded Chiciardi. They took fourteen prisoners and burned down many farmhouses. A week later, there was another raid on the village and Padula again got away by "the skin of his teeth." The Fascists and SS caught a couple more men and burned down more houses. The POWs escaped into the mountains. The Fascists and SS gave them chase initially, but turned back after the prisoners fired a few rifle shots and machine gun bursts at them. In Chiciardi the Fascists and SS rounded up the villagers, executed one of those who had been housing prisoners, and threatened the rest with more reprisals before they left the area.

Not wanting to subject the villagers to more brutality, Padula and the rest of POWs moved to another mountain range where they met three Yugoslav escaped prisoners. They decided to wage guerrilla actions against the Germans. Padula later wrote, "Whenever small columns of trucks or other vehicles came along we attacked them, burned the trucks, and took prisoners. The Yugoslavs killed the prisoners." A week after these hit-and-run operations began, the Germans sent a battalion and ran the guerrillas back into the mountains. The winter snows set in and shut them into the caves where they had taken refuge.

A snow blizzard began on Christmas Eve 1943 and lasted all night and day. The following morning, the snow was about ten feet deep. The food was scarce, and some of the men, two British majors among them, decided to attempt to go down to the village. The snow had rendered the paths invisible, so they lost their way and fell over a cliff. Most of them died immediately except for one of the British majors who broke his leg in the fall. Padula and the rest of the POWs recovered him but they did not have any medicine in the caves. They moved the major as close as possible to Isila, the nearest village, where the Fascists found him and took him to the nearby town of Teramo. A priest later told Padula that gangrene had set in on the major's broken leg. They amputated it, but the major died anyway in the middle of January.

The three Yugoslavs attempted to move down the mountain next. They took off one morning and never returned. In the beginning of April, when the snow melted, Padula and his men found their bodies about six or seven hundred yards from the cave, where they had died of exposure. They took them to Chiciardi and buried them in a small cemetery in the mountains, together with the other POWs who had died earlier.

In the beginning of May 1944, Padula and his group returned to Chiciardi, teamed up with another band of guerrillas, and coordinated a joint attack against Isila. They took the village with one heavy machine gun, about thirty-five rifles, and a lot of ammunition. They kept the area liberated for about two weeks but were forced to evacuate when the Germans sent in a cavalry company with eighty to one hundred men from Montorio, the principal town in the area situated about thirteen miles from Isila. Toward the end of May, the group established contacts with more patriots and drew up a plan to get rid of the Germans at Montorio. They attacked the town, opened up on the Germans, and kept firing all their weapons, hoping that "the Germans would believe there was a division of men attacking them," Padula wrote later. Shortly after, the Germans and the Fascist troops left the area, having lost several men between those killed, wounded, and captured by the guerrillas. Padula and his group moved in to establish control of the zone. They rounded up the "trouble makers" who were dealt with by the British authorities when they reached the area.

In the middle of May 1944, the British Eighth Army and the American Fifth Army made their decisive push at Monte Cassino, finally breaching the German defensive positions along the Gustav Line. The Germans began a precipitous withdrawal toward their next fortified line, with the Allied forces rapidly advancing northward. On May 23, 1944, Padula and his group met a small Polish motorized unit, the first Allied unit to arrive in their area. The Polish soldiers shared their cigarettes with Padula's group and directed them toward the village of Penne in the rear where a British cannon company had its headquarters. Once there, everyone felt they were safe in Allied territory and jubilation set in. Shortly after, the British brought trucks that took them to a recuperation camp where they received food, clothing, and medical attention. From there, Padula and the American POWs were transferred to Foggia, at the headquarters of the Fifteenth Air Corp Command, where they exchanged the British uniforms for American ones. After a few more days of rest in Foggia, Padula left the group of the rescued POWs and travelled to Bari, where he met Colonel Russell Livermore, head of the OG Command, and General Donovan. "Then I knew I was home," he later remembered. From Bari, Padula took a flight to Algiers, where he spent a couple of weeks on a well-earned leave before rejoining his OSS unit.

CHAPTER 6

Operations from Corsica

fter the liberation of Corsica in October 1943, the OSS moved the entire Company A of Italian Operational Groups from Algiers to L'Île-Rousse on the western coast of the island. For the next several months, the OGs used L'Île-Rousse as their training and staging area. Bastia, only thirty-five miles from the Italian mainland and ninety miles from the strategic Ligurian coast, served as the headquarters and launch base for a number of operations harassing the Germans along the Tyrrhenian coast from Genoa in the north to the islands of the Tuscan Archipelago in the south. American PT boats of Squadron 15 and a flotilla of British motor gunboats moved up from Sardinia and began to operate out of Bastia by the end of October. Until the summer of 1944, the OGs enjoyed the distinction of being the northern-most American troops in the Mediterranean theater of operations.

Among the first missions the OGs launched from Corsica were a series of raids against a group of small islands in the Tuscan Archipelago, off the Italian coast.[1] The objective of the raids was to occupy the islands and establish observation posts manned by OG personnel who monitored German air and sea activities and reported them to Bastia headquarters. The OSS established the first of these observation posts on Capraia, a small island about forty miles northeast of Bastia. On October 15, 1943, two Italian ships had arrived in Bastia with the commandant and fifty-two soldiers of the Capraia Italian garrison aboard, together with twenty-five political prisoners freed from the penal colony on the island. Also onboard was all of the island's military defense equipment that the Italians could carry away. The officers were taken to the OG base in L'Île-Rousse, where they provided detailed information about the layout of the island. In the afternoon of October 19, a small group of OGs headed by Colonel Russell Livermore set sail from L'Île-Rousse aboard a British minesweeper to reconnoiter and occupy Capraia.

They arrived off the Capraia harbor at 2200 hours and, finding no sign of activity in town, quickly secured the post office and shut down the communication lines with the island of Elba and the mainland. A handful of Italian Carabinieri still in the island expressed satisfaction at the arrival of the American troops. The OGs examined papers, journals, and records in the post office and carried a number of technical publications related to telecommunication equipment that they forwarded to the OSS headquarters in Algiers. An officer and nine enlisted men set up quarters on the central square—they would stay behind to maintain a permanent presence on the island. By 0100 hours of October 20, Livermore and his party began preparations to return aboard the British minesweeper, greeted effusively by the island's inhabitants, most of them fishermen. They left Capraia at 0130 hours and arrived at L'Île-Rousse at 0800 hours.

The OGs that remained on the island established an observation post at the Italian naval semaphore station atop the island. They transmitted weather and shipping observations by radio to the OSS headquarters in Bastia, which relayed the information via a direct telephone line to the Allied Forces war room at the 63rd Fighter Wing headquarters. At least three times a day, they sent weather reports covering sea conditions, precipitation, visibility, and wind direction and velocity. Enemy plane spotting was particularly useful for protecting the Allied airfields in Bastia and elsewhere in Corsica from surprise attacks from aircraft flying under the radar. Pilots and ground crews at the Borgo airfield on the eastern coast of Corsica, only five minutes flight time from Capraia, trained to disperse or take all the planes in the air within five minutes from receiving a warning from the island.[2]

On December 8, 1943, Livermore led a similar operation to establish an observation post on the island of Gorgona, twenty miles from Livorno off the Italian coast. The OGs captured a party of seven Fascist militia blackshirts as they slept and took them back to Bastia as prisoners. They seized useful communications equipment and codebooks. The OGs placed large binoculars at the semaphore station on top of the island, which they used to monitor enemy activity at the port of Livorno. Carl Lo Dolce, a twenty-year-old New Yorker born to a family of Sicilian immigrants, was the team radio operator who transmitted the observations daily to Corsica. In one instance, the OGs reported considerable activity at large fuel storage tanks in the harbor, which the Allies believed to be unused. An air raid was mounted and the OGs were able to report that the planes had destroyed the targets within two hours of the attack.

Shortly after, the OGs established a third observation post on the island of Elba. The heavily fortified island was firmly in German hands, so an all-out attack was out of question. Instead, a small team of OGs landed by boat and established a clandestine base on the summit of Mount Cappane, the westernmost peak overlooking Portoferraio, Elba's main city. The team reported ship movements and the conditions on the island for six weeks. The Germans, using directional finding equipment, pinpointed their location and attacked. The team was on the run for several days but were successfully evacuated on February 1, 1944.[3]

* * *

In addition to the raids against the islands on the Tuscan Archipelago, the OSS Italian Operational Groups carried out a number of reconnaissance operations and small-scale attacks on coastal installations in the last months of 1943.[4] They were intended to draw fire from enemy coastal defenses and simulate commando raids along the coast between Pisa and Livorno to make the Germans believe that preparations were in the making for an Allied landing in that area. Lieutenant Albert R. Materazzi, executive officer of the Italian OGs, led two such operations in November and December. In the first one, a group of

OGs left Bastia at 1800 hours on November 1, 1943, and at 2320 hours reached the pinpoint between Livorno and the mouth of River Arno. They lay about a mile offshore merely observing and listening. Visibility was very poor, and there was very little chance that the boat would be noticed, so they decided to make their presence known. At 0050 hours, they transmitted simulated conversations between a pickup boat and a beach reconnaissance party over the ship's radio telecommunications equipment on a frequency common to walkie-talkie radio sets that they knew the Germans monitored.

After a while, acting very distressed about the fate of the beach party, they sent up flares, flashed lights, and blinked Morse messages with the boat's signal lamp. Then they made a loud crash start sweeping the area for several minutes as if they were searching for a small boat. As a final distress signal, they fired a burst of tracer bullets vertically and sped away at full speed.

About a month later, when the moon cycle was right again, Materazzi and crew returned to the same area between the mouth of Arno and Livorno and stopped the boat a half-mile offshore. The weather was clear and the full moon setting in the ocean silhouetted the boat for an observer from the coast. To make sure they were noticed, they displayed lights on the deck of the bridge and fired tracers against the coast that was completely blacked out. Then, they turned all the engines on and headed for Bastia making as much noise as possible.

Although these initial missions were not stressful, the OGs spent the time between them exercising to stay fit and training for the more difficult missions they knew lay ahead. The training was realistic and sometime even dangerous. On December 2, 1943, several OGs were practicing landing operations with rubber boats off the coast of L'Île-Rousse. The seas were rough, and several OGs were washed overboard by a high wave. Another OG, Salvatore Di Scalfani, was walking along the beach when he heard one of the men in the water calling for help. Di Scalfani plunged into the rough sea fully clothed and went to the assistance of his fellow soldier, who had lost consciousness and was in danger of drowning. Di Scalfani battled the rough sea and fought his way to shore carrying the limp body of the soldier. For this act, Di Scalfani received the Soldier's Medal in March 1944.[5]

The OGs filled their free time with polishing weapons, writing letters home, talking to locals, and listening to the radio. They, like the rest of the Allied soldiers in the Mediterranean theater of operations, often tuned to German radio stations that mixed their propaganda broadcasts with very good music. A soldier wrote home:

As a matter of fact the best jazz programs are usually Jerry ones. Between 7–8 P.M., we always tune in to "Axis Sally" who has been broadcasting to GIs for two years now. Although she is known as "Midge" now she's the same silky babe the boys used to pick up at Anzio. First comes a German news report remarkably true, although their defeats are minimized and the number of allied losses stressed. Then follows the usual divide and conquer psychological attack. Last night the commentator explained how . . . American officers as well as British are having the time of their lives . . . carelessly scribbling out orders for the rain-soaked boys in the trenches to attack superior German positions, etc. Roosevelt is playing up to Stalin to get the huge communist vote in America, but when elections are over he will drop Stalin, who will then commence to over-run the world with Bolshevism unless Germany is spared to stave off this scourge. Their propaganda is pitifully weak now and the cornered-rat whine is all that is left.

This is followed by a sexy voice, which goes something like this: "Hello, all you GIs sitting in your wet foxholes. Are you feeling blue? Do you wish you were back in the arms of your wife and girl? Well, Midge is here to cheer you up again, calling from Berlin every night to all you brave boys crouching out there in your muddy foxholes. Come on Joe, how about a little tune like you used to dance to back in the good ol' States? Let's listen to Fats Waller playing Bye-Bye Blues." Then follows about a half hour of good jazz, mostly blues, each recording followed by comments such as "That last piece was 'I've Got the Blues' and I bet you do have them, you pooooor deae-aears." It's really a riot and a lot of fun to listen to![6]

There was one song that the men always greeted with cheers whether it came over the waves of German radio stations or the Allied ones. "Lilli Marlene" is the curious case of a song that "went viral" seventy years before the expression had any meaning. Hans Leip, a German World War I veteran, wrote simple lyrics in the 1930s that told the story of a private who used to meet the young and fair Lilli Marlene under the lantern by the barracks' gates. Then orders came for deployment and soon the private found himself in the trenches reminiscing about Lilly's sweet kisses, her sweet face haunting his dreams, and Lilly waiting for him "where the lantern softly gleams."

Norman Schultze set the verses to music in 1938 and a Swedish singer, Lale Anderson, recorded the song in 1939 with the title "The Song of a Young Sentry." Anderson's husky voice formed a perfect counterpoint to the military march theme to which the music was set. Nevertheless, the song went unnoticed and would have been forgotten had it not been for German broadcasts to the Balkans and North Africa from Radio Belgrade. One night in 1941, the director of the program for Rommel's Afrika Korps found himself short of records to play because the station had been bombed. So, he gave the song some extra playing time. Shortly after, letters began arriving from soldiers in North Africa requesting that the song be played again and again. Legend has it that Rommel himself wrote to the station asking that they incorporate the song into the regular broadcasts. After that, every night at 2200 hours Radio Belgrade played the song.

The song's popularity reached Berlin and Frau Goering, an opera singer herself, sang the song to a select group of Nazi leaders. By now, hummed by soldiers across the Third Reich, the song had gained additional lyrics with a new meaning, far different from the original one. While the private was away at the front thinking of Lilli Marlene, she kept going back to the lantern post. Soon she met a sergeant who fell in love with her, but he went to the front as well. Then it was the turn of a lieutenant, then a captain, and so on. Finally, Lilli Marlene met a brigadier general, which was what she had wanted to do all along. The irony and cynicism with which the troops now sang the song did not escape the Nazi leaders, who tried to kill the song without much success.

In 1942, the fortunes of Rommel's Afrika Korps turned and the British Eighth Army began capturing German prisoners, who brought with them "Lilli Marlene." When the Americans landed in North Africa, they picked up the song from the British. There was concern initially among the Allied authorities that a German song about a girl who did not have sterling virtues was becoming the favorite song of the British and American armies. Soon they realized that the phenomenon was out of hand. John Steinbeck, who experienced the popularity of the song among the soldiers firsthand as a war correspondent in the Mediterranean, wrote, "It is to be expected that some groups in America will attack 'Lilli,' first, on the ground that she is an enemy alien, and, second, because she is no better than she should be. Such attacks will have little effect. 'Lilli' is immortal. Her simple desire to meet a brigadier is hardly a German copyright. Politics may be dominated and nationalized, but songs have a way of leaping boundaries."[7]

In the United States, the Office of War Information overtly and the OSS Morale Operations branch covertly decided to turn the song into a propaganda tool in favor of the Allies. Marlene Dietrich, who had fled to Hollywood to escape the Nazis, recorded her own English and German versions of the song and performed it in dozens of concerts for the GIs throughout Europe during the war. Summing up the effect of the song, Steinbeck wrote, "And it would be amusing if, after all the fuss and the heiling, all the marching and indoctrination, the only contribution to the world by the Nazis was 'Lilli Marlene.'"[8]

*　*　*

The beginning of 1944 found the Allied armies in Italy stuck on two fronts, unable to penetrate the German defenses no matter how hard they tried. One of the fronts ran across Italy along the heavily fortified Gustav Line, anchored in the Cassino massif and protected by the natural obstacles of the Garigliano and Rapido Rivers. Cassino controlled the southern entrance to the broad Liri River valley, which lead straight to Rome. Field Marshal Kesselring entrusted the defense of Cassino to battle-hardened troops entrenched in strong positions and determined to hold every inch of ground. Key to the defense of the Gustav Line at Cassino was the XIV Panzer Division under the command of General Frido von Senger.

Following the successful extraction of German troops from Sardinia and Corsica, von Senger received a promotion to *General der Panzertroopen*, a rank equivalent to a three-star general commanding armored troops in the United States Army. Despite concerns about his loyalties to the Nazi regime, the German Supreme Command approved Kesselring's plan to give von Senger command of the XIV Panzer Division and entrust him with the defense of Cassino. Von Senger proved himself an excellent student of the Italian terrain and strategic use of armor and for several months frustrated the attempts of the American Fifth Army commanded by General Mark Clark to break through the Gothic Line.

The second front was at the Anzio and Nettuno beaches. The Allies had tried to make an end-run around the German defenses in Cassino by landing the US VI Corps north of the Gustav Line on January 22, 1944. The strategic intent was to roll up the German front and go straight for Rome, which lay ahead less than forty miles to the north. The landings were a complete surprise and met no opposition from the Germans, but Lieutenant General John P. Lucas, the American commander of the invasion force, decided to reinforce the beachhead before breaking inland. The momentum was lost, the Germans were able to move reserves to block the advance, and another stalemate situation was created. An exasperated Churchill, with his knack for summarizing situations said, "I had hoped that we were hurling a wild cat on to the shore, but all we got was a stranded whale."[9]

While they were holding the frontlines at Cassino and Anzio, the Germans were working hard to prepare the next defensive line using local Italian laborers and Fascist forces from Mussolini's Italian Social Republic of Salò. The project was the responsibility of the Todt Organization, the construction consortium responsible for prewar civil engineering feats, such as the Autobahn system, and for massive military works during the war, including the Siegfried Line and Atlantic Wall fortifications, built using prisoners of war and forced laborers from occupied countries. Known as the Gothic Line, the defensive fortifications started on the Tyrrhenian with strong coastal artillery positions at Punta Bianca just south of the naval base of La Spezia and ran southeast along the Apennines to Pesaro on the Adriatic. Combining heavy fortifications at strategic mountain passes with the rough terrain of that area of Italy, Kesselring created a barrier that would grind away the Allied superiority in men and equipment and force them to halt the advance.

The German High Command considered the possibility of an Allied landing from Corsica on the Ligurian coast a big threat to the German defense strategy at this time. There was fear that the Allies would attempt another end-run as they had tried to do at Anzio. To protect from this eventuality, Kesselring stood up an army group led by General Gustav-Adolf von Zangen to defend the entire territory of northern and central Italy north of Livorno, which constituted the rear area of the German forces at the time. Within Army Group von Zangen, the 75th Army Corps led by General Anton Dostler was responsible for defending the western sector along the Ligurian coast between Genoa and Livorno. Both von Zangen and Dostler had traversed a similar path to reach the position they enjoyed in the Wehrmacht at the time. They were the same age, born in 1892, had entered the military in infantry units in 1910, had received their first officer commissions in World War I, and then had served in the 100,000-men army that Germany was allowed to keep after the war. They were not members of the Nazi party—military rules forbade soldiers from joining political parties—but their careers benefited from Hitler's re-militarization of Germany and the victorious campaigns of the first years of World War II. They had commanded infantry divisions and corps in France and Russia. By the time they received their assignments in Italy in January 1944, both von Zangen and Dostler had the rank of *General der Infanterie*, equivalent to three-star general commanding infantry units in the US Army.

Along the Ligurian coast, the Germans selected strategic points and turned them into fortified long-range artillery positions intended to hold the Allies' advance from a distance and continue resistance even if the Allies overran the territory around them. The German military doctrine called these strong positions fortresses. The Germans built one such fortress on top of Monte Moro overlooking the city and port of Genoa. The artillery fortifications at Punta Bianca, the starting point of the Gothic Line near La Spezia, received the fortress designation as well. The responsibility for building and defending these strongpoints fell to the 135th Brigade, known as the 135th Fortress Brigade, a unit under Dostler's 75th Army Corps, under the command of Colonel Kurt Almers.

* * *

At the beginning of 1944, the OG operations out of Bastia packed more punch. They now targeted roads and railways along the Ligurian coast to interrupt the flow of German troops and supplies to the Cassino and Anzio frontlines.[10] On the night of January 2, 1944, Livermore and Materazzi led a group of OGs in an attack against a bridge on the Via Aurelia about five miles south of Livorno. PT Boat 216 traveled from Bastia and came to within five hundred yards of the shore at the pinpoint. At 0150 hours, the dinghy and two rubber boats were launched. Two British sailors rowed the dinghy towing the rubber boats that contained the shore party and the demolition equipment. Upon reaching the shore, the OGs beached the rubber boats and proceeded inland, whereas the British sailors rowed back to the PT boat to await the pickup signal. On the way to the target, the OGs encountered several obstacles, including an unoccupied trench, a very dense strip of woods, and a four-strand barbed-wire fence. When they emerged from the thicket, they were able to see the road and to determine the location of the bridge over a ravine that was their target. They proceeded to the bridge and found that it was larger than they had expected—a single-span masonry arch bridge about thirty feet wide. The ravine below had very steep sides, and the water in the ravine was about fifteen feet from the roadbed. The men placed a single charge consisting of 250 pounds of Composition C in the middle of the north pier, approximately two feet from the bottom of the ravine, using two-hour delay pencils to set off the charge. The OGs completed the work at 0300 hours, returned to the beach, and signaled to be picked up. All the men and equipment were back aboard the PT boat at 0340 hours. At approximately 0500 hours, the watch on the boat reported a bright flash on the mainland in the direction of the target. Upon returning to Bastia, the OGs reported the results of the mission to the 63rd Fighter

Wing, which ordered a sortie over the spot. The reconnaissance planes reported that the bridge had its railing blown away but the paving was intact, an indication that the charge had not been sufficient to cause major structural damage to the bridge.

A smaller team of OGs composed of one officer and five enlisted men attempted a similar operation that same night. With the help of an OSS intelligence team of Italian agents, the OGs would destroy a tunnel on the La Spezia–Genoa railroad about twelve miles southwest of Genoa. However, when the OGs arrived at the pinpoint, the reception party was not there to signal the landing spot, so the operation was not attempted.

A third operation of the same nature, code-named Ginny, was carried out on the night of February 27. Its objective was to destroy the tunnel entrances on the La Spezia–Genoa railroad at one of its most vulnerable points, roughly five hundred yards southeast of Stazione Framura, where the trains ran on a single-track. Because of delays setting off from Bastia and difficulties locating the pinpoint, the shore party was already one-and-one-half hours behind schedule when it landed. Delays increased after the OGs failed to locate the target immediately, thus making it highly unlikely that the team would be able to complete the mission before dawn. Lieutenant Materazzi who commanded the operation cancelled the mission and recalled the team to the PT boats, not wanting to expose the entire crew to the risks of a daylight return trip to Bastia under the threat of attacks from German coastal artillery, chase boats, or fighter planes. However the shore party had done a good reconnaissance of the target, and the OGs decided to try the operation again in four weeks at the next favorable moon cycle.

* * *

The small island of Pianosa, halfway between Elba and the island of Montecristo, became the target of several OG operations between the middle of January and the end of March 1944. It was the closest enemy-held island to the Corsican shores, and the Germans were using it to monitor the Allied shipping traffic to Bastia and flight patterns at the Borgo airfield. On January 14, 1944, an American pilot was forced to bail out of his airplane, parachuted in Pianosa, and was taken prisoner. A reconnaissance plane looking for the missing pilot flew at low altitude over the island two days later and came under fire. A team of OGs landed in Pianosa on the night of January 18 to assess the strength of enemy positions and possibly destroy the observation post. They did not see any signs of life and retreated after cutting telephone wires along the road. A follow-up reconnaissance mission landed on the night of January 30 and cut some more telephone wires. This time, they noticed a patrol of enemy soldiers on bicycles, which they decided not to engage. Upon their return to Corsica, a joint operation of American OGs and French commandos was put together to storm the island and take prisoners.

The OGs selected a team of three officers and ten enlisted men to work as part of the larger French force of the *Groupe de Commandos d'Afrique*, composed of approximately 120 officers and men, mostly Moroccans, under the command of Colonel Georges R. Bouvet. The OGs contributed to the joint effort "D" rations for the entire party of 144 men, one hundred pounds of plastic explosives, various detonating equipment, and radio communications with the Bastia headquarters. The French furnished two diesel submarine chasers to transport the entire party to and from the objective and seven large rubber landing boats. The task force conducted joint landing exercises on two consecutive nights near Saint Florent, Corsica, which included a simulation of the projected raid on the second night.

A first attempt to conduct the raid on February 28 failed due to a delay in arrival at the pinpoint and difficulties finding a suitable landing spot. The second attempt occurred on the night of March 17. Commandant Bouvet made a personal reconnaissance of the landing point two nights before the raid took place to ensure that everything went like clockwork. The two sub chasers left Bastia at 1835 hours followed closely by four escorting PT boats. They made landfall at 2220 hours at the planned pinpoint in Pianosa. A reconnoitering party went ashore and at 2245 hours gave the all-clear signal. In less than an hour, all troops were ashore and had climbed the precipitous cliff. They split into three patrols responsible for clearing the western, central, and eastern sector of the island. A fourth group assured security of the beachhead and maintained communications with Bastia.

The patrol on the western part of the island found it desolated and returned without any action. The central patrol found a penitentiary at 0300 hours and cleared it within minutes, taking twelve Italian guards as prisoners. The east patrol surrounded the village where the German garrison was bivouacked. It attacked the barracks at 0400 hours, killing several Germans in the ensuing fight, but thirty-five to forty Germans barricaded themselves in fortifications at the edge of the port. They had an 81-mm mortar, a cannon, and several light machine guns, which they used to keep the attackers at bay. They lobbed about twenty mortar rounds over the three-to-four-meter-high walls of the fortifications without causing any damage to the French and American Commandos. Commandant Bouvet judged it would be impossible to clean them out within the time limit fixed for the mission. The east patrol therefore withdrew with twenty-four Italian guards as prisoners. They arrived at the beachhead at 0600 hours and re-embarked within fifteen minutes.

The sub chasers began the return journey right on schedule at 0700 hours, just as Allied fighter planes appeared overhead and the PT boats laid defensive fire on the island. The results of the mission were positive. The French-American Commandos killed several Germans, took Italian guards prisoners for intelligence gathering purposes, and reconnoitered the island in full. The only casualty on the Allied side was a Frenchman wounded during the firefight.

The series of raids culminating with the attack on Pianosa could not help but attract the attention of the Germans to the persistent threat coming from Corsica. An incident on the night of March 21, 1944, alerted them further to the commando operations that the Allies were launching from Bastia. A group of French Commandos left Bastia at 1700 to blow up a train and block a tunnel in the Savona–Genoa line. They were aboard an Italian torpedo boat, one of the vessels that had left the Italian ports after the armistice of November 8, 1943, to join the side of the Allies. Aboard the torpedo boat, there were Italian officers and crew, French Commandos, and a group of British and French naval officers. The party was due to return to Bastia at 0800 hours the next day. When it failed to do so, reconnaissance planes searched the area all day on the 22nd and 23rd without any trace of the boat. By the end of March 23rd, the search was called off and the boat and its crew were considered lost, probably having hit a mine. Later it was learned that the Italian crew had mutinied, killed the French and British officers and Commandos, as well as their own officers, and sailed to La Spezia,[11] where they described in detail the landing operations carried from Bastia to the German naval intelligence officers stationed there.

Thus, with the vigilance of the enemy on the coast increased considerably, the odds were stacked against the success of the second Ginny operation launched on the night of March 22, 1944.

CHAPTER 7

The Ill-Fated Ginny Mission

After their unsuccessful attempt to blow up the tunnel entrances on the La Spezia–Genoa line on February 27, 1944, the OGs assigned to carry out the Ginny mission spent the time in March to further study their target and be ready to carry out the operation at the next suitable lunar cycle.[1] OSS intelligence agents in Naples were able to find construction documents and interview engineers from the maintenance section of the Italian railways that provided new information about the structure of the tunnel near Framura. Pilots from the Eighth Army Air Force's 52nd Fighter Group flew another reconnaissance of the area and delivered a number of aerial photographs of the target. Based on the new information received, the OGs decided to increase the amount of explosives from 375 pounds to 650 pounds and to concentrate the demolition charges at the tunnel entrance. Lieutenant Vincent Russo experimented with various methods for carrying this quantity of explosives and held several rehearsals with the entire team in the vicinity of L'Île-Rousse. A complete dry run of the operation was held on the night of March 20, two days before the scheduled raid date.

The plan was to arrive at the pinpoint and launch the rubber boats no later than 2300 hours. After landing, the party would proceed to the target by following a natural ravine and be ready to commence the operation no later than 0030 hours. The security party, headed by Lieutenant Paul J. Trafficante and comprising Technical Sergeant Livio Vieceli and Technical Specialists Grade 5 (T/5) Joseph Noia, Rosario F. Squatrito, and Santoro Calcara, would neutralize the signal house and perform an on-the-spot reconnaissance of the target. Upon receiving the signal to proceed, the working party, led by Lieutenant Russo and including Sergeant Alfred L. DeFlumeri, Sergeant Dominic C. Mauro, and T/5s Liberty J. Tremonte, Joseph M. Farrell, Salvatore DiScalfani, Angelo Sirico, John J. Leone, Thomas N. Savino, and Joseph A. Libardi, would set the charges to demolish the target. If Russo determined that they could not complete the work and be back onboard by 0330 hours, he would notify by walkie-talkie radio Lieutenant Albert R. Materazzi in command of the boat party and return some of the men with the rubber boats. The party remaining on shore would hide during the day and prepare the target for demolition by 2300 hours of the following night, when the PT boats would return for pickup, weather permitting. At that time, most of the men of the shore party would be at the beach with only two men left behind to set off the charges. At 2300 hours, the party on the beach would begin signaling the letter "R" with a red flashlight and repeat it at fifteen-minute intervals on the quarter hour. When they had established contact with the PT boats off shore, they would set off the delayed charges, launch the rubber boats, and head to rendezvous with the PT boats. In the event that the boats could not return the following night, the OGs would follow the same procedure nightly until the night of March 27–28. If the team had not made contact by then, it would demolish the target and proceed inland to a safe house forty miles inland, where it would contact the headquarters in Bastia to arrange for alternate return plans.

The party left Bastia at 1755 hours on March 22, 1944, and arrived at the pinpoint near Stazione Framura at 2245 hours. The PT boats came to within three hundred yards of the shore, and in ten minutes the men launched the rubber boats in the water, loaded the explosive cases in them, disembarked, and headed for the shore. Materazzi and the other members of the boat party kept watch for any activity on shore. The shore party called at 2315 hours, but the message was garbled. Ten minutes later the radio crackled and Lieutenant Russo reported that he had reached shore and was looking for a landing place.

In another ten minutes, Russo called again and said he thought he had found the target. At 2340 hours, Materazzi heard Russo say something to Trafficante and the latter replied, "We see you. Wait for us." This was the last communication received from the Ginny team.

A few minutes later, a convoy of enemy boats approached from the south and, at the same time, the lights at Stazione Framura and along the coast went off. The PT escort boat took off as a diversionary measure and attracted fire from the lead boat in the convoy. Materazzi's boat drifted about two miles south of the pinpoint and waited five hundred yards from the coast. Shortly afterward, a large green flare came from the coast clearly outlining the boat's silhouette. An answering red-and-white flare responded from the sea. The main boat moved immediately further south, but another green flare went up over its new direction. Materazzi observed what appeared to be machine gun fire coming from the shore.

At this point, the escort boat reported that the area off the coast was clear of enemy patrols. Materazzi ordered both boats to head out west for about five miles, join, and then proceed back to the landing point to reestablish communication with the shore team. The rendezvous happened at 0200 hours, but now other enemy vessels appeared on the radar between their location and the pinpoint. By 0300 hours, the area was clear again and Materazzi decided to go in. The PT boats had barely started when the escort boat reported that both the main and auxiliary steering mechanisms were not functioning. The main boat had to wait until the crew had repaired the problem. It was now 0415 hours and too late for the boats to return to the pinpoint, retrieve the men, and leave before daylight. Materazzi and the boat skippers decided to head for Bastia and return the following night to pick up the shore party per the established contingency plan.

On March 23, two PT boats returned to the pinpoint. Radar indicated the presence of several large enemy craft at sea, making it impossible for the boats to approach the shore and contact the landing party. On the night of March 24, the PT boats attempted again to pick up the party. At the pinpoint, the boat crews observed several blinking lights near the landing beach. It was not one of the prearranged signals with the Ginny team and most likely a German attempt to trap the boat party, so they headed back to Bastia again. That morning, a photore-connaissance mission flown over the area revealed no damage to the tunnel and no trace of the party. A final attempt to pick up the Ginny team was made on the night of March 25. After that, the OSS listed the fifteen OGs initially as missing in action and later as captured by the enemy.

* * *

After the fifteen OGs left the PT boats on the night of March 22, they rowed hard to reach shore only to discover sheer cliffs rising straight out of the sea. They decided to move up the coast in search of a suitable landing place, which they found around 2345 hours. The rough sea complicated the landing and the surf kicked the rubber boats around. Several OGs fell in the water and had to swim to shore; fifteen cases of the gelatinous explosive material were lost. Once ashore, they discovered that they were not at their target zone near Stazione Framura. Russo took two or three men to make a reconnaissance of the target area. Trafficante and the others remained with the boats and tried to establish contact with Materazzi on the PT boats. They had two walkie-talkie radios with them, but both failed to reach the boat party.

Russo returned and informed everyone that the target was a mile and a half away to the northwest. When he learned that Trafficante had not established contact with the boats, Russo decided that they would not demolish the target until the boats had returned. A while later, as the dawn approached, they pulled the rubber boats and the cases of explosives about fifty feet up from the beach and camouflaged them in the rocks. Then the whole party went inland about four hundred yards uphill where they found an abandoned barn and decided to hide there for the day.

* * *

In the morning of March 23, Franco Lagaxo, a sixteen-year-old Italian villager, started the day as usual preparing to go fishing. He lived alone with his mother in Bonassola, in the locality of Carpeneggio, about two miles southeast of Stazione Framura. Lagaxo was outside his house when he saw two armed men in military uniform come toward him. They identified themselves as American and asked to speak to him and his mother inside. Once they entered the house, they went near the fire to warm up because they were wet. They said they were looking for a *casetta*, little house, by the railroad tracks and asked Lagaxo if he knew where it was and whether he could take them to it discreetly. Lagaxo told them "yes," and they left after five minutes.

They followed a path in the woods for about half a mile and arrived at the place in about ten minutes. "This is not the place we are seeking," the Americans told Lagaxo as soon as they saw the guardhouse—they were on the southern exit of the railway tunnel at Bonassola, rather than at the northern entrance at Framura. They gave him some money to buy food and wine, and told him to meet back at the house. Lagaxo went into town where he bought fifteen eggs and a liter of wine and returned home to wait for the men to return. They came back around noon, ate some polenta with Lagaxo and his mother, and asked if Lagaxo could take them to another *casetta* further north. Lagaxo agreed, the men finished eating, took the eggs and wine, and told him to meet them at 1500 hours near a little stable two hundred yards from the house. Lagaxo met the Americans at the agreed time, and they walked for about an hour until they arrived at a spot on the hills from where they could see Stazione Framura down below. "This is the place where we were supposed to land," the Americans said. After about fifteen minutes, they sent Lagaxo away, while they remained behind talking among themselves.

The next day, March 24, Lagaxo left the house at 0800 hours to go fishing. He saw the two Americans climbing from the sea toward the house. When he reached the rocks on the shore, Lagaxo noticed some fishermen gathering material under the direction of a local Fascist, Vittorio Bertone. The evening before, a villager by the name of Gaetano Oneto was returning home in his boat when he noticed the bright orange rubber boats nestled among the rocks. The OGs had camouflaged them well not to be seen from the hills and from the railway embankment, but they had not been careful to cover them from the sea. Oneto went ashore to look at them and found demolition equipment in boxes with EXPLOSIVE marked on them. Upon returning to Bonassola, Oneto reported his findings to the Fascist secretary Giobatta Bianchi. In the morning, Bianchi sent Bertone with Oneto to investigate. They uncovered the three rubber boats and were in the process of inspecting them when Lagaxo happened to go by.

Instead of fishing, Lagaxo returned home and found the two Americans waiting for his mother near the door. He asked them whether they had left any materials on the rocks and told them that the Fascists were taking it in a boat. "Yes," they answered and said that they were leaving the area because they were causing too much trouble. Lagaxo's mother came out with some bread and jam, which the Americans took and returned to the stable. Out of curiosity, Lagaxo went down a mule trail that led to town and saw a group of Germans and Fascists coming up. Lagaxo ran to the little stable to warn the Americans and for the first time saw that there were several of them. Lagaxo returned home taking another path and encountered the Fascists Bertone and Giovanni Ferri, who asked him if he had seen anyone. Lagaxo said "No" and continued toward his house where he saw a group of German soldiers and Fascists who had just arrived. They dispersed and began searching the area.

Shortly after, Lagaxo saw two Fascists, Giobatta Bianchi and Bertone, about fifteen yards from a grove where the two Americans he knew were hiding. Bertone noticed them and yelled, "What are you doing here, you ugly pigs?" The Americans answered, "We are Italians." Bertone replied, "You are traitors," and asked where the others were. "It's just us. There are no others," the Americans said. Bertone knew that more than just two soldiers must have come to require three rubber boats. He took from his pocket a whistle, which he had found in one of the rubber boats, showed it to the captured soldier, and said, "Do you want to see how, if I blow this whistle, the others will come out?" Then he blew the whistle. At the sound, the rest of the American soldiers who had been hiding in a vale about one hundred yards away jumped to their feet and began firing their weapons. There was an exchange of grenades and fire from automatic guns and rifles, but only for a short time. At approximately 1030 hours, the Americans surrendered and were quickly disarmed. During the brief fight, Lieutenant Russo was slightly wounded.

Lagaxo saw the group of Americans coming toward his house with their hands raised and surrounded by Germans and Fascists with pointed guns. They were locked in the storehouse. Two Germans and two Fascists guarded them while the others continued to search the area. Around 1100 hours, being satisfied that they had caught everyone, the Germans and the Fascists returned, took away the Americans imprisoned in the storehouse, and marched them to the Fascist headquarters at Bonassola. The Fascist prefect of Bonassola, *Commissario* Guglielmini, was the first one to interrogate the two officers, Lieutenants Russo and Trafficante. He was able to learn the following:

> Following orders received from higher headquarters in Naples, they had left Corsica on a PT boat and when they neared the Italian coast they had been transferred to three rubber boats [with which] they landed about 0200 hours on 22 March [sic] at the point where the boats were found. Their mission was to blow up the portion of railroad from Bonassola to Framura. Having landed they went up the mountain and took lodging in a stable which they found empty and abandoned.

Writing to his superiors, Guglielmini took care to highlight his role in the events of that day. He asked Russo if he, the son of an Italian, did not feel ashamed to carry arms against his fatherland. "He lowered his head, became red, and did not answer but gave me the impression that my words struck home," Guglielmini wrote. As for the local Fascists who had taken part in the action, their work "was beyond any eulogy. Their initiative and courage deserve vivid recognition and I hereby inform the head of the Province of their spirit of sacrifice and their devotion to duty," he wrote.

In the afternoon, German soldiers arrived with a truck and drove the American soldiers to La Spezia, at the headquarters of Colonel Kurt Almers, commanding officer of the 135th Fortress Brigade that controlled the area. Colonel Almers included the news of the capture of the fifteen Americans in the afternoon status report that he sent to his commanding officer General Anton Dostler at the 75th Army Corps headquarters.

* * *

Oberleutnant Wolfgang Koerbitz, staff officer in the 135th Fortress Brigade headquarters responsible for anti-partisan and intelligence issues, learned about the capture of American Commandos during a meeting with prefect Guglielmini in La Spezia in the afternoon of March 24. He headed straight for the brigade headquarters located at a castle in Carozzo, a small hillside town overlooking La Spezia, about three miles to the northeast of the town center. He arrived there between 1800 and 1900 hours and saw the fifteen American soldiers dressed in field uniforms standing in front of the staff building. Koerbitz asked an orderly to get water, bread, and straw for the Americans and send them to a small building above the staff quarters that served as a prison. Hans Bertram Baumgarten, the officer in charge of the prison, received them and searched them for identification papers, weapons, and personal items. He turned over to Koerbitz four watches, several nail files, and 29,500 lire found in the pocket of one of the Americans. Baumgarten put the two officers in separate cells and split the rest of the men in three cells.

At Carozzo, Koerbitz found Corvette Captain Friedrich Klaps, head of the German Navy intelligence office in La Spezia, who had come to interrogate the prisoners. Klaps spoke some English but not well enough to conduct the interrogations himself. Therefore, he called Lieutenant Georg Sessler, one of his subordinates who spoke fluent American English, to come to the Almers headquarters. Because Koerbitz did not know English well either, Sessler conducted all the interrogations on behalf of both the army and the navy for the next day and a half.

Sessler began the interrogation with the infantry officer Lieutenant Trafficante, who refused to divulge anything beyond his name, rank, and serial number. Next, Sessler interrogated two enlisted men who simply stated their names, ranks, serial numbers, and that they belonged to an engineering company. These initial interrogations lasted two hours, but Sessler, Koerbitz, and Klaps did not learned much. They took a break and briefed Colonel Almers on their lack of progress. Around 2200 hours, a teletype message arrived from the 75th Army Corps headquarters requesting the results of the interrogation. Headquarters were particularly interested in "tactical questions" on whether the Allies were preparing for a landing from Corsica. Klaps, Sessler, and Koerbitz conferred on a strategy to get some answers to these questions. They decided to interrogate Lieutenant Russo next. Before bringing him in, Klaps suggested they use a stock interrogation ruse to trick Russo into believing that the other three Americans had talked.

When Russo came in the interrogation room, Sessler began by telling him that they had standing Führer's orders to shoot saboteurs and members of commando-raiding teams. The only way he could save himself was by giving a full account of his mission so that Sessler could verify that it was a military mission and treat them as prisoners of war. "I told Lieutenant Trafficante the same thing and he provided us the information," Sessler said pointing to a few sheets of papers on his desk. Then Sessler said, "I know you came from Bastia and first I want to know the time you left." He had only guessed that they had come from Bastia, since it was the closest port to the landing point. Russo gave him the time. Sessler, pretending to look at the papers in front of him, said, "Lieutenant Trafficante gave me a different time." Russo replied, "Well, the time I gave you is the time. It is the only time I remember exactly." "OK, continue," Sessler said, and Russo began to tell him how they left Corsica in the PT boats and then the rest of their ill-fated mission.

Based on this information, Klaps prepared the first interrogation report stating that the group of prisoners had landed from American gunboats for a military mission against the Bonassola railway tunnel, that they were American soldiers in uniform, part of a headquarters company based in Corsica, commanded by a Colonel Livermore, and with regimental headquarters somewhere in North Africa. The report was composed as a teletype at 0030 hours and was dispatched to the headquarters of the 75th Army Corps at 0215 hours.

Sessler continued with the interrogation of two other enlisted men. Both refused to discuss their mission and gave only their names, ranks, and serial numbers. Although Sessler tried to use the information he had gathered from Russo, the two men did not fall for his bluff. It was close to 0400 hours when Klaps and Sessler stopped the interrogations and left for La Spezia to refresh themselves for a few hours before returning to continue questioning the remaining OGs.

* * *

Klaps and Sessler returned in the morning of March 25 to resume the interrogations. At the same time, an official from the SD arrived to take part in the interrogations. An SD truck stood by to take the prisoners away if it was so decided. The American enlisted men were transferred from the prison to a large barn-like building with stalls to be closer to the headquarters building where the interrogations would continue to take place. Between 0900 and 0930 hours, a telegram arrived from the 75th Army Corps with the words "The captured Americans are to be shot immediately. Dostler." Colonel Almers and Klaps conferred about what to do next. Almers said that he did not interpret "immediately" to mean in the next half an hour. The case needed further consideration, and he was going to talk to General Dostler about it. In the meanwhile, Klaps and Sessler would continue the interrogations.

Between 1030 and 2000 hours of March 25, Klaps, Sessler, and the SD official interrogated one by one all the Americans who had not been questioned the day before. The men refused to provide any information about their mission or outfit. Initially, all they would give were names, home addresses, ranks, and serial numbers. Toward the end of the day, some of them stopped talking altogether—two of them would not even give their home addresses although they were plainly visible on their dog tags. Sessler interpreted this complete reluctance to talk as an indication that the whole groups had discovered from their German guards that they would be shot in any case.

Sessler recalled a curious incident that occurred around 1700 hours. He was questioning one of the Americans who must have been Joseph Farrell, given that Sessler described him later as "a person named Joe . . . of Jewish extraction." For the first ten minutes, Farrell remained silent despite Sessler's repeated questions. Then suddenly and heatedly he shouted, "Here's mud in your eye!" as if raising a toast and saying "Here's to you!" or "Cheers!" Sessler was taken aback and asked for an explanation. Ferrell told him that he had recognized Sessler as one of the naval officers of the Hamburg-American Line that provided transatlantic services to New York in the prewar days. Ferrell had worked as an ice delivery boy in 1936–1937 and had brought ice to Piers 84 and 86 where the Germans liners anchored. The conversation became friendlier and more personal with Ferrell talking about his family and personal life. Ferrell confirmed that the group knew that they would be shot rather than treated as prisoners of war. "My superior and I are doing everything we can to have you evacuated as POWs," Sessler assured him. Then Sessler dismissed Ferrell and continued with the interrogation of the remaining Americans until 2000 hours.

* * *

Throughout the day, there was confusion in the Almers headquarters about what to do with the prisoners. Some suggested sending them away to a prisoners-of-war camp; others thought they were spies who had to be shot according to Hitler's order, the Führerbefehl, on dealing with commandos and sabotage units; and others suggested to turn them over to the SD and let them deal with the problem. At 1600 hours, Klaps held a conference with Sessler, Koerbitz, and the SD representative. He asked whether they thought the Americans were members of a commando unit or whether they were soldiers. Based on the results of the interrogations and based on everyone's impressions of the Americans, the consensus was that they were not members of commandos. At this point, Klaps advised Koerbitz to submit a report to his superiors summarizing this opinion to avoid the shooting of the Americans by mistake.

Koerbitz made his report to Almers, who called the 75th Army Corps in an attempt to have the execution order postponed or delayed. Almers first talked to Colonel Kraehe, Dostler's chief of staff, and told him that the Americans were in uniform and it was impossible to execute them after capture. On the other end of the line, General Dostler took over the conversation. He said curtly, "Almers, we cannot change anything. You know the Führerbefehl. The execution is to be carried out. You know that the Führerbefehl contains a clause according to which officers who do not execute the order are to be tried by courts martial." Further arguments by Almers did not change Dostler's mind and the conversation came to an end.

Next, it was Klaps who tried to get a withdrawal or postponement of the Führerbefehl. He called Dostler's headquarters at about 1900 hours and spoke with Kraehe, who said the execution was to be carried out and a report made to General Dostler by 2400 hours. Klaps asked Kraehe to request Dostler to postpone the execution for twenty-four hours. One hour later, Kraehe called and told Klaps that the postponement of the execution had been approved until 0700 hours the next morning. Klaps insisted on speaking with Dostler personally to explain the case.

When Dostler came on the phone, Klaps tried to use code words since the line was not secure. "It is about the fifteen guests who have arrived," he said. "They are harmless and not as bad as we assumed at the beginning." Dostler answered what sounded to Klaps like "I have received other reports," or "I am of a different opinion." The conversation became heated. According to Sessler, Dostler was very angry at the whole proceedings and threatened to break Klaps if he interfered with his order and the Führerbefehl. Finally, he told Klaps to explain the case by cable and state the basis on which he asked for postponement of the execution. At the same time, he told Klaps to conclude interrogations by 0700 hours of the next morning, which Klaps understood to mean that the fifteen American prisoners would be shot at that time unless an order to the contrary was issued. Dostler ended the call by saying, "I expect you to carry out my orders. This will be confirmed by telegram which is now on its way to Almers."

Immediately after the call, Klaps wrote a cable with the following content:

> Please postpone execution of Führerbefehl, because it has not been established whether the 15 Americans belong to Commandos, or whether they are cases coming under Führerbefehl at all. There is a

possibility for repercussions against German prisoners of war. Further interrogation necessary. It should also be determined whether there are threads leading from the Americans to Italian civilian population or partisans.

Klaps prepared a second copy of the cable for the headquarters of Field Marshall Albert Kesselring, the commander in chief of all German troops in Italy, hoping that he would intervene in stopping the execution. Koerbitz took both cables personally to the cable desk and ordered the soldier on duty to send the cables as soon as possible. "Fifteen lives depend on it," Koerbitz said. After about an hour, around 2300 hours, the soldier reported that he had sent both cables and had received confirmation of their arrival at the intended destinations.

Klaps left the Almers brigade and returned to his quarters in La Spezia hoping that the cables had reached their destinations and the fifteen Americans would not be shot. Around one o'clock in the morning of March 26, he called for a status update, but no one at the Almers headquarters could give him any information. Klaps then called the headquarters of the 75th Army Corps and asked several staff officers whether Dostler had received his telegram. Nobody knew exactly whether the general had seen it. It was now between 0400 and 0430 and Klaps asked to speak with Dostler. The telephone connection was bad, and Klaps was hard of hearing from his days as an artilleryman during World War I. He could not hear Dostler's voice on the phone, but a telephone operator repeated the sentences for him.

Klaps asked Dostler to ask for his cable in case he had not seen it. Through the operator Dostler said he would do so. Then Klaps said he wanted to add to the content of the telegram. He said that people in La Spezia were talking about the case of fifteen Americans who had landed near their town. Using code words, Klaps told Dostler that if the Americans were shot, the enemy would certainly have a way to learn about it. Dostler became rather harsh, threatened him with a court martial for talking about secret matters over the phone, and terminated the call. Shortly after, Almers called Klaps and told him not to make any more phone calls. The execution of the Führerbefehl could not be avoided. "You know how this order is handled. Officers who do not comply with orders come before a court martial," Almers said.

* * *

Despite the reluctance that Colonel Almers and his staff officers had expressed in carrying out the execution order and despite their efforts to convince higher headquarters to rescind it, everyone felt they had no alternative but to comply with the order. Around 1100 hours on March 25, Almers ordered Koerbitz to make the necessary arrangements for the execution. According to Hans-Bertram Baumgarten, the officer in charge of the prison, Koerbitz ordered him by telephone to prepare a grave for fifteen men, but Baumgarten said he would not obey. Koerbitz then reached out to Lieutenant Rudolph Bolze, commanding officer of the First Company, 905th Fortress Battalion, and ordered him to prepare a grave for the fifteen Americans. Later in the day, again according to Baumgarten, Koerbitz ordered him to locate a separate cell in the prison where it would be possible to shoot the prisoners with a pistol. Baumgarten refused again and they argued for half an hour, with Koerbitz threatening to punish him for not providing the cell he had requested. Because Baumgarten did not budge, Koerbitz called Bolze again asking him to identify a spot suitable for the execution in his area. In the meanwhile, Colonel Almers ordered Captain Rehfeld, commanding officer of the 906th Fortress Battalion, and Lieutenant Seidenstuecker, commanding officer of the First Company of this battalion, to select an execution squad from this company.

At about 2300 hours on March 25, Koerbitz and Rehfeld visited Baumgarten in the prison and told him to have the Americans ready and handcuffed by five o'clock the next morning for execution. Baumgarten asked for permission to inform the prisoners a short time before the execution about their fate, but Rehfeld refused and directed him to tell the prisoners that they would be transferred to a POW camp. At 0300 hours in the morning of March 26, a telegram arrived from the headquarters of the 75th Army Corps. It was addressed to Almers and stated that the previous order was confirmed. Shortly afterward, Baumgarten informed the Americans to prepare for transfer to a POW camp. According to Baumgarten, a technical sergeant among the prisoners, most certainly Livio Vieceli who was the only member of the Ginny mission with that rank, said he did not believe his story. Vieceli asked Baumgarten to send word to their families and gave him a list of the names and addresses of their relatives for that purpose.

Sessler recalled after the war that when it became clear that the Americans would be executed, he brought Joseph Farrell back in the interrogation room. He told him that everything had been done to avoid their execution but that the decision had been made and there was no chance now to change it. They then began to talk about family affairs and Sessler asked if there was anything he could do to help Farrell's family. Sessler said he was deeply touched by the way Farrell took the news and decided to offer him the means of a personal escape. He had hung his pistol in a belt holster on the handle of the door leading from the interrogation room. He told Farrell to try to take it on his way out the room, but he had to promise not to shoot anybody. Sessler told Farrell to head for the mountains once he had gotten out of the stalls where he would encounter Italian partisans who were in touch with the Allies.

Farrell initially refused to take advantage of the offer, but eventually changed his mind. Sessler dismissed Farrell and distracted a German sergeant who was in the room to take notes of the interrogation. On his way out, Farrell pushed hard on the door handle and caused the belt to drop on the floor. He removed the gun from the holster while picking the belt from the floor and placing it on a hook on the wall nearby. When Farrell returned to the stalls, he turned the pistol over to Lieutenant Trafficante. The group must have decided to try to escape during transport. At dawn on March 26, when the trucks arrived and the Americans were led to them, Trafficante attempted to draw the gun from the pocket of his jacket. A guard nearby noted the movement and covered him immediately. A scuffle must have ensued in which Trafficante, Alfred DeFlumeri, and Farrell must have tried to overpower the guards, but without success. The Germans searched the whole group for weapons. They removed the outer clothing from Trafficante, DeFlumeri, and Farrell, leaving them only in their undershirts and underwear. They tied the hands of the fifteen Americans securely with wire behind their backs. Then, they loaded them in trucks and took them to the place of execution.

* * *

First Lieutenant Rudolph Bolze was commanding officer of the First Company, 905th Fortress Battalion, with responsibility to defend the coastal artillery fortifications built ten miles southeast of La Spezia, at Punta Bianca, along Boca di Magra, and on top of Monte Marcello. A naval artillery battalion manned the weapons installed at these positions, which included a battery of 490-mm antiaircraft guns on Monte Marcello and a battery of the formidable 1,120-mm and 3,150-mm naval guns, called the De Lutti battery.

On March 25, 1944, Bolze received orders from the 135th Fortress Brigade headquarters to dig a grave measuring three meters wide, six meters long, and one-and-one-half meters deep in which to bury dead saboteurs. Bolze called Sergeant Fritz Borowski to his headquarters and ordered him to dig the grave near an ammunition dump called La Ferrara using Italian laborers from the Todt Organization who had been building fortifications in the area. Then Bolze processed some paperwork and did some writing before going to the canteen to drink wine with his subordinates. Around 2100 hours, Borowski reported that the grave was finished. Bolze told him to be ready with six other soldiers at the grave at 0600 next morning to help bury dead saboteurs. At 2200 hours, the phone rang. Lieutenant Koerbitz from the Almers headquarters wanted to confirm that the grave had been prepared for the burial of the saboteurs the next morning. Koerbitz asked whether there was a place in Bolze's area suitable for shooting future saboteurs. "What saboteurs?" Bolze asked. "Americans," Koerbitz answered. Bolze hesitated for about thirty seconds, and then answered, "It is very hard to find a suitable place in this area, but if there is no other way and if it has to be done, they can be shot at Punta Bianca." Bolze later remembered staying in the garden outside his house until past midnight. "Thinking about the prospects for the morning, I could not sleep that night," he said. He had thought the men were already dead and that his only duty would be to bury them. Although he had fought in Russia and had seen hundreds of dead soldiers, this burial got on his nerves.

Bolze woke up at 0500 on March 26. It was dark. He washed, shaved, and at 0530 set off on a bicycle for the grave location where Borowski and six soldiers were waiting. Bolze told Borowski to bury the saboteurs as fast as possible after they arrived because he himself could not stand seeing the burial and would go away. Then Bolze rode in the opposite direction toward Punta Bianca to find a suitable execution spot. At about 0630 hours, a car arrived. Captain Rehfeld, commander of the 906th Fortress Battalion, sat next to the driver and Lieutenant Seidenstuecker, commander of the First Company, 906th, sat in the back. Two four-ton trucks covered in tarpaulin followed the officers' car. Rehfeld and Seidenstuecker came out of the car and began walking with Bolze toward the execution place. They realized that no doctor was present, so Seidenstuecker went with the car to get the medical officer of the 905th Fortress Battalion, who lived a couple of miles away. Rehfeld said that the executions would take place in two groups, and Bolze pointed out two suitable locations about fifty yards apart.

Bolze and Rehfeld agreed to place the men with their back toward the sea rather than against the stone embankment to avoid ricocheting bullets hitting German soldiers. Then, they returned to the trucks about 150 yards away. Twenty-five German soldiers with steel helmets and guns stood next to the trucks. Bolze told them to lift the covers of the trucks and noticed that seven or eight men were sitting in each truck. Bolze remembered their brown uniforms—brown shoes, brown pants, brown shirts, no headgear. "What have they done?" Bolze asked. "This is a group of American saboteurs who most likely wanted to dynamite a town," Rehfeld answered.

Bolze then walked away about 150 yards around a bend on the road to wait for the medical officer. The doctor arrived at 0715 hours in an Italian Topolino car painted white with a red cross. The doctor stopped the car in front of Bolze, got out, and greeted him, "Morning, Rudi. What's new with you?" "They are making a cemetery keeper out of me," answered Bolze. Then he told the doctor that the execution would take place farther down the road but he, Bolze, would stay where he was because he wanted nothing to do with it. The doctor got in the car and drove off. Five minutes later, Bolze heard a salvo of about ten rifles. In ten minutes, there was another salvo. Bolze said later that he sat behind the curve all this time and did not see the execution. Immediately after the second salvo, Bolze realized that the men of the De Lutti battery nearby had not been warned of the execution and might have been alarmed by the salvos. Bolze started toward their positions and walked past the executed men. They lay in a row, some fallen forward, some backward. Blood was rushing out of them in many places and "on some of them you could still hear it pumping out," Bolze recalled later. Ten feet from Bolze, the doctor was bending over the last man.

As Bolze had feared, soldiers from the battery fortifications were coming down to see what the noise was about. Bolze ordered them to return to their position and to inform their commander that American saboteurs had been executed. As more soldiers kept coming, Bolze sent them away with the remark that they should not be so inquisitive but instead should watch for saboteurs in their own battery. In the meanwhile, the soldiers of the execution details finished loading the dead in the truck. Bolze ordered soldiers from the De Lutti battery who were still around to get shovels and cover the blood that was on the ground, which they did immediately.

Bolze went in the officers' car with Rehfeld and Seidenstuecker, and they drove in the direction of the grave. The truck with the dead Americans followed behind. When they arrived at the grave, the truck pulled up right at the edge, where Sergeant Borowski and his men were waiting. Two men went into the truck to move the bodies and hand them to four solders on the ground, who carried the dead to the grave. Three or four other soldiers from the firing squad helped to move the bodies and fill the grave. As this was going on, Bolze walked toward the doctor who was standing near Captain Rehfeld. Looking into the truck, he saw four pairs of brown shoes that the German soldiers had removed from the Americans. "At what time I do not know," Bolze said later. The doctor, who had witnessed the execution, told Bolze, "The executed men died quietly and calmly and bravely." Bolze stood at the gravesite until the soldiers finished filling it. They covered the fresh earth with grass sod and tree branches for camouflage. No markers of any kind were placed on the grave. Bolze told Borowski to keep all civilians away from the grave and the area for a while. At 1100 hours that morning, he called together the whole company and said, "None of you who may fall into enemy hands is to say anything of the shooting early this morning of two American officers and thirteen men."

* * *

That same morning, Koerbitz called Sessler at the Almers brigade headquarters to interrogate him about the pistol that had been found on Trafficante. Sessler admitted that the pistol was his but explained that it had been late at night, he was tired, and had placed the pistol holster on the door handle where a prisoner could have gotten it. He was not able to explain to Koerbitz why he had not noticed the unusually light holster when he had put it on his body. After the war, Sessler said that he was interrogated for the next thirteen days about the incident.

Klaps wrote an angry report to the Abwehr Italian office about the events that had transpired, complaining that he had not been able to gather the necessary intelligence from the American prisoners. "The investigation was interrupted because the prisoners of war were shot," he wrote in the report. Three days later, the naval commandant for the Tyrrhenian Area called Klaps to his offices to explain his part in the affair. Shortly after, Klaps was removed from his position as chief of naval intelligence in La Spezia.

Two weeks after the execution of the Americans, the Abwehr offices and the Almers Brigade headquarters in La Spezia received an order from Kesselring's headquarters to destroy all the documents pertaining to the case and to report completion of the order. Clearly, someone in the higher echelons of the Wehrmacht was not comfortable with leaving traces of what had transpired in La Spezia between March 24 and 26.

* * *

On the night of March 27, 1944, two hundred German commandos raided the island of Gorgona, which OGs had taken over and held since December 1943. The strong German force overwhelmed the garrison of ten OGs and destroyed the observation post at the sema-phore. Carl Lo Dolce, the radio operator of the team, remembered shooting it out with the Germans for five or ten minutes, then, real-izing that they were hopelessly outnumbered, scattering in search of a hiding place. He spent the night lying on his back, half submerged in an icy swamp, with his .45 pistol on his chest, waiting for the Germans to find him.[2] Fortunately, the Germans withdrew before dawn. The OSS casualties included two killed and three wounded. One Italian agent was also killed. OG forces inflicted some damage to the enemy, but its extent could not be ascertained definitely because the Germans withdrew immediately.

Lo Dolce later said that he believed the Germans had pinpointed the location of the observation post by tracking his radio transmissions with triangulation equipment. It is not known whether the informa-tion Klaps and Sessler gathered from the interrogations of the Ginny team was used to prepare for the attack on Gorgona. The close timing of the two events suggests it may have been.

Reflecting on the disappearance of the Ginny mission and the Ger-man strike on the OSS garrison on Gorgona, the Allied authorities in Italy decided to put an end to the "hit-and-run" operations against tar-gets in the Tyrrhenian and the Ligurian coast. Soon, the situation at the front changed dramatically. After repeated offensives against the Ger-man defenses between January and May 1944, the American Fifth and British Eighth armies were finally able to break through the Cassino front and out of the Anzio beachhead. On June 4, 1944, they liber-ated Rome and continued their push up the Italian boot. The Germans retreated to the Gothic Line and by August 1944 had reestablished a firm frontline, cutting off the Allied advance across the peninsula.

At the end of August, the Operational Group Command left their base in L'Île-Rousse, Corsica, and on September 1, 1944, set-tled at the new OSS headquarters in Sienna, Italy. The OGs were now much closer to the areas of operations for their new missions in the Apennine mountain ranges and in northern Italy. These new missions would operate behind the frontlines in enemy-held territory for months on end.

Reflecting on the experience of the Ginny mission, Donovan and Livermore became increasingly concerned with the continued association of the OGs with the OSS. OGs were military units that operated in uniform. Everyone assumed that if taken prisoner they would be entitled to the same treatment afforded to regular members of the armed forces by the Geneva Convention about the prisoners of war. Since the Germans were fully aware of the intelligence gathering and espionage purposes of the OSS, they would consider any captured OGs as spies and shoot them outright. On August 4, 1944, Donovan reorganized the OGs in the Mediterranean theater of operations into a separate battalion. The 2671st Special Reconnaissance Battalion Separate (Provisional) had no reference to OSS and was placed under the operational control of the Assistant Chief of Staff, G-3, Allied Force Headquarters. An OG veteran after the war explained the aim behind the new name: "No enemy interrogator would be likely to figure out that this gobbledygook stood for 'Guerrilla Fighter, U.S.'"[3]

The failure of the Ginny mission drove another change in the way the OGs operated. Instead of sending teams into an operational area blind, without knowing what to expect, all future missions were coordinated closely with intelligence agents on the ground from OSS Secret Intelligence or British SOE networks. Working with local resources, these agents identified suitable landing zones for infiltrations by sea or drop zones for parachute drops. They organized reception parties, signaled the pinpoints, collected the operational team members, and were responsible for the teams' initial security until they were able to execute their mission independently.

Such improvements in operating procedures ensured that the OGs and members of other OSS Special Operations teams had an almost perfect survivability rate during the infiltration phase. During the rest of the war in Europe, the very few casualties suffered at this stage of the mission were due to equipment malfunction or rough terrain, but never to enemy action.

Thus, going into the summer of 1944, the OG personnel in Italy were ready to fulfill one of the primary objectives of their original mission—support and organize native resistance against the Germans in their rear areas. This was an objective that their brethren in the French OGs and other OSS Special Operations teams in France completed with great success between June and October 1944, as they supported the landings in Normandy and the ensuing battles on the western front.

CHAPTER 8

Operational Groups in France

The military campaigns in the Mediterranean theater of operations, beginning with the landings in North Africa in November 1942 and continuing with the protracted engagements in Italy throughout 1943 and into spring 1944, were important in paving the way for the success of the landings in France. They tied down significant German troops in Italy who would otherwise be free to deploy in France to counter the invasion. They provided combat experience for the US and other Allied troops that participated in the landings. And they allowed the OSS and its British counterparts to develop, test, and validate scenarios for the use of Special Operations units in support of regular military forces. General Eisenhower, the commander of the Supreme Headquarters Allied Expeditionary Forces (SHAEF), had been an early supporter of OSS activities in his theaters of operations in North Africa and Italy and embraced the use of Special Operations in Operation Overlord, the code name for the invasion of France in Normandy on June 6, 1944. Such operations played an even more important role in the second Allied landing in German-occupied France, known as Operation Dragoon, on August 15 in the French Riviera.

The OSS Special Operations command and its British counterpart, the Special Operations Executive (SOE), had worked together since 1942 from their base of operations in London to promote the resistance in occupied countries in Western Europe, especially in France. As D-Day approached, it became clear that their actions needed to be coordinated closely among themselves and with other military units participating in Operation Overlord. In January 1944, the SOE and OSS Special Operations organizations in London merged into a combined SOE/SO headquarters that would jointly run the resistance activities in Western Europe. This headquarters organization established close relationships with the G-3 (Special Operations) and G-2 (Intelligence) staffs of the Allied armies preparing for the invasion of France to ensure coordination between the armies and the resistance organizations behind enemy lines. On May 1, 1944, the joint headquarters was designated Special Forces Headquarters (SFHQ) to remove any distinction between British or American operations, and it was attached to the SHAEF's G-3 Branch to fully integrate the Special Operations teams with the invasion plans.

A further reorganization occurred toward the end of May, this time to accommodate the demand from General Charles de Gaulle's *Comité Français de Libération Nationale* (CFLN), or French Committee of National Liberation, that French officers direct the French resistance. De Gaulle had succeeded in unifying the different factions of resistance inside France under one organization that functioned as a Home Army and was known as *Forces Françaises de l'Intérieur* (FFI), or French Forces of the Interior. Serious problems could arise if the resistance units on the ground would receive orders from a dual chain of command, the SFHQ and the FFI.

On May 24, 1944, the commander of the FFI, General Marie-Pierre Koenig, wrote to Eisenhower's chief of staff, General Walter Bedell Smith, to recommend the creation of a tripartite staff to include "the English, American, and French elements required to manage the actions of the French resistance." "If the Supreme Commander and the CFLN agree with my opinion that the command of the French Forces of the Interior ought to be entrusted to a French general, and if they want to entrust me with this command, I am ready to serve under their orders." Such a letter would have been considered extremely pretentious six months before, but on the eve of the invasion Eisenhower wanted the full engagement of the FFI in the coming fight. On May

30, the SFHQ French operations were transferred to the *État-Major des Forces Françaises de l'Intérieur* (EMFFI), or General Staff of the FFI. Koening was named commander in chief of the FFI with a British and an American deputy to assist him in his command.[1]

The odds were against the tripartite arrangement working. At the staff level, multilingual officers with different levels of skills and experience had to learn to work together. An undercurrent of divergent political views among British, French, and Americans often created differences of opinion that had to be settled. The British were of the view that the resistance ought to be organized in small, underground cells controlled from London. They favored a limited supply of weapons and equipment out of fear that the resistance groups would use them to fight one another rather than the Germans; it had happened with resistance movements in the Balkans. The Americans were interested in accomplishing the invasion of France as quickly and with as few losses as possible. They advocated dropping large amounts of supplies and ammunition to create militarily effective resistance units capable of harassing the Germans across the country.[2] The French were very keen to appear in control and as the liberators of their country. They were also concerned with mass reprisals against the civilian population that premature armed actions against the Germans would cause. With an eye already toward post-war reconstruction, they wanted to protect key infrastructure objects either from unnecessary sabotage on the part of the resistance or from destruction by the Germans. The operators in the field had their own set of issues, too. They had to quickly assess the local resistance leaders and make decisions on how to prioritize the supply of weapons and equipment. Life-and-death decisions had to be made when deciding which resistance units to support: those that were most effective against the Germans or those that were most threatened.

The arrangement nevertheless worked, despite these odds. With regards to arming and supporting the French resistance, the American point of view prevailed. OSS and SOE undertook a massive effort to pack and drop supplies starting in May and through the end of September 1944, when the needs of the resistance dropped significantly because the Allies had overrun most of France. OSS had a packing station in Hume, England, where 326 trained personnel and prisoners of war worked around the clock to prepare containers and packages of supplies destined for northern France. A second packaging center in Algiers with a staff of 142 serviced southern France. Containers were metallic cylinders that could hold up to 220 pounds of supplies, typically arms, ammunition, explosives, and demolition devices. They were fitted with parachutes and released from the planes by aircrews. Packages were bundles of non-breakable items such as clothing, shoes, medicines, and packaged food rations. They weighed up to one hundred pounds and were dropped without parachutes.[3] Whereas fewer than three thousand containers had been dropped in France throughout 1943, more than fifty thousand containers and fifteen thousand packages were dropped between June and the end of September 1944.[4]

The supplies were delivered in close coordination between the SOE, OSS, and French staff who maintained radio contact with their operators attached to resistance units in the field. These operators submitted requests for materials and suggested several safe dropping zones with a surface area of at least two square miles each. The staff in London determined jointly the allocation of supplies based on overall strategic and tactical priorities set by the SHAEF. On the day before the drop, BBC broadcasts advertised in coded messages the drop zone where the supplies would arrive. The team in the field radioed immediately confirmation of the drop and organized a reception party with signals to pinpoint the drop area. Modified US Air Force and Royal Air Force bombers flew in the supplies, typically at night, although American pilots completed successfully at least four massive supply drops in full daylight involving 756 B-17 Flying Fortresses with escort fighters and delivering almost nine thousand containers. The largest of such drops occurred on July 14, 1944, Bastille Day, in which 349 Fortresses delivered 3,791 containers to six open resistance centers around France. The supplies delivered that day included 417 tons of equipment, sufficient to arm more than twenty thousand men.[5]

From January to September 1944, the OSS parachuted more than 3,500 tons of supplies from England and another 1,500 tons from Algiers. The SOE sent a slightly smaller amount.[6] In a report to

General de Gaulle in January 1945, Koenig estimated that the drops had supplied weapons and ammunition for 425,000 men.[7]

* * *

Coordinating the delivery of these vast amounts of supplies in the field, as well as training the resistance fighters in using the weapons and equipment sent to them, required manpower. Before D-Day, eighty-five officers, enlisted men, and civilians from the OSS French Special Operations and Secret Intelligence branches worked with their SOE counterparts to organize the French resistance. To support the resistance activities that surged after the landings in Normandy, the SFHQ called to action the Jedburghs, three-man multinational teams that had spent the months leading to D-Day in eastern England preparing for this mission. Thirteen Jedburgh teams parachuted behind enemy lines in June, ten of them in Brittany, which Eisenhower had declared an area of top priority for resistance actions. Another seventy teams went in between July and September. The majority of these teams went to the areas to the northwest and northeast of the Massif Central, the mountainous region in central France from where resistance units of the FFI attacked the German units retreating from South France towards the French-German border. In total, 286 Jedburghs—83 Americans, 90 British, 103 French, 5 Belgian, and 5 Dutch—parachuted into France, Belgium, and Holland between June and October 1944.

On the ground, the Jedburgh teams played a liaison role between the Allied headquarters and local resistance groups already organized by earlier SO and SOE efforts or by the French themselves. They assessed the strengths and needs of these groups, maintained radio communications with the SFHQ headquarters in England, arranged for delivery of supplies, collected intelligence, and received directives for military operations in their area, which they transmitted to the resistance leaders. They served as instructors to the resistance fighters and advised the local commanders on organizing attacks against German lines of communications and garrisons. Due to their small size and the nature of their assignment, the Jedburghs served primarily as liaison teams. They did not engage in independent actions behind the lines or lead resistance units in the fight against the Germans. In those situations where the SFHQ deemed it necessary to send fighting units capable of operating alone behind the lines or to lead local resistance groups in action, they called upon the Operational Groups of Company B, 2671st Special Reconnaissance Battalion Provisional (Separate), also known as the French OGs.[8]

The French OGs had arrived in Algiers in February 1944 and had spent the time there conducting extensive parachute training and preparing for the day of action. Between June 8 and September 2, 1944, fourteen French OG sections from Algiers, each with fifteen men, including a radio operator and a medical technician, parachuted behind enemy lines. OSS transferred two French operational groups to London where they joined two Norwegian operational groups, 120 men in total, assigned to support the war effort in France because of the lack of action in Norway. Seven missions departed from London between August 1 and September 9, 1944.[9]

Like the Jedburghs in northern France and Brittany, the OGs coordinated supply drops for the resistance units and trained the Maquisards in the use of weapons, explosives, and demolition devices sent to them. But, being larger in size and closer in structure to military units than the Jedburgh teams, the OGs often engaged in direct action, ambushing and harassing German units as they retreated. In implementing the Allied anti-scorched earth strategy, the OGs also captured and secured key infrastructure objects to keep the retreating Germans from destroying them. By September 10, 1944, all the OG teams parachuted into France had completed their missions and returned to England or were overrun by the Allied armies in their advance eastward toward Germany. During their engagement, the French OGs and the Maquis groups they helped train and equip killed 461, wounded 467, and captured 10,021 Germans. They demolished eleven power lines and cables, mined seventeen roads, shot down three aircraft, and destroyed two trains and three locomotives.[10] The story of team Patrick, led by Serge Obolensky, the veteran of the September 1943 mission to Sardinia, helps understand how the French OGs achieved such success in their missions.

* * *

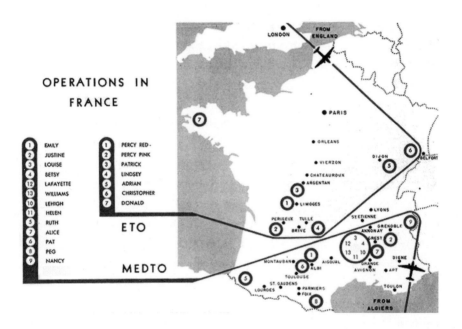

Missions of French OGs attached to the European and Mediterranean theaters of operations.

By the time the invasion of France began, Serge Obolensky had reached the rank of lieutenant colonel and had become executive officer for the French Operational Groups based in Algiers. He took charge of the French and Norwegian OGs that were transferred to England to launch missions behind the German lines from there. The OGs resided in Brockhall Hall, a country estate in Northamptonshire, a little over seventy miles north of London. It offered the perfect setting for the OSS personnel. The Manor House, property of the Thornton family since the mid-1600s, came with four hundred acres of farmland and woods that offered seclusion and privacy.[11] Yet it was only four miles from the village of Weedon, where the OGs often walked or biked for a pint of beer. It was located about twenty miles from Harrington Field, which the OGs used to fly out for their parachute missions.

A favorite spot for the OGs was a little pub called the Spotted Cow, just down the road from Weedon and a short distance from Brockhall. It became a regular hangout for the Americans, who could walk there through the fields. Darts and cribbage were the evenings' entertainment, with competitions between locals and guests where pints of bitters were at stake. Occasionally, the OGs received passes to Northhampton, a fairly good-sized city about nine miles from Brockhall, where they could watch a movie and then stop at the USO club for a cup of tea and a sweet roll.[12]

At Brockhall, the OGs kept a dog and a cat as mascots. They trained the dog to bark at airplanes when they went overhead. The dog ran across fields, looking up and barking until the plane was out of sight. The cat, on the other hand, was taught to parachute. Several of the men had fashioned a parachute that they would attach to the cat before dropping him from the roof of Brockhall. The cat would descend gracefully to the ground with claws extended and with what appeared to be a smile on his face. As soon as he touched the ground, the cat would take off and hide, but not for long. His parachute gave away his position and allowed the OGs to retrieve him. He seemed to enjoy the experience, as he never left camp. His name was Geronimo.[13]

Always a man of action, Obolensky volunteered to parachute in the Indre department in central France, four hundred miles behind

German lines, at the head of a team of twenty-five men selected from the French and Norwegian OGs. Team Patrick's primary mission was to prevent the destruction of the dam and hydroelectric plant at Eguzon, the largest one in France at the time. In addition, they were to attack railroads and highways when the Germans began their retreat from the region. In early August, Obolensky assembled the team at Brockhall and explained the operation. He passed around pictures of the dam and described a preliminary plan to approach and take the objective. He swore the team to silence and cancelled all leaves, per standard practice, to maintain the secrecy of the operation. The demolition engineers began to calculate the charges they needed to make their way through the German positions. Then the men began preparing the charges of plastic explosives that they molded by hand into packages the size of a one-pound hamburger. The explosives were made out of nitroglycerin, which after some exposure gave the men a severe headache, so they had to take turns getting fresh air outside.

The team was ready on August 14, 1944. That night, five B-24 Liberator bombers flew in formation from Harrington Field toward central France. There were five OGs in each plane with their parachutes on, gear and side arms fastened on their body. Rifles, ammunition, field rations, and other equipment were secured in containers in the bomb bay of the aircraft. When the plane approached the drop zone, the OGs assumed positions on the floor of the bomber. The ball turret at the belly of the bomber had been removed before the flight and the sixty-inch hole had been covered by a piece of plywood so no one would fall through. The engines slowed and the plane began to descend. The jumpmaster removed the piece of plywood, and the OGs could see the lights of towns and villages below as the plane raced forward.

Ellsworth Johnson, the medic of the team, remembered checking his watch before leaving the plane. It was 0120 hours on August 15, and the plane was at five hundred feet. From this altitude, the first 350 feet were in near free-fall. The jumper waited in agony for the static line to snap and pull the deployment bag out of the container on his back, thus freeing the canopy of the parachute and allowing it to deploy. Malfunctions happened and resulted in tragic accidents, because there was no time to deploy the parachute by hand or to activate the spare one. The life of the paratrooper was in the hands of the person who had packed his parachute or in those of the jumpmaster who fastened his static line to the body of the aircraft. A song that the paratroopers sang to the tune of "The Battle Hymn of the Republic" captured the agony they felt as they hurled to the ground:

> "Is everybody happy?" cried the Sergeant looking up,
> Our hero feebly answered, "Yes," and then they all stood up,
> He jumped right out into the blast, his static line unhooked,
> And he ain't gonna jump no more.

> Gory, gory, what a helluva way to die,
> Gory, gory, what a helluva way to die,
> Gory, gory, what a helluva way to die,
> And he ain't gonna jump no more.

> He counted long, he counted loud, he waited for the shock,
> He felt the wind, he felt the clouds, he felt the awful drop.
> He jerked the cord, the silk spilled out, and wrapped around his legs
> And he ain't gonna jump no more.

> Gory, gory, what a helluva way to die,
> Gory, gory, what a helluva way to die,
> Gory, gory, what a helluva way to die,
> And he ain't gonna jump no more.

> The risers wrapped around his neck, connectors cracked his dome,
> His lines were snarled and tied in knots around his skinny bones,
> His canopy became his shroud, and hurled him to the ground,
> And he ain't gonna jump no more.[14]

* * *

Everyone in Team Patrick executed a perfect landing that night. Smooth rolling maneuvers when touching the ground helped them avoid broken bones or other injuries. Once on the ground, they found Frenchmen all around eager to welcome them and help them out of their harnesses. The nylon canopies of the parachutes were quickly set aside—French women coveted their material for lingerie in those times when silk was scarce. Obolensky discovered that only three planes had dropped their cargo and men. He decided to hide in a forest nearby and wait until the next night. The Maquisards posted sentries all around in case the Germans had noticed the low-lying airplanes and decided to investigate. The following night, the two Liberators arrived on time and dropped the rest of the team and their equipment.[14]

At dawn on August 16, after the entire team had assembled, the Maquisards brought three trucks, loaded all the men, gear, and equipment, and drove to a small town of about two hundred people called Le Blanc where the team set up its base of operations. A few miles from there, they found an abandoned quarry suitable as a storage site for their explosives and demolition equipment. On August 17, Obolensky sent a patrol to reconnoiter the area near the hydroelectric plant. They came back with information that only a small company of Germans under the charge of a young lieutenant were at the plant. However, an entire regiment of Vichy soldiers was stationed at Eguzon to help the Germans protect the dam. Upon receiving this information, Obolensky moved the team to the headquarters of the local Maquis in the Muhet area about ten miles from his objective. They set up camp in the woods, half a mile from the main highway connecting Limoges and Paris, close enough to hear the German columns rolling by in trucks. The OGs began providing instructions to the Maquisards on the use of bazookas, mortars, and machine guns they had brought with them, which the French put to use in the next few days in small ambushes along the forested roads.

In the meanwhile, Obolensky met with the Maquis leaders to discuss how to attack and dislodge the Germans from the dam. They trekked to its base and recognized that the Germans had the high ground—it was impossible to take the dam without causing many casualties or risking its destruction. Obolensky sent a local Maquisard to contact Captain Clavel, the French officer in command of the Vichy regiment, and invite him to a meeting under the flag of truce. When the Frenchman arrived, he made it clear that he had orders to help the Germans defend the dam and that he planned to follow the orders. Obolensky told him that he was sent directly by General Koenig, the commander of the French Forces of the Interior. "I have orders to take and hold Eguzon for France," Obolensky said. Having realized that the tide of the war had turned, Clavel replied with some wit, "I think our intentions are identical," and agreed to switch sides.[15]

For good measure, Obolensky let Clavel believe that he had with him a large number of paratroopers standing by to attack and take Eguzon on his orders. Clavel informed Obolensky that the German commander was a young and determined officer who would not leave the area without a fight. Obolensky asked him to pass a message to the Germans that they had twelve hours to get out of Eguzon, leaving the facilities intact or else face annihilation. After the French officer left, Obolensky moved Team Patrick and about two hundred Maquisards about one mile from the dam and prepared to attack. To their delight, they saw the Germans depart the next morning toward Châteauroux in trucks and cars, leaving most of their equipment and personal items behind. Reminiscing of the operation almost a year later, Obolensky attributed the success to the fact that "They didn't know how many we were . . . and paratroopers had a very definite reputation with the Germans."[16]

* * *

Upon entering the Eguzon facility, Obolensky set up a series of concentric defensive rings to protect it from German counter-attacks. At the center, inside the facility itself, Obolensky positioned OGs from Team Patrick equipped with heavy weapons and mortars. Demolition experts from the team blew up bridges and viaducts on the roads leading to Eguzon. When they ran out of explosives and demolition equipment, they resorted to felling trees and laying them across the roads to block any German drive to retake the facility. Obolensky positioned Captain Clavel and his regiment to defend the perimeter near the dam, transformers, and turbine equipment. Maquisards set up two defensive perimeters, one at a mile and a half and the other at ten miles from Eguzon. Obolensky realized that he did not have enough troops to cover the entire area, but the Maquis put the word out for volunteers. During the next week, six hundred additional men arrived to protect the facility.

After a few days, when it became clear that the Germans had no interest in retaking Eguzon, Team Patrick moved back to Le Blanc. The area was crisscrossed with roads connecting two major highways the Germans were using to evacuate their troops from Bordeaux and points south toward Orleans and from there to Germany. The Germans often preferred these secondary roads to the major highways, which were under constant attack by the Allied air force. The French were happy to put to use the weapons and ammunition that Team Patrick had brought them. They set up small ambushes and skirmishes to slow down German movements in the area.

Medic Johnson wrote later, "The French captured very few of the enemy. There was no place to keep them and no reason to feed them. By and large, the French had had enough of the suppressive yoke of the Germans and were willing to offer a little retaliation of their own. Whatever information could be squeezed out was taken and then the captives were liquidated." On one occasion, he and a squad of men headed by Captain J. E. Cook, Obolensky's second-in-command, stopped by the Maquis headquarters during a reconnaissance patrol. There they saw a German officer whom the Maquisards had captured and questioned extensively. Johnson said, "The German was surprised to see us and when he did he pleaded for his life. Captain Cook did what he could to prevent the French from doing the very thing the German officer knew would happen. It wasn't long before we heard a shot. War is such a crazy waste of everything!"[17]

Team Patrick joined the local Maquis in looking for opportunities to ambush the Germans on these roads. On August 29, the team received information that a large German force was going to pass through the area. They prepared to ambush the Germans two miles east of the town of Tournon-Saint-Martin. The German commander, finding his way blocked, took hostages in town and sent word to the Maquis that he would shoot the hostages if they did not open the road by 2100 hours. Obolensky replied with his own ultimatum that the local priest delivered:

SUBJECT: 1. Surrender of German Troops to US Army, Le Blanc Area Headquarters

2. Reprisals against civilian population

Sir:

1. I offer you the possibility to surrender to US Army troops as your position is hopeless.

2. I warn you that you are personally responsible for any reprisals or atrocities committed on the civilian population and so are officers of units under command who perpetrate same, and that you will be judged in accordance with the statements of President Roosevelt and Prime Minister Churchill and tried by local courts.

3. I request an answer within 12 hours.[18]

When the priest returned with the Germans answer that they would fight their way out, Obolensky send word to all the Maquis groups in the area to join in setting up positions for the ambush. OGs were interspersed among the Maquisards to direct their fire and help them hold their positions. Around 2300 hours, they heard the rumble of trucks and other noises indicating that the Germans were approaching. "At this point a remarkable thing happened," Johnson remembered later. "One man came into view riding a bicycle. He must have been the advance scout. It was obvious the Germans planned to sacrifice him to warn them of any resistance. I can still see it. The French underground had bazookas supplied by us and one of them must have thought it would be a good way to start things off. As soon as the shell hit the man on the bicycle, the Germans deployed."[19]

What was initially thought to be a force of about one hundred Germans turned out to be the infantry vanguard of two divisions retreating through the area. They drove up in trucks, deployed in perfect formation, and attacked simultaneously from the front and the rear. They came up in great force around Obolensky's right flank and closed in to within fifteen to twenty yards of his command post. Several OGs and Maquisards nearby were able to push the enemy back by throwing hand grenades. Taking advantage of the dark, Team Patrick and the Maquisards disengaged and avoided encirclement without losses.

They returned to Tournon-Saint-Martin in the morning to find the Germans gone and the hostages released unharmed.

At this time, Team Patrick received orders from London to place themselves under the command of the FFI for the Indre department. They were responsible for patrolling a stretch of the road nearby with three Maquis companies, about 180 men total, under their control. It was the beginning of September, and the Germans had left the area, so all the team could find were large quantities of ammunition and equipment abandoned by the side of the road.

A few days later, the team received orders to return to London. They located a small airfield where a C-47 could land safely and radioed the coordinates to the headquarters. The pickup date was set for September 13. On that date, to their surprise, they found the field still manned by German personnel. With the help of the Maquis, the OGs quickly secured the field. Shortly after, they heard a plane's engine, and a C-47 touched down. The French had brought many bottles of champagne to celebrate the Americans' departure. Johnson remembered, "A jovial mood was in the air by the time we were ready to take off. Down the field we rumbled and became airborne in a state of rollicking laughter. The pilot, in a mood of generosity, gave us a bird's-eye view of the bombed areas that the Eighth Air Force had given to many of the cities. We had a terrific trip back! The navigator was in no position to tell us where we were. Finally, Capt. Cook took our land map and directed us toward the coast of France."[20]

As it was approaching the coast of England, the plane dropped low, flying between one hundred and two hundred feet above water to avoid detection by the coastal radars. To protect the existence of the OSS, the flight was unscheduled, and the pilot was flying without a flight plan. The men snuck into England, taking the risk of being considered an unidentified plane or, worse, an enemy aircraft that had to be shot down. Fortunately, the radars did not detect the plane and fighters did not scramble to intercept it. Once over land, the pilot radioed Harrington Field, where the team landed safely about half an hour later, having completed successfully their month-long mission behind the German lines.[21]

CHAPTER 9

Americans in Vercors

The OSS Special Operations and Operational Groups teams were involved in supporting the Maquis of Vercors during one of the best-known and much discussed episodes of the French Resistance during World War II. Vercors is a plateau situated in the pre-Alps region between the cities of Valence and Grenoble, about one hundred miles south of Lyon. Thirty miles long from north to south and twelve miles wide east to west, Vercors is a formidable natural fortress. To get inside it, an enemy had to go through an outer ring of obstacles formed by the rivers Isère, Drôme, and Drar. Next, he had to cross mountain ranges up to six thousand feet high that formed a perimeter over one hundred miles long around the plateau. At that time only eight roads led into Vercors, each of them with hairpin turns and narrow passes carved into the sides of the mountain that a defender could easily keep under surveillance, control, and if necessary destroy to prevent the advance of the enemy.[1]

After the Franco-German armistice of June 25, 1940, Vercors remained in the area of France controlled by the Vichy government, although the Germans controlled Grenoble, the main city at the northern entrance of the plateau. Being at the boundary of German-occupied zone and due to the remoteness of its geography, Vercors became a place of refuge for people on the run, including political refugees, French Jews escaping arrest, and former French soldiers who did not want to serve under the Vichy regime. The plateau came under the influence of the movement Franc Tireurs, founded in Lyon in 1941 and one of several resistance organizations that arose in France at the time.[2] Franc Tireurs, or "free shooters," was a term used in France since the early 1800s to indicate irregular soldiers who fought behind enemy lines. In Vercors, their actions began with publishing and distributing leaflets against the Vichy policies and inciting passive resistance to the government directives.

The decision of Hitler and Mussolini to occupy the south of France after the Allied landings in North Africa on November 10, 1942, caused an influx of men to the Maquis of Vercors. The majority of them took to the mountains to evade the *Service du Travail Obligatoire* (STO), or Compulsory Work Service, the mandatory labor service instituted in France that sent hundreds of thousands of Frenchmen to work in Germany. The newly arrived were young, the majority between nineteen and twenty-three years of age, and without any combat experience. They came from all walks of life, had varied motivations, and were affiliated with movements across the French political spectrum. Some attempts to homogenize the members of the Maquis were made by *equipes volantes*, or roaming teams of political agitators, who were mostly socialist-leaning members of the Franc Tireurs movement interested in keeping other resistance factions from establishing a following in Vercors. The military preparation of the new arrivals was limited to studying a manual on guerrilla warfare assembled from instructions on the use of irregular troops issued by the French Ministry of Defense before the war. They also underwent physical training despite the winter conditions and the fact that most of them wore city clothes not appropriate for life in the mountains.[3]

By the end of winter 1942–1943, four to five hundred members of the Maquis had settled in a dozen camps around Vercors. Their main preoccupation at the time was to secure provisions, including bread, meat, and tobacco. Most of the veterans remembered the time in these camps as mostly spent in boredom, filled with the drudgery of fetching water, collecting firewood, and pulling kitchen duty. They launched some raids to secure arms and munitions, but those remained marginal and most of the actions were against Italian depots to secure provisions. Here is how Gilbert François remembered the life in one of the camps:

> When it was sunny, you could see a small flock being taken to pasture in the morning and back to the stables in the evening, men lying in the shade, others toasting in the sun, in other words, a vacation colony for unemployed youth. This is what a solitary traveler would have seen venturing in that abandoned landscape. We did water duty, vegetable cleaning duty, cutting down trees, killing and preparing animals; and then there were alerts, raids in Jossaud [the nearby village], and so on.[4]

As long as the Maquisards remained in their camps and limited their actions to raids on supply depots, the Italians were happy to confine their actions to the discovery and collection of arms and ammunition dumps hidden in caves around the area. Occasional hits against Italian soldiers triggered raids on the Maquis camps or nearby villages, but no reprisals against civilians ever occurred. Both sides had developed an unspoken mutual warning system to signal each other's presence and avoid head-on confrontations. For example, on March 18, 1943, two hundred Italian soldiers left Grenoble headed toward a Maquis camp. They sang all the way to ensure that there was no surprise whatsoever in their arrival. The outcome of the operation was four Maquisards arrested. One of the leaders of the Maquis of Vercors, Eugène Samuel, later wrote that this relaxed behavior of the Italian army created bad habits among the Resistance members. When the Germans took the place of the Italians, the Maquisards learned the hard way to be more disciplined and paid the price whenever they displayed reckless temerity.[5]

The fight against the Maquis was primarily the responsibility of the Fascist secret police, the Organization for Vigilance and Repression of Anti-Fascism. Using a network of informers in the area, OVRA was able to arrest the original founders of the Maquis, which left the movement leaderless for a while and severed its connections with other Resistance groups in France and the Free French in London and Algiers.

At the end of June 1943, a new generation of leaders stepped up to reorganize the Maquis of Vercors. They embraced a strategic plan, known as *Plan Montagnards*, or Highlanders Plan, that envisioned two ways in which the Maquis could engage the Germans. In the first one, "Vercors would serve as a center of unrest and refuge for guerrilla fighters who, at the opportune moment, would attack railways, roads, bridges, electrical lines, and industrial plants in the area. The area would be a launching point for incursions in the rear of the German armies only at the time when they began their withdrawal from the Rhône valley." The second option, the most audacious one, envisioned "the transformation of the plateau of Vercors into an aircraft carrier docked on dry land." Under this option, the main task of the Maquisards would be to clear and prepare areas where Allied airplanes and parachutists could land.[6]

The leaders of Vercors found a way to brief the French leaders in Algiers about Plan Montagnards. They received the response over the airwaves when the BBC broadcast the message "*Les montagnards doivent continuer a gravir les cimes*," or "The highlanders should continue to climb the summits." It meant that the plan was approved. No further instructions arrived to indicate which of the two options was seen as more favorable, although during a clandestine visit in Vercors, a senior French officer from Algiers made it clear that "without artillery, or mortars as a minimum, there is no hope to hold the plateau for long" in the event of an attack.[7]

* * *

After the fall of Mussolini on July 25, 1943, and the signing of the armistice between Italy and the Allies on September 8, Vercors came under the 157th Reserve Division of the Wehrmacht, a unit created in November 1939 in Munich from local recruits from Bavaria. It had been located in southeast France since the fall of 1942 and did not have the combat experience that had hardened other German troops, such as deployments in the Eastern Front or in the Balkans. The division was under the commanded of General Karl Pflaum, a career officer of the German military establishment since 1910. Pflaum, born in 1890, had become a captain in 1921 and a colonel in 1937. He became general in 1941 and commanded the 258th Infantry Division in the battles for Moscow between October 1941 and January 1942.[8]

The Germans replaced OVRA with the Gestapo and the *Milice Française*, or French Militia, the dreaded paramilitary force of the Vichy regime. Known simply as the Milice, the French Resistance feared it even more than the Gestapo and the SS for its ruthlessness and cruelty.[9] The Gestapo and the Milice quickly showed that they would not tolerate any acts of defiance in the area. On November 11, 1943, when two thousand men marched to the monument of the fallen in Grenoble to commemorate the twenty-fifth anniversary of the French victory in 1918, Gestapo and French police surrounded them and deported four hundred marchers to Buchenwald. The resistance responded by sabotaging railroad and electricity lines, killing Milice members, and blowing up a depot with two hundred tons of artillery munitions.

The Germans countered with Operation Grenoble, executed between November 25 and 30, during which they arrested, killed, or deported most of the resistance leaders in the area. It became known as the "bloody week" or the Saint Bartholomew Massacre of Grenoble.[10] On January 22, 1944, about three hundred Germans responded strongly to a strike by the Maquis two days earlier that had blocked one of the gorges leading into Vercors. The Germans easily broke through their positions and moved in the village of Chapelle-en-Vercors, forty miles south of Grenoble, where they burned down half of the houses in reprisal. On January 29, the Germans attacked the Maquis at Malleval, thirty miles south of Lyon on the opposite side of the plateau. A French survivor of that engagement recalled later how the inexperienced Maquisards had fallen into a lethal trap while advancing single file to meet the enemy. A well-positioned machine gun opened up on them. About thirty Maquisards died and only five or six were able to escape the massacre. The Germans burned the village to the ground.[11]

It became clear to the Maquis leaders that the numerous camps where the Maquisards had spent the winter had become targets for the Germans and created a great risk for the civilians around them who kept these camps provisioned. A vast difference of opinions existed on whether it was best to reinforce these camps with heavy weapons that the Allies would send or to abandon them. Although all the Resistance military groups had been unified since February 1, 1944, under the French Forces of the Interior (FFI), reaching a consensus on the best way forward was very hard. Reflecting on the fate of the Maquis groups recently attacked, the FFI commander for Vercors, Albert Chambonnet, known as Didier, advised all Maquisards to "not engage in frontal battles. Be flexible, fall back, and conduct guerrilla actions without mercy against the flanks of the enemy." At the end of March, Didier ordered the camps abandoned and the men spread around Vercors in what he called "a state of dispersed defense."[12]

In early January 1944, the Maquis of Vercors came into contact with the Union mission, the first inter-allied team to be sent to France as a precursor to the Jedburgh teams that would follow after the invasion began. The team was led by British Colonel H. A. A. Thackthwaite and included American Captain Peter J. Ortiz of the OSS and the French radio operator André Foucault. The team parachuted on the night of January 6–7, 1944, near St. Nazaire-en-Royans, in the outskirts of the Vercors plateau, halfway between Valence and Grenoble. Within a few weeks, they had established contacts with the military leaders of the area from the French-Italian border to Lyon and impressed upon them that the main task of the Maquis at the time was to prepare for guerrilla activities on or after D-Day.[13]

Mission Union spend considerable amount of time in Vercors, which had the widest concentration of Maquisards in the area. They advised the French leaders to adopt a mobile defense, which meant letting the Germans move freely by day and attacking their flanks and rear by night.[14] They reported to the Special Forces Headquarters in England that there was the potential to mobilize up to three thousand Maquisards in Vercors; five hundred men were already active and lightly armed. There were many former French military among the Maquisards, with experience and training in the use of heavy arms, who could form strong fighting groups if supplied with mortars, machine guns, and other heavy weapons. When Mission Union returned to England at the end of May, they prepared detailed accounts of their activities and were debriefed for days. "Vercors has a very finely organized army," they wrote, "but their supplies, though plentiful, are not what they need; they need long distance weapons and antitank weapons."[15]

* * *

The Allies had developed elaborate plans to activate all the resistance networks and Maquis groups in France in a general national insurrection against the Germans to coincide with the landings in the Normandy beaches on D-Day. On June 1, 1944, at 1330 hours, the BBC began broadcasting one hundred and sixty so-called personal messages, which were in effect code words alerting their groups throughout France to prepare for action. The messages were repeated at 1430, 1730, and 2115 hours of that day and then again at the same times on June 2. Then, there was nothing on June 3, 4, and during the day on June 5. Finally, at 2115 hours on June 5, the BBC broadcast for sixteen minutes the code words for action directed at the twelve regional organizations of the French Forces of the Interior and sixty-one Resistance circuits controlled by the Allied Special Forces Headquarters.[16]

The code words for the Maquis of Vercors were "*Le chamois des Alpes bondit*," or "The goat of the Alps leaps." Those for the Drôme department in which the lower half of the Vercors resides were "*Dans la forêt verte est un grand arbre*," or "There is a great tree in the green forest." The military and political leaders of the Resistance received these calls to action with enthusiasm, believing that the moment had arrived to execute the Plan Montagnards, mobilize the population, and close Vercors to the Germans. They believed that "Vercors is the only Maquis in the whole of France, which has been given the mission to set up its own free territory. It will receive the arms, ammunition, and troops which will allow it to be the advance guard of a landing in Provence. It is not impossible that de Gaulle himself will land here to make his first proclamation to the French people."[17]

Calls went out to all nearby cities and villages for volunteers to join the Maquis camps in Vercors. The Communist Party printed and distributed leaflets in Grenoble calling for its supporters to take up arms. "Don't wait any longer to join the battle. There is no D-day or

H-hour for those who want to free the homeland. Let's create everywhere combat groups to support the movement and to defend ourselves against the Boches and the murderous *miliciens.*"[18] The calls were met with great enthusiasm. Within days, the number of Maquisards in the mountains increased tenfold to several thousand. This sudden influx of newcomers in the ranks of the Maquis created immediate problems: they had to be armed, fed, clothed, supplied, and trained before they could engage the enemy. Paradoxically, it worked to the benefit of the Germans who preferred to have the Maquisards concentrated in the mountains, away from the cities and main communication arteries, rather than wreaking havoc in their rear areas.

The problems were not limited to Vercors but extended throughout France. An intelligence report of the French Forces of the Interior on June 13 warned:

> The ranks have grown considerably and the recruitment cannot be stopped. Those who have arms do not have sufficient ammunition. If a considerable effort is not carried out, we will witness the massacre of the French resistance.
>
> All the partisan groups throughout France demand the same thing: arms, ammunition, money, medications. All claim to have permanent parachuting areas that they control where supplies can be sent day or night, with or without prearranged signals.[19]

FFI tried to stop the rush to insurrection especially when reports of German atrocities and reprisals began arriving. The Germans recovered quickly from their initial surprise on D-Day and moved swiftly to restore order. Reinforcement divisions on their way to Normandy often went out of the way to sweep the areas of Maquisards and leaving a swath of blood on their wake. On June 9, in the city of Tulle, ninety-nine hostages were hanged from trees and balconies. On June 10, the Germans massacred and burned alive 634 inhabitants of Oradour-sur-Glane, twenty miles northwest of Limoges.[20]

On June 10, General Koenig issued the following clandestine order to his subordinates in France: "Rein in to the maximum guerrilla activity. Impossible at this time to provide you with arms and ammunition in sufficient quantities. Break contact with the enemy everywhere to reorganize. Avoid big gatherings. Operate in small isolated groups." On June 17, Koenig further instructed to avoid gatherings around armed groupings of elements who were not armed and ready to fight. The focus of the guerrilla had to shift away from mobilizing the population in general insurrection and toward classical objectives such as disrupting enemy communications, railroad traffic, and long-distance telephone lines.[21]

The efforts to throttle back the enthusiasm of the Maquis had little effect in Vercors. On July 3, 1944, the civilian authorities in the massif announced the restoration of the French republic in Vercors. A proclamation posted in all the towns and villages of the area informed the citizens that "starting from this day, the decrees of Vichy are abolished and all the laws of the republic have been restored. . . . People of Vercors, it is among you that the great Republic is being born again. You can be proud of yourself. We are certain that you will know how to defend it. . . . Long live the French Republic. Long live France. Long live General de Gaulle."[22] The flux of would-be fighters from the cities continued. Most of them had little experience and there were many who had never fired a weapon.

An initial conflagration with the Germans, a harbinger of things to come, did not bode well for the Maquis of Vercors. On June 10, two companies of German soldiers attacked Saint-Nizier, a key mountain pass in the northern extremity of the Vercors, which dominated the city of Grenoble in the valley below, only a few miles to the northeast. Saint-Nizier was an excellent observation point for all the automobile and railroad traffic into and out of Grenoble. The Maquisards holding the pass had little military experience but were able to hold out for several hours until more seasoned and better-equipped men arrived from other camps. The Germans retreated but returned on June 15. This time, there were between 1,000 and 1,500 German soldiers against 300 Maquisards stretched along a front of 2.5 miles. Within a few hours, the Germans broke through their defenses, entered the town, and burned it down.[23]

Throughout June, the Germans assembled forces and equipment for the final assault on Vercors, which they gave the code name Operation Bettina. Over 1,500 reinforcements arrived in Valence, a city west of Vercors, among them troops specialized in mountain fighting and anti-guerrilla operations. Seventy airplanes and armored equipment were positioned at the airfield of Chabeuil, just south of Valence.[24] General Pflaum took special care in retraining and preparing the 157th Reserve Division for the upcoming battle. He restructured the division around mobile columns who could operate more effectively in Maquis territory. He supervised personally the instruction of each unit of infantry and insisted on special drills at night and in camouflage. He was able to change completely the division's state of mind, which resulted in a marked improvement in the ability of his soldiers to fight.[25]

The German preparations did not go unnoticed by the French Maquisards. Spotters observing the German movements from the mountains reported in detail the preparations to the Vercors military commanders. They in turn sent appeals for help of increasing intensity to their superiors in Algiers and London.

* * *

To strengthen the Maquis of Vercors and to coordinate guerrilla attacks against the German lines of communications, the OSS dispatched a team, code-named Justine, of two officers and thirteen enlisted men from the French OGs based in Algiers. Captain Vernon G. Hoppers and First Lieutenant Chester L. Myers led the team. They left Algiers in the evening of June 28 and reached the designated drop zone near Vassieux at 0100 hours on June 29. The sky was clear, the weather was calm, and the entire team parachuted in perfect form to the reception area organized by the Maquis on the ground. They moved all the containers dropped with them to a farmhouse nearby and began distributing the supplies to the Maquisards.

They had been there for a few minutes when the excited Frenchmen brought in another five parachutists. They belonged to an inter-allied team, code name Eucalyptus, commanded by British Major Desmond Lange. It included another British officer, Captain John Houseman, two Frenchmen of the FFI, and a French-American member of the OSS Special Operations branch, First Lieutenant André E. Pecquet, the radio operator of the team. The French reception committee and the villagers were impressed and excited by the presence of twenty Allied soldiers in their midst. They served coffee, dark bread, and rich butter, which everyone took with gusto. The paratroopers passed around their cigarettes and a lively conversation ensued. After a while, vehicles arrived to transport the paratroopers—a smart private car for the Eucalyptus team and a special bus for the American OGs. They were taken to Vassieux and accommodated in villagers' houses where they were able to rest for a few hours.[26]

The next day, Commandant François Huet, the Maquis leader in the area, arrived early. He had coffee with the paratroopers and asked them to attend the hoisting of the flag, a short ceremony that nevertheless astonished the new arrivals for the strict military procedure with which it was conducted. Houseman described in his diary what happened next:

> On the way back the people of the village had turned out to welcome us. We were shaken by the hand a score of times. The children kissed us, and the infants were held up also to be kissed. Bouquets were pressed into our arms—the whole unrehearsed greeting was very touching. They behaved as though our very arrival had liberated them from the burdens and fears of occupation.[27]

The two teams began conducting their assigned missions immediately. Eucalyptus acted as liaison between the Vercors commanders and the Special Forces Headquarters in London. The OGs began training the Maquisards on the use of British and American equipment at hand and in planning strikes against the Germans. The news of the arrival of the Allied paratroopers spread fast, and the FFI commanders wanted them to visit the area to boost the morale and confidence of the Maquisards. On June 30, Captain Hoppers and a corporal from Team Justine, Houseman from Eucalyptus, and a Maquisard escort went on a three-day "see and be seen" tour in the southern part of Vercors in the department of Drôme.

In contrast with the sharp-looking military personnel in Vassieux, the Maquisards in these areas were "young and middle aged men, tough and rough-looking from months of hard living, some dressed in what remained of their wartime uniform, others in any civilian clothes they had managed to scrounge." They had only a fair supply of arms, ammunition, and explosives. Throughout the villages they visited, they—the first Allied officers to visit the area—were treated as the saviors of France. People simply did not know how to express their delight and gratitude. Houseman wrote about the reception they received in the town of Aouste, the last town they visited at the southern end of the Vercors massif:

> As we entered by some smallish streets I happened to see a young girl staring at us—she stared for a moment only. Turning round on her bicycle she shot off into the town itself—the news was out. No town crier can have had such a response.
>
> We stopped at a small shop and shook hands (I think we were kissed as well) with the people inside. Wine appeared, and I had scarcely raised my glass, when I heard a seething mob outside in the street—the people of Aouste had come immediately to welcome us. They surged round us, shaking our hands and hugging us—all were talking at once, and my very poor French met its Waterloo. Armed with flowers and carrying children, they kept on streaming in, telling us of their experiences, asking us when the invasion armies would come and thanking us time and again for coming to their country and to their town. The bouquets of red, white and blue flowers by now covered the large table in the shop—more wine was brought up and the children reappeared with red, white and blue ribbons in their hair.
>
> After an hour or so we left the shop to make what proved to be nothing less than a regal procession through the town. We had to walk at the head of this excited ever-growing crowd along the main street to an outpost at the far side of the town. Men saluted us, the women clapped, children ran to kiss us and give us more flowers to carry. People rushed into the road and held up the cavalcade to grasp us by the hand and to embrace us. On our way back, an elderly woman ran across the road with tears in her eyes, to tell me about a relation she had lost and to ask the ever-expectant question "when will the invasion from the south begin?"[28]

* * *

Upon return of the inspection group to Vassieux, both teams, Justine and Eucalyptus, reported through their channels the need to send arms and supplies to Vercors. They also advised the FFI military staff on measures they could take to strengthen the ranks and discipline of the Maquisards. In early July, Commandant Huet decided to militarize the volunteer force and return to the military tradition of regular troop units. "In the past two years," Huet wrote to his subordinates, "the flags, the standards, the pennants of our regiments and our battalions have been asleep. Now, with a magnificent drive, France has risen against the invader. The old French army that has shone in the course of centuries will reclaim its place in the nation."[29]

The old camps and companies of civilians were reorganized into alpine battalions and even an armored battalion, which included a section of irregular African riflemen from Senegal. Efforts were made to standardize the uniforms, using in part battle dress uniforms that had arrived with teams Justine and Eucalyptus. Requests were made to send more uniforms as well. In a report to London, Lieutenant Pecquet, the French-American radio operator of Eucalyptus, said that proper uniforms were a question of self-respect for the French, who were very sensible to the enemy propaganda that described the Maquisards as terrorists.

In the first days of July, Eucalyptus settled at the Huet's headquarters in Saint-Martin-en-Vercors, twelve miles north of Vassieux. The team became the primary channel of communication between Huet and the outside world, with Pacquet exchanging hundreds of messages with Algiers and London. On the other hand, Captain Hoppers and the OGs of Team Justine took a much more visible role among the Maquis as they began preparing their first action against the Germans. They also equipped and trained a group of Maquisards to add strengths to their own group.

The French proposed a location suitable for an ambush at the southeastern extremity of Vercors, near the village of Lus-la-Croix-Haute, about forty-five miles south of Grenoble. On July 7, Hoppers and his men travelled to that location, a strip of road about three hundred yards long, shaped like a horseshoe and flanked on the east by an escarpment thirty feet high. It was perfect for an L-shaped ambush. On the short end of the L the OGs placed only two men armed with a bazooka and a Browning machine gun. The remainder of the group took positions along the long end the L. After waiting for about an hour, they saw a column of six trucks and a bus carrying about 120 Germans approaching. A bazooka round hit and disabled the leading truck as it came around the bend of the road. The machine gun fire stopped the second truck that attempted to drive around the disabled truck. The remainder of the convoy had nowhere to go and came under a barrage of fire from the OGs and the Maquisards lined up along the kill zone. Particularly effective were Gammon grenades, bags of canvas-like material and a fuse, which the OGs filled with one pound of C-2 explosives and one pound of scrap iron. The Gammon grenade was activated by removing the fuse and throwing the bag toward the enemy. Upon impact, it exploded, sending shrapnel in all directions and killing or maiming everyone in the vicinity.

In true guerrilla fashion, the attack ended almost as soon as it began. By the time the Germans had taken cover, set up mortars, and began to return fire, Hoppers gave the order to withdraw to the pre-arranged rendezvous point ten miles from the ambush location. They had destroyed three trucks and one bus, killed sixty Germans and wounded another twenty-five. One Maquisard was killed in action, and another one was missing. The next day, they learned that the Germans had captured the wounded Frenchman and had tortured him to death in front of the villagers of Lus-la-Croix-Haute.[30]

This operation was the only successful combat operation the Maquisards had conducted since the Germans had dislodged them from Saint-Nizier near Grenoble. It added to the fascination the Maquisards had developed with the Americans' appearance, their weapons, and the aura of abundance and modernity that seemed to surround them. It also added further credit to rumors of a massive arrival of Allied soldiers in Vercors, rumors that puzzled Pecquet who wondered about their precise origin in a report to Algiers. The diary of Henri Audra from the town of Die, about twenty miles south of Vassieux, allows us to trace the progression of these rumors among the population of the area. On June 19, he noted, "the imminent parachuting of 2,000 Canadians coming to support the dissidents in Vercors." On June 25, hearing airplanes flying overhead, he wrote, "most certainly, they are parachuting the Canadians we have been expecting for several days." On July 10, he noted that he saw passing though the town "trucks carrying Canadians to attack a German convoy." Then, on July 13, he noted that it was not Canadians after all, but "Americans from New York!"[31]

* * *

The Germans were well informed of such rumors, as well. In its orders for the final preparations for Operation Bettina, issued on July 8, 1944, the headquarters of Army Group B responsible for defending South France said:

> The concentration of important enemy troops in the zone of Vercors, their increasing equipment with heavy weapons, their probable reinforcement by Canadian paratroopers, and a considerable number of enemy forces expected to be transported by air in the plateau of Vassieux, make us think that in case of further landings by the enemy we should expect greater offensive actions launched from this region aiming to occupy Valence and the valley of Rhone, and perhaps at the same time to take the city of Grenoble.[32]

The Germans tightened the stranglehold on the region in preparation for the final assault. General Pflaum began concentrating his men for the attack on Vercors. He set the D-day for operation Bettina on July 21, 1944. The initial striking point would be the town of Vassieux. The German soldiers were ordered to "hit fast and hard" and to show no mercy because Vassieux harbored the supreme command of the Resistance and considerable forces protecting it.[33] The Luftwaffe flew multiple reconnaissance missions every day over the plateau photographing the terrain, roads, towns and villages.

Through communications with Team Eucalyptus, French authorities in Algiers sent warnings to the leaders of Vercors to expect a major attack at almost any moment. Local intelligence services of the Maquis confirmed this information: three German divisions were closing in on Vercors from Valence, Romans-sur-Isère, and Grenoble. The command of Vercors issued a general mobilization order on July 11. Six hundred men volunteered as laborers to prepare an airfield in Vassieux where Allies could land troops and supplies if they decided to come. Another one thousand men were called to the colors, but arming and equipping them remained a problem.

On July 12, the Germans were on the move. Chapelle-en-Vercors, in the heart of the plateau, was bombed on July 12 and 13 while surveillance airplanes flew over the plateau constantly during that time. In the evening of July 13, London sent word to expect a mass parachute drop the next day. On July 14, Bastille Day, at 0900 hours, eighty-five Flying Fortresses flew in formation over Vassieux in three waves and dropped 1,457 containers with red-white-and-blue parachutes in honor of France's national holiday. The inhabitants of Vassieux celebrated in the streets, waiving at the planes and thanking the members of Eucalyptus and Justine for their efforts.

It was a sight to celebrate, but the joy was short-lived. Thirty minutes later, German airplanes began to bomb and strafe the town, and continued to do so for three days in a row, from dawn until well into the evening hours. The Germans used explosives during the day and incendiaries in the evening. The town was set ablaze, and the planes machine-gunned people trying to salvage belongings out of their homes. By July 16, Vassieux was completely in ruins, and the Germans began to destroy Chapelle-en-Vercors, seven miles to the south. From all the containers dropped to them, the Maquisards were able to retrieve only about two hundred during the night.

On July 17, the 157th Reserve Division and selected mobile units of the Ninth Panzer Division moved in on the Vercors triangle and began engaging the Maquisards at a number of outposts and mountain passes. The bombing and strafing of the towns and villages continued incessantly. According to estimates, seven hundred Germans closed in from the east, three thousand from the south and west, and four thousand from the north. No other Maquis group in France had drawn this many enemy troops against them.[34]

Commandant Huet proclaimed martial law throughout the Vercors and all units were put in battle positions. The Maquis counted in their ranks two thousand fully armed men, one thousand partially armed men, and another one thousand unarmed men.[35] Desmond Lange and John Houseman, the officers of Team Eucalyptus, sent requests to London and Algiers for heavy weapons and additional support troops, without effect. Houseman noted in his diary entry of July 18, "Commandant H[uet] maintaining extraordinary calm. He seemed (as in fact he had) to have the situation completely in hand. Signs of nervousness in the P. C. [command post] among the junior officers—Desmond and I trying hard not to show signs of alarm!"[36]

In the morning of July 21 at 0930 hours, French volunteers working at the airfield in Vassieux saw twenty airplanes carrying enormous gliders approaching from the south. The sight lifted their spirits with the hope that these were the much-expected paratroopers and heavy equipment coming to the rescue of Vercors. The hope disappeared moments later when the gliders began their final approach and the Frenchmen noticed the Luftwaffe markings on them. One by one, twenty DFS 230 troop gliders touched ground, some of them in the airfield itself and the rest in the plateau outside Vassieux. Within minutes, two hundred German paratroopers of special commando units of the Luftwaffe stormed Vassieux under the protection of Stuka fighters overhead. Each glider had a machine gun mounted in front, which the pilot used to cover the exit of the paratroopers from the aircraft and their rapid advancement toward the objective. The element of surprise was complete, just as it had been when Germans had used the same technique to take the Belgian fortress of Eben Emmael in 1940, occupy Crete in 1941, and rescue Mussolini in 1943. "It was as if lightning struck Vassieux," was how a number of Frenchmen described those initial moments.[37]

The shock did not last long, however. The Maquisards around Vassieux rushed to block the German paratroopers. The officers and men of the OG mission Justine organized the Frenchmen into surrounding the Germans in town and attacking them with all the weapons at their disposal. According to German sources, during the first day of fighting, the German paratroopers suffered over 25 percent casualties,

ABOVE: Major General William J. Donovan circa 1944.

BELOW LEFT: The compound at 25th and E Streets, NW, in Washington, DC, was OSS headquarters from 1942 to 1945 and CIA's headquarters from 1947 to 1961.

BELOW RIGHT: The OSS Memorial Wall in CIA's Lobby commemorates the 116 OSS officers who died in the line of duty during World War II. Donovan's statue stands to the right.

ABOVE: Area F at the Congressional Country Club in Bethesda, Maryland, served as training ground for the OGs.

RIGHT: William Fairbairn demonstrates the correct stance with the stiletto knife designed for the OSS.

BELOW RIGHT: Two paratroopers practice close combat. Note the almost perfect fighting stance of the soldier to the left.

BELOW LEFT: OGs aboard a Skytrain C-47 transport airplane prepare for a practice parachute drop.

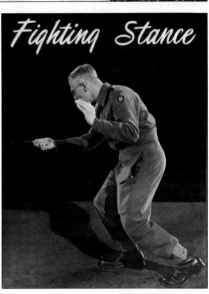

LEFT: French OGs at the Brookhall Estate in England in 1944.

RIGHT: Lieutenant Colonel Serge Obolensky, executive officer of French OGs and leader of Team Patrick.

ABOVE: Team Patrick in a victory parade in a French town they helped liberate in August 1944.

BELOW RIGHT: Supply drops over Vercors on Bastille Day, July 14, 1944.

BELOW LEFT: Team Justine in Vercors.

ABOVE: A member of the Greek OGs with weapons to be distributed to Greek partisans in the background.

LEFT: Rescued nurses arriving in Italy from Albania.

BELOW (L–R): Lieutenant Nick Lalich, Master Sergeant Michael Rajacich wearing a chetnik cap, and Lieutenant George Musulin of mission Halyard in Pranjani, Serbia.

ABOVE LEFT: PT boat at harbor in Bastia in February 1944—one of several PT boats that carried the Italian OGs to their missions in Italy.
ABOVE RIGHT: Captain Albert Materazzi, executive officer of the Italian OGs.

RIGHT: A group of Italian OGs in Corsica.

BELOW (L–R): Three unidentified members of the Italian Sixth Zone command, Anton Ukmar (Miro), commander of the Sixth Zone, and Captain Les Vanoncini, leader of the OSS Peedee mission at the victory parade in Genoa, on May 2, 1945.

ABOVE: Members of the Chrysler-Mangosteen team and three OSS Italian agents who parachuted on September 26, 1944, near Lake Orta, in Italy. Rear (L–R): Major William V. Holohan, Lieutenant Aldo Icardi, Sergeant Carl Lo Dolce, Tullio Lussi, and Lieutenant Victor Giannino. Front, center: Sergeant Arthur Ciarmicoli with two Italian OSS agents.

RIGHT: Holohan in his US Army Captain uniform.

BELOW (L–R): Aldo Icardi, Carl Lo Dolce, Aminta Migliari, and communist leader Vincenzo Moscatelli.

TOP: Major Frederick W. Roche, Judge Advocate, swears in the military commission at the trial of Lieutenant General Anton Dostler in Rome, Italy.

ABOVE (L–R): Lieutenant Georg Sessler, Lieutenant Hans-Georg Schultz and Lieutenant General Gustav-Adolph von Zangen testify at the trial.

BELOW (L–R): Anton Dostler, Sergeant Hirschman, interpreter, Lieutenant General Frido von Senger, Colonel Claudius O. Wolfe, defense counsel, and Major Cecil K. Emery, assistant defense counsel, look over the *Fuehrerbefeh*.

TOP: Major General Lawrence C. Jaynes reads the verdict of "Guilty" to Anton Dostler.

MIDDLE LEFT: At the execution site, MPs secure Anton Dostler to the post while military chaplains offer last prayers.

MIDDLE RIGHT: Medical Officer, Captain Arthur N. Lieberman, pins an oval white target over Dostler's heart.

RIGHT: Chaplains administer the last rites to the lifeless body of Dostler.

twenty-nine dead and twenty wounded.[38] The attacks on all sides, the constant bombardment of towns and villages, and the fierce battle in Vassieux rattled the nerves of the Maquisards. Houseman described "an oppressive atmosphere of confinement in our house with bombing and machine gunning off and on all day." When assistance from the outside failed to materialize, a feeling of abandonment if not betrayal set in. Eugène Chavant, the civilian leader of Vercors, who had traveled to Algiers in May 1944 to meet with De Gaulle's military staff and believed he had received assurances of help from them, fired off a message on the night of July 21:

> La Chappelle, Vassieux, Saint-Martin bombarded by German aircraft. Enemy troops parachuted on Vassieux. We demand resupplies in men, foodstuffs and supplies. Morale of population excellent but will turn quickly against you if you do not take immediate measures and we will be in agreement with them in saying that those sitting in London and Algiers have understood nothing of the situation in which we find ourselves and are considered criminals and cowards. Let us be clear on this: criminals and cowards.[39]

The next day, the Americans and Maquisards continued their attacks on the German paratroopers, helped by the rain that prevented the Germans from reinforcing their men. But the following day, on July 23, the weather cleared and another 250 German paratroopers landed in Vassieux aboard twenty DFS 230 gliders. While the Maquisards and the American OGs were going through their last reserves, the Germans used larger Go242 gliders to bring supplies and ammunition for their beleaguered paratroopers. The Germans dropped in a 20-mm Flak 38 antiaircraft gun, which could fire eight hundred rounds per minute from four independent guns at a range of 2,200 meters. They used the gun to destroy the Maquisards' positions and force them to withdraw.

The Germans came out of the three-day battle victorious, losing 101 paratroopers and four glider pilots.[40] Elsewhere around Vercors during these three days, two heavy mountain battalions took all the mountain passes to the southeast of Vassieux from ill-equipped

Maquisards. German infantry pushing south from Grenoble broke through the northern positions in the key town of Valchevrière. Armored columns from the Ninth Panzer Division moving from Valence breached the southern defenses in the town of Die. On July 23 in the afternoon, the battle was over.[41] In a telegram to Algiers sent on the night of July 25–26, Huet summarized the situation as follows:

> Defenses of Vercors pierced on the 23rd at 1600 hours, after 56 hours of battle. Have ordered the dispersion in small groups with the hope to resume the fight when possible. All did their duty courageously in a desperate struggle and all carry with them the sadness of having succumbed to superior numbers and having been left alone in the moment of battle.[42]

* * *

What followed is the most bloody and tragic chapter in history of the Maquis of Vercors. The Germans cordoned off the entire area and set up surveillance posts on all the roads, primary, secondary, and even forest tracks. Airplanes constantly flew overhead searching for movements in the mountains and woods. The German command ordered:

> It is now the time to mop up Vercors methodically, to find the bands and the terrorists dispersed in their hiding places and to exterminate them completely, to discover the stockpiles of ammunition and provisions of the enemy, and to destroy their depots and hiding places, to make impossible any future resurgence of the enemy in Vercors. A period of seven days is envisioned for the mopping up. . . . The houses that have been points of support and supply for the terrorists, especially in the Vercors proper, shall be burned."[43]

Thus, seven days of reprisals and barbarity were unleashed upon Vercors. The toll mounted to 840 killed, of which 639 were Maquisards and 201 civilians.[44] In Vassieux alone, the Germans massacred one hundred civilians, often killing entire families on sight. Only seven houses remained inhabited out of the 120 houses that the town had before the operation.[45]

On July 27, a surveillance plane noticed a Red Cross flag spread at the entrance of the cave of Luire, three miles east of Vassieux. A German infantry unit arrived around 1700 hours to discover that the cave had become a temporary refuge for the military hospital of Saint-Martin, evacuated since July 21 to escape the bombing and strafing of the Luftwaffe. Most of the wounded were Maquisards, but they also included First Lieutenant Chester L. Myers of the OG team Justine, who had come down with appendicitis and was recovering from surgery,[46] four Wehrmacht soldiers from Poland, and two women from Vassieux.

The German soldiers sprayed the walls of the cave with bullets and began searching the place for hidden resistance fighters and arms. They ripped off bandages of the wounded to make sure they were not fake. The Poles tried to intervene, explaining that they had been treated well, but without success. The Germans marched everyone down the ridge where they shot thirteen gravely wounded Maquisards as they lay in their stretchers. They took the rest to the nearby village of Rousset, where they executed twenty-five lightly wounded Maquisards. They considered the four Poles deserters and shot them as well. Then they unleashed reprisals on Rousset and the nearby town of Saint-Agnan, where they interrogated, arrested, or killed several civilians.

The Germans took the rest of the prisoners to the Gestapo headquarters in Grenoble. An aerial bombardment was going on when they arrived, and, in the confusion, one of the doctors managed to escape together with his wife, daughter, and a Red Cross nurse. The rest were not so fortunate. The Gestapo interrogated and then executed Lieutenant Myers that night. They executed two French doctors and a priest on August 10. They sent eight nurses to the concentration camp in Ravensbrück where one of them died of disease and the rest managed to survive until liberation.[47]

* * *

When Commandant Huet gave the order to disperse on July 23, Team Eucalyptus split up. The French-speaking members of the team, including the OSS radio operator, André Pecquet, moved up the mountains, where they hid the W/T equipment in caves. Pecquet changed into civilian clothes and made several dangerous reconnaissance trips into villages and towns in the area, collecting information about the disposition of enemy troops in the area that the Allied command used to great benefit during the landings in the south of France in mid-August.

During one of these trips, Pecquet went to a post office outside Vercors to buy stamps. He was an avid stamp collector and showed great interest in the stamps issued by the Vichy government, although they had been in use in that area of France for almost four years. His unusual interest attracted the attention of the man standing in line behind him, who could tell that Pecquet had not lived long in the country. The girl at the post office winked. Pecquet realized his error and left the post office in a hurry with the man following him. Pecquet was able to get rid of his pursuer but only after a great deal of trouble.[48]

On August 21, 1944, when the German 157th Infantry division retreated and the US forces arrived in Grenoble, Pecquet assumed a liaison role between the FFI and the US Army command. The French considered Pecquet one of the heroes of Vercors, and he was awarded the Distinguished Service Cross for "his devotion to duty, perseverance and courage displayed throughout his hazardous assignment" in Mission Eucalyptus.[49]

The two British officers of Eucalyptus, Major Lange and Captain Houseman, travelled through the mountains and woods with a small group of four Frenchmen, including a young girl who had worked for the mission as a cipher clerk. The journey was harrowing, with hair-raising escapes from German and Milice patrols, which forced the members of the party to talk in the mildest whispers. Houseman wrote in his diary, "every unusual sound in the woods caused an instant silence among the party—a hunted dog look, as everyone strained his ears and slowly, but with calculated intention, reached for his gun."[50]

Further complications came from scarce food, and especially lack of water in the mountains. "The meagre ration of half a cupful of water a day (sometimes) and two table-spoons of goat's milk were not much help." Houseman wrote. "So I settled down to squeeze water out of moss irrespective of the physical effort which it entailed. After two or three hours of hard work, sometimes with the assistance of one or another member of the party, I had perhaps 3/4 of a pint which, though muddy and having an unwelcome taste, was nectar."

On July 26, the party decided to split to make it easier to move undetected and to find food and water. Lange, Houseman, and a French guide left in the afternoon to climb down in the valley in search for food and water. "We were to learn later that the remainder of the party were surprised by a German patrol." Houseman wrote. "The men, after castration, were beaten to death with rifle butts and the girl disemboweled and left to die with her intestines wound round her neck. I saw the photographs later—they were unrecognizable." Throughout the night, Lange, Houseman, and their French guide, made their way through the valley and across German lines, "running, walking, crawling and rolling" under bursts of fire and pursued by attack dogs, until they were able to reach the mountain ridge and forests on the other side.

After several days of experiences like this, the team was finally able to exit Vercors on August 3 from the north by crossing the river L'Isère. There, Lange and Houseman established contact with the local Maquisards who guided them on a 125-mile journey through the mountains to the city of Chamonix on the Swiss border. On August 11, 1944, Lange and Houseman crossed into Switzerland.

The OG team Justine had a similar harrowing escape. After breaking off the engagement with the German paratroopers in Vassieux, the members moved to the northeast to the plateau of Presles in an attempt to break the encirclement toward the town of Saint-Marcellin. When four hundred Germans appeared on Presles, the OGs took to the woods, where they remained in hiding for eleven days, subsisting only on raw potatoes and occasionally a little cheese. They were never allowed to speak above a whisper. Not more than one man moved at a time, and then never more than fifty feet. Finally, on August 9, when the situation had calmed down a little, a French guide went to Saint-Marcellin and stole a truck that the OGs used to drive outside the

Vercors plateau to the west across the L'Isère. From there, they moved along the Isère valley for ninety miles to the Chartreuse Mountains, twenty miles to the north of Grenoble. Then the team crossed L'Isère again this time eastward to the Belledonne Mountains. By this time, the American army had arrived in Grenoble, and Team Justine moved into the city. They were all in poor condition. Many had severe cases of dysentery, three men were unable to walk and all had lost weight, including Captain Hoppers who had lost thirty-seven pounds.[51]

* * *

The experiences of the Maquis of Vercors, the pitched battle it put up against the Germans during the assault of July 21–23, 1944, and the bloody reprisals that followed have been a source of debate and controversy in France since the end of the war. The prosecutors in the Nuremberg trials, under the charge of "senseless destruction of cities, town, and villages, and devastations unjustified by the military necessity," cited the example of numerous villages destroyed in their entirety in France, among others "Oradour-sur-Glane, Saint-Nizier, and in the Vercors: La Mure, Vassieux, La Chappelle-en-Vercors." Nevertheless, not a single soldier of the Wehrmacht who participated in the operations against Vercors was held accountable for war crimes.[52]

Countless accounts have been written to discuss whether the French authorities in Algiers gave false hopes to the leaders of Vercors on their support for the Plan Montagnards. The fact is that this plan was never part of the Allied strategy for using the French Resistance in coordination with the landings in Normandy and Provence. The reprisals in Vercors left the participants in the Resistance with a feeling of having been misunderstood, abandoned, and even betrayed by the Allies. Historians have established that there were not sufficient means among the French officials in Algiers or among the Allies who supported them to match the enthusiasm of the members of the Resistance.[53] Several members of the Resistance have pointed out that shortly after the reprisals, the region rose up again when the Allies landed in the south of France, which they would not have done had they felt betrayed.

The military choices of the Maquis leaders have been questioned as well, and their decision to engage in frontal battles against a much stronger enemy has been called in various degrees a tragedy, a disaster, and a mistake. Alain le Ray, one of the proponents of the original Plan Montagnards, rejected the aura of disaster and strategic error. In a debate in 1975, he suggested that guerrilla tactics in Vercors might have provoked even more reprisals and that the battle of the Vercors tied down an important section of the Germans army. It "induced in the German war machine a kind of paralysis, both moral and material in the very locality where the Allied forces would penetrate into France after the landings in Provence."[54]

In the end, General Koenig probably summarized best the story of the Maquis of Vercors when he told an enquiry commission in 1961:

> Due to circumstances that were quite unfortunate at the time, you became soldiers assigned with a true sacrificial mission. You became, pardon the expression, "laboratory rats . . ." I tell you this to remove a little bit of the bitterness that you who lived through those hours feel. There are moments when we find ourselves, pardon the expression, in deep s . . . and unfortunately the story has a sad ending, meaning no one is able to escape.[55]

CHAPTER 10

Mission *Walla Walla* in Italy

The declaration of the armistice by the Italian government on September 8, 1943, marked the beginning of the partisan movement in Italy to resist the German occupation as well as the reborn Fascist state, *Republicca Sociale Italiana* (RSI), or Italian Social Republic, which Mussolini proclaimed on September 14, 1943, two days after Skorzeny's commandos liberated him from captivity. The first partisan bands popped up spontaneously and included former Italian officers and soldiers who took to the mountains to avoid capture by the Germans. Their ranks grew with former prisoners of war and political prisoners who escaped detention in the first days after the armistice. A third major source of recruits was Italian civilians who wanted to escape forced conscription into the new Fascist military structures or in the Todt Organization. Armed resistance was not limited to the mountains and remote villages. Urban guerrilla groups, known as *Gruppi di Azione Patriottica* (GAP), or Patriotic Action Groups, operated in all the major cities of occupied Italy by the beginning of 1944.

Like elsewhere in Europe where partisan movements developed, partisan units in Italy were affiliated with political parties, most of which were anti-monarchist as well as anti-Fascist in nature. Formations linked to the Communist Party were called Garibaldi units; those affiliated with the Action Party were known as *Giustizia e Libertà* (Justice and Liberty) units; those affiliated with the Christian Democratic Party were called *Fiamme Verdi* (Green Flames); and those affiliated with the Socialist Party were called Matteotti units. Other minor political parties that supported the resistance included the Liberal and Republican parties. Despite their differences, these parties coordinated their actions in local national liberation committees that reported up to the *Comitato di Liberazione Nazionale per l'Alta Italia* (CLNAI), or National Liberation Committee for Upper Italy with underground headquarters in Milan. By April 1944, CLNAI had become the supreme authority for resistance in occupied Italy and it assumed the stature of an underground government.[1] CLNAI partitioned the territory into operational zones in which all partisan formations coordinated their actions. One of the largest zones was the Sixth Zone, an area centered around the city of Genoa that covered parts of the Piedmont, Lombardy, Liguria, and Emilia regions of Italy.

Early partisan activities consisted of aiding downed Allied airmen, passive resistance to occupation directives, and minor acts of sabotage. Starting in the early months of 1944, these activities became increasingly more organized and with tangible effects. Between March 1 and 8, the resistance coordinated labor strikes in all the major centers of Northern Italy, in which hundreds of thousand of workers shut down factories and production sites despite strict measures put in place by the Fascist government and the German occupation authorities who had a keen interest to keep Italy's industrial machine running at full capacity. Over two hundred thousand workers participated in the strikes, according to the estimates of the Fascist Ministry of Interior, whereas post-war accounts by Italian historians put the numbers between 500,000 to 1.2 million. The Germans arrested and deported about 1,200 workers, including 400 to 600 from Fiat factories alone.[2]

The Germans countered the armed resistance in Italy with ferocity. With the Allies stalled at Cassino and Anzio, units of the Wehrmacht, with the support of the SS and Fascist blackshirt troops, spent the early months of 1944 methodically cleaning up the areas in the rear of the partisans and their supporters. Raking operations, known as *rastrellamenti*, aimed to kill as many partisans as possible but also to terrorize the civilian population in the mountains. The Nazi-Fascist troops killed on the spot family members of the partisans and other civilians suspected of aiding them. They burned thousands of houses, farmhouses, stables, and other property to punish any sign of solidarity with the partisans.

In the area around La Spezia, units of the 135th Fortress Brigade conducted such operations with an ever-increasing regularity. Between May 3 and 5, 1944, Colonel Kurt Almers himself lead a joint operation of troops from his brigade, the "Herman Goering" armored parachute division, and several Fascist units in the area of Fivizzano in the Apuan Alps about twenty miles northeast of La Spezia. The German monthly report of activities in the area summarized the results of the operation. The German losses included one dead and two wounded; Fascist losses were similar. The operation resulted in "143 dead, 170 prisoners including a lieutenant colonel of the US Air Force; the Italian prisoners were shot the day after."[3] In the village of Mommio, the Germans destroyed seventy out of seventy-two houses. Erminia Pierotti, a survivor from the village of Sermezzana described the actions of the blackshirts on May 4 as follows:

> At Sermezzana, they went to the house of Pietro and Geremia Gherardi near the church. Pietro was married with two children and the wife expected a third one. Both of them worked for the Todt but it rained that morning so they were home. The blackshirts wanted to know the whereabouts of the partisans and the Gherardi's third brother, Otta-vio, who was with the partisans. Pietro and Geremia said they knew nothing, and how could they give up their brother! Given that they were not telling, the blackshirts cut off one ear from each brother then took them near the cemetery where they shot them. They put the ears in a little bag for their commander. The two brothers Trippalla, also Todt workers, suffered the same fate. They threw one out of the window, shot him on the ground and cut off the ear. They took the other brother, 19 years old, to show them the way to the next village. They shot him in the pinewoods and off with his ear as well![4]

Through terror, the Germans were successful in dispersing some of the most important partisan units especially in the mountainous areas where the partisans had to contend with the winter weather in addition to the ferocity of their Nazi-Fascist pursuers. Despite the heavy losses, the partisans who survived the rastrellamenti had become by the end of spring 1944 a serious fighting force, with the experience and skills necessary to absorb and organize the new influx of volunteers that headed to the mountains as soon as the weather improved. More importantly, they were hardened in battle and thirsting for vengeance.

* * *

In the first half of 1944, the OSS established and nurtured contacts with several partisan units along the Tyrrhenian coast. Initially, these contacts were mainly for intelligence-gathering purposes. The OSS Secret Intelligence branch put ashore from fast boats or parachuted into the mountains several teams of Italian agents, most of them recruited from SIM, the Italian military intelligence service. Along the Ligurian coast alone, there were several teams composed of an agent and a radio operator each, with code names Lobo, Valentine, Otto, Piroscafo, and Maria Giovanna. Italian SI agents working for the OSS also organized two networks, known as Locust and Meridien, each counting about thirty individuals among agents, informers, sympathizers, and guides.[5] At the beginning of the summer, these teams reported a significant increase in the numbers of partisans in the Sixth Zone. The reports came at a time when the area had become of strategic importance for the Allied command.

After finally breaking through the Cassino and Anzio fronts, the Allied forces liberated Rome on June 4, 1944, and moved swiftly up the Italian peninsula. Fighting delaying actions, the Germans fell back toward the heavily fortified Gothic Line on the Apennine Mountains, where at the beginning of August they stopped to make their next stand. The Sixth Operational Zone was immediately behind the Gothic Line and in the rear of the German units countering the advance of the American Fifth Army. General Mark Clark, commanding officer of the Fifth Army, recognized that the partisans could tie down significant enemy troops who would otherwise fight his men at the frontline. Clark welcomed any relief he could get at this point. Almost overnight, he had lost half the strength of his army when seven battle-hardened divisions of the French Expeditionary Corps commanded by General Alfred Juin and the American VI Corps commanded by General Lucien Truscott left Italy to conduct Operation Dragoon, the Allied invasion of southern France that began on August 15, 1944.[6]

The Italian operational groups were finally able to step in and fulfill a significant part of their original mission and became "instrumental in harnessing resistance groups throughout northern Italy and forging them into a weapon that created a major diversion of the German military effort on the Italian front."[7] The first OG operation to establish contact with Italian partisans was a fifteen-man team, code-named Walla Walla, under the command of Captain William C. Wheeler, Jr., and First Lieutenant Quayle N. Smith. It also included Technical Sergeant Angelo Galante, a veteran of the OG operation to rescue Allied prisoners of war in September 1943.[8] The team departed for the mission at 2100 hours on August 11 from Brindisi airport. In the early hours of the morning, they parachuted on Mount Aiona, about thirty miles northeast of Genoa, where the OSS SI team Locust had arranged the reception with the help of two squads of local partisans. About fifty containers with war materials for the partisans followed the OGs to the ground.

The terrain was rocky and filled with crevasses and precipices. A light but troublesome wind from the mountains complicated the descent. The wind blew the parachutes, with their men and containers, away from the drop zone onto locations that were hard to get to among the cliffs. Some of the OGs were hurt upon landing, but a doctor was at hand among the reception party to offer first aid. The partisans prepared rudimentary stretchers to help evacuate the wounded parachutists. It took until eight in the morning to collect all the men and material and move them to sheltered storage areas that the partisans had built near the drop zone. The Americans were welcomed with great joy and open arms. There was an immediate spirit of fraternizing and, after the preliminary introductions, Captain Wheeler ordered his men to distribute chocolate, whisky, and cigarettes among the partisans.

The OGs wasted no time in teaching the partisans how to use the weapons they had brought with them, including 60-mm mortars, bazookas, and Bren guns. After a while, the equipment and the wounded OGs who could not walk were loaded on sixty mules. In the early afternoon of August 12, the entire column, including eleven of the fifteen Americans and thirty partisans escorting them, set off from the barracks at Mount Aiona. Lieutenant R. T. Smith and three OGs remained on Mount Aiona to set up the radio transmitter for the mission and provide follow-up training in the use of arms, plastic explosives, and preparing booby traps for sabotage.

When Albert Materazzi, the executive officer of the Italian OGs, briefed the team for the mission before departure, little was known of the partisan activity in the area. He told them to expect to contact a small band of partisans, live with them in the mountains, and make raids upon targets as they presented themselves. So Wheeler and his men were surprised when, once they reached the roadway, the partisans unloaded the equipment by the side of the road and dismissed the muleteers and their mules. In a short while, a modern passenger bus and several trucks arrived to transport the group over nearly twenty miles of road to the partisan headquarters in the town of Rovegno. Several partisan commanders welcomed them to "liberated Italy," which the OGs soon learned comprised an area fifty miles long by thirty miles wide between Genoa and Piacenza from where Nazi-Fascists had been completely driven out. The partisans were in full control of the area, which they called the Republic of Torriglia, and could move freely throughout the region by motor transport.

The partisan activities included raiding enemy garrisons and attacking major highways and secondary roads. The actions were limited due to the acute shortage of arms, ammunition, and explosives, although the partisans hoarded a lot of material that they kept for defensive actions against the enemy during their mop-up operations. The partisan commanders regarded the OG mission as their saviors and asked them to do their best to secure adequate supply drops and air support during fights. When the OGs asked to get involved in the fighting, the partisans said they had the men to do the fighting as long as the Americans would supply and train them. Lieutenant Smith and the three OGs that remained at Mount Aiona coordinated daily drops of war materials, equipment, food, and medicine between August 12 and 26.

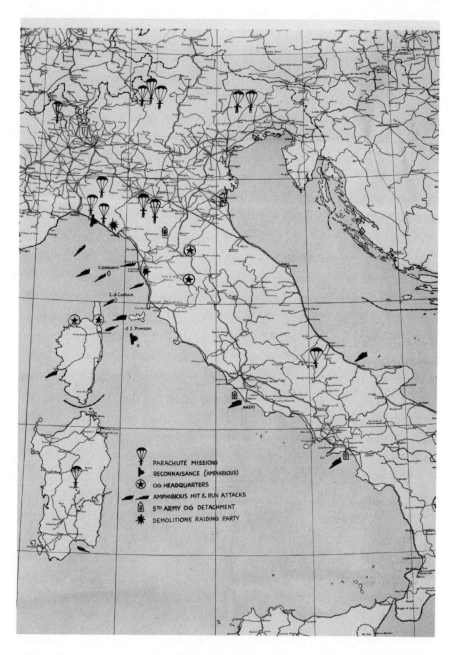

OSS map depicting Italian OG operations between August 1943 and May 1945.

On August 26, the Germans began a serious cleanup operation aimed at retaking control of areas they considered of strategic importance for the defense of their positions. The Germans were particularly weary of the liberated areas behind the Gothic Line, which the Allies could use as bridgeheads for end-run operations that would bypass the German fortifications. Two German divisions went into attack, supported by artillery and mortar fire, against five to six thousand partisans defending the territory. The partisan units dispersed in different directions to avoid annihilation. The OG mission split up into groups of two or three attached to different partisans to evade capture. The parachuting of supplies at Mount Aiona stopped in order not to attract undue attention of the enemy to the storehouses and hiding places the partisans had built around that drop zone.

The German all-out assault made clear the limitations of partisan warfare. An eyewitness of the events at the time wrote, "500 men carried the brunt of the battle, 2,500 (a generous number) participated marginally but remained with their units, and the remaining 2,000 threw their weapons away and ran without firing a shot."[9] As usual, the fights with the partisans gave way to reprisals against the population, in which the Fascist units often distinguished themselves for their ruthlessness. Nuto Revelli, one of the partisan commanders, wrote in his diary:

> The Fascists we hate, I emphasize, "we hate," because they arrive always after the battle, they arrive always after the *rastrellamenti*, following the Germans. The Fascists are ferocious in their reprisals against the population, against the defenseless. They surpass the Germans these clumsy Italians, scoundrels that specialize in burning, blackmailing, and hanging, dirty in their souls as in their uniforms, with their black shirts of mourning and terror on their grey-green uniforms.[10]

* * *

The Italian partisans showed a lot of resiliency. By the end of September, with the wave of rastrellamenti receding, they regrouped and resumed their actions against the Germans. At this time, the OGs of Walla Walla began again receiving drops of supplies for the partisans of the Sixth Zone. The supplies were initially dropped during the night, but the mountainous terrain made it very difficult to retrieve all of them. During a drop on November 4, for example, the materials were dispersed over eight kilometers, with the nearest container landing seven kilometers from the designated drop zone. As the partisans began to re-occupy the ground they had lost during the summer, the drops began arriving during the day.

The mission used the promise of supplies and support to implement the policy of military unification of all resistance fighters under the common command of the Sixth Zone and the CLNAI. Those groups that refused to accept the common command were dissolved and the personnel absorbed into the regular units. At the time, there were two major partisan divisions in the zone, a Garibaldi division under Anton Ukmar, also known as Miro, and a Giustizia e Libertà division under the command of Fausto Cossu, known simply as Fausto.

Anton Ukmar was born in 1900 in Prosecco, Trieste, in a family of farmers of Slovenian descent. He joined the Italian Communist Party in 1926 and was sent to Genoa to organize the railroad workers there. Pursued by the Fascist police, he escaped to Yugoslavia, then moved to France and the Soviet Union. Ukmar went to Spain during the Spanish Civil War, first as a counterespionage officer and then as political commissar of the 12th Garibaldi Brigade. After the defeat of the Republican cause in 1939, he fled to France. Ukmar returned to Italy after the fall of Mussolini and assumed command of the Sixth Zone under the battle name Miro.[11]

Fausto Cossu was born in 1915 and had been an official of the Carabinieri, the Italian military police, in Yugoslavia since 1942. The Germans captured him after the armistice of September 8, 1943, and deported him first to Zagreb, Croatia, and then to Germany. He was able to escape and return to Italy where in January 1944 he organized a resistance unit affiliated with the Action Party in the mountains near Piacenza, which later grew to become a full-size division.[12]

The word about the Walla Walla mission spread, and partisan leaders from outside the Sixth Zone contacted the OGs to request supplies.

One of these leaders commanded a division in nearby Lombardy and went by the name of Americano. His true name was Domenico Mezzadra, and he was born in Windsor Lochs, Connecticut, in 1920 to a family of Italian immigrants. When his father died in 1933, the family, mother and three children, returned to Italy. Mezzadra was drafted in the Italian army in 1941 and became an officer in 1943. He was able to evade capture by the Germans after the armistice of September 8, 1943. He joined the resistance in February 1944 as a commander of a Garibaldi platoon and by the summer of that year had taken command of an entire brigade in the area around Pavia, in the region of Lombardy known as Oltrepò Pavese, south of the River Po from Pavia and southwest of Piacenza.[13]

At Americano's request, Captain Wheeler met with him to assess the strength and needs of his brigade. He coordinated a drop of supplies for Americano's division, but the supplies were accidentally sent to a drop zone that belonged to the Fausto division. Efforts by Wheeler to convince Fausto to share the supplies with Americano were not fruitful. At one point, Fausto said he did not need Allied aid, after which drops to Fausto's zone were suspended. On November 19, the "Big Three"—Miro, Americano, and Fausto—met to try to resolve the issues. Americano was invited and agreed to join the Sixth Zone command at which point Fausto boiled over and said he was considering an armistice with the enemy. After the war, Fausto said that the armistice had been a hoax by one of the partisans under his command. It had been so convincing that the Germans and the Fascist authorities had sent money and emissaries to negotiate the terms of surrender for twenty-five thousand partisans,[14] but he did not share any of this information during the conference. Afterward, the CLNAI considered Fausto a collaborator and severed the ties with him. Cut off from American supplies and the headquarters of the CLNAI, Fausto dissolved his Giustizia e Libertà division at the end of November. After the worst of the winter passed, he reconstituted a new division in the Piacenza area in February–March 1945, which operated independently of the Sixth Zone command or the CLNAI until the liberation of Piacenza.[15]

The enemy too had gotten word of the presence of the Walla Walla mission among the partisans. Partisans guarding the mission captured a Fascist spy near the Sixth Zone headquarters who was asking the civilian population questions about the whereabouts of the mission. They took him to the headquarters and promptly shot him.

* * *

At the beginning of November, the Nazi-Fascists prepared another mop-up operation. In a speech commemorating the anniversary of the march on Rome that brought him to power, Mussolini announced an amnesty for all those who had dodged the draft in military service, deserted, or failed to enroll in the obligatory labor service of the Fascist republic. He gave all the partisans across northern Italy until November 11, 1944, to surrender, promising that all would be forgiven. The partisans took no notice but began to prepare for the strong action that would come after the deadline. Mission Walla Walla coordinated a massive drop of almost six thousand pounds of supplies on November 16. Thirty planes flew over the drop zone in the mountains, sending down 195 containers and 13 packs that dispersed over a large area. It took thirty-six hours to collect all the supplies, but in the end, they accounted for 100 percent of the containers due to excellent partisan cooperation.

An early onset of cold weather and fierce resistance of the Germans all along the Gothic Line forced the Allies to stop their efforts to push through the Apennines and settle for a second winter of bitter fighting in Italy. The lull in the frontlines was propitious for the Germans and their Fascist allies in that it allowed them to concentrate their forces in cleaning up the rear areas from the partisan bands. The German operation in the Sixth Zone began on November 23 initially against the Giustizia e Libertà division. After offering scattered resistance, Fausto withdrew, leaving the Americano division's north and east flank exposed. Miro rushed reinforcements to the north to plug the gap. Heavy battles occurred between November 23 and 30 in the Americano zone.

The Walla Walla mission made desperate attempts to secure a flow of supplies to reinforce the partisans. On November 28, seven aircraft flying two separate sorties dropped over 240 packages with over twenty-eight thousand pounds of material. A daylight drop of mortars went to Americano on November 29, in plain view of enemy troops of the 162nd Turkoman Division, composed of Soviet prisoners of war and deserters from the Caucasus fighting under German officers and NCOs. These units were particularly cruel against the population in the area, looting and raping the town of Zavaterello in a vicious manner. There and elsewhere, the Germans massacred civilians with pitchforks and meat hooks, leaving the corpses exposed and forbidding the burial of the killed. "You could see that it didn't make a difference to them, partisan or not, we were all rebels for the Germans," recalled a survivor.[16]

The Americano and Miro divisions put up a strong resistance through the middle of December. They met every thrust of the enemy with determination, unlike the meek opposition and the quick collapse of the partisan units that occurred during the August rastrellamenti. Even though the partisans lost control of the liberated areas when faced by an enemy equipped with armor and artillery, they made the Germans pay a heavy cost for their operations measured in hundreds killed and wounded. As the partisans retreated up the mountains again, they made sure this time to destroy all the strategic bridges in the area, which effectively blocked the roads to enemy traffic for the remainder of the war.

On December 15, the Walla Walla mission received urgent orders from the Sienna headquarters to head south immediately toward the Allied lines. Traveling with the help of partisan guides, they trekked through the mountains, leaving the Sixth Zone on December 20 and arriving at an American outpost near Carrara at 0930 hours on December 26, 1944. All fifteen OGs of the Walla Walla team returned safely.

During their nineteen weeks with the Italian partisans, the OG team accomplished all the objectives of its mission. The Sixth Zone command considered the officers of the mission, Captain Wheeler and Lieutenant Smith, as its own staff officers, frequently consulting them and adopting their recommendations about the overall strategy and organization of the units in the zone. The support that the team provided to the partisans of the Sixth Zone brought a notable increase in activities and a marked improvement in the efficiency of their operations against the Nazi-Fascists in occupied Italy. In addition to the supplies provided to the partisans, weapons specialists with the mission instructed partisans in the function and use of Allied weapons being sent to them. Demolitions specialists demonstrated the use of explosives and demolition devices for sabotage. The OGs gave instructions in scouting, patrolling, and setting up raids and ambushes. Aside from the military considerations, the presence of an American mission served as a constant reminder of the Allies' desire to aid the partisan cause and also as a significant factor in unifying their efforts against the common enemy.

The German mop-up operations and the onset of winter would have been valid reasons for the headquarters to order the withdrawal of the Walla Walla mission. What influenced the decision the most, however, was very disconcerting news from northern Italy about the fate of another mission, code-named Mangosteen-Chrysler, that had operated in the area north of Milan since the end of September 1944.

CHAPTER 11

Mission Mangosteen-Chrysler

In mid-August 1944, under the supervision of General Donovan himself, the OSS Secret Intelligence branch in Siena, Italy, planned a mission, code-named Mangosteen, to be parachuted in northern Italy in the area between Milan and the Swiss border. The objective of the mission was to establish contact with the CLNAI leaders in Milan and facilitate their communications with Allied headquarters. Donovan trusted the command of Mangosteen to Captain William V. Holohan, a forty-year-old cavalry reserve officer who had joined the OSS only recently. Holohan was born and raised in New York City. He graduated from Manhattan College in 1925, entered Harvard Law School in the same year, and earned his law degree in 1928.[1] He went into government service and successfully tried the first Securities and Exchange Commission's stock manipulation case.[2] Holohan was called into service shortly after Pearl Harbor and served in Fort Riley, Kansas, and then in the Army Air Forces before volunteering to join the OSS.

Donovan knew Holohan personally and put him in charge of the mission despite the fact that he lacked the training, experience, or language skills of OSS operatives sent behind the lines for this type of mission. On the other hand, Holohan was trim, fit, calm, and had a commanding personality. He was a devout Catholic and a fervent anti-communist in politics. In Donovan's view, "the mission might come under pressure, and Holohan could be counted on not to play any political games."[3] To boost Holohan's standing with the CLNAI, Donovan promoted him to major on the spot, which allowed Holohan to wear the golden oak leafs on his uniform before he left, although his promotion was confirmed in October when he was already deployed on the mission.

The second member of the team was Lieutenant Aldo Icardi, a twenty-three-year-old Italian American from Pittsburgh who had been one of the early recruits of the OSS Special Operations and Secret Intelligence Italian branches. Icardi was fluent in Italian and spoke it with the Piedmont accent of his parents. Because of his language skills and operational experience, Icardi was to be Holohan's translator and right-hand man in the field. In early September, the Mangosteen team merged with a team of three OGs, code name Chrysler, composed of Lieutenant Victor Giannino, Technical Sergeant Arthur Ciarmicoli, and Sergeant Carl Lo Dolce. They had tried a dozen times to parachute into the mountains north of Milan and organize the partisan units in that area. Each time they had to return to their base because of bad weather, enemy activity along their flightpath, or failure to identify the drop zone. Giannino was a veteran of the Italian OG operations in the Mediterranean, including the liberation of Corsica and other islands in the Tuscan Archipelago. Ciarmicoli was a demolition and explosives expert. Lo Dolce was a skilled radio operator who had participated in a number of raids behind enemy lines. He had spent several months in a rest camp recovering from a close encounter with the Germans on the island of Gorgona during a raid at the end of March 1944.[4]

The combined team Mangosteen-Chrysler left the Maison Blanche Airfield in Algeria in the evening of September 26, 1944, aboard two B-17 Flying Fortresses. Three Italian intelligence agents working for the OSS shared the ride on the way to their own assignments in northern Italy. One of them, Tullio Lussi, a professor of literature and philosophy at the University of Trieste who went by the code name Landi, would provide the initial introductions between Holohan and the CLNAI leaders in Milan. While the three Italians were in civilian clothes, the five Americans were in military uniform and had orders to remain so throughout their mission.

In addition to the eight men, the Flying Fortresses carried several containers of arms, ammunition, and supplies for the mission and for the partisans on the ground that had organized their reception. Giannino carried $4,000 on him. Holohan carried another $16,000 worth of currency, most of it in Italian lire but also in Swiss francs and US dollars, hard currencies that were in high demand in northern Italy. The Americans carried $3,000 worth of gold in Louis d'Or coins, rolled in cartridges. They called this "blood money," to be used to bribe their way to freedom in case they fell into the hands of Germans, especially the Gestapo, who were known to covet gold.

On the night of September 26, the team parachuted on Mount Mottarone, between Lake Maggiore to the east and the smaller alpine Lake Orta to the west. It was a pristine area then, as it is today, with a number of hotels that the Germans used as convalescing and rest centers for their troops. It was also teeming with partisans, who held remote villages, like Coiromonte, where the mission set up base after landing. Only a dozen miles to the north of their location began the free territory of the Republic of Ossola, which stretched to the border with Switzerland. Partisan brigades of multiple affiliations, including Christian Democrats, Socialists, and Communists, had liberated the area and declared it a republic on September 10, 1944. They had set up a civil administration in the regional capital, Domodossola, and ran the zone like a functioning democracy under the eyes of international journalists who could enter the liberated territory from Switzerland.

Giannino and Ciarmicoli immediately began training the partisans in the Coiromonte area in using the explosives and weapons they had brought with them and from a second drop that arrived on October 2. Holohan and Icardi met with the partisan commanders in the area, all of whom asked for more arms and ammunition. Ferruccio Parri, one the three leaders of the CLNAI, arrived from Milan to meet with Major Holohan. Everyone believed the end of the war was imminent, so the discussion focused on how the CLNAI would take control of the area immediately upon the surrender of the Germans and protect key assets of the infrastructure there.

But the Germans had no plans to quit fighting any time soon. At the beginning of October, they began amassing troops in preparation for a mop-up operation of the entire area. Alfredo Di Dio, the partisan leader of the Christian Democrat "Val Toce" division, came to visit the American mission with a plea for arms that his men needed to protect the Ossola valley. Di Dio was only twenty-four years old but had been leading his group of partisans since 1943.[5] He told Holohan that British SOE and American OSS contacts from Switzerland had encouraged him to launch his insurrection in Ossola. Now, he asked for supplies, arms, ammunition, and air support from the Allies to protect his men and his positions. Holohan transmitted the request to the OSS Italian headquarters in Sienna, but the Allied headquarters did not find the objective strategically important enough to satisfy Di Dio's request.[6]

From the beginning, Holohan noticed signs of friction between Di Dio's Christian Democrat partisans and Communist partisans led by Vincenzo (Cino) Moscatelli. Moscatelli was thirty-six years old at the time. He had joined the ranks of the Communist movement when he was still a teenager and had been sent by the party to attend political courses in Switzerland, Berlin, and Moscow in the late 1920s. He returned in 1930 to organize the communist resistance against Mussolini but fell into the hands of police and spent thirteen years in Fascist prisons until the fall of the regime in 1943. Immediately after the armistice, he began to organize the partisan movement in the area between Novara and the Swiss border. He became the political commissar of all the Garibaldi units in that area and earned a reputation for showing no mercy toward the Germans and Fascists.[7]

In a message sent to Sienna, Holohan wrote, "The Communist chief Moscatelli is putting pressure to take control of all the patriots in Val d'Ossola but is unlikely to succeed because his group is in minority. Communist bands have much more money that the others because they receive funds from Russia and Tito." Although Holohan could not do much to help Di Dio, he consented to allow Giannino and Ciarmicoli to go with him to Ossola to offer what assistance they could in preparing to defend the area. They left on October 8 and arrived in Domodossola the next day.

On October 10, the enemy launched the attack against the Republic of Ossola with thirteen thousand troops, only five hundred of which were Germans and the rest Italian Fascists. From the heights of Mottarone, Holohan, Icardi, and Lo Dolce could see the troops advancing from Lake Maggiore through valleys leading to Ossola. Giannino, who was caught in the valley with the partisans, later described six days of heavy fighting during which the partisans were under continuous fire from 88-mm artillery and mortar pieces. The Germans brought an armored train to shell the partisan positions in the mountains. Commander Di Dio fell into an ambush and was killed on October 11. On October 14, facing an enemy that enjoyed a four-to-one superiority in numbers, the partisans began an organized retreat toward Switzerland. Delaying fights allowed the evacuation by train of thirty-five thousand civilians from Domodossola, half the population of the city, which was semi-deserted by the time the Fascist troops arrived. On October 23, the last partisan units, with Giannino and Ciarmicoli among them, crossed into Switzerland after exhausting their last ammunitions. The Fascists had the entire area under control.[8]

* * *

After clearing the Ossola valley, the Nazi-Fascists turned their attention to the areas they had bypassed, including Mount Mottarone and Coiromonte, where the Mangosteen-Chrysler mission resided. Holohan made a fateful decision not to attach the team to any of the partisan units in the area, most likely to maintain independence of the mission. This created the impression among the local partisan commanders that the mission was aloof and did not support their needs at a time when they insisted on having arms and supplies parachuted to them.

The only close contact for the mission became Aminta Migliari, who went by the battle name Giorgio. He had been in charge of the intelligence services for Di Dio's brigade and offered to help the Americans find secure lodging and collect information about the enemy movements in the area, but he expected to be paid for his services. Giorgio also provided two local men to assist the Americans in their movements and carry their equipment. They were Giuseppe Manini, who called himself Manin, and Gualtiero Tozzini, who went by the nickname

Pupo. Later Icardi described Migliari as a thin, small man, quite unlike the other partisans in the area, who were very strong mountaineer types. He was very intelligent, fervently Catholic, and violently anti-communist, like all the men under his supervision. Manini and Tozzini were strong, quiet, and self-controlled men, without an education or profession. Both were in their thirties, had been with the Italian army alpine troops, and knew all the paths and tracks in the area.[9]

On October 19, 1944, Migliari came with the news that it was dangerous for the Americans to continue to stay in Coiromonte. He had found a place in a village called Egro, on the western side of Lake Orta. Late at night, the team, guided by Migliari, Manini, and Tozzini, left Coiromonte carrying one change of clothing, the radio, personal weapons, and sleeping bags. They hid all the other equipment and clothes in a small shed high up in the mountains. They crossed the lake that night and arrived at a small house in Egro, about a mile from the lake's shore. They had to move out soon because the house was iso-lated, the radio could not get reception, and the family hosting them became increasingly concerned that their presence would leak out.

After four days, Migliari found a villa on the southwestern shore of Lake Orta, called Villa Maria. It belonged to a Milanese industrialist close to the Fascist regime who wisely stayed away from the property given the partisan activity in the area. After Lo Dolce verified that the radio reception was good from that location, the entire mission moved to the villa. It was located about thirty feet from the lake and it offered a magnificent view of the town of Orta on the other shore and Mount Mottarone behind it. Directly across from Villa Maria was San Giulio, a tiny picture-perfect island with a medieval seminary on it.

At Villa Maria, the team set up the radio and reestablished com-munications with the headquarters, transmitting weather observations and the occasional information about enemy movements that Migliari collected from his network of contacts. From the villa, they observed the Germans moving in on Mount Mottarone at the end of October. They received news that the enemy had searched Coiromonte and found the equipment and personal belongings they had hidden before fleeing the area. The Germans now could confirm rumors they had heard about the presence of Americans in the area. Fearing a German search on this side of the lake, the team left Villa Maria and hid in the hills overlooking the lake. The weather was cold, wet, and miserable and they could not last long in it.

Don Carletto and Don Giovanni, two friendly priests in charge of the seminary at San Giulio agreed to give them refuge there. After three or four days, a group of Germans and Fascist officers came to inspect the island. The priests showed them around and managed to keep them from entering the seminary, but it was clear that the Germans could return any time. At night, the team left the island and went back to Egro, where they found a family who agreed to host them. They had been there for about an hour when a partisan brought the news that the enemy had entered the town after them and was sweeping the houses in search of partisans. They left Egro in the opposite direction and stayed in the woods until the following night when Migliari arrived and took them to Grassona, a town at the southern tip of the lake, where the team found refuge in the attic of the local church. There they hid for six days, subsisting only on bread and apples that the village priest sent for them, while over fifteen hundred Germans and Fascists combed the area, looking for partisans and the American mission.

* * *

When the enemy pressure eased, the mission moved from the church attic to a house across the street from the church. Lo Dolce activated the radio again and began communicating with the head-quarters to coordinate a supply drop on Mount Mottarone for the partisans who were trying to rebuild their strength after the German drive through the area and against Ossola. Holohan and Lo Dolce remained in town while Icardi and Migliari traveled to Mottarone to determine the status of the partisan units there and to look for a suitable drop zone.

On the way, Icardi received news that the partisans in Mottarone had captured four suspicious men hiking in the area. Guessing that they were German spies, the partisans took them to their headquar-ters for search and interrogation. When the men removed their heavy overcoats, the partisans noticed that two of them had radio equipment strapped around their waists, antenna wire coiled around their bodies, and batteries in their pockets. They were German radio technicians turned into living radio directional finding devices. The third man, responsible for their security, carried a detailed map of the area with various triangulation lines that intersected at the location of another OSS radio transmitter that the Germans had eliminated during the mop-up in Mount Mottarone. The fourth man, a Swiss national, served as the guide and the translator for the Germans.

Icardi arrived in Mottarone on November 22, interrogated the Germans and took pictures of them wearing and using the equipment, which he eventually sent to headquarters in a report that described the means and methods used by the Germans to track Allied agents. When Icardi inquired about the fourth man, one of the partisans said, "We sent him to Switzerland without shoes." Perplexed at the expression, Icardi asked for an explanation. The partisan told him that a court martial had sentenced the Swiss collaborator to death. The partisans shot him and buried him headfirst in a grave they had dug in haste. The foxes had dug into the shallow grave at night and had gnawed at his shoes and feet. The expression took hold and was used each time they talked about eliminating someone who could not be trusted.

In Mottarone, Icardi organized a meeting with partisan leaders to discuss the process for receiving and distributing the supplies. It included Luigi Fusco, known as Cinquanta, the leader of the independent bands, and Arias, leader of the Communist bands in the area. Arias gave Icardi an earful, accusing Giorgio of isolating the Communist partisans from the American mission to prevent them from receiving arms and supplies. Migliari was a fierce anti-Communist and bragged that the Communists would not receive any help from the allies. Moscatelli had grave suspicions about the Americans and their exclusive relationship with Migliari and the Christian Democrats.[10]

Icardi returned to Grassona to brief Holohan about the developments. The position of the Mangosteen-Chrysler mission was very precarious at this point, with threats coming from all sides. The people in Grassona and other towns around the lake knew about their presence there. This was certainly due to the propensity of the villagers for gossip, but also due to Holohan's insistence that they appear at all times in military uniform. People who were close to the mission at the time recalled later that Holohan had been very strict in enforcing this requirement and had chewed Icardi out when he had suggested they change in civilian clothes. Lo Dolce, who had experienced firsthand in Gorgona the ability of Germans to pinpoint radio locations, was terrified to come on air after Icardi talked about the Germans captured in the mountains. Moscatelli's suspicions about the Americans' willingness to help the Communists rattled their nerves because Moscatelli had earned a reputation for showing no mercy to those who stood in his path.

When Migliari arrived that afternoon, Holohan and Icardi confronted him with what they had heard from the Communist partisans in Mottarone. Migliari did not make excuses about his position. He was trying to arm non-Communist partisans to bring them at the same level of strength as the Communists, who, he said, intended to take power by force at the end of the war.

With these words, Migliari touched a raw nerve for Holohan. In a terse voice, he told Migliari in English, with Icardi translating in Italian, that the purpose of his mission was to help all those who fought the enemy. "Quit acting like an exclusive contact for the mission," Holohan said. Migliari quickly assured him that he was in favor of Holohan meeting Moscatelli as soon as he wished. Then he added that he had found a good drop point in the mountains where the first supplies could arrive. He also suggested that the team move to a different location, given that everyone in town knew where they were. The next day, Migliari moved them to another villa by Lake Orta, Villa Castelnuovo, one of the most luxurious villas in the area, about half a mile from Villa Maria. Lo Dolce set up the radio and transmitted the coordinates of the drop point in the mountains, which they called Blueberry. On November 27, the headquarters responded that the drop was being prepared and would arrive on the night of December 2.

Preparations to receive the drop got complicated when the Fascists arrived in Orta on November 29 and began searching the hills and forests around Mottarone. December 2 brought worse news. Commandant Cinquanta had revealed himself as a Fascist provocateur and had led the enemy in rounding up his former comrades. The Fascists rewarded him with a captain commission in the Fascist army and now Cinquanta roamed the streets of Novara in Fascist uniform. Cinquanta knew personally Holohan and Icardi and the news of his betrayal added to the stress under which team Mangosteen-Chrysler operated.

Late in the day, Moscatelli sent word that he wished to meet that evening. Around 2000 hours, one of his men came by Villa Castelnuovo in a car and drove Holohan and Icardi along dark country roads. The men felt that Moscatelli had sent the car, a rare luxury in those areas, as a show of strength and to impress the Americans. The car stopped at the entrance of a secluded gravel path that ended in a cul-de-sac where a group of silhouettes were barely visible. The driver pointed at the figures in the dark and said, "Moscatelli is waiting for you." Icardi later described the encounter:

> True to his evasive and mysterious personality, our meeting was arranged so that we never got a good look at Moscatelli. As we walked the short distance to the group of men, they came toward us. The puff of a cigarette threw a momentary glow on a thin, rugged face. The face was Moscatelli's. The other men walked away from us, leaving Moscatelli, Major Holohan, and me alone.
>
> I tried to peer through the shadows to see what he looked like, but the moonlight was only strong enough to throw his body into outline, nothing more. An "alpine star" metal insignia glinted on his lapel. This was the distinctive emblem used by the Communist Garibaldini partisans. Moscatelli was wearing a uniform, and his hat was the peaked felt of the Italian Alpini, with an eagle feather jutting up along one side.
>
> He spoke softly, steadily, and surely. This was not the quick, dynamic genius we had felt in Alfredo Di Dio. Here was maturity and confidence, based on experience and the ability to produce and control his calculated position.[11]

Holohan and Moscatelli discussed at length the partisan situation, with Icardi translating for the two men. Moscatelli complained that he had heard from Migliari that all the American supplies were going to the Christian Democrats. Holohan responded that only a small drop was for the partisans of Migliari to compensate for the heavy losses they had suffered in Ossola. Other drops were in the works, and they would be distributed equally among all the partisans, without regard of their political orientation. Holohan said bluntly that his mission was not to establish a Communist regime in Italy but to kill as many Germans as possible.[12] If the partisans wanted supplies, they had to prove their ability and intentions to use the arms against the Germans. For this, Holohan said, he needed specific information about the operations Moscatelli intended to carry out, his actual forces, and their equipment.

Moscatelli promised to send this information, although he must have perceived Holohan's request as a stalling tactic to gain time. Moscatelli's misgivings about Holohan's attitude toward the Communists must have gotten only stronger when, as they were speaking, two airplanes lumbered overhead and dropped the first supplies at Point Blueberry for the Christian Democrat partisans of Migliari. They parted ways with vague promises of collaboration in the near future. Holohan doubted it, but he felt that they had taken some steps in the right direction.

* * *

Two days later, in the evening of December 5, the American team was in Villa Castelnuovo when the friendly priests from the seminary of San Giulio arrived. A thick fog covered the lake, but Don Carletto and Don Giovanni were expert rowers. They knew the waters like the palms of their hands and could make the crossing by compass in total darkness. The reason for the urgency was that they had heard people in the market of Orta mention that the American mission was located at Villa Castelnuovo. A Fascist unit was stationed in Orta at the time and the priests were certain that it would hear the same rumors soon and send a patrol to search the place. The Americans needed to move again. They sent word to Migliari to find them a new location. Giorgio arrived the next day and told them to be ready to leave at 2200 hours.

He would display a light signal from the island of San Giulio when it was safe for them to move.

Marina Duelli, a young girl of twenty-three who acted as a secret courier for Giorgio, visited Villa Castelnuovo in the afternoon of December 6. She recalled after the war sitting with Holohan in the villa's drawing room looking out at the lake and Mottarone in the distance. The afternoon was miserable and sheets of rain came down from thick dark clouds that hung over the gray lake. "He was gloomy and gray like the landscape," said Duelli about Holohan, "as if he knew what awaited him."[13]

* * *

The OSS headquarters in Sienna did not hear from the mission for the first two weeks in December. Then on December 14, it received a brief radio message that the team had come under attack and Major Holohan had disappeared. Then silence again. The biweekly report covering the OSS activities for the period December 1–15 noted for the team, "This team recently was forced to suspend contacts because of enemy action in the zone. It is believed that the mission is moving to a safe zone." The report for the activities in the second half of December noted, "No intelligence since December 17." Headquarters asked an Italian secret agent operating in the area to inquire about the team's whereabouts. His report noted that "the mission was fraught with danger because its presence was known to the residents of the nearby villages, its transmissions could be heard by the enemy, and its movements were hampered by the fact that its personnel was operating in US military uniforms."[14]

Finally, in early January, a pouch arrived from the OSS office in Switzerland that contained Icardi's detailed description of the events. In the evening of December 6, the Chrysler team, Holohan, Icardi, Lo Dolce, and their two Italian fixers, Manini and Tozzini, had waited anxiously for Migliari's light signal from San Giulio. A thick fog descended on the lake, and it was impossible to see any lights. Around 2230 hours, Holohan decided to wait no longer and move out. "It is better to be out in the open than to end up in a trap in this villa," he said.

Within a few minutes, they collected all their belongings and cleaned up any sign of their presence from the villa. Then they exited through the back door and crossed the backyard toward a rowboat on the lake's shore. After Tozzini and Manini had loaded the equipment in the boat, Holohan sent Manini to the villa for a final check to make sure everything was in order. They were waiting for Manini to return when gunfire erupted from the villa. Icardi returned fire with his .45-caliber pistol then ran in the dark on the path along the lake. As he was running, he could hear shots being fired. Then, the shooting stopped as suddenly as it had started. Icardi kept running until he arrived at the house of Giorgio, a couple of miles away from the location of Villa Castelnuovo.

Icardi wrote in his report that he was reunited with Lo Dolce and Tozzini three days later. They said they too had fired in the dark toward the house when they had heard the first bursts of gunfire. Then they had run along the lake in the opposite direction from Icardi until they had reached Villa Maria, a half mile further, where they decided to hide until things quieted down. Manini reappeared five days later, on December 11. He said that when he had gone toward the villa for a final check, he had heard steps on the gravel path of the gardens. He called out to the people in the darkness but received gunfire in response. He too returned fire and then retreated toward the lake. He jumped on the boat and rowed in the dark to the opposite shore of the lake. He hid the radio and the team's other equipment in a cemetery and laid low until he was certain the danger had passed.

Icardi reported that when Major Holohan had failed to show up, he had searched the area for his body. The friendly priests from the seminary of San Giulio had taken a group of children in the area pretending to be on a field trip and had spent an entire day looking for any traces of the major. Icardi concluded his report saying he assumed Holohan was captured by the enemy. He had included in the report a map of the Lake Orta area indicating the location of the attack that lead to Holohan's disappearance.

The disappearance of Holohan was seen at the OSS headquarters as an unfortunate incident not out of line with the nature of secret operations. A thorough investigation into Holohan's fate would have to wait until the end of the war. But the OSS had to avoid situations in which its missions were caught between the competing interests of the different political currents that made up the Italian resistance. It pushed the leaders of the CLNAI to take responsibility for the distribution of supplies sent in to their partisan units. In the Mangosteen-Chrysler area of operations, an Italian Army career officer took charge of the distribution of any future supplies among the Italian partisan units. The American mission, now under the command of Icardi, assumed the sole role of coordinating the drop of supplies between the Allied headquarters and the CLNAI representatives. "We were no more than a telegraph agency, watching only to see that no abuses developed," said Icardi later.[14]

On January 18, 1945, a massive supply of twenty-four tons of weapons arrived in a day drop on the alpine village of Quarna, perched high up in the mountains a mile from the northwest shores of Lake Orta. Icardi and Lo Dolce were present at the drop, but the collection and distribution of supplies was handled entirely by Italian partisans from Communist and Christian-Democrat units. Shortly afterward, Icardi and Lo Dolce received the order to get out of the Lake Orta area and move to the town of Busta Arsizio, thirty-five miles to the southeast, halfway between Lake Orta and Milan. There they shed their military uniforms and, dressed in civilian clothes, spent the remaining months of the war setting up and running an intelligence network that collected and passed information about the strength of enemy troops to the allies through radio communications and through the OSS mission in Switzerland.

CHAPTER 12

Rescue Missions in the Balkans

As the experience of missions like Ginny, Justine, Walla Walla, and Mangosteen-Chrysler showed, the operational success of the OSS teams behind enemy lines depended on a number of factors, including their training, the support they received from their headquarters, and the partnerships they were able to forge with the resistance groups on the ground. Enemy forces clearly had a big vote into the performance and livelihood of the teams, since they determined the rate and severity of mop-up operations and made life-or-death decisions for those men who fell into their hands.

What is often overlooked is the dependency of these missions on the aircrews that flew the modified bombers deep into enemy territory initially to parachute the teams into their operational areas, and then to drop supplies for them and the resistance units they were organizing in the ground. The dependency became mutual very quickly and developed into a full-fledged symbiotic relationship. As the war efforts intensified in 1944, the number of bombing runs over targets in enemy-held territory increased. The toll of enemy fire on equipment and personnel climbed proportionally. Many airmen lost their lives, but a number of them were able to bail out. Once on the ground, enemy forces captured a good number of them and confined them in prisoners-of-war camps. Quite a few though, managed to evade capture and remain hidden with help and support from local resistance groups or populations friendly to the Allied cause. The OSS mounted a number of daring operations behind enemy lines to rescue these aircrews and bring them back to safety.

* * *

In the Mediterranean theater of operations, the United States strategic air assets were organized under the 15th Air Force, which was established on November 1, 1943, and operated out of airfields in southern Italy. Its first commander was General Jimmy Doolittle, the daredevil pilot who on April 18, 1942, led a squadron of sixteen bombers from the aircraft carrier *Hornet* in a one-way mission to bomb Tokyo and other Japanese targets for the first time in World War II.[1] Starting in January 1944, it fell under General Nathan F. Twining, who was also the overall commander of the Mediterranean Allied Strategic Air Forces.[2] The key objectives for the 15th included enemy oil facilities, air force assets, air defenses, communications nodes, marshalling yards, and enemy ground forces. Its area of responsibility covered Italy, southern France, Austria, southern Germany, and all the Balkans. The 15th consisted of five bomb wings flying B-17 Flying Fortresses and B-24 Liberators. Each bomb wing had three to six bomb groups, and each group had three to four bomb squadrons. A separate fighter command flew P-37, P-48, and P-51 fighters that escorted the heavy bombers to protect them during their runs.

A separate group, the 2641st Special Group, had as its primary mission the insertion and supply of OSS teams in Italy and the Balkans, as well as the supply of partisan forces in these areas. The squadrons of the Special Group operated specially modified B-17 and B-24 aircraft painted all black with very limited identification markings. The aircrews were trained to conduct low-altitude night operations in which the pilot, navigator, and bombardier worked together to guide the aircraft to the drop zone. Such operations required flying over mountainous terrain followed by descents into deep valleys, in darkness, guided in the final approach by the eyes of the bombardier and the hands of the pilot. Final approach to the drop zones was at an altitude of a few hundred feet at near stall speeds.[3]

The crews of the heavy bombers had a different set of challenges. Their flights lasted several hours with the majority of that time spent over enemy territory. Although they flew and carried their bombings from altitudes of eighteen to twenty thousand feet, they were very vulnerable to enemy fighters that preyed on them and to the formidable German 88-mm and 128-mm antiaircraft guns. Known as flak, from the German acronym for *FlugzeugAbwehrkanone*, or aircraft-defense cannon, these guns fired shells as heavy as fifty pounds each. They exploded in shrapnel mushrooms around the Allied bombers, riddling their fuselage, taking out one or more of their engines, and causing significant losses in aircraft and personnel.

At the beginning of 1944, the Allies saw the disruption of oil supplies to the German military machine as a key strategic objective of the air campaign. To implement this objective, the 15th Air Force focused on destroying the complex of oil refineries and depots in Ploesti, Romania, which contributed about 30 percent of the entire Axis oil and gasoline supply. In a sustained campaign that lasted until August 19, 1944, bombers from 15th Air Force in daylight raids and night bombers from the Royal Air Force 205th Group crippled the refineries, reducing them to only 10 percent of their normal rate of activity and cutting their production rate by 60 percent. Four days later, Romania switched to the Allied sides and joined the war against Germany.

Over the course of the campaign, 15th Air Force and RAF bombers flew 5,287 sorties, dropping 12,870 tons of bombs. The cost was 237 heavy bombers, fifteen of them RAF, ten P-38 dive bombers, and thirty-nine escorting fighters downed all over the Balkans. More than 2,200 American airmen were lost.[4]

Hundreds of the downed airmen were captured and held as prisoners of war. Hundreds others bailed out over areas in Yugoslavia controlled by Communist-led partisans under Josip Broz Tito. In the summer of 1944 both the British and the OSS had large missions attached to Tito's headquarters and his partisan brigades. These missions located the downed airmen and arranged partisan escorts for them to the Adriatic coast where they were picked up by fast boats and evacuated to Italy. Nevertheless, there were still hundreds of men whose fates were not known and were listed as missing in action. There was a large swath of Yugoslav territory in the mountains of central Serbia under the control of anti-Communist forces lead by Drazha Mihailovich. There was hope at the 15th Air Force headquarters that some of their airmen had taken refuge in this area. The problem was that in the summer of 1944 the Allies considered Mihailovich a collaborator and maintained no connections with his headquarters.

* * *

It had been a stunning reversal of fortunes for Mihailovich. Only two years earlier, he had been the leader of the only resistance movement in Europe actively fighting and bloodying the Germans. He launched his movement right after the Germans conquered Yugoslavia in April 1941. After their quick victory, the Germans kept enough troops in the country to allow them to control the major cities, highways, and railroads, but left the countryside alone, especially in the mountainous areas of Serbia and Bosnia. This lax attitude gave an opening to members of the Yugoslav Royal Army, most of whom were Serbs, to move into these areas and establish control over them with relative ease. They revived the cherished Balkan tradition of harassing a much stronger enemy with small bands of warriors, who ambushed isolated enemy troops and quickly dissipated into the mountains whenever reinforcements arrived. The Serbian word for these small fighting units was *cheta*, so these men became known as chetniks. They wore the traditional Serb peasants' black lambskin cap with a skull-and-crossbones emblem in front.[5]

Mihailovich, an army staff officer himself, earned worldwide recognition as the leader of these bands. In 1942, *Time* magazine featured him on its cover and portrayed him as "the greatest guerrilla fighter in Europe." He received the most votes from the magazine readers for the Man of the Year Award.[6] Twentieth Century Fox began filming a movie, titled *Seventh Column* about the exploits of Mihailovich, in which Phillip Dorn played Mihailovich and Linda Darnell played his wife.[7] On the day when the Italian Armistice was announced, the *New York Times* opined, "In the event that Italy is completely knocked out of the war, the Adriatic Sea would be open to the British fleet. With air cover from bases on the east coast of Italy only 150 miles from Yugoslavia, any Allied attempt to join hands with Mihailovich, whose resistance to the Axis remains as unrelenting as ever, would be likely to prove a less hazardous operation than the initial Allied landings in Sicily."[8]

But the war took a different course. The Allies decided to open the front in Italy rather than in the Balkans. *Time* gave Stalin the Man of the Year award. At the Teheran Conference in December 1943, Churchill and Roosevelt decided to place their support behind Tito, who eventually became the only leader of Yugoslav resistance that the Allies recognized. And, by the time Twentieth Century Fox released its movie in 1943, Mihailovich had been completely erased from it. The Allied support for Mihailovich faded away rapidly. Even though his troops did not relent in their war against the Germans, Allied communications downplayed their role and portrayed Tito's partisans as the only ones doing the fighting.

When Mihailovich refused to step aside, civil war erupted in Yugoslavia, with chetniks and partisans spending more energy fighting each other than the Germans. In the spring of 1944, the Allies branded Mihailovich a Nazi collaborator. On May 29, 1944, the last Allied personnel attached to Mihailovich's headquarters and about forty airmen rescued by his forces left aboard transport airplanes from a secret airfield in the mountains. Airmen flying missions over the Balkans received instructions to bail out only on Tito partisan-held areas and avoid the chetniks who were said to turn shot-down Allied crews over to the Germans.[9]

The experience of many airmen who were shot down shows that the rumors were not true. On July 9, 1944, Lieutenant Richard L. Felman and nine other crewmembers of the B-24 *Never a Dull Moment* bailed out over chetnik territory on their way back from a strike at the Ploesti oilfields. When they fell into chetnik hands, they fully expected to be handed over to the Germans, or worse. Before every mission, the bomb crews were briefed to seek men with red stars on their hats, Tito's Communist partisans. Intelligence reported that Mihailovich and his chetniks were "cutting off the ears of American airmen and turning them over to the Germans." The Americans were surprised to find refuge and support among these people they were told to avoid. Felman said, "The Germans had seen us hit the silk, and immediately demanded that the local population surrender us. The peasants stood fast: they refused. The reprisal—their village was burned to the ground."[10]

The chetniks took Felman's group to Mihailovich's headquarters at Pranjani in the mountains of central Serbia, about ninety miles south of Belgrade. There were other rescued Americans there, and more kept arriving every day. They were divided into small groups and billeted at peasants' farmhouses, where they idled without much to do. Lieutenant Thomas K. Oliver, a pilot with the 756th Squadron, 459th Bomb Group, who had been in chetnik territory since the beginning of May, wrote, "We had lots of time to kill and would whittle out corncob pipes and smoke whatever local blend of tobacco we could lay our hands on." Oliver remembered that gypsy bands moving from village to village were the only entertainment available. "They would come into the village carrying an accordion and a couple of violins. Then that evening the whole village had a party. Food was brought out and everyone had dinner. Then the gypsies played and there was dancing in the public square. Next day the gypsies moved on." The stream of flights over their heads reminded them that the war continued. "It was an impressive event each time the 15th Air Force flew overhead on the way to targets in the Ploesti area," Oliver wrote. "We would first hear a faint buzzing sound, like bees. The sound would get louder and louder until it became a roar and the sky was filled with airplanes. We knew we could count on another two or three crews to join us on the ground."[11]

* * *

By the end of July 1944, there were close to 150 allied airmen in and around Pranjani. They wanted to get back to Italy as soon as possible, but there was no longer a direct communication channel between the chetniks and the Allied headquarters. Chetnik commanders said they had reported the presence of the Americans to their government in exile in Cairo who, in turn, had forwarded the information to the British. But they had received no response from the British. Gradually, the idea rose among the Americans of finding a way to send a direct message to the 15th Air Force in Italy. If they knew how many Americans were stranded in chetnik territory, they would be more likely to act than the British in Cairo. Oliver, who had become the unofficial leader of the group, met with Mihailovich and asked him to use one of his radio transmitters. Mihailovich was very willing to help the Americans establish communications with their headquarters.

The formulation of the message was a challenge in itself. The message would go over an open channel that the Germans could be monitoring. They had no prearranged signal security plans, so they had to find a way to let the headquarters recognize the message as an authentic one coming from American personnel and not an attempt from the Germans to draw them into a trap. They also had to establish a challenge and response code to ensure that any message they received was genuine from the headquarters and not from the Germans. The message could not be encoded and was formulated in plain English. So, they had to obfuscate the content enough for a German listening in to miss its meaning, but not to the point where the Americans would fail to understand it. Using Air Force slang and data points known only to a handful of people at his bomb group headquarters, Oliver sent the following message:

Mudcat driver to CO APO520

150 Yanks in Yugo, some sick. Shoot us workhorses. Our challenge first letter of bombardier's last name, color of Banana Nose's scarf. Your authenticator last letter of chief lug's name, color of fist on wall. Must refer to shark squadron, 459th Bomb Group for decoding.

Signed, TKO, Flat Rat 4 in lug order.[12]

The Yugoslav radio operator sent the message on the air as soon as it was ready. A British radio operator in Italy picked it up, recognized APO520 as the routing code for the 15th Air Force, and forwarded the message to its headquarters. There, they recognized the keywords "shark squadron" as a reference to the 756th Squadron of the 459th Bomb Group—all the airplanes of this squadron had shark teeth painted on their noses. So, they referred the message to Walt Cannon, the commanding officer of the squadron who decoded the message and recognized it as genuine.

The challenge—"first letter of bombardier's last name, color of Banana Nose's scarf"—could only be "B-White." Banana Nose was Sam Benigno, a pilot in the 756th Squadron who always wore a white scarf. The authenticator—"last letter of chief lug's name, color of fist on wall"—was "M-Red." The commander of the 459th Bomb Group, Colonel Munn, once wrote on the wall of the officers' club, "Each lug in the 459th sign here," and then signed, "M. M. Munn, Chief Lug." The "fist on the wall" in the message was a red fist on the club wall, part of the 15th Air Force emblem. Finally, there was no doubt that Oliver had sent the message. He had signed his name on the wall of the officers' club as "T. K. Oliver, Flat Rat 4" and had named his plane *The Fighting Mudcat*, because the catfish was a survivor.

As to the content of the message itself—"150 Yanks are in Yugo, some sick. Shoot us workhorses"—it was clear that 150 Americans were stranded in Yugoslavia and were asking for C-47 troop transporters to take them back. A workhorse was a C-47 in the US Air Force slang and not the draft animal. But, Oliver wrote later, "We hoped the literal-minded Germans would picture us executing old dobbin."[13]

Once the headquarters was satisfied with the authenticity of Oliver's message, they asked him to encode the following communications using his radio operator serial number, which made the exchange of messages easier. Oliver sent the coordinates of Pranjani. The headquarters sent word that they were preparing a team to come on the ground to assess the situation and prepare the evacuation. They directed preparations for a reception area and recognition signals.

The message that the airmen had waited for so long finally arrived: "Prepare reception for July 31 and subsequent night." A feeling of relief mixed with anxiety came over everyone, because no one could be certain that the effort would succeed. There was always fear that the Germans could get wind of the presence of such large numbers of Americans in the area and could attack at any moment. Pranjani, although free of Germans, was in a very precarious situation. Forty-five hundred Germans were garrisoned in the town of Chachak, only fifteen miles south. Just five miles from the landing zone as the crow flies there were another twenty-five hundred troops. The only security for the Americans came from the mountains around Pranjani and the Serbian population that sheltered and protected them. Lieutenant Felman described those anxious moments:

> The 31st finally came. General Mihailovich himself and about one thousand of his ragged troops came to visit us at our encampment near the tiny airstrip from which we expected to be evacuated. He held a review of his troops in our honor, and then talked to us through an interpreter. He told us how much he loved America and how sorry he was that he had not been able to do more for us, though his people had given us the best of everything they had. He also assured us that he had eight thousand troops deployed over a twenty-file mile area around our airstrip with orders to hold off the Germans at all costs until we were evacuated.
>
> That night at ten P.M. we were all down at the field. We waited for forty minutes silently. Exactly at 10:40 came the sound of motors, but we were afraid that coming so late it might be a German plane, so we decided not to light up the flares, since that might give up the whole show. Nothing happened the rest of that long night—nor on the next. Our spirits hit rock bottom.[14]

* * *

With the 15th Air Force's campaign against the Ploesti refineries reaching a crescendo at the beginning of summer 1944, the number of unaccounted aircrews grew significantly. General Nathan Twining created a special organization, the Air Corps Rescue Unit, under the command of Colonel George Kraigher, focused on organizing rescue and evasion missions to help the downed airmen. Kraigher had plenty of resources and materiel, but he needed men with experience in missions behind enemy lines and especially in chetnik territory.

The OSS office covering the Balkans, based in Bari, Italy, at the time, had experience getting American personnel stranded behind enemy lines to safety. One of the early successful operations came as a result of the efforts of Captain Lloyd G. Smith in Albania. On November 8, 1943, a Dakota C-53 medical transport plane was flying from Catania, Sicily, to Bari to pick up wounded personnel. There were thirteen nurses, thirteen medical technicians, and a crew of four aboard the plane. En route, the plane ran into stormy weather over the Mediterranean. The pilot lost his bearings and flew by mistake across the Adriatic Sea over Albania, where he was hit by antiaircraft fire. He managed to crash land in a field in central Albania, saving life and limb of the men and women aboard, but wrecking the plane. A group of Albanian partisans picked up the Americans and transported them over circuitous routes into the mountains to the south where the partisans were in firm control.

As in Yugoslavia, a civil war was going on in Albania at the time, with Communist-led partisans battling a loose coalition of nationalist forces for control of the country after the war. While the partisans controlled the interior of the country, the nationalists controlled the coastal areas—the only place where the Americans could hope to get a boat to return to Italy. The British Special Operations Executive had several missions attached to the partisans at the time. By the end of November, the Albanian partisans turned the American party over to one of these missions, who notified their headquarters in Cairo, who in turn notified their American OSS counterparts in Bari. They agreed that the British mission would accompany the Americans through partisan territory toward the coast. The OSS sent Captain Lloyd G. Smith, a Special Operations officer, to the Albanian coast with the task of cutting across nationalist territory, connecting with the British and American party, and bringing the Americans back to the coast where they would be evacuated by fast boats.[15]

Using a network of agents in nationalist territory and a supply of gold coins he had brought with him, Smith was able to travel inland, cross into partisan territory, collect the American party, and return with them through nationalist lines to the coast. The British officer who accompanied the Americans to the coast later paid tribute to "the people of the villages through which we passed, most of whom were extremely hospitable, even when a reprisal by the Germans would be the price to be paid." On January 9, 1944, two months after they had flown out of Sicily to pick up wounded GIs, a boat carrying ten nurses, thirteen medical technicians, four airmen, and Captain Smith of the OSS arrived at Bari, Italy. All were safe, except for three of the nurses who had been separated from the larger group during a German raid and were still in Albania.[16]

Smith told later a story of being in the washroom next to his office on January 9, 1944. He had just finished making his report on his trip to Albania and was shaving when he heard the door to his office open and footsteps approaching. He turned to see none other than General Donovan who had come to congratulate him on the mission. "President Roosevelt has followed the situation daily and will be most pleased to learn of the group's safe return," Donovan said. He paused, then continued, "That is, all but the three nurses who are still in Albania." After Smith reported that he had learned the whereabouts of the three nurses when he was in Albania, Donovan seated himself on the edge of Smith's desk and told him to choose any place he wanted to go on furlough for a week or two. "Pick something good," Donovan said, "because when you get back, you'll be going back to Albania for the three nurses left behind."[17]

At the beginning of February 1944, Captain Smith was back in Albania. From his refuge on the coast, he contacted his informers among the Albanian nationalist circles who confirmed that the three nurses were hiding in Berat, a city in central Albania under nationalist control. They had been there with a local family since mid-November, when a German raid forced them to lose connections with the rest of the American party. With the assistance of his Albanian contacts, Smith wrote a letter to the nationalist leaders, Mithat Frashëri and Kadri Cakrani, urging them to guarantee the safety of the three American nurses and conduct them safely to the coast for evacuation.

German operations in the area where Smith had taken refuge delayed plans for a quick exit. In the meanwhile, the nationalist leaders had provided local credentials and civilian clothes to the American nurses and kept them hidden from the Germans. When the situation in the coastal area returned to normal, they secured an automobile for the nurses and provided a truck full of their troops to escort them. Whenever German patrols stopped the convoy, the Albanians showed a letter by their leaders authorizing the trip toward the coast for the purpose of fighting partisans. Under this cover and protection, the three nurses were able to travel most of the way to the coast and met Captain Smith on March 19. They left the Albanian coast in the evening of March 21, and in the early-morning hours of March 22, 1944, they arrived in Italy after almost five months behind enemy lines.[18]

* * *

When Colonel Kraigher of the 15th Air Force's Corps Rescue Unit came asking for men with experience with the chetniks, the OSS provided a team of three operatives, code-named Halyard. Lieutenant George Musulin was the natural choice to command the team. He was born in the United States to parents who had emigrated from Yugoslavia and spoke Serbo-Croat very well. A bulky, 250-pound, five-foot-eleven former University of Pittsburgh tackle, steelworker, and physical education teacher, Musulin was far heavier than the 185 pounds that was the official limit for Army paratroopers. Yet he had no problems going through the rigorous physical regimen during the OSS training. The parachute instructors at Fort Benning placed bets each time he was due to jump as to how many panels in his chute would break. But Musulin had no problems earning his paratrooper wings, either. After completing the training in the United States, Musulin arrived in Algiers in June 1943 and on October 19, 1943, parachuted into central Serbia to assist the British liaison mission attached to Mihailovich's headquarters. At the time, he was the third American officer to parachute into Yugoslavia. Musulin remained with the chetnik forces until May 29, 1944, when the Allied mission received orders to withdraw.[19]

Musulin added to the Halyard team two fellow OSS operators who like him had completed missions in Chetnik territory. Master Sergeant Michael (Mike) Rajacich was his second-in-command and Arthur (Jibby) Jibilian would handle the radio communication. Rajacich was of

Serbian descent and spoke the language. Jibilian, the youngest member of the team at twenty-one years old, was of Armenian descent. An orphan at young age, he was raised by cousins in Toledo, Ohio. He was drafted in the Navy in March 1943 and was training as a radioman, learning Morse code and Navy signals, when OSS recruiters came to his base looking for volunteers for extremely dangerous missions in enemy territory. Jibilian volunteered, because, as he explained later, "I was more expendable as I had no immediate family and I might, just possibly, be more valuable with OSS than if I were on a ship."[20]

Musulin did not waist time in preparing his team for the Halyard mission. On July 3, he reported that they were ready to go and were prepared to drop blind if there was no time to prepare proper reception. But sending a mission into Mihailovich territory raised serious political concerns. If the Halyard team went in and rescued the airmen, could Mihailovich still be called a collaborator? The British and the Russians were vehemently opposed to anyone going into chetnik territory on any pretext. Legend has it that when Donovan described the proposed rescue plan to President Roosevelt, the president mentioned that the British would be unhappy with it. Donovan replied, "Screw the British, let's get our boys out."[21]

Several attempts to parachute the team in July were not successful. Musulin was convinced the British were sabotaging his mission. On one occasion, when they were above a landing area that a reception party in the ground had supposedly arranged, bright glares suddenly illuminated the plane followed by heavy small arms fire. This was either a trap or they had flown completely off their pinpoint and had almost dropped into the hands of Germans.[22] The failure to make the rendezvous on the night of July 31, 1944, over Pranjani raised further concerns. Musulin said later:

> By that time the three of us on the team were nervous wrecks. I was
> very worried about getting our mission off and about the morale of
> the team. I kept thinking about the plight of those airmen and I knew
> that their danger would increase with every flight we made to the
> area. The terrific tension of those long dangerous flights, the strain
> of being constantly alerted at the airfield, the unnerving knowledge

that each successive flight might mean being shot down, or a jump to
death, had us all pretty groggy. We had nearly had it a dozen times,
and we weren't even inside yet. I haven't enough praise for Mike
and Jibby, who kept taking it and were still game for another trip on
August 2.[23]

Musulin had no way of knowing that Lieutenant Oliver's men on
the ground did not light the recognition signals out of caution. He considered the failed contact as yet another British foul-up. For their next
flight, scheduled on August 2, 1944, Musulin requested and received
an American plane, an American crew, and an American jumpmaster.[24]

* * *

On the evening of August 2, Oliver and the rest of the American
airmen were again at the airstrip in Pranjani. At 2210 hours, they heard
airplane engines in the distance. As before, they could not be certain
whether it was friend or foe, but at that point they decided to risk it.
They lit up the flares in the prearranged signal and waited. The plane
flew overhead, and after about thirty seconds, it turned around and
headed for the airstrip. Everybody hid in the bushes, just in case it was
a German plane coming in to strife them. Oliver later remembered:

> The plane circled for about ten minutes, then came in very low over
> our strip. As it zoomed over our heads, we could see the big white
> star of the Air Force under the wings. With one voice the men let
> out a yell—the most terrific cheer I have ever heard went up in those
> Yugoslavian mountains. It was just like Ruth hitting a homer with the
> bases loaded in the World Series. The sight of that American plane
> was the first tangible evidence of rescue that we had seen since land-
> ing, and the boys nearly went crazy.[25]

The Chetniks collected the containers and packages that had parachuted from the plane. Musulin, Rajachich, and Jibilian arrived soon
after. They had landed in a cornfield two miles from the pinpoint—
Musulin crashed on a chicken coop and destroyed it, but a payment of

15,000 dinars ($10) was sufficient to compensate the Serbian farmer for the damage.[26] The Americans immediately began distributing the cigarettes and chocolates they had brought, but found that the airmen had far greater needs. Over two dozen of them were wounded or hurt, the majority were barefoot, and many of them had peasants' clothes mixed with their worn-out uniforms. Jibilian established contact with the headquarters in Bari that very morning, reported the safe arrival in the area, and requested an immediate airdrop of clothes, shoes, food, and medicine for more than two hundred airmen that had assembled around Pranjani. On the night of August 5, a large supply drop arrived, which improved the situation immensely.

As soon as he arrived, Musulin reviewed the condition of the airstrip where he had landed. It was nothing more than a natural plateau nestled among mountain peaks that surrounded it only a mile and a half to two miles in the distance. It was 150 feet wide and approximately 1,800 feet long. There were woods on one side and a sheer drop on the other. At one end of the strip there were some large trees and at the opposite end, a huge depression. Lieutenant Oliver and other Air Corps officers doubted an airplane could use it in its condition. They knew of at least two other fields more suitable than the one in Pranjani, but they were a fourteen-hour walk away. It was not practical to move all the airmen, including the sick and the wounded, over that distance. Furthermore, these remote locations did not have the strong defenses that the Chetniks had organized around Pranjani. On Mihailovich's orders, they had set up an outer and an inner protective ring around the mountains that surrounded the airstrip. Roadblocks controlled every road that the Germans could take to attack Pranjani. Sergeant Rajacich inspected the defenses and was satisfied to find hundreds of men in the outer and inner defensive positions ready to block any German attempt toward Pranjani.

For these reasons, Musulin decided to stick with the airstrip at hand and improve it to meet the minimum requirements for a C-47 transport plane to land. Under the guidance of the Air Corps officers, all the able-bodied airmen and three hundred local Serbs worked for days to improve the airstrip. The villagers provided sixty oxcarts, which they used to haul stones and dirt from nearby streams. Within a few days, they managed to extend the airfield by another seventy-five yards to give it the absolute minimum length for C-47 operations. On August 8, Jibilian radioed the headquarters that they were ready to receive the transports. Bari responded that the planes would arrive on the night of August 9.

Musulin set up an order of evacuation that made no distinction between officers and enlisted men. The sick and wounded had the highest priority. The rest of the airmen would board the planes based on the length of time they had been behind enemy lines. Musulin radioed Bari the concerns about the length of the airstrip. To enable the planes to take off on such a short runway, they needed to minimize the weight of the planes. They decided that only twelve men would board each plane. The flight crews stripped down the airplanes of all unnecessary materials and fueled them with only half a gasload, barely enough for the roundtrip flight from Bari to Pranjani.

There was a scare on the afternoon of August 9, when three German fighter planes suddenly appeared in the skies and buzzed the airstrip. Fortunately, all the laborers had finished work by that time. Sheep and cattle were grazing peacefully on the airfield and the fighters disappeared as quickly as they came. Nevertheless, Musulin was concerned that the Germans had discovered that there was something in the works down below. Unlike B-17 and B-24 heavy bombers that had their own protective guns and crews, C-47 planes were stripped-down transport planes with no protection of their own. They would fly in on the night of August 9 without fighter escort and would be easy targets of German night fighters if discovered. The image of these planes loaded with airmen blown to bits over the skies of Yugoslavia was a nightmare that hunted Musulin for the rest of the day. He received some reassurance when one of his Chetnik contacts reported in the evening that all was quiet in the closest town where the Germans had stationed a garrison. Afterward, Musulin described those tense hours as follows:

> By ten o'clock the designated first seventy-two airmen assembled at the strip. I had a Chetnick soldier stationed at each flare, ready to light them up at my signal. The airmen were all in top spirits,

but unfortunately, we of the Halyard Mission were not able to share in their exuberance. We waited there in the darkness for another hour and then in the distance we heard airplane engines. Everyone strained his ears and then the airmen began to cheer—they sounded like American planes.

Jibby was standing by me with an Aldis lamp to blink the proper identification signal. As they circled over for the first time, he blinked '*Nan*' and to our great joy received the correct reply, '*Xray*.' So far, so good—at least they had found us, and there had been no German interference. Now to get them down and off again. I gave the order to light up the ground fires and shot up a green flare, our signal that the landings were to commence.

The first plane started down with his landing lights on and headed toward our strip. The airmen were cheering and shouting, but as that plane came in the noise died down. Everyone was holding his breath and more than a few praying. Down and down he came, and then just before he put down his wheels, he gave it the gun and roared off, having overshot the field. The next plane, however, made a perfect landing and pulled at the end of the strip. The rest of them were supposed to stay aloft until I had the strip cleared, but they disregarded our signals and kept coming right in. I was afraid that there would be a pile up at the end of the strip, and had some of the Chetniks and airmen wheel the first plane down into a slopping depression off to one side at the end. This was done just in time, because the wings of the next plane just passed over the top of this first one as it wheeled about to taxi to one side. It missed by inches, and I could see that these night landings were too dangerous. The slightest mix-up, and the whole show might be ruined.[27]

Four C-47 transports brought in fresh supplies and a medical crew that would set up a field hospital for the airmen and the local villagers. In addition, Lieutenant Nick Lalich, another OSS officer of the Yugoslav section, arrived to assist Musulin in the evacuation operation. It took only a few minutes to empty the cargo from the planes and to board the departing airmen. Most of them stripped off their shoes and clothes and tossed them to their chetnik friends as they boarded the planes. No more than twenty minutes after landing, the first airplane started down the airfield to take off. Everyone watched anxiously as the plane began climbing in the air at the last possible moment. The other three planes followed, one of them brushing the trees at the end of the runway, but all were able to take off safely. Only forty minutes from the time they first noticed the engines of the approaching airplanes, Musulin and his men heard their noise fading in the horizon as the airplanes headed toward Bari.

* * *

Musulin sent a message to Colonel Kraigher with the returning airplanes requesting that the airlift operation resume that morning and continue until all the airmen at Pranjani were evacuated. Time was of the essence, because the Germans could discover the operation at any moment, and the conditions of the airstrip made night operations extremely dangerous. Jibilian spent the entire night at his radio trying to confirm that Bari had received the message and approved the request. Although they did not receive a positive response, Musulin send couriers around Pranjani, asking all the airmen to be ready at the airfield at 0800 hours on August 10. At just about that time, they heard a tremendous roar of engines in the distance. They thought it was a bombing party heading for Ploesti, first. Then, cries of jubilation went up when they recognized the shapes of six C-47s in the center of a protective umbrella of twenty-five P-51 Mustang fighters.

General Twining and Colonel Kraigher entrusted the mission of protecting the unarmed C-47s to fliers of the 332nd Fighter Group, known as the Red Tails, because of the distinctive bright red color they used to paint the tailfin of their planes. The Red Tails had a tremendous reputation among bomber crews of the 15th Air Force for not having lost a single bomber under their escort. They stuck close to the planes under their protection, unlike other escort fighters who often ventured away looking for enemy planes to add to their kill list while leaving the bombers exposed to surprise attacks. They were part of the contingent of African American fighter pilots that later became better known as the Tuskegee Airmen.[28]

As the flight formation approached the airfield, a number of the Red Tail fighters peeled off to strafe the roads leading to Pranjani and German installations nearby. Another group bombed the Kraljevo airfield, about thirty-five miles southwest. These diversionary actions kept the German fighters on the ground and left the impression that they were the main objective of the flights overhead. In the meanwhile, each of the six C-47s came in at a five-minute interval. Some of the pilots had to ground-loop their planes, turn them rapidly left and right after the wheels touched down, to slow down and stop before they ran off the end of the airstrip. Musulin described the jubilant atmosphere on the ground:

> The minute each plane taxied to a stop, it was surrounded by scream-ing women and girls who showered the planes, their crews, and the embarking Americans with garlands of flowers. The airmen going aboard were shouting boisterously, and as each group of twenty entered their designated plane, they would peel off their shoes and most of their clothing, and toss it to the cheering chetniks.
>
> The pilots and crews of the evacuating planes were caught up with the excitement of the occasion. All of them wanted souvenirs— daggers, guns, chetnik caps and *opankas*, the Serbian sandals made out of goatskin. None of them was in any hurry to leave, and I had trou-ble getting them to take off to clear the strip for the other planes.[29]

And yet, within minutes, all six C-47s had landed, loaded the air-men, and were back up in the air, circling slowly up the funnel of the surrounding mountains to gain altitude. Then, they formed a loose V formation, dipped the wings in salute to their friends on the ground, and headed toward Italy with the Red Tail fighters roaring around them. On the night of August 9 and the morning of August 10, the Halyard mission sent to safety 289 Allied personnel, including 251 Americans, six British, four French, nine Italians, seven Yugoslavs, and twelve Russians.

* * *

As soon as the planes left, the mission retreated into the mountains fearing a German attack against the airfield. It was the first time in five weeks that Musulin, Rajicich, and Jibilian felt relaxed. Evidently, the operation had gone undetected, so, as more airmen were rescued, they mounted another evacuation. In two consecutive nights, on August 27 and 28, fifty-eight Americans came out, together with two British officers attached to Tito's partisans that the chetniks had captured in battle.

Musulin received orders to return to Bari on the flights of August 28, as well. Officially, the reason was that he would work with the Air Force to prepare updated escape maps and proper briefings instructing the airmen on how to evade capture over chetnik territory. The real reason was that Musulin was too vocal a supporter of Mihailovich to suit the political line of the time, which continued to treat Mihailovich as a collaborator and Tito as the sole leader of Yugoslav resistance. Lalich took command of the Halyard team and remained with the chetniks until the end of December 1944, when the partisans finally overran their territory. Throughout its operations in Yugoslavia, the Halyard mission rescued 432 Americans and another 80 Allied personnel of other nationalities.

The achievements of the Halyard mission in Yugoslavia and the rescue of American nurses in Albania were examples of the networks that the OSS established to rescue thousands of airmen trapped behind enemy lines, which the *New York Times* compared to the Underground Railroad that had helped slaves escape during the Civil War. The numbers were impressive and included almost 1,800 personnel rescued in Yugoslavia, Albania, and Greece; 1,350 in Romania; 342 in Bulgaria; 275 in Switzerland; and 226 in Italy. In a letter of commendation to Donovan, General Henry H. Arnold, commanding general of the Army Air Forces, hailed the OSS work, declaring: "The success of the rescue missions has been directly dependent upon excellent OSS cooperation. Please accept my sincere thanks for the assistance your organization has rendered to the Army Air Forces."[30]

* * *

General Mihailovich remained with his Chetniks until the end. He turned down an OSS offer presented through Lieutenant Lalich to take the last American flight out of his areas in Yugoslavia to Bari at the end of December 1944. Tito's Communist regime captured him in

1946 and put him on trial. Dozens of the American fliers who had been rescued by his men petitioned the State Department to intervene with the Yugoslav government on behalf of Mihailovich. It was a fruitless effort. Mihailovich was sentenced to death, executed by a firing squad on July 17, 1946, and buried in an unmarked grave.

The Truman administration awarded Mihailovich the Legion of Merit in 1948 for his support for the Allies, especially during Operation Halyard. The citation read, "Through the undaunted efforts of his troops, many United States airmen were rescued and returned safely to friendly control." The award remained secret in order not to antagonize Tito who, at the time, had become a wild card in the Cold War by breaking ranks with Stalin and taking Yugoslavia out of the Soviet bloc. Almost sixty years later, on May 9, 2005, a group of participants in Operation Halyard, including Arthur Jibilian, traveled to Serbia and formally presented the award to Mihailovich's daughter, Gordana.[31]

CHAPTER 13
Mission Peedee-Roanoke

The end of 1944 was the low point in the struggle of the Italian partisans across northern Italy and especially in the Sixth Operational Zone. The Nazi-Fascist rastrellamenti or cleanup operations of November–December 1944 had forced the partisans to abandon the liberated areas and retreat to the heights of the Apennine Mountains. The Germans elevated the terror policy to a level never seen before to drive a wedge between the resistance and the local population. They planned raids with a scientific precision to cover the entire territory the partisans once controlled. Where before they shot civilians, now they hanged them; where before they hanged people on the noose, now they hung them on the meat hook. Whereas before they arrested family members of the partisans, now they pillaged their houses, as well. The Fascists created special units specializing in antipartisan warfare. Field tribunals, the dreaded Cogu (*Contro-guerriglia* or anti-guerrilla), roamed the countryside passing swift judgments and showing no mercy.[1] The Germans offered special inducements to soldiers for *Baenderkampftage*, or days of service in antipartisan operations.[2]

The morale of the partisans suffered another blow when British General Harold Alexander, the Allied theater commander, broadcast over the airwaves on November 13 his new instructions to the Italian patriots:

The summer campaign that began on May 11 and continued without interruption until the Gothic line was breached is over. Now
begins the winter campaign. . . . The patriots should cease their
activities and prepare for the new phase of the war and to face the
new enemy, the winter. . . . General Alexander's orders to the patriots are as follows: cease large-scale organized operations, conserve
the ammunition and materiel, and be ready for new orders . . . be
guarded, be in defense, but at the same time be prepared to attack
the Germans and the Fascists. . . . The patriots should be prepared
for the approaching advance.[3]

The announcement was well-meaning and reflected the realities of
the situations at the time. The bad weather had curtailed the ability of
the theater air force to fly supply missions over the partisan-held areas,
and there was fear that it would not be possible to provide adequate
food, clothing, and equipment to the partisans during the cold months.
But the effect it had on the morale of the partisans was devastating. It
lead to accusations, repeated with much more vigor after the war, that
Alexander had intentionally tried to sabotage the position of the Communists in Italy with this move.

The OSS protested the curtailing of aid and made all efforts to
deliver as many supplies as possible. Beginning in December, the
aid was provided under the umbrella of the tripartite agreement
forged between the Allied Command for the Mediterranean theater, the Italian government, and the CLNAI (National Liberation
Committee of Upper Italy). The agreement recognized the CLNAI
as the de facto government in German-occupied Italy. To support
the activities of the CLNAI, the OSS and SOE funded in equal
parts a monthly budget of 160 million lire ($1.6 million), which
increased to 350 million lire in March 1945. They distributed funds
to partisan groups under the command of the CLNAI according
to regional priorities established by the Allied command. Monthly
expenses per partisan were estimated at 1,500 lire per month.
The funds also covered couriers, transportation, and relief for the
families of fallen partisans or civilians who had suffered from the
Nazi-Fascist reprisals.[4]

The Sixth Operational Zone remained one of the most important areas for the Allied command given its position in the rear of the Gothic Line. While the American Fifth Army prepared for the coming spring offensive, it looked to the partisans in the zone to continue to harass the Germans and disrupt their communications and the flow of troops and supplies to the front. In addition, the partisans were expected to counter the scorched-earth tactics that Germans were likely to follow as they retreated north. German engineers had demonstrated a great mastery in mining key infrastructure installations and setting booby traps all over before abandoning cities or positions.

General Mark Clark, the Fifth Army commander, had seen the destructive genius of the Germans at work in several occasions. When the Fifth Army entered Naples on October 1, 1943, Clark found a city in ruins. Describing his drive through the deserted streets, he wrote in his memoirs that "there was little triumphant about our journey." The Germans had left behind "a city of ghosts."[5] To make matters worse, the Germans had hidden a series of time-delayed mines in the city's central post office building, which had become a shelter for homeless civilians. On the morning of October 7, a series of violent explosions ripped through the building, leaving it in ruins and killing at least a hundred, mostly civilians but also members of the 82nd Airborne Division.

When the US 34th Infantry Division liberated the city of Livorno on July 19, 1944, it found the port in ruins and the city covered in explosive devices that took days to clear. Clark described the situation as follows: "As soon as we mastered one trick, we immediately discovered that the Germans had another up their sleeve . . . bars of chocolate, soap, a packet of gauze, a wallet, or a pencil, which, when touched or disturbed, exploded and killed or injured anyone in the vicinity. Others were attached to windows, doors, toilets, articles of furniture, and even bodies of dead German soldiers. We found over twenty-five thousand of these hideous devices, and many of our lads were killed or injured as a result."[6]

There was a serious concern that the Germans would follow the same scorched-earth tactics against the port city of Genoa, the maritime gateway to northern Italy, which the Allies needed to capture in working conditions to ship food and other supplies to the civilian population after the liberation. The Allied command determined that the partisans of the Sixth Operational Zone, with support and training from the Allies, could play a key role in protecting the port facilities, factories, electric power plants, and other infrastructure objects in and around Genoa. Thus, immediately after the Walla Walla mission returned at the end of December 1944, the OSS activated another team of OGs, code-named Peedee, to be parachuted on the mountains where the Sixth Zone command had retreated.

* * *

The Peedee team was headed by Captain Les Vanoncini and included five NCOs.[7] The team completed a dry run over the target drop zone on January 17, 1945, but was unable to see the ground signals due to the snow that was falling at the time. They flew in the next day in clear weather and found the drop zone easily with clear landing signals prepared by the reception party on the ground. Three feet of snow that covered the ground made the landing very easy for all except for Technical Sergeant Ignatius Caprioli, who landed on the only bare spot in the area, slipped on the ice, and hit his head hard. He was immediately placed under the care of the zone doctor and confined in bed for five days.

The Peedee assignment was to work closely with a SOE mission that parachuted with them on the same night. They would work with seven thousand partisans of the Sixth Zone to prevent the Axis troops from retreating into the Alpine redoubt where the Nazis were rumored to be preparing for their final stand. The SOE team had the responsibility to collect intelligence about the enemy forces and provide the information to the advancing Allied forces, whereas the American OGs would provide combat training and military instruction, as well as coordinate the dropping of arms, ammunition, and supplies to the partisans.

When Peedee arrived in the area, they found the partisans in total disarray, lacking weapons, and low in morale. A general confusion existed in the zone as a result of the German drive against the partisans that had started in December and continued through the month of February. Just three days after the team's arrival, the Germans probed the partisan positions near the Sixth Zone headquarters in Carrega, about forty miles northeast of Genoa. The six OGs and a group of thirty partisans responded with bazookas, heavy machine guns, and other weapons the team had brought. The Germans held for half an hour, then took civilian hostages in a nearby village and retreated, using them as shields. They returned in force five days later, on January 26, when six hundred Germans and Fascists attacked Carrega from two directions and forced the mission and the Sixth Zone command to take to the mountains in three feet of snow and under a temperature of twenty degrees below zero. Over the next several days, the OGs and thirty to forty partisans from the Sixth Zone command were constantly on the run, moving from one mountain location to the other, leaving everything behind except for the clothes and the equipment they could carry.

The Germans controlled the major highways—Route 1 between La Spezia and Genoa, Route 35 between Genoa and Alessandria, and Route 45 between Genoa and Piacenza—and all the important secondary roads in the area. In addition, they captured all the major towns and villages across the zone and pushed the partisans into remote areas in the mountains and forests. The Sixth Zone command sent half of the partisans home for the winter and struggled to provide food, clothing, and shelter for the remaining ones. Captain Vanoncini, or Captain Van as the OGs and the partisans called him, wrote about patrols out on duty with only burlap sacks wrapped around their feet.

Under these conditions, the Peedee team had their own share of hardships. Their movements were limited during the months of January and February due to the German operations, and the very cold weather, with temperatures often between 0 and -10 degrees Fahrenheit. The deep snow covering the ground had rendered the mountain paths impassible except for emergencies. The living conditions were very poor. Fleeing from an enemy attack, the six OGs lost their sleeping bags within a few days of their arrival and had to spend many a nights in barns and stalls with only straw for cover. Bathing was infrequent and there were no facilities or warm water. Lice infections and scabies rashes became a constant nuisance and presented serious health hazards.

* * *

Despite the difficulties, the six OGs remained preoccupied in the first weeks of their mission with establishing and maintaining contact with the division commanders in the zone to assess their needs, provide encouragement, and coordinate as many supply drops as possible. They split into groups of two and three, visited with the partisan brigades and divisions in the zone, and identified suitable drop zones closer to the units where supplies began to arrive. They located and prepared twelve new pinpoints, which, in addition to six pinpoints that Team Walla Walla had identified earlier, made for a total of eighteen drop zones used to fly in resources for the partisans.

From the beginning, the team set up a rigorous procedure for handling the material parachuted into the drop zones, to ensure accountability and fair distribution of the supplies. The first rule that Vanoncini established was that at least one mission member would always be present at the pinpoints during the drops. This often required that the OGs attach themselves to the partisan units for extended periods of time and travel for three to four hours to reach the pinpoints where the supplies arrived. The OGs took with them thirty to forty armed partisans to organize the reception, set out the signals, and provide security around the drop zone. Two men counted the number of parachutes and free bundles as they left the plane to ensure later that the partisans retrieved and accounted for all of them.

After the planes had completed the drop, groups of partisans first collected the containers attached to parachutes, then all the bundles, and counted them. They loaded everything on mules and took them to a protected and well-hidden place nearby that served as a makeshift logistics depot. Here, the Peedee team member responsible for the drop zone supervised the opening of containers and bundles and made an accurate inventory of all the material received. He allotted the material to the partisan brigades in the area based on requests that they had filed with the mission. Mule trains were loaded with these allotments and began the trek to take the newly arrived supplies to the various partisan brigades. The goal was to have all the supplies received, accounted for, and on the way to the partisans within a matter of hours, not only because they were badly needed but also to prevent the Germans from raiding the drop zones and seizing the materials.

The parachutes were a prized commodity in Italy at the time, just as they were in France. Vanoncini gave strict orders to the OGs to never give away or sell any chutes. Instead, they were turned over to the zone command to do with them as they wished. The zone command traded them for money or used the material to make clothes for the partisans or sheets for the area hospitals. Sometimes, they gave them to the families whose houses had been burned down, whose sons were killed or injured, or whose daughters had been raped by the Nazis and the Fascists.

Another rule that Vanoncini set from the beginning was that all material coming into the zone was for the partisans unless explicitly marked for the mission. This meant that all the food that came by plane was off limits for the OGs because it was not specifically marked for them. Throughout the four-month mission, the Peedee men received only eight boxes of 10-in-1 food parcels, field rations that provided one meal for ten men. Vanoncini insisted on purchasing food for his staff in towns and in villages nearby or at discounted prices from the partisan organization responsible for distributing the supplies among the partisan units. Partisans tried to give the Americans some of the supplies coming in, but they always refused. "The impression this attitude made on the partisans was everlasting," one OG wrote later, "even though our stomachs were getting smaller and smaller."

Even when the OGs were on assignment to the drop zones, they had to pay their way for food and shelter, not only when they could find accommodation in an occasional hotel room but also when they stayed in private homes or even barns with nothing more than straw for cover. A detailed accounting by Vanoncini at the end of the mission noted that the Peedee team spent 1,634 man-days behind the lines, and food costs ran close to six dollars per man per day, which also covered housing when available. When their cigarettes ran out, they bought them at a rate of 110 lire for ten cigarettes. Most men smoked at least twenty cigarettes a day, which amounted to $12 per day or $600 in total spent for cigarettes. Hiring the mules at $10 a day cost $400. Local shoemakers made three pair of shoes for the OGs at $35 a pair. The mission also provided $100 each to two American prisoners of war to carry them through the lines. They paid $600 to couriers, informers, and guides they hired during the four months in terrain. Vanoncini gave $150 each to two families mistreated by Wehrmacht soldiers from the Caucasus, known as Mongols, for sheltering the Americans in their houses. "The ladies of the house were badly beaten about the face and back by waist belt," Vanoncini wrote. "All dishes were broken and clothes taken away. For this suffering, we gave them the money, only a small token for the damage the Mongols committed."

Securing the money was the chief worry for the OGs. When Sergeant Caprioli landed hard and hurt himself on the night of January 18, he also lost his wallet with $500 in Swiss francs and 50,000 lire. During German pursuits in the first few weeks, the team lost nine pieces of gold and $400 worth in lire. During a visit to one of the partisan units, two OGs stayed in a hotel to sleep. During the night, someone entered the room through the latrine and took both wallets containing eight pieces of gold and 72,000 lire. The money "gave us more bother than it was worth," said Vanoncini after the mission ended.

* * *

Between the end of January and the end of April 1945, Peedee organized the reception and distribution of 115 planeloads of arms, ammunition, explosives, clothes, and food supplies for the partisans. The partisans received 1,100 Sten and M3 machine guns, 2,000 automatic and semiautomatic M1 and Mauser rifles, 35 mortars, 73 bazooka rocket launchers, and 25 Piat bomb launchers.[8] With the arrival of spring and the intensification of the fight against the Germans, supply drops included propaganda materials, movie reels, motorcycles, gasoline, and even a printing press and printing paper, which the zone command put to use to print daily newspapers for the liberated areas.

At this time, there was a considerable increase of partisan activities in the Sixth Zone and the demand for the services of the Peedee mission far outpaced what Vanoncini and his team of five could provide. In addition, partisan commanders from neighboring regions to the north were asking for Allied teams to parachute into their areas. The Italian OGs headquarters in Sienna decided to expand the size of the Peedee team and to send a new team of thirteen OGs, code-named Roanoke, to the Garibaldi formation commanded by Domenico Mezzadra, known by the battle name Americano. Mezzadra had grown the brigade he commanded at the time when he met Captain Wheeler of the Walla Walla mission into a full division, the Alliotta division.

On March 7, 1945, Lieutenant Rawleigh Taylor, commanding officer of Roanoke parachuted alone into a drop zone the Peedee team prepared. He traveled with two OGs from Vanoncini's group to the Oltrepò Pavese area to assess the partisan movement there, which he found stronger than originally thought. Americano's Alliotta division was the best in the zone. It counted six hundred men organized in three brigades. Taylor described Americano as "an aggressive leader, very quiet, who fought only for liberty, and was well loved by his men and the people in the area." In addition to the Alliotta division, three other divisions operated in the area with another 1,200 partisans in their ranks.

The overall commander of the partisan divisions was Italo Pietra, battle name Edoardo, who had just been nominated deputy-commander of the Sixth Zone under Miro. Taylor described Edoardo as "an effective band leader who claimed he was no politician," although later events would make clear to the American mission that Edoardo was a politician first and a partisan second. Italo Pietra was born in 1911 and served in the Italian army during the war in Ethiopia in 1935 and in Albania in 1940. He joined the resistance after September 8, 1943, and functioned as the inspector general of the Communist-affiliated Garibaldi brigades in the Oltrepò Pavese before assuming command of all the partisan units in the zone.[9]

Upon making his initial assessment, Taylor radioed for the full Roanoke team to arrive as soon as possible. They parachuted in two drops on March 21 and April 9, 1945. With these same drops, another eleven OGs arrived to reinforce Vanoncini's Peedee team. Thus, by the beginning of April 1945, about thirty OGs were organizing supply drops and supporting close to ten thousand partisans in a one-thousand-square-mile area between Genoa, Pavia to the north, and Piacenza to the northeast.

* * *

In addition to coordinating supplies, the OGs set up weeklong training schools that they held at each partisan brigade location. The focus of the schools was the maintenance, use, and practice of firing the weapons supplied by the drops, especially mortars, machine guns, bazookas, and Piat guns. The goal was to make the partisan crews operating these weapons familiar to the point of being able to strip and put them together blindfolded. The instruction also included teaching of sabotage techniques, manipulating explosives, and setting up booby traps. In addition, the OGs covered tactical topics related to guerrilla warfare, such as setting up ambushes, positioning weapons for maximum effect, and withdrawing quickly to minimize losses.

Frequently, the OGs joined the partisans in action to demonstrate in practice what they taught during training and to instill courage and confidence in their men. On one occasion, on March 24, 1945, the partisans attacked an enemy stronghold in the village of Loco, which controlled the important Route 45 between Piacenza and Genoa. The attack had been bogged down because the Germans had fortified a building and taken civilian hostages for protection. One of the OGs, Sergeant Mario Tarrantino, took a bazooka, exposed himself to enemy fire, and fired two rounds near the target to draw the Germans' attention. Observing carefully the return fire from the Germans, Tarrantino was able to pinpoint one of their defensive strongpoints. Still under fire, he fired two more rounds directly at this position, killing five Germans and forcing the remaining thirty-two to surrender without harming the civilians. Eliminating this stronghold removed the last point of control the Germans had on this important highway, which remained in the hands of the partisans until the end of the war. After the war, Vanoncini recommended Tarrantino for the Silver Star award for the courage he displayed in the action.

The efforts of the Peedee and Roanoke missions to equip and train the partisan units had a strong effect on the morale of the partisans and on their ability to stand up to the Germans and the Fascists. Vanoncini compared the remarkable change in the performance of one partisan division in the zone, the Garibaldi Pinan Cichero division, between the end of January 1945 when he first met them and the end of April. In January, "thirty Germans came through the entire division and got as far as the Zone command headquarters, absolutely raising havoc among the partisans," Vanoncini wrote. "Three months later, 1,500 Germans and Mongols made the same attack against only one brigade of this division, and after six days of heavy fighting, the enemy retreated leaving behind many dead and wounded."

By this time, the division had 1,400 men in uniform organized in three brigades; another six hundred sympathizers in civilian clothes worked in the cities and towns around the area to collect information on the enemy movements and to secure provisions for the armed fighters. Between January 18 and April 15, 1945, the Pinan Cichero division conducted seventeen attacks against enemy positions, command posts, headquarters, and supply dumps. They carried out 119 raids against telecommunication and transportation lines, destroying five locomotives, eighty-eight railroad cars, and twenty-six trucks. They inflicted almost 1,200 enemy casualties, including 281 killed, 341 wounded, and 569 taken prisoner.

* * *

The members of the OG missions influenced the partisans in another important way: quietly and through actions more than words, they demonstrated the values and moral principles of the American way of life. The majority of the Italian partisans around them were young and had been under Fascism all their lives. They had no idea how democracy or other forms of government worked. They understood well how Fascism had wrecked Italy and were excited at the prospects of rebuilding a new life for their country after the war. Speaking with and interacting with the Americans soldiers of their age and with

with similar background was a way for the partisans to visualize what their future might be like.

Philip Francis, the medic of the Peedee team, told a vignette fifty years after the war that provides a glimpse of how this intellectual transfer happened. On April 12, 1945, Francis traveled to the town of Varzi, halfway between Genoa and Piacenza, where the headquarters of Team Roanoke were located. He was excited to make the trip because the medic of the Roanoke team was Leo Francis, Philip's identical twin brother, whom he had not seen since leaving Sienna ten days before. "What a heartwarming event for both of us to meet behind the enemy lines!" Philip wrote. "Twins from a small rural area of Pittsburgh, sons of a farmer, coal miner, and Italian immigrants named Francesconi helped Italy free itself from the Nazis and Fascists. To my knowledge, this was the first time American twins had ever met behind enemy lines."[10]

After greeting his brother Leo, Philip was introduced to Lieutenant Robert Gallagher, deputy commander of Roanoke, Corporal David Waggoner, and other members of the team who had been parachuted just three days ago on April 9. They all went inside the headquarters, and Philip Francis described what happened next:

> We were in a room when an officer of the partisans burst in with an electrifying announcement, "The war is over, we surrender, President Roosevelt died." Lieutenant Gallagher acted quickly to calm the partisans, not knowing if the rumor was true. He said, "Let us all stand for two minutes of silence to honor our departed Commander-in-Chief, Franklin D. Roosevelt." After two minutes, Lieutenant Gallagher spoke, "And we will continue the fight under our new Commander-in-Chief." He hesitated for a moment because we had all left the USA prior to the election and most of us did not know who held the office of the Vice-President.
>
> The voice of Dave Wagonner from Missouri said, "I believe it is our former Senator, Harry S. Truman." Lieutenant Gallagher then stated, "We will continue the battle against the enemy under our new Commander-in-Chief, Harry S. Truman." About ten more partisans burst into the room, amazed that we could so soon forget our great

leader. We explained that Roosevelt was not elected for life but for a period of time and that our Constitution provides for an immediate replacement in case the President dies. The partisans looked at the Americans with great surprise and enthusiasm and were ready to go destroy the enemy. Thank God for the wisdom of Lieutenant Gallagher that was able to calm down the partisans that day![11]

Partisans at all levels recognized and appreciated the contribution of the OGs in strengthening the partisan units in the Sixth Zone. In a letter to General Truscott, commanding general of the US Fifth Army, on March 9, 1945, Miro, commander of the zone, expressed the deepest thanks on behalf of his commanders and partisans for the work done by the Peedee team:

> The behavior of the mission and of its commander has generated the full sympathy and admiration of everyone. These men, besides working day and night to enable us to receive drops of arms, munitions, clothes, and food, after enduring great risks and pains during the mop up operations, volunteered to participate in battles in our area, showing their courage and ability, especially with the bazookas. After coming victorious from the recent engagements, our formations are well armed, supplied, and ready for the decisive battle: no obstacles will stop the impetus of our brave Garibaldini and your men will be at our side, welcomed guests and precious comrades.

* * *

The presence of strong partisan formations behind the German lines that were well-equipped, trained, and willing to fight was a welcome development for the Allied planners as they moved into the final stages of preparing the spring offensive in Italy. Through the end of March 1945, the instructions of the Allied command to the partisans transmitted through the OG missions were to strengthen their bands and conduct sabotage activities but not to engage in large-scale actions until the order came for the all-out assault. At this time, the front line was in approximately the same positions as it had been in October

1944, when the Allied halted their advance. It ran from a point about twenty-five miles south of La Spezia, on the Ligurian coast, generally northeast to the southern tip of Lake Comacchio on the Adriatic Sea. General Clark who now commanded the 15th Army Group, set April 9, 1945, as D-Day for the assault. Fifth Army, on the left, was to make the main effort to take or isolate Bologna and round up the German armies south of the Po River before crossing it. The plan called for the 92nd Infantry Division to launch a diversionary attack along the Ligurian coast toward Massa and La Spezia four days before Fifth Army's main attack toward Bologna.

In early February 1945, the 92nd had tried to take the city of Massa, which would bring the key port city of La Spezia, twenty miles to the north, within striking distance of American artillery and create an opportunity to break through the Gothic Line at its easternmost point. The Germans put up a ferocious resistance, deploying thousands of troops supported by field artillery and tanks. For the first time, the Germans put to use the coastal gun batteries at Punta Bianca, which could lob deadly shells onto the American positions ten to twelve miles away. Shells from these guns left craters on the ground so large that tanks literally fell into them. Within days, the 92nd lost 1,100 men, including fifty-six officers, and twenty-two tanks. The assault was called off and the 92nd had to be refitted in preparation for the spring offensive.[12]

The immediate objective for the 92nd's diversionary attack was Massa. To avoid the heavy coastal guns at Punta Bianca, whose fire had largely been responsible for smashing the February attempt to cross the flat plain before Massa, the attack would be made to the east through the mountain ridges to capture heights dominating the town and then force the Germans to evacuate their positions. The attack would then proceed toward La Spezia.

The offensive began at 0500 hours on April 5 with air attacks on enemy positions and on the coastal guns at Punta Bianca and with supporting fire from British destroyers off the coast. After a ten-minute artillery barrage, two regimental combat teams, the 370th on the left and the 473rd on the right, moved out abreast. The Massa outskirts were only five miles ahead, but the Germans put up a staunch resistance, beating back repeated assaults by the American infantry units and their supporting armored battalions. While the fighting raged in the plains, a third regimental combat team, the 442nd, battled the enemy in the mountains ridge by ridge, blowing away bunkers and fortifications with bazookas and grenades.

On April 10, the 442nd outflanked Massa from the hills to the east and the Germans evacuated the town. The 442nd continued its advance through nearly impassable mountain terrain and reached Carrara of the famous marble quarries on the morning of April 11.[13] La Spezia lay less than twenty miles to the north, but it took the 92nd another two weeks of bitter fighting to capture it. The Germans poured reserve infantry units of the 135th Fortress Brigade and a battalion of the 90th Panzer Division to reinforce their positions and slow down the advance of the 92nd. These reserves were committed just in time to prevent their use against the main attack of the Fifth Army that began on April 14, 1945.

On the coast, the guns at Punta Bianca had survived the aerial and naval bombardment and continued to pound the 92nd positions, especially on Massa and Carrara. But soon these guns came within range of the American artillery units. All thirty-six 76-mm guns of the 679th Tank Destroyer Battalion were assigned to neutralize the coastal guns. An 8-inch howitzer was brought up to aid them. When a German gun fired, the tank destroyers, operating on prearranged signals, answered with 60 to 180 rounds, the first landing within forty-five seconds after forward observers called for it. In six days the tank destroyers fired 11,066 rounds on the coastal guns. By April 19, the guns on the east side of the German strongpoint had stopped firing, but fire continued from those on the west side. It took another twenty-four hours of close-range fire to destroy them, but on April 20, the guns at Punta Bianca finally fell silent.[14] Shortly after, the Germans evacuated La Spezia to avoid being trapped behind the lines.

While the 92nd Infantry Division was fighting its way north along the Ligurian coast, the rest of the US Fifth Army and the British Eighth Army punched through the German defenses along the entire length of the Gothic Line. Bologna fell on April 21, and by the 23rd the Allied units were rolling down the northeastern slopes of the

Apennines into the flatlands of the River Po Valley. Both the Fifth and Eighth Armies were now able to take advantage of the flat terrain and excellent road network in the Po Valley. Using mobile and armored units, they launched a fast-paced offensive to reach the Po River and the Alpine foothills ahead of the Axis forces, encircle, and destroy surviving enemy troops before they escaped through the Alps.[15]

The Allied planners left the entire northwestern Apennines area to the partisans of the Sixth Zone to liberate. On orders from the Fifteenth Army Group transmitted through the Peedee and Roanoke Missions, the partisans moved to block the main communication routes between La Spezia, Genoa, Alessandria, and Piacenza, forcing the Germans to concentrate their forces in garrisons in the major cities. On April 23, Italian partisans entered La Spezia. Elements of the 92nd arrived in the city the next day on their way toward Genoa.[16]

* * *

The big prize was the city of Genoa, and the Sixth Zone command assumed the responsibility of coordinating the military preparations in the mountains with the actions inside the city undertaken by Genoa's *Comitato di Liberazione Nazionale* (CLN), or National Liberation Committee. Captain Vanoncini had held several planning meetings with the Sixth Zone command to discuss how to take the city and prevent the Germans from destroying it and the important port facilities there. In April 1945, the German and Fascist forces in and around Genoa amounted to the strength of an entire division. Strong detachments of the German navy reinforced by mobile artillery units defended the port. The 135th Fortress Brigade had set up heavy artillery batteries on the heights of Mount Moro that loomed over the city. The Germans had placed demolition charges throughout Genoa and the entire port area, including the main bridges and tunnels leading into the city, the water and power plants, and all the main industrial objects in the city. Ships, piers, and cranes in the port had been mined to render it unusable.[17]

The breakthrough of the 15th Army Group along the entire Gothic Line became the catalyst for the events that led to the liberation of

Genoa. In the evening of April 23, after the Fascist authorities had abandoned the city, the German commander, General Günther Meinhold, sent word through the church authorities that the German troops would abandon the city and the region in four days. They would not destroy the city as long as they had freedom of movement to complete their evacuation. The CLN leaders met overnight to discuss the offer and decided to launch the pre-agreed operational plan to take the city.

Between four and five o'clock in the morning of April 24, the first shots rang in Genoa. By 1000 hours, the insurgents controlled the city hall, the post office, police headquarters, and the prison. By nightfall, action squads had paralyzed all train transportation in Liguria and toward Piedmont, effectively cutting off the main routes of retreat for the German forces. Civilians armed with weapons they had captured from fleeing Fascists or German soldiers set up ambushes to prevent German columns from leaving the city. Fighting raged in the city center, at the port, and in different suburbs where Germans units held strong positions. There was a serious risk that the Germans would overcome their initial surprise, begin to coordinate their actions, and suffocate the insurgents in a bloodbath. Disconcerting news came of German regiments approaching from La Spezia. The atmosphere became ominous when an emissary from General Meinhold arrived with an ultimatum: the Germans would open fire on Genoa with the heavy guns from Mount Moro and mobile artillery from the port unless they were allowed to retreat in an orderly fashion.

The CLN leaders found themselves in a precarious situation. The Americans were at least sixty miles away and the partisans of the Sixth Zone had yet to arrive from the mountains to offer assistance. Nevertheless, the city leaders held fast. They responded to the ultimatum by threatening to kill over one thousand German prisoners already in their hands and to execute all those taken thereafter as war criminals. The cardinal of Genoa also intervened and after long conversations with the German consul, convinced him to intercede with the German command to avoid the bombardment of the city.

The fighting resumed the next morning, April 25, with action groups expanding their control over the city block by block. The radio station fell into the hands of the insurgents and began broadcasting on behalf of the CLN. A big breakthrough came when General Meinhold himself traveled in an ambulance from his headquarters outside the city to the see of Genoa's cardinal and requested to meet directly with the leaders of the CLN. The negotiations lasted from 1500 to 2000 hours on April 25 and concluded with an agreement to surrender all the German armed forces under General Meinhold to the volunteers of the Military Command of Liguria in return for their treatment as prisoners of war under international laws and their transfer to the Allied command in Italy. The agreement went into effect on April 26, at 0900 hours. It was the only case during World War II when regular military units surrendered to volunteer forces.

Not all the Germans abided by the terms of the surrender. The German navy commander holding the port sent two officers to say that they had sentenced Meinhold to death on orders from Hitler and they were ready to begin bombing the city with the heavy guns on Mount Moro if the insurgents continued their attacks. By this time, hundreds of partisans were streaming into the city, including seven hundred of the Pinan Cichero division, and most of the Peedee team that had traveled with them. With these reinforcements, they made a decisive assault on the port forcing the German troops there to surrender.

Next, they focused on implementing the anti-scorch plan that Vanoncini and the Sixth Zone command had worked on for the past two months. They searched for and disabled the demolition charges in the city and in the port, keeping the infrastructure intact. On the way to Genoa, the Peedee team had met the Second Battalion of the 442nd Regiment twenty miles outside the city. They informed them on the situation in the area, letting them know that the road was clear all the way to Genoa. Advance units of the 92nd Division were at the outskirts of Genoa by nightfall, marveling at seeing a functioning city with running lights, which was in sharp contrast with the destruction the Germans usually left on their wake. On the morning of April 27, the 473rd Regimental Combat Team entered Genoa, riding through town on still operating streetcars. General Edward Almond, commanding officer of the 92nd Division, arrived in the afternoon and met with the leaders of the CLN to congratulate them on the great feat they had just accomplished.

By this time all the German units in and around Genoa had laid down their arms, with the exception of units of the 135th Fortress Brigade manning the harbor defense guns high up on Mount Moro. Colonel Kurt Almers, the brigade commander, had two 381-mm, three 152-mm, and four 90-mm guns looking down on the city and threatened to fire them if Allied soldiers approached the German positions. On the moonless, rainy night of April 27–28, in complete darkness, soldiers of Company A, 679th Tank Destroyer Battalion, moved twelve guns up steep streets barely wide enough for a halftrack. When halftracks failed to make the final turn, they carried the guns by hand into position. By daylight, they laid their guns for direct fire four hundred yards from the enemy concrete emplacement openings. The Germans could not lower their gun tubes to fire on the 679th's guns. At 1430 hours on April 28, with the American guns trained on his positions and surrounded by all sides, Almers surrendered. It was the last episode of the battle for Genoa.[18] Men from the Peedee team, acting as intermediaries between the 92nd and the Italian partisans participated in the disarming of Germans. They distributed the material taken from the five battalions of the 135th Fortress Brigade to the partisans in Genoa proper. They turned over to the 92nd division 150 fortress guns captured on Mount Moro and at the port.

* * *

While the Peedee team moved to Genoa with the Pinan Cichero division, the OGs of the Roanoke mission remained in the area southwest of Piacenza with the Americano's Alliotta division. Lieutenant Taylor received orders from the 15th Army Group that the partisans in his area were to take the city of Voghera, halfway between Alessandria and Piacenza and a gateway to the Po River only five miles to its north. In the evening of April 25, Taylor arrived in the outskirts of Voghera, where the Germans had set up an outpost. Only a handful of partisans were at that location. A detachment of fifty former Wehrmacht soldiers from Czechoslovakia who had deserted and joined the Italian partisans was supposed to support the Americans in the attack, but they had not arrived yet. Taylor and one of his OGs, Technical

Sergeant Fred Orbach, removed their weapons and approached the German lines under a white flag. They were taken to the command post to negotiate terms with the officers in charge. The Germans said they would not fire as long as they were not fired upon. They promised to give up Voghera without a fight, provided they were allowed to use the roads at night so that they might cross the Po River and join other Germans forces there. Taylor told the Germans that all the roads were blocked. The American army was only a few hours away. He was in command of one thousand fully equipped parachutists, and had the support of three thousand partisans, also fully equipped. Taylor told the Germans that they had one of two choices: surrender unconditionally or fight and be killed. The talks continued until 2230 hours. The Germans refused to surrender, so Taylor told them he would attack at midnight.

He retreated, pondering his situation and wondering whether the Germans would call his bluff. At 2330 hours, two German officers appeared. They said they had changed their mind, wanted to surrender, and agreed unconditionally to Taylor's terms. At 0130, the Germans marched out of Voghera with all their equipment and arms. There were 340 men in total, twenty-one of them officers, including one colonel. It took until 0500 to disarm them of weapons and equipment that filled eight trucks and twenty-four wagons. There was some excitement around 0200 hours when the glow of cigarettes and flares of matches attracted the attention of an American B-17 Flying Fortress that dropped three bombs in a field two hundred yards away, without causing any casualties.

On April 26 at 0700, Taylor and his men entered Voghera. In the afternoon, reports from partisan intelligence showed that there were several hundred Germans about twelve miles north of Voghera. Taylor sent them word that the Allied armies had already bypassed them and he had four thousand men under his command. The Germans, a total of two hundred officers and men, surrendered immediately and unconditionally. The partisans disarmed them and distributed the weapons and ammunition among themselves. As the evening came, Taylor set up outposts around Voghera, and everyone settled in for the night.

The next morning at 0730, an excited partisan reported to Taylor that nearly one thousand Germans were marching on Voghera and were already within the city limits. Taylor immediately called the men of the Roanoke team into formation and set out to meet the Germans. Many partisans were at the main square, all talking chaotically and not sure what to do. Taylor sent Sergeant Orbach with two hundred partisans to the city limits, where they set up three lines of defense and placed machine guns and Brens in positions. They learned that the Germans were about three miles away, preparing to attack after an all-night march. After he had set up the city's defenses, Orbach, with a white flag on a stick, rode a bicycle to the German positions to negotiate their surrender. A little later, Taylor arrived and joined the discussion. Eventually, the Germans agreed to surrender. "Not because they were afraid," wrote Taylor later, "not because of lack of weapons or ammo, but because they were well informed on the course of the war and knew that it would not last long."

This was the last contact the Roanoke mission had with German forces. During their action on Voghera, they captured eight hundred men, thirty-six officers, sixteen motor vehicles, and forty wagons with equipment and ammunition. In the next few days, they continued to hold the town with a token force of partisans awaiting the arrival of regular Allied troops. Their actions allowed the bulk of the Alliotta division, under the command of Italo Pietra, or Edoardo, to leave Voghera on April 27 for Milan, to reinforce the position of the Italian patriots there who had taken over the city and confined the Germans in their garrisons. Alliotta was the first partisan unit to enter Milan in the afternoon of April 27, 1945.

* * *

Already on April 25, CLNAI, the National Liberation Committee for Upper Italy based in Milan, had issued a decree calling for the general uprising against the Germans and the Fascists. Under the decree, the CLNAI assumed all the powers, civilian and military, in the cities and regions across Northern Italy. The decree established war tribunals, ordered the dissolution of all Fascist armed units, and promised to treat as prisoners of war all German military personnel who put down their arms. A second decree issued the same day set the terms for the administration of justice against Italian Fascists and collaborators. It declared: "The members of the Fascist government and the Fascist hierarchs, guilty of contributing to the suppression of the constitutional guarantees, destroying the popular freedoms, creating the Fascist regime, compromising and betraying the fortunes of the country, and leading it to the current catastrophe, are punished to death or, in less severe cases, to imprisonment for life."[19]

In the evening of April 27, word arrived at the headquarters of the CLNAI that a group of partisans had arrested Mussolini near Dongo, on the shores of Lake Como, sixty miles to the north. He had been traveling with other Fascist hierarchs in a German convoy headed toward Switzerland. He had tried to disguise himself by putting on the coat of a German soldier, but an alert partisan, Urbano Lazzaro, had recognized him. The leaders of the CLNAI had decided long time ago that Mussolini must not fall into the hands of the Allies for fear that they would show leniency or drag his case for months in judicial proceedings. The decrees they had issued on April 25 implied the death sentence for the Fascist dictator and the hierarchs. The CLNAI leaders wished to carry out a quick execution of such a sentence, "without process, without theatrics, without historical phrases," in the words of Luigi Longo, one of communist leaders of CLNAI at the time.[20]

The CLNAI gave Edoardo, as the first partisan commander to enter Milan, the task of traveling to Dongo to carry out the provisions of those decrees. In the absence of a written order from the CLNAI headquarters, Edoardo limited his involvement to assigning a group of partisans from the Alliotta division to assist in the operation. Walter Audisio, known by the battle name Colonel Valerio, took charge of the group of partisans and traveled to Dongo overnight.[21] In the morning of April 28, the partisans separated Mussolini and his lover, Claretta Petacci, from the rest of the Fascist officials and took them to Giulino di Mezzegra, a hamlet outside Dongo. Colonel Valerio and two partisans placed Mussolini and Petacci against the wall at the entrance of Villa Belmonte. Colonel Valerio described what happened next:

I began to read the text of the death sentence to the war criminal Benito Mussolini: "By order of the General Command of the Corps of Freedom Volunteers, I am charged to render justice to the Italian people." I believe Mussolini did not even understand these words: his gaze was fixed on the gun pointed at him. . . . I discharged five shots on his body. Petacci, out of her wits, dazed, and confused, began to move; she was hit and fell to the ground forthwith. Mussolini was still breathing and I gave him a last shot in the heart with my pistol. It was 1630 of April 28, 1945.[22]

A little later, a partisan firing squad executed fifteen Fascist leaders in the main square in Dongo. They loaded the bodies, including those of Mussolini and Petacci, in the back of a truck and took them overnight to Milan. In the early hours of April 29, 1945, they dumped the bodies in Piazzale Loreto, a square in Milan where in August 1944 Nazis and Fascists had executed fifteen political prisoners in reprisal for a partisan hit. The bodies remained for hours exposed to the fury, violence, and cruelty of the crowd. Then, the crowd hanged them from their heels and left them dangling from the girders of a gas station in what is probably the most iconic image in modern Italian history, the brutal epilogue of the Fascist regime.

Ferruccio Parri, leader of *Partito d'Azione* and one of the leaders of the CLNAI described the spectacle as "an exhibition worthy of a Mexican slaughterhouse." Sandro Pertini, the Socialist Party leader who had declared he would gladly kill Mussolini with his own hands, wrote, "The insurgency has been dishonored." Indro Montanelli, one of the most distinguished Italian journalists, wrote, "The spectacle, which left me with a vague sense of shame, is a lesson on what happens when someone intoxicates the crowd with a passion and instills in me a profound hatred against all those who seek to intoxicate it."[23]

* * *

The atmosphere of retribution, acts of vengeance, and summary executions, especially against the Fascist security forces and those who had collaborated with the Germans, was pervasive in the initial days after the liberation and continued unabated until the Allied forces arrived in force and established the structures of the Allied Military Government. It presented difficult moral and ethical choices to the few Americans, most of them members of the OSS, who had supported the Italian resistance and found themselves in the eye of the storm.

In Genoa on April 28, Captain Vanoncini and the men of the Peedee mission moved to Hotel Verdi. The partisans had set up a prison in the basement of the hotel for high-ranking Fascists and Nazi officers. For some partisans it was time to settle old scores, an eye for an eye. Vanoncini saw a risk that his men could be drawn into acts of brutality and retribution. After all, the enemy had treated the American OGs as terrorists, had tortured and even murdered them whenever it had a chance. Medic Philip Francis said, "Van loved his men and could see what might happen. He called his men together and explained that we should not go into the basement of Hotel Verdi, or any other torture chamber. This was not the American way to seek revenge by torture. This proved to us all that Van was a great leader and a man of great love for all people, friend or foe. To my knowledge, Capt. Vanoncini's request was kept by all members of mission Peedee."[24]

In Milan on April 29, the partisans of the Alliotta division captured Colonel Felice Fiorentini, the cruel leader of the notorious *Sicherheits Abteilung*, or Security Office, of Voghera, composed of Italian Fascists working for the SS. The men of this unit helped the Germans in operations against the partisans and carried out reprisals against the civilians. They were responsible for the deaths of 130 Italians, only 10 percent of whom fell in combat. The rest died after arrest and included wounded or sick partisans of the Alliotta division that fell into the unit's hands. The *Sicherheits* men called themselves "Brotherhood of the Well" because they would often dump the bodies of their victims in wells. They left other victims exposed for days in village squares or crossroads to terrorize the population.[25] The partisans' desire for revenge once they had Colonel Fiorentini in their hands was understandable. They took Fiorentini in front of Edoardo at the partisan headquarters in a school in Milan. One of the partisans, Paolo Murialdi, who had escorted Fiorentini, described the scene:

Tall, thin, pale, defeated. Edoardo and I fear a lynching or a blast of
automatic gunfire from the agitated partisans who have gathered in
the atrium and are clamoring to see him. Edoardo comes up with the
idea of showing him to the partisans with the two of us standing next
to him, elbow to elbow. Edoardo asks for silence and says that we
have to teach him a lesson. We will have a special tribunal in Voghera
judge him, but, in the meanwhile, let us sing him a partisan song.
And it so happens. An emotional and even theatrical scene, but the
partisans sing and do not shoot.[26]

Captain Taylor of the Roanoke mission wrote laconically about
the fate of Fiorentini after the partisans took him to Voghera: "Killed
while trying to escape," he noted in his mission report for the OSS.
The same phrase appears in the reports of several other OSS missions in Italy at the time and indicates that such events were not isolated cases. Italian historians today estimate the number of Fascists
killed during the insurrection and in the days after at between ten
thousand and twelve thousand, as opposed to three to four thousand
killed during the war against the partisans. This phenomenon was not
unique to Italy and occurred in all the countries that experienced soci-
etal divisions between collaborators and those who opposed the Nazis.
For example, historians place the number of summary executions in
France in August to October 1944 at between seventeen and eighteen
thousand.[27]

What was unique to Italy is that the immediate aftermath of the
liberation brought to the surface not only the short-term memories
of the civil war that began on September 8, 1943, but also all the
memories of violence, persecution, and murder inflicted on the Italians by the Fascist regime in the twenty years before the armistice. In
the words of an Italian historian, Enrico Gorrieri, "There was a lot of
anger accumulated in people's hearts. It was impossible for it not to
explode after April 25. Violence begets violence. The crimes that hit
the Fascists after the liberation, even though they were in part acts of
summary justice, are not justifiable, but nevertheless can be explained
with what had happened earlier and with the inflamed climate of that
time. The Fascists are not entitled to play the victims."[28]

* * *

In the last few days of April, after the American Fifth Army and British Eighth Army erupted from the Po River bridgeheads, the war in Italy entered its final stage. The goal was to roll up the disintegrating German units before they had a chance to retreat and regroup into the Alps. The Allied advance now looked more like a tactical march than a combat operation. The Fifth Army sliced through the plains to capture Verona on April 26, then it pushed further north to close the Brenner Pass, the main gateway for German forces trying to retreat into Austria.

To the west, Fifth Army's First Armored Division penetrated the Po Valley to the Alpine foothills at Lake Garda then turned westward toward Brescia and Como to seal off all possible escape routes to Switzerland and Austria before entering the liberated Milan on April 30. To its left, the 34th Infantry Division drove west, taking the towns of Parma, Fidenza, and Piacenza in quick succession, and then turned left toward the French border. The 92nd Infantry Division, after arriving in Genoa on April 27, continued its sweep along the coastal highway toward the French Riviera. The 442nd Regimental Combat Team entered Torino on May 1.[29]

The British Eighth Army, supported by elements of the Fifth Army, pushed to the northeast to capture Padua and Venice and link up with the Yugoslav Liberation Army in Trieste and Goriza. One of the American units supporting the British Eight Army was the 85th Infantry Division. It thrust deep into the Dolomite Mountains toward Innsbruck to link up with American units that were pushing south from Austria. On May 2, advance units of the 85th Division arrived at the village of Calalzo di Cadore, twenty miles from the Austrian border, in the middle of a pitched battle between Italian partisans and German forces of the 73rd Army Corps. The Americans arranged a cease-fire, demanded, and received the unconditional surrender of the Germans. The senior German officer that surrendered the troops was General Anton Dostler who had been in command of the 73rd Army Corps since November 1944.[30]

The overwhelming success of the Allied offensive across Northern Italy caused the rapid disintegration of the Axis forces at the end of April. General Heinrich von Vietinghoff, commander in chief of all German forces in Italy, moved to end the fighting and avoid further bloodshed. German emissaries arrived at the Supreme Allied headquarters for the Mediterranean theater in Caserta on April 28 to arrange a cease-fire and the unconditional surrender of all the Axis forces south of the Alps. They signed an armistice agreement at 1400 hours the next day and agreed to a cease-fire along the entire Italian front to take effect at 1200 hours on May 2, 1945.[31]

There was a bit of drama on April 30 when Kesselring, commander in chief of all German forces in the West, heard about the agreement. He dismissed von Vietinghoff and his chief of staff for exceeding their authority in negotiating with the enemy and sent written instructions to all senior officers in Italy prohibiting negotiations without special orders. But the events were beyond the control of Kesselring or anyone else in the German High Command at that point. The German troops were utterly defeated and cut off from the homeland in northern Italy. Without weapons, fuel, ammunition, and provisions, any further resistance was futile. Hitler's suicide in Berlin freed the senior generals from the vestiges of the personal oath of allegiance they had pledged the dictator. Now they felt they could keep to the agreement signed in Caserta and settle "in a very honorable manner." Kesselring, faced with a *fait accompli*, relented and begrudgingly allowed the surrender to go forward.[32] On the evening of May 2, the 15th Army Group headquarters and the German Army Group C headquarters transmitted the cease-fire orders throughout northern Italy. So shattered were the German command and control structure and communications networks that it took forty-eight hours for the orders to trickle down and for all the units to lay down their arms.

On May 4, 1945, General von Senger and a group of German staff officers arrived at General Mark Clark's 15th Army Group headquarters in Florence. He reported to General Clark who was standing in his tent under the Stars and Stripes flag, with General Truscott, commander of the American Fifth Army and General McCreery, commander of the British Eighth Army, at his sides. Von Senger gave Clark the military salute, and then delivered a formula that had been agreed-upon before the meeting, "I have been authorized by General von Vietinghoff, my superior commander, to receive your orders for the surrender of the Army Group C." There was no mention of unconditional surrender, but there was no illusion that the surrender was anything but full capitulation in view of the complete inability of the German forces to continue to fight. Von Senger wrote:

> I could not escape the impression that the Allied officers found this a painful scene. I had to respect them as opponents, whereas they could see in me only a representative of the Hitler regime. How could they know that this setting evoked in me little of the bitterness that they themselves felt? For me it marked the end of twelve years of spiritual servitude as well as a very personal turning point in life, whatever my eventual fate might be.[33]

* * *

After the OG missions and the partisan units they supported connected with regular Allied units, they spend a few more days in their operational areas before returning to the OG headquarters in Sienna. During this time, they turned their attention toward immediate reconstruction projects to reopen routes of communication. Already on April 27, Captain Vanoncini and the Peedee team had put six hundred Germans to work repairing the tarmac and bridges of Highway 45, between Genoa and Piacenza. They also played the role of liaison between the partisan commands, the Allied commanders, and the Allied Military Government officials who moved in to take over the civil administration of the territories. Efforts went toward the proper treatment of the prisoners of war held by the partisans and their transfer to concentration areas and prisoners of war cages that sprang up throughout Italy at the time.

Another sensitive area that required the OGs' attention was preventing frictions among the partisan units affiliated with different political movements that began to position themselves for the governance of postwar Italy. The Communists were very strong in the partisan movement throughout Italy and the Allies greatly feared they would use the strength of arms to take over the country. A similar situation in Greece had sparked a bloody civil war in November 1944, a scenario that the Allies wanted to prevent happening in Italy at all costs. They saw disarming the partisan units as a key measure to enable the discussions about the future of Italy to go forward through peaceful and democratic means. The Allies organized disarmament parades throughout northern Italy in the first few days after the war ended. These parades began with speeches from partisan leaders and senior Allied commanders. Then the partisan units marched to the ovations of the Italian population displaying their colors. At a designated area at the end of the route, they deposited their weapons and marched off with their flags flying. The entire Peedee mission participated in the partisan parade in Genoa on May 2, and the Roanoke mission participated at a similar parade in Pavia on May 12.

One of the last acts of the missions in the field was supporting investigations already under way of war crimes committed by the Germans or the Fascists during the war. As early as April 27, Captain Vanoncini of the Peedee mission received two visitors from the OG headquarters in Sienna: Captain Nevio J. Manzani and Captain Albert G. Lanier were investigating the fate of the fifteen men of the Ginny team who had disappeared more than a year ago. Manzani and Lanier were particularly interested in identifying and interviewing Germans and Fascists who knew about those events. Vanoncini assigned men from the Peedee team to help them with the investigation and to track persons of interest in the prisoner of war cages in and around Genoa, where the 135th Fortress Brigade officers and men were being held.

CHAPTER 14

OSS Investigations into War Crimes

After the Ginny men failed to return from their mission of March 22–23, 1944, the OSS initially reported their status as "Captured by the Enemy" on a Battle Casualty Report dated April 26, 1944.[1] Then, on May 9, 1944, they updated the status of all fifteen men to "Missing in Action." They forwarded the information to the Military Personnel Casualty Branch in the Adjutant General's Office of the War Department in Washington, DC. On January 23, 1945, the Casualty Branch began a review of the status of the men to determine whether they could issue a "finding of death" under the provisions of Section 5, Public Law 490. Findings of death were made twelve months after a soldier had been declared missing in action, if there were no indications that the person was still alive. The military bureaucracy used findings of death to terminate the deposits of pay and other allowances into the soldiers' accounts and to issue payments of death gratuities to their next of kin.[2]

In response to a query from the Casualty Branch at the end of January 1945, Colonel Livermore and Captain Materazzi, respectively commanding and executive officers of the Italian OGs, compiled all the information they had at the time about the fate of the Ginny mission. After they lost contact with their men, they had arranged through OSS channels to send a message to an OSS agent, code name Youngstown, operating in Genoa, "Some American soldiers in uniform landed a few nights ago in close vicinity of Stazione di Framura. Please find out through intermediaries and most cautiously what happened to them and where they are now." The agent answered on April 1, 1944, "Thirteen American soldiers plus two American officers made prisoners after a brief battle the night of 26–27 near Framura. They are now in La Spezia."

Several broadcasts from German and Italian radios that OSS monitored at the time provided conflicting information. A broadcast in German from Vienna on March 27, 1944, reported, "On the eastern side of the gulf of Genoa, an American Commando Group consisting of two officers and thirteen men, which landed northwest of La Spezia, was wiped out in combat." The Wehrmacht communiqué of the same day mentioned the operation and reported the men as "wiped out." The next day, an Italian station broadcast proclaimed "Fascist Captures American Rangers: The head of the Spezia Province commended the Fascist Giovanni Bianco who together with other Fascists captured a group of Americans, including two officers who landed on the Ligurian coast." A similar message was broadcast the next morning by another Italian station.

At the beginning of February 1945, an Italian civilian from Sarzana crossed the frontlines some forty miles south of La Spezia. He was taken prisoner and transferred to a prisoner of war camp. Captain Nevio J. Manzani of the Italian OGs, on assignment with the 92nd Division at the time, interrogated him on February 2 and obtained the following information: "In March 1944, eleven Americans landed above La Spezia in the area of Framura and were captured. They were subsequently executed by a unit of a German Marine Company commanded by a Captain De Suti. Said execution was believed to have taken place near Ferrara and the bodies were buried in the vicinity. The only witness is a person known as Don Greco, parish priest of the cathedral of Sarzana."

This was the first information the OSS had received about the men in the Ginny mission that had specific names of people and locations. Most of it sounded plausible. Sarzana was a town on the other side of the Magra River from La Spezia, where the Germans could have taken the Ginny team if they had captured them at Framura. So it made sense that a civilian from Sarzana and the local priest had heard about them. One thing that left everyone puzzled was that the execution place was Ferrara, a city 155 miles northeast of Sarzana and La Spezia. Why would the Germans have taken the men on the other side of the Apennines to execute them? Manzani reported that he would investigate the information and would try to contact the priest for more precise details. But at the beginning of February 1945, the Allies were still stuck in front of the Gothic Line and Sarzana was in firm German control. Following up on the details of the story would have to wait until the military situation changed.

* * *

In April 26, 1945, as soon as the frontline moved north of La Spezia, the OSS sent Captain Manzani and Captain Albert G. Lanier to La Spezia to find out what had happened to the Ginny team. Within days, they learned that Italian Fascist and German soldiers of the 135th Fortress Brigade had captured, interrogated, and executed their men in the morning of March 26, 1944, near the positions of the De Lutti battery at Punta Bianca. Witnesses told them that the Germans had dumped the bodies in a common unmarked grave near the munition depot "La Ferrara" by the sea. Manzani and Lanier traveled to Genoa as soon as it was liberated and with the assistance of Captain Vanoncini and men from the Peedee mission began looking for German soldiers who had information about the case.

They came upon Lieutenant Rudolph Bolze who had assisted in the execution of the Americans and had overseen their burial. Manzani and Lanier interrogated Bolze between May 10 and 13, 1945, at the 92nd Division prisoners-of-war cage in Genoa. At the end of the third day, Bolze asked for time to write the story in longhand in his own words. On May 15, Manzani and Lanier had a final interview with Bolze at the Genoa POW cage in which they reviewed the written version of his story. They asked Bolze to raise his right hand and be sworn, but Bolze refused on the grounds that he was not accustomed to swearing. Then the Americans asked him, "Will you give your word of honor as a German officer that you did not see the execution of these men described in your story?" Bolze showed very obvious and extreme confusion and did not answer for some time. He fumbled around with excuses like "a long time ago—I cannot really remember—much has happened—very unpleasant, etc."

Finally, he stated, "I have never seen anybody executed." After this, he signed the statement containing his story. He also drew a map of the site near Punta Bianca where the Germans had buried the fifteen Americans.

With this information, Manzani and Lanier returned to La Spezia and Bonassola to continue their investigation and interview witnesses. They took the deposition of the young fisherman, Franco Lagaxo, and his mother who had met and sheltered the OGs before their capture. In the archives of the Fascist office, they found a laudatory report from the prefect of Bonassola, *Commissario* Guglielmini, describing the contribution of his local Fascists in the capture of the fifteen Americans. Manzani and Lanier found several villagers who had seen the fifteen Americans in Bonasola when the Germans and the Fascists had brought them after the capture. "The soldiers walked with the hands up and locked behind their heads. They were pale and there was anguish in their faces," one remembered. Another one remembered taking Lieutenant Russo to the village doctor for a slight wound in his face. "Why did you not go up into the mountains?" he managed to ask him. Russo told him that they had been captured before they were able to escape.

Other Italians in La Spezia helped Manzani and Lanier pinpoint the location where the fifteen Americans had been buried. Staff from the Graves Registration and local laborers began excavating the grave on May 20, 1945. After three days, they located fifteen bodies at the bottom of the hole, fifteen feet below the surface of the road. Major Clifford M. Bassett and Captain Robert J. Willoughby, medical officers from the 103rd Station Hospital arrived at the site and assisted in the exhumation of the bodies from the common grave, taking notes on their condition. Each man had the hands secured tightly behind the back with strong wire. None of the men wore shoes. Most of the men had their military olive drab shirts, jackets, and trousers on. Three of the bodies wore no outer clothing—they were in undershirts and underwear.

The bodies were badly decomposed, and it was hard to identify the men. Manzani and Lanier were able to identify only seven men upon disinterment. Some men still had laundry tags on their clothes with the last name's initial letter followed by the last four digits of their serial number. Some others had their sergeant stripes on their jackets. Only one had his dog tags still around his neck. They used dental records to identify another one. Major M. Pedro Souza, the medical officer of the Italian OGs, who had known the men personally, identified six additional men based on their dental records and personal features that he was able to recognize. They identified the men found without outer clothes as Lieutenant Paul Trafficante, Sergeant Alfred DeFlumeri, and John Farrell.

The medical officers were appalled at the conditions of the bodies. Bassett and Willoughby wrote in their report, "Two skulls were crushed to such an extent that no statement can be made as to whether or not these had been perforated by bullets. . . . Ten skulls showed extensive fractures, usually unilateral and located over the temporal bone. There was no perforation of the skulls on the contralateral side, such as would be produced by a bullet. The clothing, anterior chest and abdomen of all fifteen bodies were examined for perforations, which could have been caused by bullets. None were found."

Souza was less succinct in his report. "I found that the fifteen bodies had extreme fractures (unilateral) of the temporal bone; the opposite temporal bone was intact. This excludes the possibility of the personnel having been shot in the head. The bodies showed no bullet perforations (thorax, abdomen, and extremities). Also, the clothes did not show any perforation that could have been caused by a bullet. In my opinion, in all fifteen cases death was caused by a severe traumatism in the temporal region, extensive fractures of the temporal bone, severe brain injury, and hemorrhage."

The reported conditions in which the bodies of the Ginny mission men were found, without shoes, some of them without clothes on, with shattered skulls and without telltale signs of bullet holes through their bodies outraged the OSS personnel. They were convinced that the Germans had tortured and bludgeoned their men to death. Captain Materazzi offered to head the firing squad that would execute the

EXHIBIT L

DESCRIPTION AND DIAGRAM OF BODIES WHEN DISINTERRED

1. The following diagram and findings give a picture of how the bodies were found upon excavation. Each body was numbered and the following individual notations were made:

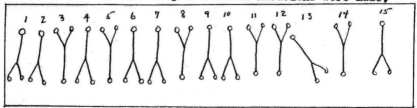

2. Positive identification of seven bodies was made by Capt. Manzani on 23 May as follows:

    a. Body No. 1 – By laundry markings (S-3008), it was identified to be T/5 Angelo Sirico, 32543008.

    b. Body No. 2 – By laundry markings (L-2732 on drawers), it was identified to be T/5 Joseph A. Libardi, 31212732.

    c. Body No. 5 – By T/Sgt. stripes on OD shirt and size of body, it was identified to be T/Sgt. Livio Vieceli, 33037797.

    d. Body No. 7 – By 2 large plates, it was identified to be Sgt. Alfred L. DiFlumeri, 31252071.

    e. Body No. 8 – By laundry markings on drawers (M-0582) and by Sgt. stripes, it was identified to be Sgt. Dominic C. Mauro, 32650582.

    f. Body No. 11 – By dog tags and laundry markings on drawers (6119), it was identified to be T/5 Joseph Noia, 32536119.

    g. Body No. 13 – By laundry markings (T-399) and cotton T shirt, it was identified to be 1st Lt. Paul J. Traficante, 01308399.

Diagram and identification notes that OSS investigators made upon exhuming the bodies of the fifteen Ginny team members.

Germans responsible for the massacre. The outrage was still present forty years after the war when a number of the Italian OG veterans gathered in Italy to reminisce about those events.[3]

* * *

Immediately after the war ended, the OSS created a special unit to investigate war crimes in Italy. At the end of May 1945, Captain Robert Blythin, the unit's lead investigator for the Ginny mission case, assembled and reviewed all the evidence that Manzani and Lanier had collected up to that point. Based on their information, Blythin pieced together how the Ginny men had spent their first forty-eight hours near Bonasola, until the local Fascists discovered them and handed them over to the Germans. He also knew the conditions in which they were buried in the common grave. Captain Georg Sessler of the German naval intelligence helped the OSS investigators understand the events that transpired in La Spezia that lead to the execution of the Americans.

Sessler was in Milan when the Italian patriots launched the general insurrection on April 25, 1945. Fearing for his safety, he crossed the Swiss border near Chiasso. On May 2, 1945, Sessler requested a Swiss friend who was in contact with British intelligence agents in Milan to notify them that he was willing to return to Italy from Switzerland if he could be of assistance. He was ready to cooperate with the Allied intelligence forces. On May 3, Sessler returned to Milan and began a series of intelligence debriefings with British and American officers. On May 5, Sessler wrote down all the information he knew about German intelligence forces in Italy for an American officer. The information included the first mention of the execution of the fifteen American OGs. On May 12, the British sent Sessler to Florence and handed him over to the Americans who interrogated him for the first time on the case of the Ginny mission. Sessler recounted in detail the events he had witnessed in La Spezia. It is not clear why in these initial interrogations Sessler attributed the order to execute the Americans to General Rudolph Toussaint, who had been the commissioner of the Wehrmacht in Italy at the time.

On May 24, Livermore summarized the results of the investigation for Donovan in Washington. Based on the interrogations of Sessler, Klaps, and Bolze, Livermore reported that the Ginny men had been shot by orders of Colonel Almers who had acted under orders from his commanding officer, General Toussaint. The shooting was done because of Hitler's order that all persons engaging in sabotage would be executed. Livermore queried Washington as follows: "Are the subordinate commanders and soldiers of the firing squad guilty war criminals when they are carrying our orders of colonels and generals? The latter, if apprehended, will probably say they got orders from the higher up." Washington replied within the same date as follows:

> Defense of superior orders NOT valid, although it may be considered for lenient sentence. All implicated in crime, irrespective of rank, station, or involuntary character of their acts, are to be regarded as war criminals, and full information on all is required. For international trials, especially interested in all from commissioned officers up as defendants. Soldiers of firing squad, etc., may be material witnesses in international trial and also defendants before American military commissions. Army Field Manual 27–10 now being amended to conform to foregoing.

At the end of May, Sessler revised his story and explained that he had erroneously named Toussaint as the general who had ordered the execution of the fifteen Americans. It was Anton Dostler, commanding general of the 75th Army Corps, who had sent the orders for the execution. Dostler at the time was in custody of the British at a POW camp in Taranto, in the south of Italy. On June 7, 1945, the Americans took Dostler under their custody and sent him to the Combined Services Detailed Interrogation Center (CSDIC) at the Cinecittà complex for detailed interrogations.

Mussolini had inaugurated Cinecittà in 1937 as a complete movie making and production facility intended to rival Hollywood studios. Within the first six years, the Italian film industry produced six hundred movies there, most of them toeing the Fascist propaganda line.[4] When the Germans took over Italy in 1943, they looted the film studios and turned Cinecittà into a holding center for British prisoners. A British intelligence officer who visited the facility shortly after the liberation of Rome said about it, "The floors were deep in straw and alive with fleas. It took some weeks before the place became habitable—thanks to DDT, which the Germans did not have."[5] In 1944–1945, the Allies used the complex as an interrogation center and holding area for prisoners of war.

Captain Blythin interrogated Dostler for the first time at the CSDIC camp in Cinecittà on June 9, 1945. A British-American intelligence agent by the name of Alexander Golodetz served as the interpreter. Dostler recalled immediately the incident of the fifteen Americans captured in this sector. He said that he had received word from the Almers Brigade that they had captured a group of Italian-speaking American saboteurs. Dostler said he asked his chief of staff to pass the message to the higher echelon, the headquarters of the army group commanded by General von Zangen, and to query whether the prisoners fell under the Führerbefehl, Hitler's order on the treatment of commando groups captured by the German army. The army group replied in the affirmative so Dostler ordered the men shot. He did not remember whether von Zangen himself or his chief of staff, Colonel Nagel, gave the order but he believed the chief of staff would not have given such an order without referring it to the army group commander in person. Dostler said that, independently of orders from the army group, he read the Führerbefehl, and it appeared that this party came directly under it. "I cannot remember the exact details," Dostler said. "All I do know is that I read the Führerbefehl at the time and that according to its wording it seemed clear that these men were saboteurs as defined therein. I would not, however, assume the responsibility for having the prisoners shot, but referred it to the Army, who took the decision." Repeatedly during that interrogation, Dostler emphasized these two points. He expressed anxiety about producing the Führerbefehl itself and hoped a copy of it would surface.

On June 10, Livermore sent the following telegram to Donovan, "I have interrogated General Dostler who commanded 75th Corps. He freely admits that he gave orders to Colonel Almers to have the Ginny men executed. He states that this was in compliance with the

Hitler order that all persons apprehended while engaging in sabotage would be executed. He also said he received orders from Army commander General von Zangen to execute them."

After their first interrogation of Dostler, Blythin and Golodetz crosschecked his story with the information that Sessler was providing. On June 12, they interrogated Dostler again. Golodetz told him, "According to information on hand, the Almers Brigade received a first teletype message ordering the execution from your HQ as early as 1000 hours of the day following the capture of the Americans. As they had only reported the case to you during the afternoon of the day of capture, it looks as if the decision was taken at your HQ without reference to Army."

Dostler replied, "It is possible that I may have issued a preliminary order, but the men were not executed until the morning of the day after, by which time I had received definite orders by phone from the Army on the subject." Blythin later described Dostler's demeanor as uneasy and nervous when he posed the question. "The thing that I noticed particularly was that beads of perspiration appeared on his neck and his brow," Blythin said.

Blythin arranged the transfer of General von Zangen from Western Europe, where he was captured at the end of the war, to Rome for interrogation. Von Zangen categorically denied any involvement in the execution of the Americans. "It is simply impossible that I should not remember the shooting of fifteen men, especially members of the American army in uniform, had it taken place on my own, or the order of a member of my staff," von Zangen told Blythin. During interrogations, he explained very methodically that he had never heard of the execution before. Due to the large area under his responsibility, he was away from his headquarters most of the time. Colonel Nagel, his chief of staff, had authority to take action on routine matters, but on all matters of higher importance, he had orders to wait for von Zangen's decision or, if the matter was urgent, to ask for a decision at the next higher echelon, Kesselring's headquarters.

The execution of fifteen Americans, von Zangen said, was not a matter Nagel could have handled and Nagel had not reported to van Zangen that he had ordered the execution. The logical conclusion then was that the higher authority that had ordered Dostler to execute the Americans must have been either Kesselring's headquarters or the High Command of the Wehrmacht itself. Von Zangen urged strongly that the investigators locate the Führerbefehl and interrogate Nagel and Kraehe, Dostler's chief of staff, who could clarify the matter.

The record does not show what efforts Blythin made to interrogate Nagel or Kraehe, although they were available in the prisoner of war enclosures where German soldiers and officers were confined at that time. He tried to locate Colonel Almers, but without results. Almers had been in a POW enclosure near Pisa until the end of May 1945, when he assumed the identity of a noncommissioned officer and disappeared. Someone said that Almers had talked about hiding in a villa by the sea, in a rather isolated spot near La Spezia where he had lived during the war. Blythin located the villa, searched it, and interrogated its inhabitants to no avail. When a report arrived that Almers had been spotted in a POW enclosure in Taranto, Blythin traveled there, taking Koerbitz, one of Almers's staff officers, with him. "We examined I would say twenty thousand Germans in several cages, trying to locate Almers," Blythin said later. In Taranto Blythin found Hans-Georg Schultz, the adjutant to Almers, who had detailed knowledge of the events surrounding the execution of the Americans and was willing to testify.

By mid-June, Blythin believed there was sufficient evidence to take to trial and convict a dozen German Army and Navy intelligence officers, ranging from noncommissioned officers to three-star generals. However, in early September all the regular personnel of the office of the judge advocate, including Brigadier General Adam Richmond, the theater judge advocate, received orders to repatriate to the United States. The turnover in personnel required that the case be brought to trial quickly and without delay. In a letter to the OSS headquarters in Washington, Captain Lanier wrote:

> OSS has about given up hope of finding Col. Almers and General Richmond does not think there is any case against General von Zangen. Also, he thinks there is not much of a case against the various small-timers down the line who merely obeyed superior orders. So, the plan is to try General Dostler alone on the main charge that he

exceeded discretion in giving the execution order. In other words, he took it upon himself to interpret the Hitler Saboteur order and to decide that our Ginny Mission men came within its purview. That exercise of personal discretion will be the War Crime of which he is guilty.

Thus, at the beginning of September, when the US Army decided to send the case to trial, only Anton Dostler was on the docket, the first German general to be tried for war crimes committed during World War II.

* * *

The fate of Major Holohan, commander of the Mangosteen-Chrysler mission, remained a mystery for the OSS. Besides Aldo Icardi's initial report on the disappearance of the major, the OSS headquarters in Sienna received information from other sources, as well. One of them was from Tullio Lussi, the Italian professor-agent who had parachuted with the American mission and had introduced Holohan to the leaders of the CLNAI. Lussi had been in the Lake Orta area by chance right after the events of December 6. He wrote in a report prepared for the OSS, "I remained in the area for a day to conduct an exhaustive investigation, but I failed to come up with any positive elements."[6] British officers of Mission Cherokee that operated in the area reported rumors they had heard from their Italian sources. According to them, Holohan had been murdered to rob him of large sums of money, as high as $400,000, which he carried with him in a suitcase at all times. The OSS in Sienna could not have believed such reports, but they asked the British to meet with Icardi anyhow and check these rumors.[7]

At the beginning of April 1945, Aminta Migliari crossed the border into Switzerland and then traveled to Florence. The OSS had special interest in talking to him, since he had been responsible for the personal security of the mission. Max Corvo, the OSS Secret Intelligence officer in Sienna, debriefed Migliari and asked him to prepare a written report of the events. When Corvo received the report, including a map of the Lake Orta area that Migliari drew, he found them very similar to the first report that Icardi had sent in January 1945. "Reading the text and comparing the map, there was no doubt that both reports were written by the same person," Corvo wrote. When asked about it, Migliari admitted that he had written both reports. Corvo felt that the security of the mission had been lax, especially since they had operated in military uniforms, and that the mission should have been attached to one of the partisan units in the area rather than leave its security in Migliari's hands.[8]

At the end of April 1945, as soon as Milan was liberated, an OSS team assigned to probe the disappearance of Major Holohan arrived in the Lake Orta area to investigate. Icardi made a full report to the investigators, explaining the numerous lines of inquiry he had pursued after Holohan's disappearance and in the months since, providing the names of all the people that had been involved with the mission before that event, and presenting an analysis of the situation at that time. The group questioned Icardi at length and asked him to relate in narrative fashion the events of that night. "I was happy to offer what assistance I could to find Major Holohan," wrote Icardi later.[9]

The working hypothesis was that the major had been hit during the firefight and had either fallen in the lake or hidden in the mountains and died of his wounds. The investigators dragged the lake, set off explosives in the water, dug up the mountainside, and checked every lead in the area but found no trace of Holohan. In early August 1945, Icardi was preparing to return to the United States when the OSS investigating team called him again for questioning about Major Holohan. Icardi said he spent an entire day with the officer investigating the matter, recounting the events leading up to and that transpired during the night of December 6, 1944. After this interview, Icardi received clearance to return to the United States. The investigators continued to interview everyone who might have been involved in the case. Cross-checking of records revealed that there had been no German or Fascist operations in the area around December 6, 1944. This reinforced the sentiment expressed by several locals who had never believed the story of a Nazi-Fascist ambush and had attributed the disappearance of Holohan to individuals who saw Holohan as an obstacle to their political ambitions or were after the money he carried with him.[10]

Icardi wrote that, as soon as he arrived in Washington, army officers called him into a conference to relate his experience and the results of the investigations in Italy. Before returning to civilian life, army investigators questioned Icardi once more. Icardi recalled:

> They asked me to tell my story all over from the beginning. Numerous questions followed and the interview finished up with an explanation that all efforts to shed some light on the fate of Major Holohan had been fruitless. The numerous interrogations were designed to find some lead, which might assist in learning the whereabouts of Major Holohan. With apologies for the inconvenience I had been caused, the investigators told me that I was free to go home and become a civilian citizen again.[11]

Like many returning veterans, Icardi used scholarship money from the GI Bill to go back to school. The American investigators in Italy, finding themselves at an impasse, left it to the Italian authorities to look for the thread that would unravel the Holohan mystery.

CHAPTER 15

Swift Justice for the Ginny Men

In September 1945, the office of the judge advocate general began formal proceedings to try General Anton Dostler for the murder of the fifteen Americans of the Ginny mission. Major Frederick W. Roche of the JAG presented the formal charge to Dostler at his confinement area in Aversa, near Naples, on September 10, 1945. Roche would base the government case mostly on witness testimony; there was very little documentary or other type of evidence available. One group of witnesses included American officers who had knowledge of the mission or had conducted the investigations after the war. Other witnesses were a number of former Fascists and German officers, all prisoners of war, who had first-hand knowledge of the capture, interrogation, and execution of the fifteen Americans. The scant documentary evidence included a two-page document, which was a translation of the Führerbefehl of October 18, 1942. French intelligence had discovered the document in December 1944 and had shared it with the OSS at the beginning of January 1945. The document was a facsimile of the original order that Hitler had issued, but it did not include the supplement that provided further instructions on how the order was to be implemented.[1]

On September 23, 1945, General Joseph T. McNarney, commanding general of the US Army forces in the Mediterranean theater, issued Circular Number 114, "Regulations for the Trial of War Crimes." It laid out rules under which military commissions would conduct trials of war crimes and therefore was the legal foundation for Dostler's trial. The circular began by defining what constituted a war crime. A large body of work would develop following Dostler's trial regarding the definition of war crimes, and it continues to expand to these days. McNarney's rules very laconically stated, "As used in these regulations the expression 'war crime' means a violation of the laws or customs of war." Next, the circular made it clear that while a military commission had to follow procedures deemed necessary for a free and fair trial, it had wide latitude in defining these procedures and did not have to follow the rules prescribed for general courts-martial proceedings. In particular, technical rules of evidence would not apply. Any evidence was admissible if, in the opinion of the president of the commission, it had "any probative value to a reasonable man." If witnesses were dead or otherwise unable to testify before the commission, the commission could "receive secondary evidence of statements made by or attributed to such witness." Documents could be admitted as evidence without proof that they were signed or issued officially by proper authorities. Confessions did not require proof that they were made voluntarily. If the accused raised questions about the circumstances surrounding the taking of a confession, the commission might weigh those questions but the accused could not use such questions to prevent the confession from being admitted.

Most importantly, the rules stated, "The fact that an accused acted pursuant to order of his Government or of a superior shall not free him from responsibility, but may be considered in mitigation of punishment if the commission determines that justice so required."

Thus, going into the trial, the rules laid out in Circular 114 guaranteed that the commission would find Dostler responsible for the execution of the Americans. He had admitted to ordering the execution of the fifteen Americans in compliance with the Führerbefehl and with orders from higher command. The only question that the trial would resolve was what sentence Dostler would receive. The circular listed the sentences that the military commission could impose: death by hanging or shooting, confinement for life or lesser term, or fine.

On September 26, 1945, General McNarney issued Special Order 269, which appointed a military commission to try Dostler's case. The president of the commission was Major General Lawrence C. Jaynes. The other members included Brigadier General Thoburn K. Brown, Colonel Harrison Shaler, Colonel James Notestein, and Colonel Franklin T. Hammond, Jr. Major Frederick W. Roche would be the trial judge advocate with First Lieutenant William T. Andress as his assistant. Colonel Claudius O. Wolfe was appointed as defense counsel with Major Cecil K. Emery as his assistant.

The trial was set to begin on Monday, October 8, 1945, at the Palace of Justice in Rome. The members of the commission met in General Brown's office the day before to review the set of rules under which they would conduct the trial, as defined in General McNarney's Circular 114. They discussed the need to keep methods of operations of the OSS out of the trial as much as possible, given the secrecy that surrounded most of what the organization had accomplished during the war. Everyone was aware of the momentous precedent that the trial would set, since it was the first trial in Europe for crimes committed during the war. The trial would be open to the public and the press to serve as an example of fair justice for the new Italian and German societies being born from the ashes of World Word II. The venue of the trial itself was symbolic—Hall Number 4 of the Palace of Justice had housed Mussolini's Special Tribunal for the Defense of the State, which had passed judgment on political prisoners and enemies of the Fascist regime.

* * *

The trial began on October 8, 1945, at 1000 hours. The courtroom was packed with reporters and members of the public. The US Army Signal Corps had set up cameras to record the proceedings. Dostler arrived dressed in the Wehrmacht uniform of the general of infantry, stripped of all insignia and marks of rank. He was accompanied by his defense lawyers and General Frido von Senger, whom Dostler had asked to assist during the trial given his knowledge of English.

Major Roche, as trial judge advocate, swore in the members of the military commission, the prosecution team, and the defense team. Then, he began the trial by reading the charges and specifications against Dostler, accusing him of violating the law of war by issuing the order that lead to the execution of fifteen members of the United States Army. At this point, defense counsel Colonel Wolfe entered several pleas challenging the jurisdiction of the commission to try the case and asking that the trial be conducted in accordance with the rules of evidence and procedure applicable to courts-martial or United States federal courts. General Jaynes overruled each objection and the trial continued with the deposition of the prosecution witnesses.

The first prosecution witness was Captain Albert R. Materazzi, the executive officer of the Italian OGs, who had mounted the Ginny mission and had personally trained the fifteen Americans for the mission. Materazzi provided a description of the operation as he had experienced it and established that the men had been on a military mission assigned by the Special Operations section, G-3, of the Allied Forces Headquarters. They had worn regulation field uniforms and the insignia of rank with the exception of the two officers who had left their insignia with Materazzi and wore their jackets inside out. On cross-examination, Wolfe tried to get Materazzi to expand on the fact that he and his men were part of the OSS, whose primary mission was espionage, sabotage, and "cloak and dagger" operations, but the commission quickly stopped that line of questions. "Let us not put into the record any such terms," Jaynes said. "Let us keep it military."

The next witness, Giobatta Bianchi, one of the Bonassola Fascists who had captured the Ginny team, described how they had seized the Americans, taken them to the village, and handed them over to the Germans. Georg Sessler, the German naval intelligence officer who interrogated the OGs in La Spezia, followed Bianchi on the witness stand. He described the interrogation sessions on March 24 and 25 at the 135th Fortress Brigade headquarters, how he had gotten the information about the mission from Russo, and how he, Klaps, and Koerbitz had tried to prevent the execution of the men. During Sessler's deposition Roche introduced into evidence the Führerbefehl, Hitler's order for the execution of saboteurs and commandos. He asked why, despite knowing about the Führerbefehl, Sessler had joined Klaps and Koerbitz in protesting the order to execute the Americans. Sessler said, "As an intelligence officer . . . I am of the opinion that a man

SECRET
OFFICE OF STRATEGIC SERVICES

Country: Germany   Original Report No. FF-2175
Subject: German Order to Kill Captured   Date of Report   16 Dec 1944
          Allied Commandos and Parachutists   Evaluation   Documentary

Source: French Intelligence

Date of Information: See text   Number of pages   2
Place of Origin: Paris   Attachments
                              Theatre   MEDTO

The first of the following two orders was issued by the Fuehrer
Headquarters on 18 October 1942 and reissued, together with the
supplementary order, on a date not indicated, following the
invasion of France. The German classification of the orders is
"Most Secret". A covering note found with the two orders, dated
10 October 1944, indicates that the order was distributed to
regimental commanders and staff officers of corresponding rank.

1. Order of 18 October 1942:

    1. Recently our adversaries have employed methods of warfare
    contrary to the provisions of the Geneva Convention. The atti-
    tude of the so-called commandos, who are recruited in part among
    common criminals released from prison, is particularly brutal
    and underhanded. From captured documents it has been learned
    that they have orders not only to bind prisoners but to kill
    them without hesitation should they become an encumbrance or
    constitute an obstacle to the completion of their mission.
    Finally, we have captured orders which advocate putting prisoners
    to death as a matter of principle.

    2. For this reason, an addition to the communique of the Wehrmacht
    of 7 October 1942 is announced: that, in the future, Germany will
    resort to the same methods in regard to these groups of British
    saboteurs and their accomplices - that is to say that German
    troops will exterminate them without mercy wherever they find
    them.

    3. Therefore, I command that: Henceforth all enemy troops
    encountered by German troops during so-called commando operations,
    in Europe or in Africa, though they appear to be soldiers in uni-
    form or demolition groups, armed or unarmed, are to be extermi-
    nated to the last man, either in combat or in pursuit. It matters
    not in the least whether they have been landed by ships or planes
    or dropped by parachute. If such men appear to be about to
    surrender, no quarter should be given them - on general principle.
    A detailed report on this point is to be addressed in each case
    to the OKW for inclusion in the Wehrmacht communique.

Copy

FF-2175

s agents,
rmacht, through
lice in co-
to the Sicher-
idden to keep
ion (for example,

iers who surrender
its of normal
or seaborne
aptured during
led out to save

ll leaders and
ns - either by
ience of this

ture illegible.

rance, the Fuhrer's
tion of saboteurs
and terrorists, remains fully valid. Exceptions to this order
are enemy soldiers in uniform within the actual combat zone, i.e.
in the front-line sectors as far as the post command. (of No. 5
of the original order of 18 October 1942).

    2. All members of terrorist and saboteur bands, including (on
    general principle) all parachutists encountered outside the
    immediate combat zone, are to be executed. In special cases they
    are to be turned over to the SD (Sicherheitsdienst).

    3. All units outside the Normandy combat zone are to be given
    precise and succinct instructions on the duty incumbent upon them
    to destroy groups of terrorists and saboteurs.

    4. Commencing tomorrow, the Oberbefehlshaber will report daily
    the number of saboteurs thus liquidated. This measure is, above
    all, valid for operations conducted under direction of the
    Militerbefehlshabor. The number of executions must appear in
    the daily communique of the Wehrmacht to serve as a warning for
    potential terrorists.

                              Signature illegible -

                              Lieutenant..........

SECRET

Copy of the Führerbefehl of October 18, 1942, ordering the killing of captured Allied commandos.

from a commando raid or from a team like this one, of the two officers and thirteen men, is better than any other soldier." He explained that the German Army and Navy considered a saboteur a man put behind enemy lines in civilian clothes but not in the uniform of his country.

The next witness was Friedrich Klaps, Sessler's superior in the German naval intelligence organization at La Spezia. Klaps described his understanding at the time that the American men were military personnel in uniform and his doubts that they fell under the definition of saboteurs or commandos of the Führerbefehl. Klaps described his efforts to rescind the execution order that had arrived from the 75th Army Corps, including his "camouflaged" telephone conversations with Dostler, and the telegrams he had sent to Dostler's headquarters and Kesselring's headquarters to that effect. Klaps also told of the order from Kesselring's headquarters to destroy all the records about the events, which came two weeks after the Americans had been shot. Klaps was the last witness for the day and the commission recessed until 1000 hours the next day.

The trial resumed on October 9, 1945, with Wolfe introducing in the record the fact that Dostler had requested as witnesses Colonel Almers, commanding officer of the 135th Fortress Brigade, and three members of his staff in March 1944: Colonel Kraehe, chief of staff, Major Koepper, staff officer, and Captain Fuerst zu Dohna, intelligence officer. Roche explained that he had done every effort to locate the witnesses Dostler had asked for, but General von Senger, present at the trial, was the only one he had been able to locate. Almers had been in custody but had escaped from a prisoner of war camp in early July and had not yet been apprehended. There was no trace of the other three officers in the Mediterranean or European theaters of operations.

Next, Hans-Georg Schultz, an aide to Colonel Almers, appeared in front of the commission. He was a key witness for the prosecution because as part of his duties he read all the incoming and outgoing messages between the 135th Fortress Brigade and the 75th Army Corps. Schultz was the only one who had actually seen the first order for the execution of the Americans that the Corps sent to the Almers brigade in the morning of March 25, 1944. But he could not remember whether the order was sent by Dostler himself or by Kraehe, his chief of staff. Shultz also had listened in on the conversation that Almers had with Kraehe and Dostler in the evening of March 25, which he described as follows:

> Colonel Almers tried to have the order of execution which had been received by telegram postponed or delayed. He talked about it with Colonel Kraehe. Communications were poor and I listened in in parts. He talked about the fact that after the capture it was impossible to execute the men. On the other end of the line, the conversation was taken up by General Dostler who said briefly, "Almers, we cannot change anything. You know the Führerbefehl. The execution is to be carried out. You know that the Führerbefehl contains a clause according to which officers who do not execute the order are to be tried by courts-martial." Further attempts were without result and the conversation came to an end.

Shultz described the second telegram that came from Dostler's headquarters in the early hours of March 26, ordering the execution, "The carrying out of the Führerbefehl is indispensable. The execution is to be reported by seven o'clock." Shultz was also the only officer who had witnessed the destruction of the records related to the matter in compliance with the order they received two weeks later from Kesselring's headquarters.

The next prosecution witness was Rudolph Bolze, who had chosen the execution spot and arranged the burial detail for the fifteen Americans. Although Bolze described in detail the events before and after the shots were fired, he denied having seen the actual execution of the men. It was the next witness, Wilhelm Knell, who provided that piece of the puzzle. Knell was a corporal in Bolze's company who was out to fetch coffee in the morning of March 26, 1944, when he was stopped by Bolze at a bend of the road in Punta Bianca. Soon after, he saw two trucks arrive and American prisoners climb out of them. Knell remembered noticing an officer who was without his shirt and shoes and "rubbed his wrists quite probably because he had been tied." When Roche asked what made him think the men was an officer, Knell said, "I assumed that from his looks," and he pumped his chest out to show a figure of authority in charge of the situation.

There were about twenty to twenty-five German soldiers in the execution detail, Knell recalled. They split the Americans in two groups and lined up the first seven along the road on the side of the mountain. Captain Rehfeld and Lieutenant Seidenstuecker stood next to the execution squad, turned their backs to the soldiers, and one of them gave the command to fire. After the first volley was fired, Bolze ordered Knell and other soldiers from his detail to move the bodies aside, cover them with planks, and throw sand on the blood.

"Did you do that?" Roche asked.

"Yes," Knell said. "I did that, but before that every one of the Americans was given a security shot."

"What do you mean by a security shot?"

"I have never assisted before in an execution, but I believe it is done to make sure that the soldier is really dead," Knell explained. During the interrogations, he had said that some of the men were still alive, yelling in pain, and all seven had received security shots.

"In what part of the bodies of these soldiers was the security shot fired?"

"I have seen several cases where the shots were given in the neck," said Knell, pointing behind his right ear at the base of the skull.

It was Lieutenant Seidenstuecker who had administered the security shots. The second group of Americans was executed in the same manner, four to five minutes after the first group had been shot. In the end, Knell saw the bodies loaded on a truck and driven down to the village where they were buried.

Up to this point, Roche had established the chain of events from the moment the men of the Ginny team left Bastia on the night of March 22, 1944, to the moment they were executed and buried. Next he introduced into evidence the testimony of Captain Albert G. Lanier who had conducted the initial investigation into the fate of the men and returned to Washington by the time the trial started. Together with Lanier's testimony, Roche introduced into the evidence the identification report that Lanier had prepared at the time the bodies were exhumed.

Major Clifford M. Bassett testified next. He had been one of the two medical doctors present in the exhumation of the bodies who had done the first examination. Bassett reiterated the findings in the exhumation report that they had not been able to find bullet wounds and attributed that to the advanced stage of decomposition of the bodies. There was also an explanation now for the splintered skulls they had seen, after Corporal Knell's testimony earlier about the security shots applied to each man after the execution. Throwing the bodies into a grave fifteen feet deep would have only added to the injuries on the bones and the skull. Major Bassett's testimony concluded the proceedings for the second day of the trial.

When the trial resumed the next morning, the prosecution presented as witnesses the two investigators who had interrogated Anton Dostler between June 9 and 12, Captains Alexander Golodetz and Robert Blythin. Golodetz was sworn in under the assumed name of Alexander Kennedy to protect his identity. Golodetz and Blythin described Dostler's unease and state of discomfort at certain points during the interrogations, such as when he was shown that he had issued the first execution order on his own initiative and without waiting for higher headquarters' decision. On cross-examination, Wolfe established that neither Golodetz nor Blythin had warned Dostler before beginning the interrogation that as a prisoner of war under the Geneva Convention he did not have to provide any information beyond his name, organization, and serial number. Wolfe also established the fact that Dostler had signed only a brief statement in German recounting the basic events. The other interrogation reports introduced in evidence were summaries in English prepared by the interrogating officers.

The last witness for the prosecution was General Gustav von Zangen. With a firm and authoritative voice, he reaffirmed that he had first heard of the execution of fifteen Americans in his area during the interrogations in June 1945. He remembered only having received a very short report on an act or attempt of sabotage near La Spezia around March 1944, after the matter was closed, upon his return from one of his numerous trips away from his headquarters. "If the report had mentioned the execution of American soldiers, fifteen of them, and in American uniform, I would have a recollection of that fact," von Zangen said. When Roche asked whether he had ordered the execution of the fifteen Americans, von Zangen very firmly said, "No, I could not have possibly done that."

With that, the prosecution rested.

* * *

Wolfe chose not to make an opening statement for the defense. He called back von Zangen as his first witness to testify about Dostler as an officer. Von Zangen described him as "very exact" and "very reliable in the execution of his duties," adding that Dostler "was a general who, as opposed to his outer appearance, was absolutely a soldier with a heart."

General von Senger, the second defense witness, also testified to Dostler's very good reputation as an officer during peacetimes. Wolfe used von Senger's testimony to establish the fact that all German soldiers and officers were bound by the oath given to Hitler when he rose to power, which, in von Senger's words, was "very short and it contained practically only the expression of loyalty and strict obedience to the Führer, Adolf Hitler himself." There was no question of disobeying orders issued by Hitler or under his authority, von Senger said. Generals, especially toward the end of the war, were punished not only for disobeying strict orders but also for acting on their own initiative, without clearing their actions with the Supreme Command of the Wehrmacht first.

In cross-examination, Roche asked von Senger whether the oath he and Dostler had given to Hitler bound them to carry out orders even when they were in violation of well-established principles of international law, including orders like the Führerbefehl, which demanded the summary execution of prisoners of war. Von Senger explained that it was the responsibility of the government to issue orders that complied with the international law and not of the individual officers who had to execute them. "I am convinced that, as things were, the Führer gave out orders which in some way interfered with international law," von Senger said. "We on the front who had to execute these orders were certain that he would make a statement or by some other means inform opponent governments of his decisions, so that we would not be responsible for carrying out his orders." When Roche asked whether von Senger or any other general could have refused to take the oath or resign if they objected to the orders, von Senger explained that before the war doing so would have led to "great disadvantages, both economic and personal, and for my family also." After the war started, there was a special order from the Führer that forbade a general from resigning because he disagreed with the decisions of the Supreme Command. "He was to remain on duty and he was bound to carry out the orders," von Senger said.

Next, Wolfe informed the commission that Dostler desired to take the stand as a witness and give sworn testimony. General Jaynes, the president of the commission, explained to Dostler that he had the right to do one of three things. First, he could remain silent and the court would not presume that he was guilty merely because he remained silent. Second, he could provide an unsworn statement, oral or written, personally or through his counsel, about the matters in front of the commission. Finally, he could take the stand, be sworn like any other witness, and testify on his behalf. Statements he made under oath carried greater weight with the commission than those made in an unsworn statement. However, if he chose to take the stand, he was subject to cross-examination by the trial judge advocate and the commission could allow greater latitude in the questions than in the cross-examination of other witnesses. Dostler replied that he understood his rights and desired to be sworn in as a witness.

In the first part of the examination, Wolfe asked Dostler to summarize his career in the military since the time he joined the army in 1910 and up to the point where he surrendered to the American troops on May 2, 1945. Then, the questions moved to the Führerbefehl. Dostler explained that the Führerbefehl the prosecution had introduced in the trial was not the complete order that had lain on his desk in March 1944 when the Americans had been captured. "The complete Führerbefehl has as its subject commando operations and there was a list of what it construed as commando operations," Dostler said. "I know exactly that a mission to explode something, to blow up something, came under the concept of commando troops. . . . In addition, there was something said in that Führerbefehl about the interrogation of men belonging to sabotage troops and the shooting of these men after their interrogation."

Then, Wolfe asked Dostler to recount the sequence of events related to the fifteen Americans. According to Dostler, he learned about the capture of the commando troops from the morning report of the Almers Brigade on March 25, 1944. Dostler remembered the terms "commando troops" and "English-speaking Italians" from that report. He discussed his report with his chief of staff, Colonel Kraehe, and his chief of intelligence, Captain zu Dohna. Since it appeared that this commando unit would come under the Führerbefehl, Dostler "had the Führerbefehl brought to us and studied it in a detailed fashion and we studied again the morning report. As it appeared without a doubt that the operations came under the Führerbefehl, an order was given by me and sent out that the men were to be shot." This was between nine and ten o'clock in the morning of March 25.

Dostler said he reflected about the matter and had a telephone conversation with Colonel Almers, who gave him further details about the commando unit, telling him that they were soldiers in uniform and that the matter should be examined further. As a result, Dostler said, "I told Colonel Almers the order which had been given out is not to be carried out. I shall examine the matter further and you shall hear from me." Dostler had another meeting with his staff officers Kraehe and zu Dohna and decided to ask von Zangen's headquarters what to do with these men, since the Führerbefehl explicitly forbade sending them to a prisoners of war camp.

Kraehe called about noon and spoke with Nagel, von Zangen's chief of staff. Late in the afternoon, Kraehe reported that a telephone call had arrived ordering the men to be executed. Dostler ordered Kraehe to forward the order to the Almers's headquarters. In the evening, while they were in the mess hall, a telephone call came for zu Dohna. After taking the call, zu Dohna reported that it had been an inquiry from Kesselring's headquarters about why the Americans had not been shot yet. Later that evening, Dostler had another telephone conversation with Almers in which he told him that the matter had been ordered. Then, at three o'clock in the morning of March 26, he received a call from Klaps asking for more time to interrogate the men. "I answered he is allowed to interrogate the men until early in the morning but he could not go further as the execution had been ordered by higher headquarters," said Dostler.

In cross-examination, Roche got Dostler to concede that troops under his command had executed the fifteen American soldiers on March 26, 1944, without trial or judicial proceedings. Dostler also admitted that his first order to Almers, sent in the morning of March 25, said, "The captured Americans are to be shot immediately." When pressed further, he admitted knowing that the captured men were Americans and not "English-speaking Italians" as he had said earlier. Dostler also admitted that he had issued the first order without taking the matter up with any higher headquarters. Thus, Roche implied, Dostler had sealed the fate of the Americans in the morning of March 25 and the fact that they had not been executed until the following morning was only due to the intervention of the subordinate officers in La Spezia, as recounted in the testimonies of Koerbitz, Schultz, and Klaps. When Roche asked Dostler whether he had any reason to disbelieve their testimonies, his answer was, "No." Roche then brought up the Führerbefehl, but Dostler held firmly his position that the document presented in the trial was only a partial version of the order as it existed in March 1944.

"Would you have ordered the execution of these fifteen American soldiers if it had not been for the Führerbefehl?" Roche asked.

"No," Dostler said. "I have waged war in many fronts, and I have never ordered the execution of any prisoners of war."

"Do you believe that if in this case you had not carried out the execution of these fifteen American soldiers that you yourself would bave been shot?"

"I had to count on being referred to courts-martial because of nonexecution of the Führerbefehl."

At the end of the cross-examination, a member of the commission, Colonel Notestein, referred Dostler to a paragraph of the Führerbefehl which said that if commando troops fell in the hands of the Wehrmacht through indirect means they were to be turned over immediately to the *Sicherheitdienst*, or the Secret Police. Dostler explained that zu Dohna, his chief of intelligence, had contacted the SD to transfer the

men, but the SD had refused to take them. When pressed by Notestein, Dostler admitted that he had issued his first order to execute the
Americans before attempting to contact the SD to turn over the men,
as called for in the Führerbefehl.

Dostler's testimony marked the end of the defense case. By the
end of the depositions, Dostler's main line of defense that the order
for the execution of the Americans had come from upper echelons had
been thoroughly undermined. By Dostler's own admission, his direct
commander, General von Zangen, had not given the order and Nagel,
von Zangen's chief of staff, did not have the authority to give such an
order on his own. If Nagel had received approval from Kesselring's
headquarters, why would Kesselring reverse himself with the telegram
sent to Klaps the day after the Americans had been executed? When
Wolfe asked Dostler to explain this contradiction, he said:

> I heard for the first time about that telegram in this trial. Something
> must be wrong here. I spoke to Almers on the day after the execu-
> tion and we talked about the matter, and Almers did not mention
> anything relating to that telegram. In addition, it is very unusual that
> a telegram of that sort would have come directly to the Almers head-
> quarters instead of passing through me or my headquarters.

There was a possibility that Kesselring's headquarters had confirmed the order based on verbal conversations over the telephone with
Nagel. Then, when they received the written cable from Klaps, they
sent the order to stop the execution, either because they truly wished
to stop it, or simply to provide cover for themselves by establishing for
the record that they had been against it. The fact that the same headquarters ordered all records related to the matter destroyed two weeks
later is certainly an indication that someone in Kesselring's circle had
considered the issue to be damning enough that it warranted burying.

* * *

When the trial resumed the next day, October 11, 1945, it was time
for closing arguments. Roche summarized the witnesses' statements

that the fifteen men of the ill-fated Ginny mission had been members of the United States Army on a military mission and in uniform when they were captured. Instead of being treated as prisoners of war, the men were executed, their execution was summary, without a trial or judicial proceeding, and Dostler had given the order or command for the execution.

This was a flagrant violation of the international laws of warfare, not only as set by The Hague and Geneva Convention, but going back hundreds of years. Roche said, "This court is sitting in the city of Rome where it was once the custom to seize captives and drag them along through the triumphal arch up to the Forum and then slaughter them. That custom has long died out. It is abhorrent to the decent feelings of civilized man. It had been against the law for at least five hundred years. It is against the law today, as all concerned agree."

Roche told the commission that there was no argument with the points he had summarized thus far. "The accused had conceded most of them," Roche said. "His guilt is thereby established. The only question which you must answer, the only question left unsolved or unanswered is this: To what extent is his guilt mitigated by the fact that he was acting under superior orders?" Roche said that there was no mitigation. Not only could Dostler not hide behind the Führerbefehl but a strict reading of it showed that he had not obeyed with its provision to hand over the captured Americans to the SD. And, there were grounds to believe that he had never consulted with General von Zangen or his chief of staff on the matter. What aggravated the matter was that Dostler had issued the original order to execute the men and had stuck with his decision, despite the efforts of Almers, Klaps, and others to change his mind. "It is pretty obvious that with the exception of the accused, no one had the stomach for this execution," said Roche.

Roche concluded his argument with these words: "For a violation of any of the laws of war, international law provides the penalty of death as a possible penalty. As a result of this particular violation of the law of war, fifteen American soldiers died. I leave to this commission the drawing of the conclusion from these two propositions."

There was a lunch recess, and when the trial resumed, it was Wolfe's turn to make his closing argument. Wolfe began by accepting that there

was no question that the execution of the Americans had been a violation of the Geneva Convention. The issue was whether Dostler was
the criminal responsible for the crime. "It cannot be denied in this case
that the Führerbefehl was the reason why the execution was carried
out," Wolfe said before proceeding to walk the commission through
the different paragraphs of the order that substantiated Dostler decision. Then, he evoked the testimony the German officers, especially
the generals among them, to the fact that "obedience to orders as they
understood them was an inherent requirement of any officer in the
German Army" and that to disobey the orders subjected them to trial
by a German court-martial.

Wolfe's argument was that obedience to superior orders was at the
heart of the matter. He reminded the commission that according to policy, principle, or legal and military precedent of the United States, "a subordinate officer is never treated as a war criminal or is punished or tried
for an act which he has been ordered to commit by competent authority."

As far as the prosecution's statements that Dostler had acted in
violation of the requirement to turn over the prisoners to the secret
police, Wolfe explained that the Americans had fallen into the hands
of the Wehrmacht from the beginning, they were not handed to them
by the police, and therefore, that clause of the Führerbefehl did not
apply. Besides, Wolfe said, "if reports of the activities of the SS are to
be believed, of what they had done to prisoners, these men are much
more fortunate to have been executed than turned over to the SS."

Those who complained about Dostler's initial order—Sessler,
Klaps, and Koerbitz—did not do so because they had a better understanding of the Führerbefehl than Dostler. They could not have had
access to the Führerbefehl, Wolfe argued. It was kept extremely secret,
to the point where no true copy of it had been found as of the time of
the trial and the document produced as evidence was a copy of uncertain provenience secured from the French intelligence. Sessler, Klaps,
and Koerbitz, Wolfe argued, were engaged in exactly the same kind of
work as the fifteen captured Americans. They realized that carrying
out the Führerbefehl would expose them to the same treatment at the
hands of the Americans someday. "They felt that as a matter of local
ethics, courtesies of their profession, of their own trade, that these men

should not be executed because of the danger of reprisals on them," Wolfe said, adding, "and I agree with them."

When presented with the complaints, Dostler rescinded his order of execution and passed the matter to higher command for a decision. Had he been acting in a vindictive and cruel manner, he would have simply ignored them and asked that the prisoners be shot, Wolfe said. With regards to which higher authority had sanctioned the execution, Wolfe pointed out that Dostler's inquiry must have gone up to the Supreme Command of the Southwest, Kesselring's headquarters. The absence of the witnesses that Dostler had requested hurt his ability to prove this conclusively, but there were two facts that nevertheless were convincing. The first one was that the order not to carry out the execution came to the Almers headquarters several hours after the fact. Had they intended to the stop the execution, Wolfe implied, they could have sent the order in time to stop the execution, which they knew was imminent. The most convincing fact was that Kesselring's headquarters had ordered the destruction of all records two weeks after the execution. "Somebody knew they had done wrong," Wolfe said. "Somebody wanted to cover up their tracks and it was not General Dostler. He never ordered the Brigade to destroy a single record. If we had those records today we would know the truth perhaps." Driving home this point, Wolfe told the commission, "The only conclusion you can draw from that is that we are not trying the right man in this case. I think General Kesselring's headquarters knew of this; that they ordered the execution and that they intended to fix the responsibility on some intermediate commanding general if they could do so."

Wolfe spoke for close to ninety minutes and then came in for a strong finish.

> Judge not lest ye be judged. . . . This time we won the war; next time we might not win it. Next time, you gentlemen, might be sitting here and this gentleman might be sitting there. . . . It would be most unfortunate indeed were we to hold General Dostler as a war criminal, and to be treated as a common felon because he performed what he thought to be his duties as a soldier and as an officer. . . .

The United States as a nation has a glorious background. We are protectors and defenders of the law and the right. . . . Trying in an unlawful and illegal manner this general here, convicting him contrary to the precepts upon which our great nation was founded, would be no more than what Adolf Hitler did when he executed these fifteen men in violation of law. Whatever the true facts may be, I don't know. The trial judge advocate, the defense counsel, and the members of this court are only trying to do their job, but I say this:

That if we don't do our duty, that if we simply find a man guilty because of political pressure or because he lost the war or he is in our power and we can do what we want to do to him—we might as well not have won the war. We might as well not have won the war unless we are going to make a bigger and better contribution to civilization, and unless we are going to establish the sacred laws and enforce those laws governing the rules of warfare and the living between nations.

* * *

After Wolfe finished, Roche stood up for a rebuttal. "I have listened to the most eloquent argument of the defense counsel," Roche said. "The prosecution cannot hope to match the defense in eloquence. I trust that what we lack in eloquence is made up by the soundness of our position, not only on the law but also on the facts." Roche went on to counter Wolfe's arguments that the responsibility for the crime fell on the Führerbefehl, Kesselring's headquarters, or Dostler's duty to obey superior orders. Then, Roche came in for his own strong closing. Picking up on the fact that Wolfe had said several times that at the time that the fifteen Americans had been executed, thousands of men were being killed each day at the fronts of Cassino and Anzio, he said:

In view of that undisputed fact, the defense says and would have you believe that the execution of these fifteen soldiers was quite insignificant. It must be an awful thing to be in the position of any of these fifteen men when he know what was going to happen to him; it must have been a terrible thing. I doubt very much that any one of the fifteen deemed the matter insignificant. I doubt very much if the wives, mothers, fathers, sons, daughters, and friends of any of these fifteen men deemed the matter insignificant. I doubt very much if the United States Army deemed it insignificant, and I know the people of the United States, of the United Nations, do not think it insignificant. It is not a pleasant thing to stand here or anywhere and cold-bloodily say to a fellow man that you must die for an offense. Nor is it a pleasant thing to stand here and say to a commission that your duty so dictates: you must condemn that man to death.

I ask you to approach the task which you are about to undertake not in a spirit of blood-thirsty revenge but rather with a determination that the voice, and the feelings, and the aspirations of civilized peoples, which have been soundly crushed for the past six or seven years, will at least be heard and clearly heard.

After the closing arguments, the commission met behind closed doors for the rest of the day. The next morning, October 12, 1945, at 0900 hours, the commission entered the room to hand down its verdict. Everyone stood up. Dostler came to the center of the room facing the commission at attention with the interpreter to his right. General Jaynes informed the spectators that no public expression of approbation or disapprobation of its action in the case would be permitted in the courtroom. Then he read the verdict:

General Dostler,
As president of this commission, it is my duty to inform you that the commission in closed session and upon secret written ballot, at least two-thirds of all the members of the commission concurring in each finding of guilty, find you of the specifications and of the charge:
Guilty.
And again in closed session and upon secret written ballot, at least two-thirds of all of the members of the commission concurring, sentences you:
To be shot to death by Musketry.

Dostler, who could not understand English, waited patiently until the translator found the words to translate the decision. Then, with a barely perceptible bow of the head he acknowledged the commission. The commission adjourned and the trial was over at 0905 hours.

* * *

On October 23, 1945, there was a change in leadership at the US Army Mediterranean Theater of Operations Command. General McNarney left the theater for the United States and Lieutenant General Mathew B. Ridgeway assumed the role of acting theater commander in his absence. It fell upon Ridgeway to review the trial record, consider any appeals for clemency, and act upon the sentence against Dostler. There were very few pleas for clemency on behalf of Dostler. On October 14, General von Vietinghoff, who had been the supreme commander of the German armies in Italy at the end of the war, wrote a letter to Lieutenant-General Frederick E. Morgan, the British supreme Allied commander of the Mediterranean theater of operations. "Dostler is well known as an excellent regular soldier who has paid the strictest attention to the carrying out, without questioning, of all orders," von Vietinghoff wrote. "He has become a sacrifice of the Führerbefehl mentioned in the trial. I would therefore request you to make use of your right to pardon him."

Dostler's daughter, Annemarie Dostler, wrote an emotional letter urging Ridgeway and those with power to decide life or death for her father to consider the larger meaning of mercy and justice. Quoting Shakespeare, she wrote that mercy comes by naturally, like "gentle rain from heaven." It blesses both those who receive mercy and those who grant it. It is especially powerful when given by the powerful. Mercy fits the king better than his crown and makes him stronger than his earthly authority vested in his scepter, because it is "an attribute to God himself." Although we may be entitled to justice, justice alone will not be our salvation. It is when "mercy seasons justice" that we are the strongest and most closely resemble God, she wrote.

Against these appeals for clemency stood passionate letters that family members of the murdered soldiers sent to different levels of the

US government. The father of Santoro Calcara wrote to the adjutant general in Washington, DC, and called his son "a loving Son, an excellent Boy . . . [who] was my only support in my old age, a real soothing consolation by his irreproachable behavior and the only helping Companion of my life. As a Father, and so tremendously thrown out of balance, I would for my part recommend and invoke the extreme penalty on the vile assassin and butcher."

Private First Class Joe DiScalfani, brother of Salvatore DiScalfani, wrote to the War Department asking that they communicate with him regarding the outcome of the trial rather than his mother, who was too fragile to handle the news. He also asked to be "among those to execute the guilty, and there can be no other punishment for them than execution. I have not killed a man before but I assure you it would be a pleasure to kill these Germans who took the lives of my brother and 14 other Americans."

Josephine Russo, sister of Lieutenant Vincent Russo, wrote to President Harry Truman to complain about Dostler's defense counsel, Colonel Wolfe. She wrote:

> My temper became infuriated to read that an American Colonel of his standing should try and save the life of this monstrous Nazi criminal who so brutally took the lives of fifteen young American boys. . . . Did Gen'l Dostler show any leniency to my poor unfortunate brother? No! Neither should he be given any leniency. . . . Those boys fought hard for their country and joined a Commando outfit which very few boys join knowing that their lives are at stake at all times. They showed true patriotism to their country by risking their lives on such a dangerous mission and the loss of their lives should not be in vain by acquitting this monstrous Gen'l Dostler and also to have a greedy and inconsiderate Colonel such as Col. Wolfe serve in the American Army.

A lengthy response from the office of the judge advocate general explained that Wolfe served as Dostler's counsel not because of any personal desires but because he was ordered by his commanding officer to perform a military duty and he "should not be censured for ably performing an assignment that must have been distasteful to him."

* * *

Dostler himself wrote a long petition to Ridgeway submitted on October 24, 1945, in which he outlined a number of factors for his consideration. Dostler began with a summary of his unblemished record in all theaters of operations where he had served. Then, he highlighted the fact that with the exception of von Zangen, no other material witnesses had appeared during the trial who could testify to what had transpired at his, von Zangen's, or Kesselring's headquarters. "It was not possible for me to successfully defend myself before this Commission," Dostler wrote, "since the Commission heard only certain witnesses against me, but did not hear witnesses who could have aided me." Dostler's petition also discussed the fact that the Führerbefehl used in the trial had not been complete and the same one he had reviewed when deciding the fate of the Americans. Finally, Dostler raised the point that he should have been tried by a court-martial, in accordance with the Geneva Convention provisions, rather than by a military commission. Given these facts, Dostler asked Ridgeway to commute the sentence to a term of confinement or suspend the execution of the sentence until further evidence was gathered from witnesses who had not been available at the trial. "It was not my order who caused this unfortunate incident," Dostler wrote in conclusion, "but it was the order of a higher headquarters. As an officer of the German Army, it was my duty to obey orders and I obeyed them. For this reason, I feel that I am neither legally nor morally responsible for any breach of international law."

Neither Dostler nor Wolfe was aware that both Kesselring and his chief of staff, General Siegfried Westphal, were interviewed in Nuremberg in relation to the Dostler case. Westphal, interviewed on October 4, 1945, was very evasive in his responses but recollected that the daily report of Army Group von Zangen included the capture near La Spezia of commando troops. The report had been forwarded as usual to the OKW, the Supreme Command of the Armed Forces.

When asked whether he recalled an order by OKW as to what was to be done with these troops, Westphal said, "It is very difficult for me to testify to this under oath, but I believe that an order had come down from OKW that these troops should be treated according to the Führer's decree. . . . I want to say this: That if the report had been given to the OKW, as I believe it was, I am sure that the order to shoot these people came from the OKW." Westphal also remembered the Führerbefehl as consisting of two parts. The first part was very brief and signed by Hitler. The second part contained rules for carrying out the order and was signed by either Keitel or Jodl.

Kesselring was interviewed on October 6, 1945. He denied recalling the execution of the fifteen Americans. "Due to the mass of reports that came to me about terrorist partisan activities, one incident or another might have escaped my attention due to the fact that I was frequently away from my headquarters," he said. When the interrogator asked him whether he would like to say anything in defense of Dostler, Kesselring said:

> General Dostler was a very smart, energetic, and wise leader. He had tried to carry out the task that was given him one hundred percent. He had made himself valuable particularly in two fields: a) coastal defense, and (b) fight against the partisans behind the lines. I recall that he had carried out one particular action against a group of partisans in a masterly way, so that it was considered by me as a model action. It is possible that, due to the great number of partisan actions, the personal excitement played a certain role. I also know that the railroad to La Spezia was subjected to frequent interruptions, which embittered us, particularly because this railroad also served to bring food and other necessities to the civilian population in the area.
>
> According to his military principles, I believe that General Doslter would have taken execution measures only if he was properly backed up by orders from higher sources. If the case had not been entirely clear, he would certainly have asked for orders from higher up. If in this case the intermediate higher headquarters, or my own headquarters, had been approached (I cannot say whether they

were or not), one of these higher headquarters would have to take the responsibility.

* * *

On November 6, 1945, Colonel Tom H. Barratt, acting theater judge advocate, reviewed the trial record, as required by law, and found nothing in the appeals for clemency to warrant further hearings in the case. On November 27, 1945, Ridgeway issued General Order Number 301, which approved and confirmed the sentence against Dostler. The sentence was to be carried into execution on or before December 1, 1945, at or in the vicinity of Aversa, Italy.

On November 28, 1945, at 1400 hours, four US Army officers visited Dostler at his confinement cell at the Peninsular Base Station (PBS) Garrison Stockade 1 in Aversa, near Naples. They read Ridgeway's order to Dostler and asked him whether he had anything to say or any request. Army records do not indicate what Dostler said, but show that "Subject prisoner's last request was carried out." Chaplain Franz Gruber, a German prisoner of war himself, was with Dostler. He had been with him since November 15 and would be by his side until the last moments of his life. Frido von Senger visited Dostler on November 30. He remembered spending some time with the condemned man while outside they could hear the firing squad rehearsing. Von Senger wrote:

> He was his usual self, cheerful and relaxed, explaining that he only wanted to thank me for my friendship and good offices and to bid me farewell, as he was due to be shot. Too moved to speak, I stood there a while looking him in the face, this comrade with smiling eyes who in adversity had become my friend.[2]

In a last minute attempt to delay the execution, Colonel Wolfe, Dostler's defense counsel, requested that Ridgeway consider granting a three-month grace period before the execution of the death sentence, which paragraph 139 of Army Field Manual 27–10, The Law of Land Warfare, accorded to condemned prisoners of war. Ridgeway met with Barratt on November 30, 1945, to review the request. Barratt expressed the view that Dostler was classified as a war criminal, a person who had performed an unlawful belligerent act, contrary to the laws and usages of war, and, therefore, was not entitled to the status of a prisoner of war and the privileges accorded to prisoners of war. Ridgeway let his execution order stand.

Dostler also sent an appeal for clemency to the pope. On November 30, the Vatican's secretary of state delivered a letter to Harold Tittmann, the Unites States representative to the Holy See, which said, among other, "His holiness in accordance with those sentiments of Christian charity and mercy with which he regards all men cannot but bring this appeal to the attention of the competent authorities." Records show that Titman had at least two conversations with Ridgeway about the Vatican request, the last one on December 1 at 0710 hours, without being able to change the course of the events.

In the morning of December 1, Second Lieutenant Walter L. Willie, Corporal Gordon W. Wilkinson, and Corporal James W. Murray prepared Dostler for execution. He was dressed in regulation uniform, with all decorations, insignia, and other distinguishing marks removed. Willie recalled Dostler telling him that his trial could have been more just by having his witnesses there, but he said, "I understand the American people believe in justice and I want you to thank each and every person concerned for the courtesies extended in my case."[3]

Shortly before 0900 hours, Lieutenant Willie, the prisoner guard, Dostler, Chaplain Gruber, and Captain H. B. Crummins, a US Army chaplain, left the cell block and headed to the place of execution. A special guard of twelve enlisted men from Company B, 803 Military Police Battalion, was lined up in two ranks facing one another at the entrance of the firing pit. Ten officers designated as official witnesses to the execution and several others, including photographers and motion picture camera operators from the Army Signals Corps, were lined up behind ropes. It was a sunny but chilly morning, and the condensation of breaths created the impression that men were blowing out smoke.

Willie led the way, followed by Dostler, the two chaplains, and the two corporals. They walked between the ranks of the special guard, down a flight of steps, and into the firing pit. Then, they headed toward the far side of the pit where a post had been erected. Dostler walked to the post, halted, turned around, and leaned against it. Chaplain Crummins stood to his left and Chaplain Gruber stood to his right, reciting prayers. The two guards tied Dostler's hands behind the post, and then secured him against the post with ropes that went around his chest, thighs, and ankles. The officer in charge of the execution, Lieutenant John H. Magnocavallo, read the charge, finding, sentence, and execution orders aloud. Then, he asked Dostler if he had a last statement. "No," said Dostler, adding, "*Es lebe Deutchland!*" (Long live Germany) and in a quieter voice, "My soul in God's keeping, my life for the Fatherland."[4] One of the guards removed Dostler's hat and the other one placed a black hood over his head. The medical officer, Captain Arthur N. Lieberman, placed a four-inch-wide oval white target over his heart. Then, the prisoner guard, the chaplains, and medical officer walked to the opposite side of the firing pit.

Magnocavallo ordered the firing squad to enter the pit. It was composed of one sergeant and eleven enlisted men. One by one, they came down the steps and retrieved their weapons from a rack of rifles positioned next to the steps. Earlier in the morning, Magnocavallo had personally prepared and tested the weapons in the firing pit. He had supervised the loading of the weapons. Per regulation, at least one, but not more than four of them, were loaded with blank ammunition. Then, Magnocavallo had placed the weapons at random in the rack.

The men in the firing squad stood in two rows three feet from one another at order arms. On Magnocavallo's command, they turned to face the prisoner and positioned themselves at arm's length. The men in the second row took one step to the right and stood between the men in the first row. Magnocavallo raised his right arm vertically overhead, palm forward, fingers extended and joined. The execution party came to the ready position. The first row took a knee to the ground while the second raw remained standing. The men unlocked the weapons. Magnocavallo lowered his arm to a horizontal position in front of his body. The firing squad aimed the rifles at Dostler. Magnocavallo dropped his arm directly to his side and commanded: "Fire!" The execution squad fired the volley simultaneously. It was 0909 hours, December 1, 1945.

The bullets hit the white target over Dostler's heart and cut the rope that secured him to the post. He leaned slowly forward and to the right. His body stopped at a forty-five-degree angle, and then, as Dostler gave his last breath, it bent to almost ninety degrees. Steam rose from the exit wounds in his back. The chaplains came forward, followed by the medical doctor who began inspecting the condemned man. Magnocavallo stood nearby prepared to administer the *coup de grace* with his side arm, if the medical officer so decided. At 0911 hours, the medical officer declared Anton Dostler dead. At this point, the men in the firing squad, who had turned their back to the condemned after firing their volley, placed their rifles in the rack and left the firing pit. Magnocavallo ordered the removal of Dostler's body from the post. Three enlisted men wrapped him in a white mattress cover, laid him on a stretcher, and took him away in the back of a truck for burial.

* * *

Anton Dostler was buried near the place of execution in Aversa, Naples. His remains were later moved to the German War Cemetery in Pomezia near Rome, where they are to this day.

The fifteen men of the ill-fated Ginny mission were buried at the US military cemetery in Florence, Italy. Eight of them were later brought to the United States by their families. They were all awarded the Bronze Star for gallantry in combat operations in 1946. In 1990, the town of Ameglia, located between La Spezia and Punta Bianca in Italy, placed a plaque in the main town square commemorating the members of the Ginny mission. They also placed bronze markers at Punta Bianca where the team had been executed and at La Ferrara where they were buried. A group of OSS OG veterans led by Albert Materazzi traveled to Italy in 2004 and on March 26 led commemoration ceremonies on the sixtieth anniversary of the execution of the Ginny team.

After the execution of Anton Dostler, the wave of death sentences against former German officers abated. General von Falkenhorst who applied the Führerbefehl numerous times in Norway stood trial in front of a British-Norwegian military court in Brunswick, Germany.

He was found guilty of war crimes on seven counts and sentenced to death in August 1946. The sentence was commuted to twenty years' imprisonment in November 1946. Due to ill health, von Falkenhorst was released as an act of clemency in 1953. He died in 1968.[5]

In 1947, Marshal Kesselring faced his own trial in Venice in front of a British military tribunal for his role in the Ardeatine Caves massacres in Italy on March 24, 1944. His possible role in ordering the execution of the fifteen American OGs around the same time went unnoticed. The court's initial sentence of death was commuted to life in prison by the reviewing judge. Eventually Kesselring was allowed to leave prison on health grounds and died in 1960.[6]

CHAPTER 16

No Justice for Major Holohan

Major Holohan had a brother in Brooklyn, New York, with whom he had maintained a close relationship since childhood. His name was Joseph E. Holahan, a spelling of the last name different from Major Holohan's due to a confusion in school records that dated back the days of elementary school. Before Major Holohan had left for the Mangosteen-Chrysler mission behind the lines in Italy, he had written his brother to let him know that he may not hear from him for a while. He had also asked that if anything happened to him, and "if there is anything left of me" to bring his body home and bury him with their parents at Gate of Heaven Cemetery in Pleasantville, New York. That was the last time Holahan heard from his brother.

When the Army declared Major Holohan "Missing in Action" in February 1945, his brother began contacting and writing to everyone who might have known Holohan overseas. In December 1945, the War Department notified Holahan that it had listed his brother officially as "Killed in Action." That did not stop Holahan from continuing his search for his brother's whereabouts. "There was something that kept gnawing at me," he said later. "I could not put my finger on it but I knew, somehow, that I had not heard the truth about my brother."[1]

Unbeknown to Holahan, the Army's Criminal Investigating Division (CID) had continued to look into the mystery of Hoholan's disappearance. In 1947, they had gone to the area in Lake Orta where the mission had operated and interviewed local Italians who had been in contact with the mission. A strange document had appeared in their search showing that Aldo Icardi had invested a sum of money in return for a share of ownership into a woodworking business that Aminta Migliari and his father operated.

In August 1947, Icardi was attending law school at the University of Pittsburgh when an agent of the CID contacted him to ask questions about this transaction. Icardi wrote that the agent questioned him at the CID offices for two hours. At the end, he asked Icardi if he was willing to take a lie detector test. Icardi agreed and returned in a week for the examination. Icardi described a tense session that lasted the entire day during which the CID investigators repeatedly asked questions about the disappearance of Major Holohan. Then, they asked him to come back the next day for more questioning. After three hours of additional questions the next morning, the CID investigators told Icardi the case was closed and he would not hear about it again.[2] The CID report summarizing the outcome of the two sessions indicated that the polygraph tests showed a lot of agitation around questions related to the financial transaction that Icardi had concluded with Migliari but did not indicate that Icardi was lying about the whereabouts of Major Holohan.[3]

Icardi went on with his law studies, graduating in June 1948, then passing the Pennsylvania Bar Exam on March 1949. Two weeks later, he left for Lima, Peru, with his family to study international law.

* * *

When the CID investigation failed to discover any new leads, the War Department turned the Holohan case over to the Italian authorities, which continued their investigation in secret. A breakthrough came in early 1949, when Lieutenant Elio Albieri took over command of the local Carabinieri post in Lake Orta. Albieri was young and energetic and he quickly zoomed into Aminta Migliari, the local man who had monopolized the relationship between the Italian partisans and the OSS mission from the time they had parachuted in and until the disappearance of Major Holohan. Beginning in

February 1949, Migliari began talking and told Albieri about tensions between Holohan and Icardi.

Migliari pointed Albieri toward Gualtiero Tozzini and Giuseppe Manini, the two local men he had provided to escort the American mission in those days. Albieri called both of them for questioning. Initially, they told conflicting stories about the ambush of December 6, 1944. It was a clue for Albieri that they were not telling the truth. He reported the new leads developed in the case to his superior command, which notified the American consul in Milan and the American military command in Trieste. Henry Manfredi, on the staff of the Army's Criminal Investigations Division in Trieste, arrived in Lake Orta to participate in the Italian investigation.

After continued interrogations, Manini and Tozzini opened up and told Albieri and Manfredi a horrid story of betrayal and murder that pointed to Icardi as the mastermind of a plot to eliminate Holohan and Lo Dolce as the one who had pulled the trigger. The two Italians said they had no choice but to assist the two Americans in killing their superior officer and getting rid of his body. They had feared that they might suffer the same fate if they did not.[4]

Based on the testimony of Manini and Tozzini, the Italian authorities had a story for the disappearance of Holohan, although not a clear motive for why Icardi and Lo Dolce had killed their commander. Albieri and Manfredi focused next on finding the body of Holohan. At the beginning of June 1950, they hired local bargemen with makeshift hooks to comb, they combed the bottom of the lake in the area where Manini and Tozzini said they had dumped the body. The depth of the lake varied between sixty and one hundred twenty feet and the efforts proved fruitless for several days, but persistence paid off. In the afternoon of June 15, 1950, the Carabinieri fished a backpack out of the lake. A thunderstorm rolled in from the mountains and forced them to suspend the search for the day. But they returned to the same spot the next morning and, after one hour of searching, brought to the surface first pieces of a sleeping bag and then a corpse.

Albieri took the remains to the morgue of the cemetery in the nearby village of San Maurizio d'Opaglio where the local doctor performed an initial inspection of the body. Parts of it were in an

advanced state of decomposition. The right hand was missing, perhaps severed when they had pulled the body from the lake. On the
left wrist, the doctor noticed a wristwatch that had stopped at 10:35.
It was easy to notice that at least two bullets had hit the head. The first
one had made an entry hole in the left temple with an exit hole in the
opposite side of the skull. The second one had hit in the back, at the
base of the skull.[5]

* * *

With the new developments from Italy, CID investigators in the
United States began looking at the case again. Icardi was still in Peru at
the time, but Lo Dolce was in Rochester, New York, working for a lock
manufacturing company there and attending the Rochester Institute
of Technology under the GI Bill of Rights. At the end of July 1950,
two investigators visited Lo Dolce at his workplace and interviewed
him over two sessions. They described the events surrounding Major
Holohan's disappearance that had surfaced from the Italian investigation and pressed Lo Dolce to confess to his role in the murder of
his commanding officer. Lo Dolce refused and cut short the second
interview by asking the agents to leave. They did so, but returned the
next day, August 3, 1950, in the morning, accompanied by the chief of
detectives of the Rochester Police Department. They took Lo Dolce
to the police headquarters for questioning and spent several hours trying to get him to admit to his involvement in the case.

Lo Dolce, who had come out of the war in a particularly fragile
physical and mental state, was under additional stress at the time. His
brother had been killed in Korea a few weeks earlier, his wife was in
the hospital having just given birth to their youngest baby, and he suffered from back pain due to injuries he had received during the mission
in Italy. According to Icardi, the interrogators took advantage of the
hardship Lo Dolce was under by repeatedly telling him what he was
supposed to have done and pressing him to confess everything. After
three hours of continuous interrogation, they pushed him to take a lie
detector test. "Under those conditions," Icardi said, "it's not surprising
that the machine indicated agitation."[6]

The interrogation resumed with vigor afterward. In the end, Lo Dolce wrote in his own hand and signed an eight-page statement in which he corroborated the story that Manini and Tozzini had told in Italy. Lo Dolce wrote that Holohan and Icardi had never been friendly and an air of friction and tension had developed between them. Icardi and Lo Dolce began to feel that the major was hampering them from performing a useful service. Rather than sending messages to the headquarters with information about the strength and movements of Germans and Fascist troops that could save the lives of hundreds of American soldiers, the mission was preoccupied mainly with reporting about Italian politics. Lo Dolce wrote:

> It all (the plan to rid ourselves of Major Holohan) began in a joking way. For instance, at times when the major had been overly authoritative with one of our partisan attendants and left the room, someone would say in a joking way, "Should I send him to Switzerland without his shoes?" which means to kill someone. Somehow, from being just a saying the thing became serious. Icardi suggested that we give the major something that would make him sick for a while so that we could get the underground to send him to Allied territory via Switzerland, but no one took him seriously.
>
> On the 6th of December 1944, one of our Italian attendants, Manin, brought something that looked like sugar in a piece of paper and said that it was poison and could be used to kill the major. By this time, the major was held in an intense aversion by myself, Icardi, Manin, and Pupo, and means of getting rid of him had been discussed. It may have been a means of getting off steam—the fear caused by being in the general situation may have made us want to direct it against something tangible, and wild and impossible plans had been discussed and discarded. On the 6th of December, 1944, things suddenly seemed to become serious. Manin said he had tried the poison on a cat and that it had died instantly. Icardi said we would have to use the poison right away—that night.
>
> Manin and Pupo prepared a meal of soup and rice and Manin placed some of the poison in the soup. The major was called to dinner, and we all set down to eat. When the major had taken a few

spoonfuls of the soup he remarked that it burned. Icardi said, "Yes, it's hot." Manin and Pupo were silent (to the best of my memory) throughout the meal. I felt sick and could not bring myself to look up during the meal, forcing myself to eat. I think the major ate all his soup and then suddenly rose and left the room. Manin remarked that he probably went upstairs to vomit.

The major came back. I don't remember whether he ate rice— soon after he came down he said he didn't feel well and was going to bed. When he had left, Manin remarked that I had been extremely pale during the meal and that the major surely knew something was wrong. Icardi and I sat in front of the fireplace and wondered what was going to happen. Icardi said something like, "If he lives through this, he will send a message to headquarters, so we'll have to make sure he doesn't live."

He asked Manin and Pupo if they would shoot the major and they said they absolutely refused, so Icardi said it had to be me or him. I don't remember clearly my movements from then on. I remember Icardi tossed a coin and I called and lost. Manin gave me a gun, his Beretta. We walked in. The major sat up and said either "What is it?" "Who is it?" or "What's the matter?" I walked to the side of his bed and fired two shots.

Icardi, Manin, and Pupo rushed in. Icardi opened the major's haversack and removed some money in bills which were rolled up. I'm not sure exactly what was taken because I stood there dazed and weak and couldn't think well. Manin, Pupo, and Icardi picked up the major. He was heavy and Manin told me to help but I couldn't bring myself to do anything. The major was carried to the boat, which Manin had waiting on the lake. I took my radio equipment and followed them and placed it in the boat. Icardi and I waited on the shore while Manin and Pupo rowed him out to deeper water and dropped his weighted body.

When they returned, Icardi told the partisans to go get the rest of our stuff. I don't remember whether they had two trips back to the house or one, or whether Icardi told Manin to go fire some rounds into the house then, or whether Manin did this in accordance with a pre-arranged plan. Manin went back and when he started firing, we fired too, so that people would think that we were being ambushed. A hand grenade that had belonged to the major was set off, but I don't remember who threw it. After the firing, Pupo and I left for Villa Maria, while Icardi and Manin left for the town of Pella by water.[7]

One would think that with Lo Dolce's confession in hand, the CID investigators would move quickly to bring closure to the case. Instead, nothing happened. They told Lo Dolce that he was "cleared."[8] The Rochester police told Lo Dolce's employer, Sargent & Greenleaf, "Lo Dolce was absolutely innocent of any irregularity of any nature whatsoever, and that everything in regard to this case was clear and above question."[9] The government investigators had no further contacts with Lo Dolce. They did not contact Icardi about these latest developments in Peru, where he lived until April 1951, or after his return to the United States.

* * *

The American public knew very little about this story until August 1951. Some Italian American newspapers that followed the Italian press had reported on the developments of the Italian investigation, but the story did not go beyond their niche audience. This all changed in the summer of 1951. Michael Stern, European correspondent for Fawcet Publications and *True, The Men's Magazine*, picked up threads of the story in Rome. He interviewed a number of sources in the Lake Orta area and prepared an account of the mystery surrounding the disappearance of Holohan.

The story portrayed Icardi as the mastermind of the crime and Lo Dolce as the material executor. Stern identified politics and greed as the two motives for the slaying of Major Holohan. Icardi, according to the story, had advocated for dropping of supplies to the Communists, while Holohan wanted to support the Christian Democrats in the area. Once Icardi eliminated Holohan, Stern wrote, dozens of supply missions had been flown to the partisans in the area, most of which went into the hands of the Garibaldi units. Besides political motivations,

Stern charged that Icardi had killed Holohan to appropriate $100,000 worth of mission funds that he carried on him.

Stern's story was included in the September issue of *True* magazine. The publisher sent advance copies of the issue to subscribers in early August. One such copy arrived at the Pentagon on August 9, 1951. Less than a week later, on August 15, 1951, the Department of Defense issued a press release recounting a chilling cloak-and-dagger story of two American servicemen who had murdered their commanding officer behind enemy lines in a struggle to arm Communist partisans in Italy. The Pentagon's press release borrowed heavily from the *True* magazine story, including factual errors that Stern had reported and which the Army could have easily verified. Such errors included the amount of funds that Holohan had carried for the mission and the number of drops before and after his disappearance. Ken W. Purdy, editor of the magazine, accused the Defense Department of copying the story from his magazine and issuing it as its own press release to preempt the impact that its publication would have. At the same time, he charged the Department with suppressing the story from reaching the public. "Government officials have long known who killed Major Holohan and by every device at their command have tried to keep the story from reaching the public," Purdy said.[10]

For the next few days, the story made the headlines around the country. The most shocking twist was that neither Icardi nor Lo Dolce could be prosecuted under United States civil or military law. Since the crime had occurred overseas, it was outside the jurisdiction of American civilian courts, which can prosecute only crimes perpetrated in US territories. It was also outside the purview of the military justice system because both Icardi and Lo Dolce had been honorably discharged from service in 1945. According to military laws in effect when the crime was alleged to have occurred and until 1951, the jurisdiction of the United States military authorities over servicemen terminated when they separated from the military. The Supreme Court had ruled that servicemen, even though separated from the service for as little as one day, could not be court-martialed for a crime committed while on active duty. The new Uniform Code of Military Justice, which had become effective in May 1951, had plugged this loophole in the old law, but it was not retroactive. Thus, the only legal recourse against Icardi and Lo Dolce seemed to be their extradition to Italy to face charges there.[11] The Pentagon cited this inability to take legal action as the main reason why they had not gone public with the story sooner, even though they had obtained a confession from Lo Dolce over a year ago.

* * *

Aldo Icardi immediately called the charges "absurd, vicious, and completely untrue." He said that if the Italian partisans had confessed to the murder of Holohan, they were simply trying to shift the blame to him and Lo Dolce. "The vagaries and complexities of Italian politics are such that all kinds of trumped-up charges could be made against us," he said. Rather than being tried by a magazine, radio, and press, "contrary to every concept of due process of law and freedom that we have fought with blood to preserve," Icardi said he would accept a trial by jury "at the drop of the hat." He even offered to reenlist to face a military tribunal. But he vowed to fight any attempts to extradite him to Italy, where he would not stand a chance for a fair trial due to the nature of his espionage activities during the war. "I am the victim of enemies in Italy who are striking back at me because they did not understand the work we were doing or were disgruntled in failing to get arms we were not able to supply. I have been caught in the cross-current of Italian politics. These enemies are trying to Shanghai me into standing trial in a country where I served as a spy for the Allies."[12]

Carl Lo Dolce came out in public as well after the Rochester Police Department released to the press his eight-page confession to the murder of Holohan from a year ago. In a press conference in Rochester on August 17 with his wife and lawyers by his side, Lo Dolce admitted that the confession he signed a year earlier was in his own handwriting. But, he added, "I refute and repudiate the confession as it appeared in the press. It is incomplete and the facts will prove that I am completely innocent of those charges. There is no doubt in my mind that when the proper authorities reveal the complete and true story, the disclosures will prove that I am innocent."[13]

Other people came to the defense of Icardi and Lo Dolce. Arthur P. Ciarmicoli, the OG technical sergeant who had been a member of the original Chrysler mission told reporters, "As far as Lo Dolce and the lieutenant [Icardi] murdering anyone, I don't believe it. As for the motive—money—that's silly. As far as saying there was any bad feeling between Icardi and Holohan, that is not fair. We all didn't particularly like the major. He was older than the rest of us and was content to sit back and take things easy. He endangered our lives on several occasions with his attitude."[14]

General Donovan spoke to reporters from his law office at 2 Wall Street and said that the sum Holohan carried with him was closer to $14,000 and not the $100,000 reported by the Pentagon and in the press. He praised Holohan as a "very upstanding, serious, brave guy," assigned to the difficult mission of working with pro- and anti-Communist partisans, "whichever could at a given time deliver a more effective blow at the Germans."[15]

Vincenzo Moscatelli, the wartime Communist partisan leader, who in 1951 was a member of the parliament in Italy, spoke to the press there and described his dealings with Major Holohan. "The major came to me accompanied by Icardi and asked the number of my forces," he said. "Because of his attitude toward us, I did not give him detailed information. What I firmly told him was this: 'Send us more arms. For any information about my men, apply to the British missions, who know us better than you do.'" He said that propaganda from Christian Democratic partisan groups had caused Holohan to take an anti-Communist attitude. When Icardi took command of the OSS mission after Holohan's disappearance, Moscatelli said, his Communist partisans received a larger proportion of the arms dropped.[16]

By some strange coincidence, as the story of Holohan's murder behind enemy lines made the headlines around the country, his body arrived on August 20, 1951, at the Brooklyn Army Base on a transport ship from Trieste. It was in a bronze casket encased in a wooden crate draped with the American flag. A requiem mass for Major Holohan was celebrated at the Saint Patrick's Cathedral on August 27. General Donovan, Colonel Suhlig, and other former military associates, friends, and family members attended the funeral service. A military honor guard accompanied the funeral cortege after the service to the Gate of Heaven Cemetery in Pleasantville, New York. Major Holohan was buried next to his parents, according to his wishes, with full military honors including the traditional three volleys that the honor guard fired over the grave.[17]

* * *

On the same day that Holohan's burial ceremony was held in New York, magistrate Carlo Rama in Italy finalized the investigation on the circumstances of the major's death. He named Aldo Icardi, Carl Lo Dolce, and the two Italian ex-partisans, Gualtiero Tozzini and Giuseppe Manini, as his murderers. He issued warrants for the arrests of Icardi and Lo Dolce, which was the first step for their extradition to Italy to face trial under the terms of an 1868 treaty between Italy and the United States. On January 1952, the Italian government submitted a formal extradition request to the State Department, together with over one hundred pages of evidence, including the affidavits from Manini and Tozzini confessing to participating in the murder. After the State Department completed the review of the request, Secretary Dean Acheson signed orders for the arrests of Icardi and Lo Dolce for being fugitives from the justice of Italy. These orders were forwarded to the Italian General Consul in New York on January 31, 1952.[18]

With these orders in hand, Italian consular officers tried for several months to get federal courts in Pennsylvania and New York to issue warrants for the arrests of Icardi and Lo Dolce. Their efforts were frustrated at every turn on the grounds that the 1868 extradition treaty between the United States and Italy was not in force in December 1944 because the Italian government did not have physical control and authority over northern Italy. Italy was still the enemy of the United States at the time and courts had repeatedly upheld the immunity of US military forces in enemy territory from the laws and tribunals of the occupied hostile country.[19]

At the end of August 1951, Italian authorities abandoned efforts to extradite Icardi and Lo Dolce. Lo Dolce, who at the time was undergoing treatment for his back injuries at the Buffalo Veterans Hospital, said when hearing the news that "this is the most beautiful day of my life." Icardi sent him a telegram that said, "Our hour approaches to tell the world we served the country well and honorably." He told the Associated Press in Pittsburgh, "I've been taking a beating for over a year and I'm going to start punching back. I am going to take my story to the American people in the form of a book which I am completing."[20] The book, *Aldo Icardi, An American Spy*, came out in 1954 and provides Icardi's version of the events and his rebuttal to the accusations levied against him and Lo Dolce in the Holohan case.

* * *

When the Italian government's efforts to extradite Icardi or Lo Dolce failed, the judicial authorities there moved to try them in absentia for the robbery and murder of Major Holohan. According to the indictment, Icardi was the mastermind of the plot, Lo Dolce pulled the trigger, and three Italians—Aminta Migliari, Gualtiero Tozzini, and Giuseppe Manini—were accessories to murder and had assisted in getting rid of the major's corpse.

The trial began on October 19, 1953. At 8:45 a.m., a closed van escorted by two Carabinieri trucks stopped at the steps of the Court of Assizes of Novara. The first to come out was Migliari, in his early thirties, extremely pale, very thin, with a bony face and myopic eyes. He was stunned for a moment by the flashes of dozens of cameras but then lowered his head and proceeded up the stairs into the building. Tozzini and Manini followed, both in their forties. Handcuffed and chained together, they ignored the photographers but greeted friends and family waiting for them in the steps of the courthouse. At 9:30 a.m., the Carabinieri brought the defendants into a cage inside the courtroom, which was packed with ex-partisans, journalists, lawyers, and other members of the public. Vincenzo Moscatelli, the ex-partisan leader of the area and Communist member of the Italian parliament, set the mood of the audience by shouting, "Let the Italians go free. They were only obeying American orders. They couldn't do otherwise." Then, he called out to the three defendants, "The comrades won't forget you."[21]

A few minutes after 9:30, the eight-member court presided by Judge Francesco Sicher entered the room and the trial began. After the opening formalities, one of the court-appointed lawyers for Icardi and Lo Dolce rose. Reading from a letter that Icardi had sent him, he argued that based on international law the Italian judicial system did not have jurisdiction to try two foreign military personnel accused of murdering a co-national. The court took a brief recess and when it returned, it rejected the argument.

The next order of business was to interrogate a minor defendant in the case, a farmer by the name of Edoardo Maulini, who three years earlier had purchased from Tozzini the pistol that had been used to kill Holohan. Now, he stood accused of illegal possession of a firearm. Under interrogation from Sicher, he quickly admitted his culpability. Sicher asked him to come back in fifteen days for sentencing.

Finally, the public prosecutor came to the point of reading the charges against the two American fugitives and three Italian detainees. They were accused of "homicide with multiple aggravating circumstances by having caused the death—through poison put in the soup followed by two revolver shots while he was sleeping—of major William Holohan, head of the Chrysler mission, for the purpose of robbing him of three thousand dollars."[22]

In the afternoon, Judge Sicher began interrogating Gualtiero Tozzini. "Lieutenant Icardi hated Major Holohan because of his severity, but also because the major had displaced him in the command of the mission," Tozzini said. "His feelings were based on loathing of discipline, jealousy, and perhaps also the desire to take the money."[23] After Tozzini, Judge Sicher interrogated Manini. He repeated a similar story and admitted to having procured the potassium cyanide used to poison the major, under orders from Icardi.

The next day, Migliari came in front of the judge to answer questions. When asked when he had begun planning with Icardi to take out the major, Migliari said, "I never heard of such a thing. Lieutenant Icardi only told me he would like to have some men dressed as Fascists capture his superior and send him to Switzerland." Migliari maintained that he had not known what had happened to Holohan and had been the first one to doubt the story of an ambush in the area.

The most painful part of the deposition for Migliari was when he had to explain the large sums of money he had accumulated during the war. He said that the Americans gave him one hundred thousand lire ($1,000) per month for him and his network of informants. Once, Major Holohan had given him one and a half million lire ($15,000) to reward him for exchanging three and a half kilograms of gold Louis d'Or coins. With this money, he founded a commercial venture in November 1944, in partnership with Icardi.[24]

After the court finished interrogating the defendants, the prosecutor began presenting his witnesses. The first one on the list was the Communist leader Moscatelli who told the judge about his meeting with Holohan at the end of November 1944. "Holohan as an officer was always collected, courageous but prudent," Moscatelli told the judge. "Whereas Icardi was a dynamic type, cordial, effusive. Their diverse mindset was the foundation for their divisions. In my opinion, Icardi freed himself from Holohan to take over command. But perhaps he acted in obedience of an order from his superiors. I know that the Allied command ignored the reports against him. Not only that, but they nominated him as chief of mission and promoted him to captain."[25]

A parade of prosecution witnesses followed Moscatelli over the next three days, including local villagers who had interacted with the mission, the priests who had sheltered them, and former partisans. Everyone painted Icardi as the diabolic schemer driven by greed and ambition to kill his superior. Lo Dolce was the spineless dimwit who followed the lieutenant blindly. Tozzini and Manini were the poor souls who had no choice but to follow Icardi's orders if they did not want to suffer the same fate as the major. And Migliari was the complete innocent dragged into the story by confused witnesses who retracted in court depositions they had made during the investigation phase.

By the end of the day on October 23, the attorneys for the defense told Judge Sicher it was superfluous to call their own witnesses given the favorable, often laudatory depositions that the prosecution witnesses had given toward the accused. Judge Sicher agreed. "I have never seen the Carabinieri so patient and prosecution witnesses so generous with the accused as in these proceedings," he said at the end of the session.

Then he postponed the trial for several days to give the prosecution and the defense time to prepare the closing arguments.[26]

* * *

When the trial resumed on October 28, the public prosecutor rose for his closing arguments. In the hushed courtroom he stared for a moment at the three defendants, then exclaimed, "Anyone would be perplexed with these proceedings: three Italians are in the cage, two Americans are free and undisturbed in their country despite being clearly responsible for killing a senior officer, a fellow American. Feelings of pity and national solidarity, even of Italian nationalism, play in favor of Migliari, Manini, and Tozzini. All the witnesses I brought in this courtroom turned their back to me. But I, for the love of justice, will continue to support the case." The prosecutor continued to speak for the rest of the day, summarizing the case and calling in the end for the judges to give life sentences to the two Americans, twenty-four years in prison to Migliari, and twenty-two years in prison each for Tozzini and Manini.[27]

The following day, October 30, it was the turn of the defense layers to make their case on behalf of their clients. There were nine lawyers assigned to the defense and each one of them could not pass the opportunity to display their oratory skills in the courtroom. The lawyers for Lo Dolce, Icardi, and Tozzini talked for the entire day on the October 30, those for Migliari took October 31, the lawyers for Manini spoke for the whole day on November 3, and those for Icardi and Migliari returned for another full-day session on November 5. The lawyers asked the court to absolve the three Italian defendants. "Open wide the prison gates for poor Manini and Tozzini. Let Aminta Migliari leave the jail with his head held high, with his honor as a citizen and a partisan intact," exclaimed one of the lawyers.[28]

For Icardi and Lo Dolce, even their defense lawyers would not claim their innocence. Instead, they portrayed them as having committed the crime for political reasons and necessities of the war. "Icardi was the true and only commander of the Chrysler Mission which was ordered to work with the partisans and to give them arms so they could fight and help shorten the war," Icardi's lawyer said. "Holohan obviously had other instructions. The fact is he was mainly concerned in gathering political information and did not want to be bothered with anything else. Icardi had to eliminate him as an obstacle in the fight for victory." The lawyers for the Americans asked the court to grant them amnesty, as the Italian law provided.[29]

* * *

By the afternoon of November 6, 1953, all sides in the Holohan process in Novara had run out of things to say. At 1500 hours, the president of the court, Judge Sicher, addressed the three defendants with the ritual words, "Do you have anything else to add?" "Nothing, nothing," replied Migliari, Manini, and Tozzini. The court retired to the council chambers to deliberate. After one hour, it announced it had reached a verdict. At 1610 hours, the eight judges returned to the packed courtroom. An absolute silence fell in the room.

Judge Sicher read the court decision with a calm voice articulating carefully each word. Aminta Migliari was fully absolved of all charges—he had no involvement whatsoever in any of the alleged crimes. Gualtiero Tozzini and Giuseppe Manini were absolved because they participated in the crime against their will and under threat of death. The two Americans were found guilty. Lieutenant Aldo Icardi received a life sentence and Sergeant Carl Lo Dolce seventeen years in prison. The farmer Edoardo Maulini, involved in the case by accident, received eight months' probation and a fine of ten thousand lire for abusive possession of a firearm.

The judge had barely finished reading the court's decision when the crowd erupted in a loud and continuous ovation. The austere magistrate tried to control the room by shaking his bell to no avail. In front of him, there were hundreds of people tightly packed against each other. They had managed to raise their arms over their heads and now were all applauding and cheering, "Long live the Court! Long live the Justice!" Seeing that they could not calm the enthusiasm of the public, the president and the popular judges whose faces radiated with joy left the podium precipitously and retired in their chambers. The

Carabinieri tried to empty the courtroom but it was not an easy task because now everyone was trying to get to the cage to congratulate Migliari, Manini, and Tozzini who were in tears. That same afternoon, they were released from jail and returned to their families in time for dinner.[30]

* * *

The last act in the Holohan-Icardi tragedy began shortly after *True* magazine published Michael Stern's account of Holohan's murder in its September 1951 issue. Representative Sterling W. Cole, Republican of New York, charged that the Defense Department had tried to cover up the Holohan death. By December of that year, Cole was named chairman of a House Armed Services subcommittee to investigate the circumstances surrounding the disappearance of Major Holohan and the Defense Department's handling of the matter.[31]

Cole conducted the first hearing on December 19, 1951. In a closed-door session, Michael Stern told the committee what he had learned during the eighteen months he had spent investigating the case. He also showed the subcommittee that the Defense Department's press release had borrowed liberally from his article, including errors or guesses he had made. For example, the government press release described Villa Castelnuovo as a twenty-two-room villa, the same way as Stern described it in his article. Stern explained that he had simply guessed at the number of rooms in the villa—he had never counted them. Likewise, Stern had guessed the value of mission funds to be $100,000—a number the government repeated without bothering to verify that the true amount had been only a fraction of that.[32]

On January 9 and 10, 1952, Cole took testimony from Henry L. Manfredi, who had investigated the matter in Italy for the Army's Criminal Investigation Division. The subcommittee received copies of statements from Tozzini and Manini to the Italian investigators and a copy of Lo Dolce's confession, which fixed responsibility for Major Holohan's death on Icardi and upon which Stern and Manfredi apparently based their hearsay statements in large part. The committee also had other information from the files of the OSS and CID, including Icardi's own statements during the investigation by military authorities of Major Holohan's disappearance, as well as Icardi's statements to the press with respect to the charges against him.

There were no further hearings until March 26, 1953, when Icardi appeared in front of the subcommittee. He was not under subpoena and could have refused to come—Lo Dolce rejected three invitations to testify.[33] Icardi could have also claimed protection under the Fifth Amendment against self-incrimination. Instead, for four and a half hours, he answered questions by Cole and the subcommittee counsel, despite being warned at the beginning that anything he said might be used against him in a "future proceeding or tribunal." Throughout the hearing, he substantially reiterated his former statements concerning the disappearance of Major Holohan.

On May 19, 1953, the subcommittee heard the fourth and final witness, Colonel Ralph W. Pierce, former chief, Criminal Branch, Provost Marshal's Office, who had conducted the polygraph test of Icardi in 1947 to determine whether Icardi had any knowledge of Major Holohan's disappearance. Colonel Pierce testified that at the time he had concluded that Icardi did not kill Holohan and probably did not know who did, although he could not give a conclusive opinion on the basis of the tests made.[34]

In mid-July 1953, Cole and Representative Paul J. Kilday, Democrat of Texas, ranking member of the subcommittee, completed their report and submitted it to the full Committee on Armed Services, which approved and adopted it on July 24, 1953. The report concluded that a careful review of the evidence "clearly reveals that probable cause has been established against Aldo Icardi and Carl Lo Dolce for the murder of Maj. William V. Holohan." John J. Courtney, subcommittee counsel clarified for the journalists that "probable cause" was a legal term meaning sufficient evidence for indictment. The report also said that Icardi probably could be tried for embezzlement of perhaps thousands of dollars, but that a conviction on this charge would be difficult to obtain. The report affirmed that Icardi and Lo Dolce were not subject to prosecution under existing civil law or under the Uniform Code of Military Justice and suggested that legislative amendments to the Federal Criminal Code be recommended to the Judiciary Committee, to prevent this situation from happening again.[35]

* * *

The report marked the end of the two-year investigation into the Holohan affair by Representatives Cole and Kilday. But the matter did not end there. In summer of 1955, a Federal grand jury was summoned in Washington, DC, to review the evidence collected by the Cole committee. The idea was to go after Icardi on perjury charges by proving that he was involved in the Holohan murder, which he had denied under oath in front of the Cole committee. The government presented to the grand jury all the evidence amassed over the years. It even arranged for seventeen witnesses to fly from Italy. They included Gualtiero Tozzini and Giuseppe Manini, who received guarantees that they would not be entangled in the American legal system if they came to the United States. The priests who had sheltered the Chrysler mission were part of the group. A notable absence was that of Aminta Migliari, who refused to come to the United States.[36] At the end of August 1955, the grand jury indicted Icardi—but not Lo Dolce, who had not appeared in front of the Cole committee—on eight counts of perjury. Each count carried a maximum penalty of five years, so Icardi faced a stiff prison sentence if convicted.

At this point, Icardi turned to Edward Bennett Williams for help. Williams was a thirty-five-year-old lawyer who had earned fame for representing Senator Joe McCarthy during his meteoric rise in Washington and the sudden downfall, which resulted in his censure by the Senate in December 1954. At the time, Williams was described in the press as "probably the most talented young trial lawyer in town," "a young and tough battler," but at the same time as "extremely personable" and as someone with "a relaxed, casual manner . . . [and] a disarming, boyish air."[37]

A friend remembered that Williams had once said, "There are three things in life, money, power, and public relations. My wife is rich, and I wouldn't know what to do with power, but give me those press clippings!"[38] Williams saw Icardi's case as a David and

Goliath story that was sure to give him the headlines and publicity he sought. On one hand, he reminisced later, there was Icardi, "a short, bespectacled, bald-headed man, [who] looked anything but the central figure of the most widely publicized spy melodrama of World War II. . . . He was a desperate and despondent man and years of living under the accusation of murder had taken a toll on him." Against him "was arrayed the majesty of the United States government," which had spent a half-million dollars investigating all angles of the case over the past ten years. Williams wrote a letter to the Attorney General of the United States requesting that the government make available to the defense the results of its investigation, citing Icardi's lack of funds and inability to access witnesses in Italy. When the government refused his request, Williams said that his "sense of fair play was so offended that he decided to conduct his own all-out investigation into the facts."[39]

Williams called for help an old friend, Robert Maheu, a former FBI agent who ran his own international investigative agency. He also enlisted Giuseppe Dosi, former head of the Italian branch of Interpol. In March 1956, they traveled 12,500 miles in four countries meeting with former partisans who had knowledge of the events of December 1944 in Lake Orta. They met Giuseppe Manini who lived with his wife and sons in abject poverty in a one-room house. Manini was first scared but quickly grew angry when Williams confronted him with the conflicting statements he had made over time regarding the events of December 6, 1944. Williams described the meeting:

> It was apparent that he was a violent and unstable man. He sat before us flicking the blade of his switchblade knife. Finally, he exploded in a burst of profanities and shouted that Migliari and Tozzini were responsible for all his trouble and that Tozzini was a "*Communista*." When he ordered us from his home, we left. The switchblade was very persuasive.[40]

Tozzini was more stable and less unwilling to talk. The real breakthrough came when Williams and Maheu met Vincenzo Moscatelli in Rome. They visited him at his offices in the Italian parliament and then continued the conversation over a laid-back lunch with wine flowing freely at Ristorante da Pancrazia. Williams recalled the meeting:

> Moscatelli was completely open and frank about the whole matter. As far as he was was concerned, the incident was just another war story, and he could not understand how it could be the subject of a criminal case. He readily conceded that the Communist partisans had eliminated Holohan, and he defended it as a necessary act. He ridiculed the selection of a man who did not speak Italian as the head of a behind-the-lines mission in Italy. He told in dismay of Holohan's insistence on wearing this uniform at all times. Moscatelli's position was that Holohan was an obstructionist who had to be removed. There was no way to remove him except by murder. He absolved Icardi and Lo Dolce of any knowledge of or involvement in the killing, and was ready and willing to testify in court. He gave us details which checked out in every instance, and we were able to prepare a documented line of proof.[41]

Williams felt so confident in his ability to convince the jury of his version of events that he laid out his entire case in his opening statement at the trial on April 17, 1956. Williams told the jury that the Army had been correct in its initial investigation after the war, when the CID had concluded, "The disappearance of Major Holohan was a political move engineered by the Communist group headed by Moscatelli, a man of few scruples who was capable of weakening the opposite party to enrich his group." He promised to show the jury that "Major Holohan was liquidated after a meeting that he had with Vincenzo Moscatelli on December 2, 1944. He was liquidated because Moscatelli believed that he constituted an obstruction to Moscatelli's plans after the war."[42]

When the investigation was open again in early 1950, it came too close to Moscatelli and his brigands for their comfort. The Communist Party of Italy devised a line of action to point the investigators away from the role of the Communists. Tozzini and Manini were coached to pin the blame on Icardi who, according to the party line, had killed Holohan under orders from the State Department and higher

American authorities.[43] "Lieutenant Aldo Icardi is not a murder, or a thief, or a liar, but one of the real heroes of World War II," Williams said as he concluded his opening statement.[44]

Williams's opening argument was strong, but it served only as a smokescreen to hide his true plan to win the case. The plan unfolded as soon as the first witness for the prosecution, Congressman Cole, took the stand. Confident in himself, Cole described the proceedings of his subcommittee, which had given rise to the perjury charges against Icardi. On cross-examination, Williams focused on making Cole admit that the purpose of his investigation had not been to identify inadequacies in the existing legislation that Congress needed to address, which is within the bounds of a congressional committee's responsibilities. Instead, Cole had exceeded the constitutional powers of a congressional committee by carrying out a legislative investigation against Icardi with the mere goal of finding a way to punish him in face of the inability of civilian or military courts to prosecute him. Williams delivered his decisive blow when he had Cole admit that he had discussed with his staff the possibility of perjury charges against Icardi even before they had invited him to testify. The line of questioning went like this:

> **Williams:** Didn't you have a conversation with your counsel and with Mr. Kilday during which you discussed inviting Icardi to testify, during which you discussed that you would swear him if he accepted the invitation, and during which you discussed that a perjury case could be spelled out against him if he testified in accordance with the reports that you then had in your committee files obtained from the Army?
>
> **Cole:** I cannot deny that that happened. On the other hand, I cannot swear that it did happen. I could very readily say that in all probability it did happen.
>
> **W:** And you best recollection here today is that it did happen?
>
> **C:** It could very well have happened.
>
> **W:**And that is your best recollection here today?
>
> **C:** I could not swear that it did, but it is my recollection.
>
> **W:** It is you recollection that it did, is that your answer, sir?
>
> **C:** Yes, sir.
>
> **W:** I have no further questions.[45]

At this point, Williams asked the judge to dismiss the charges. He explained that the investigation conducted by the Cole commission had been totally unrelated to its constitutional duty because the Congress had already closed the loophole that had existed in the Icardi case by passing the Uniform Code of Military Justice. The investigation had been a show for the sake of headlines and, worse than that, a carefully laid perjury trap, a preconceived plan by members of the Congress to get to Aldo Icardi. Judge Richmond B. Keech presiding over the trial suspended the proceedings and took the case under advisement for the night.

When the trial resumed the next morning, April 19, 1956, Judge Keech read a long opinion that essentially agreed with Williams's position that the Cole subcommittee had not acted for legislative purposes. Citing language from the Cole report of 1953 calling Icardi as the "accused" and concluding that there was "probable cause" to charge both Icardi and Lo Dolce for murder and embezzlement, the judge said that the subcommittee had functioned as a "committing magistrate." Citing from Cole's testimony, Judge Keech said, "neither affording an individual a forum in which to protest his innocence nor extracting testimony with a view to a perjury prosecution is a valid legislative purpose."[46] Congress, he said, had the right to inquire whether a crime has been committed and to "ascertain whether an executive department charged with the prosecution of such crime had acted properly." But, he added, "this authority cannot be extended to sanction a legislative trial and conviction of the individual toward whom the finger of suspicion points."[47]

Countering the government suggestion that "frequently individuals are adjudged guilty of an offense by a congressional committee in the exercise of its functions," the judge said that "such practice should not be condoned, as it denies to the accused the constitutional safeguards of judicial trial." Judge Keech ended his opinion with the words:

> For the foregoing reasons the defendant's motion to dismiss, which . . . I must treat as a motion for judgment of acquittal must be granted.
>
> I shall ask the Marshal to call in the jury and I shall direct a verdict of acquittal for the defendant.[48]

It was a stunning end right at the beginning of a trial that was
supposed to last for days. One of the Italians called to testify, unhappy
that his trip to America at the United States government's expense was
cut short, mused that someone must have gotten to the judge. Icardi
collapsed in Williams's arms, sobbing.

"What do I owe you?" he asked.

"You don't owe me anything," Williams said. "Go back to your
family."[49]

* * *

Aldo Icardi lived with his family near Pittsburgh, Pennsylvania,
until 1969 when he moved to Maitland, Florida. He was admitted to
the Florida bar in 1972 and practiced law until he was eighty years
old. He died in 2011. He never wavered from the story he told about
his role in the OSS and Operation Chrysler-Mangosteen and always
denied any involvement in Holohan's death.

Vincenzo Moscatelli retired from active participation in the Italian
legislature and the Communist Party of Italy in the early 1960s for
health reasons. He dedicated himself to the glorification of the resistance and its ideals and founded the Institute for the History of the
Resistance, which today bears his name. He died in 1981.[50] Giuseppe
Manini committed suicide in 1965. His body was found hanging from
a stair rail at his home. He was said to be ill and faring poorly in his
construction business.[51] Aminta Migliari considered the 1953 trial in
Novara the most terrible experience of his life. He lived quietly afterward working as a land surveyor for many years. He proudly spoke
of the network of 354 agents he had run during the war as the largest
intelligence net of the resistance in Italy. When he died in 1991, the
local press called him the "007 of the Resistance" and described him as
"a champion of intelligence without having the body of Sean Connery
or the drive of Charles Bronson."[52]

Epilogue

The Operational Group Command, formally known as the 2671st Special Reconnaissance Battalion (Separate), was among the most successful components of the OSS and, as such, earned recongnition both at the individual and unit level. Out of 805 officers and men who made up the OGs, 335 received individual decorations for heroism in battle. The awards included three Distinguished Service Crosses, sixteen Legions of Merit, thirty Silver Stars, and nine decorations by foreign governments. Company A—the Italian OGs, Company B—the French OGs, and Company C—the Balkan OGs, received unit citations for outstanding performance of duty in action against the enemy in Italy from April 15 to May 1, 1945, in southern France from August 1 to 15, 1944, and in Greece from August 15 to September 1, 1944. In an official commendation of the Italian OGs for their work in the Italian campaign, General Mark Clark, commanding officer of the US Fifth Army and the 15th Allied Army Group in Italy, said:

> Their attacks on enemy supply lines, dumps, convoys, and similar targets . . . were a constant and harassing problem for the enemy . . . With the knowledge that if captured they probably would be tortured and executed by the enemy, these men volunteered for these extra-hazardous missions. The outstanding success of partisan operations where they operated, and the excellent intelligence as to enemy dispositions

received was in large measure due to the presence of these men and their leadership of partisan formations.[1]

Lieutenant General Alexander M. Patch, commanding officer of the US Seventh Army, offered similar praise for the 27 officers and 155 enlisted men of Company B who carried out missions in widely scattered areas of strategic importance in southern France in preparation for and during Operation Dragoon. "In performing this extra hazardous mission, the members of the unit inflicted heavy casualties upon the enemy, destroyed enemy installations of great military importance, and stimulated notably the morale of the French patriot groups with which they came in contact," Patch wrote.[2]

With the end of the war in Europe, there were plans to deploy the OGs in China against the Japanese, after a period of rest and refitting in the United States. The Japanese surrender announced on August 15, 1945, made such a deployment unnecessary and triggered the rapid demobilitzation of the OG personnel. There was broad consensus at the time that specialized unorthodox warfare practiced by the OGs in particular and special operations in general belonged in open conflict and were not useful to the nation at peace. There was hope, at best, that the experience gained during the war would be preserved and studied. In a letter addressed to each officer and soldier of the 2671st Special Reconnaissance Battalion on August 22, 1945, Colonel Livermore wrote:

> The war is won. Our job is done. Each of you can be proud of your individual contribution to a unique achievement. The Operational Groups of this battalion were a wholly new idea in the US Army, and their success has far exceeded expectations. The potentialities of resistance and partisan groups in supplementing operations of the armies was developed further in each successive campaign in the Mediterranean Theater. The experience of and new techniques used by this battalion are an important development in military tactics.[3]

At the time, however, there was very little effort to capture and reflect on the experience of the OGs, Jedburghs, and other special operations that the OSS conducted. Donovan was locked in a fierce struggle with the Washington establishment to transform the OSS into a peacetime central intelligence service reporting directly to the president. Donovan began advocating for the consolidation of postwar intelligence functions as early as 1943, but he formalized his proposal in a memorandum to President Roosevelt on November 18, 1944. He described the intelligence field at the time as:

[A]nalagous to a large industrial plant producing parts of a complicated product without an assembly line. Our intelligence system consists of a number of disparate agencies, each trying vainly to satisfy national requirements. The ill-defined functions of each permit confusion, duplication, and inevitable competition. The resulting waste of manpower and talent, while deplorable, is not the worst aspect. None of the agencies had both adequate resources and logical scope of activity to satisfy national requirements.[4]

Donovan recommended the creation of a "focal agency where all subject intelligence material is finally evaluated, analyzed, and synthesized." This new Central Intelligence Service would not be permitted to carry out police or law enforcement actions at home or abroad, but it would engage in subversive operations abroad or any other functions related to intelligence as directed by the president.[5]

In the early days as coordinator of intelligence, Donovan had been very mindful of the opposition that his ideas would encounter in the intelligence establishment. He advised his subordinates, "being a new outfit, we don't want to be presumptuous. There is a great deal of sales resistance to this kind of thing." At the time, he said, he had sense enough to understand that if he had tried to coordinate all intelligence activities, "we would just start a thirty-year war that would be fiercer than any war we are in now. So that all I proposed is that we would try to coordinate the information that was brought in—and that exists in every department of the government."[6]

With his November 1944 proposal to transform the OSS into a permanent peacetime central intelligence service, Donovan triggered the all-out struggle he had managed to avoid in 1941. His opponents leaked the proposal to the press where some columnists characterized

Donovan's efforts as an attempt to create an American Gestapo—loaded words that preempted any desire FDR may have had to support the idea.

When Roosevelt died on April 12, 1945, Donovan lost his strongest supporter in Washington. The new president, Harry Truman, a fiscally conservative Democrat, considered the OSS one of the many government agencies that had mushroomed in Washington as a result of the war and that had to be eliminated as soon as the conflict was over. At his first meeting with Donovan on May 18, 1945, Truman said, "The OSS has been a credit to America. You and your men are to be congratulated on doing a remarkable job for the country, but the OSS belongs to a nation at war. It can have no place in an America at peace."[7] When Donovan tried to argue the case for a continued use of the OSS after the war, Truman said:

> I am completely opposed to international spying on the part of the United States. It is un-American. I cannot be certain in my mind that a formidable clandestine organization such as the OSS designed to spy abroad will not in time spy upon the American people themselves. The OSS represents a threat to the liberties of the American people. An all-powerful intelligence apparatus in the hands of an unprincipled president can be a dangerous instrument. I would never use such a tool against my own people, but there is always the risk, and I cannot entertain such a risk.[8]

At the end of that meeting, Donovan had no doubts that the OSS would not last after the war. On September 20, 1945, Truman issued Executive Order 9621 dissolving the OSS, effective October 1, 1945. The functions of the Research and Analysis and Presentations Branches were transferred to the State Department. The War Department subsumed the rest of the organization and the Secretary of War received the authority to discontinue any of its activities deemed no longer necessary. In the transfer, the military preserved most of the Secret Intelligence (SI) and Counter-Intelligence (X-2) functions, but eliminated those related to paramilitary operations and unorthodox warfare, including Special Operations, Jedburgh, and Operational Group capabilities. Most of the personnel from these branches of the OSS was demobilized and entered civilian life.

DECLASSIFIED AND APPROVED FOR RELEASE
BY THE CENTRAL INTELLIGENCE AGENCY
DATE: 2001

#8

20 September 1945

My dear General Donovan:

I appreciate very much the work which you and your staff undertook, beginning prior to the Japanese surrender, to liquidate those wartime activities of the Office of Strategic Services which will not be needed in time of peace.

Timely steps should also be taken to conserve those resources and skills developed within your organization which are vital to our peacetime purposes.

Accordingly, I have today directed, by Executive order, that the activities of the Research and Analysis Branch and the Presentation Branch of the Office of Strategic Services be transferred to the State Department. This transfer, which is effective as of October 1, 1945, represents the beginning of the development of a coordinated system of foreign intelligence within the permanent framework of the Government.

Consistent with the foregoing, the Executive order provides for the transfer of the remaining activities of the Office of Strategic Services to the War Department; for the abolition of the Office of Strategic Services; and for the continued orderly liquidation of some of the activities of the Office without interrupting other services of a military nature the need for which will continue for some time.

I want to take this occasion to thank you for the capable leadership you have brought to a vital wartime activity in your capacity as Director of Strategic Services. You may well find satisfaction in the achievements of the Office and take pride in your own contribution to them. These are in themselves large rewards. Great additional reward for your efforts should lie in the knowledge that the peacetime intelligence services of the Government are being erected on the foundation of the facilities and resources mobilized through the Office of Strategic Services during the war.

                              Sincerely yours,

                              HARRY S. TRUMAN

President Truman's letter to General Donovan on September 20, 1945, informing him of the dissolution of the OSS.

* * *

It would not take long for interest in paramilitary and special operations capabilities to be revived. The alliance between the Soviet Union and the Western democracies that defeated the Axis powers shattered immediately after the war. In the cold war that ensued and that lasted for the next forty-five years, covert warfare became an important component of operations designed to counteract Soviet and Soviet-inspired activities throughout the world. The Central Intelligence Agency, America's first peacetime intelligence agency, came into existence on September 18, 1947, mostly by bringing under one roof the functions and capabilities of the old OSS that still survived in the areas of research and analysis, intelligence, and counterintelligence. These capabilities were expanded with the creation of the Office of Policy Coordination on September 1, 1948, tasked to conduct covert paramilitary operations that included:

> Any covert activities related to: propaganda; economic warfare; preventive direct action, including sabotage, anti-sabotage, demolition and evacuation measures; subversion against hostile states, including assistance to underground resistance movements, guerrillas, and refugee liberation groups, and support to indigenous anti-Communist elements in threatened countries around the world.[9]

The ranks of OPC were quickly filled with former OSS staffers, who dusted off and adopted the OSS training methods and procedures as they set about recruiting, training, and organizing agents for action behind the Iron Curtain. Over the years, these capabilities evolved through trial and error, through successes and failures to today's National Clandestine Service Directorate of Operations, whose paramilitary operations officers regularly engage in unconventional warfare, including training and leading guerrilla units.

The advent of the Cold War caused the armed forces to reevaluate the need for special operations behind enemy lines, as well. In a paper written for the Joint Chiefs of Staff on October 20, 1948, Colonel Russell J. Livermore, the former head of the Operational Group Command, pointed out that while the intelligence functions of the OSS had found a home in successive organizations, its operational side had been lost. Livermore wrote:

> Nothing had been done to perpetuate it or to be ready for a war with Russia, which may be staring us in the face. The personnel who learned the techniques of special operations have disappeared into thin air and unless they hold army reserve commissions even their whereabouts is unknown. . . . The army has no organization for Special Operations, either as part of the regular army or its reserve. No forward planning is being done and no research and experimentation is being carried on in the technical skills of radio and other means of communication, use of light planes and helicopters, packing of arms and supplies, and improving air drops of personnel and supplies. We started from scratch in our knowledge of these things in the last war and learned by the hard slow costly way of trial and error. Do we have to repeat this in case of another national emergency?[10]

Livermore urged the JCS to direct the Army, the Air Force, and the Navy to immediately set up sections devoted to special operations. Each component would have its specialty areas, but all three would work jointly in training, infiltration, and evacuation methods, use of weapons, and communication equipment. The Korean War provided urgency for the idea. In 1952, Colonel Aaron Bank created the first formal unconventional warfare unit in the United States Army, the Tenth Special Forces Group (Airborne), or the Green Berets, at Fort Bragg, North Carolina. A veteran of the OSS Special Operations Command and a former Jedburgh, Bank set up the initial training curriculum of the Special Forces Group based on the OSS manuals and experience. Bank is celebrated as the father of Special Forces. To this day, the US Special Operations Command traces its lineage to the OSS and regards Donovan "as the spiritual godfather of modern-day special operations," in the words of Admiral Eric Olson, commander of the US Special Operations Command from 2007 to 2011.

One of the key factors for the success of the OSS Operational Groups, Jedburghs, and other special operations teams during World War II was the close coordination between the intelligence and operations arms of the organization. In his 1948 paper to the JCS, Livermore wrote, "Obviously, there must be the closest liaison between them as the operations produce a vast amount of intelligence, and the OGs must depend on an intelligence network for initial penetration of enemy-held areas."[11] With the dissolution of the OSS, intelligence operations, represented by the CIA, separated from special operations, represented by the US Special Operations Command. They followed separate paths that intersected occasionally but in general moved forward independently. If the attack on Pearl Harbor served as a catalyst for the creation of the OSS, the attacks on September 11, 2001, had a similarly profound effect in bringing the CIA and the US Special Operations Command much closer together, thus reuniting the two halves of the OSS legacy. In the words of the CIA director, John Brennan, "This Nation's response to the attacks of 9/11 brought the two main branches of the OSS back together. Intelligence officers and special operators are once again working hand-in-hand to take the fight to our adversaries."[12]

This convergence began immediately after the 9/11 attacks, when one hundred CIA paramilitary officers entered Afghanistan, laid the groundwork for 350 Special Forces soldiers, and, together, led fifteen thousand Northern Alliance fighters to drive the Taliban out of power.[13] It proved successful in a number of operations since, including the May 2011 raid to kill Osama bin Laden. It also drove the reorganization of the CIA announced on March 6, 2015, in which the National Clandestine Service was renamed the Directorate of Operations, and the Directorate of Intelligence was renamed the Directorate of Analysis. These directorates maintain the responsibility for developing officers with the specialized skills unique to the directorates, for developing tradecraft, and for maintaining a strategic perspective that cuts across all issues and regions. However, the day-to-day operations are conducted in mission centers, which are integrated pools of assets, people, and resources from the agency's direcorates that "bring the full range of operational, analytic, support, technical, and digital personnel and capabilities to bear on the nation's most pressing security issues and interests." Not unlike the way OSS operated out of London, Algiers, Caserta, Bari, Sienna, and other locations during World War II.[14]

Notes

Prologue

1 Captain Robert J. Bulkley, Jr, *At Close Quarters: PT Boats in the United States Navy* (Washington, DC: Naval History Division, 1962), 277. NavSource Online, *Motor Torpedo Boat Photo Archive, PT-203.*

2 The Bureau of Ships, *Know your PT Boat* (Washington, DC: Navy Department, 1945), 2.

3 Bulkley.

4 The Bureau of Ships, 26.

5 National Museum of the Pacific War, *PT Boat Virtual Tour.*

6 The Bureau of Ships, 20–22. National Museum of the Pacific War.

7 National Museum of the Pacific War.

8 National Museum of the Pacific War. NavSource Online.

9 NavSource Online.

10 The Bureau of Ships, 4.

11 NARA, RG 226, Entry 99, Boxes 45–46.

Chapter 1: Office of Strategic Services

1 United States Department of State, Office of the Historian, *American Isolationism in the 1930s*, n.d.

2 Byron Darnton, "Vast Throng Jams the Mall to Cheer American Day Fete," *New York Times*, May 19, 1941, 1.

3 "Bill Robinson," *Biography.com*, n.d.

4 Lisa Belkin, "Lucy Monroe Dies; A Celebrated Singer Of National Anthem," *New York Times*, October 16, 1987, B5.

5 "God Bless America," *Library of Congress*, n.d.

6 Darnton.

7 "Lindbergh Joins in Wheeler Plea to U.S. to Shun War," *New York Times*, May 24, 1941, 1.

8 Allen W. Dulles, "William J. Donovan and the National Security," *Studies in Intelligence*, Summer 1959.

9 Elizabeth R. Valentine, "Fact-Finder and Fighing Man," *New York Times*, May 4, 1941, SM8.

10 Dulles.

11 Dulles. Valentine.

12 Ibid.

13 "Drive Begun Here for Polish Relief," *New York Times*, February 26, 1940, 2.

14 "Bids Convention Back Cabinet Appointees," *New York Times*, June 22, 1940, 10.

15 "House of Commons Debate, May 13, 1940," *Hansard 1803–2005*, n.d.

16 "House of Commons Debate, June 4, 1940," *Hansard 1803–2005*, n.d.

17 "House of Commons Debate, June 18, 1940," *Hansard 1803–2005*, n.d.

18 William J. Donovan and Edgar Mowrer, "Germans Said to Spend Vast Sums Abroad to Pave Way for Conquest," *New York Times*, August 23, 1940, 5.

19 "Col. Donovan Back, Has Seen 'A Lot,'" *New York Times*, March 19, 1941, 9.

20 Dulles.

21 Franklin D. Roosevelt, "Executive Order Designating a Coordinator of Intelligence," The White House, July 11, 1941.

22 Ibid.

23 Arthur B. Darling, "Origins of Central Intelligence," *Center for the Study of Intelligence, Volume 8, Number 3* (1953).

24 NARA, Troy Papers, Box 2, Folder 19.

25 Darling.

26 Arthur Krock, "The War in Pictures," *New York Times*, October 8, 1941, 4.

27 Darling and Troy Papers, Box 2, Folder 19.

28 Kermit Roosevelt, *War Report of the OSS* (New York: Walker and Company, 1976), 80.

29 Troy Papers, Box 2, Folder 19.

30 Franklin D. Roosevelt, "Military Order Office of Strategic Services," The White House, June 13, 1942.

31 Troy Papers, Box 3, Folder 22.

32 Ibid.

33 Ibid.

34 "General Joseph T. McNarney," *US Air Force*, n.d. "Horne," *Naval Historical Center*, July 11, 2007.

35 Roosevelt, *War Report of the OSS*, 83–84.

36 Eleony Moorhead, "The OSS and Operation TORCH: The Beginning of the Beginning," *Tempus: The Harvard College History Review, Vol. X, Issue 1*, Summer 2009.

37 Kermit Roosevelt, *The Overseas Targets: War Report of the OSS, Volume II* (New York: Walker and Company, 1976), 11–18.

38 Roosevelt, *War Report of the OSS*, 105.

39 Ibid.

Chapter 2: Irregular Warfare in the Early Years of World War II

1 Russell Miller, *The Commandos* (Chicago: Time-Life Books, Inc., 1981), 129–141.

2 Gordon Williamson, *German Special Forces of World War II* (Oxford: Osprey Publishing, 2009), 4–19.

3 Miller, 20.

4 Winston S. Churchill, *London to Ladysmith Via Pretoria* (London: Longman, Green, and Co., 1900), 449–466.

5 "Boers Traits and British Traits," *New York Times*, March 6, 1900, 8.

6 Miller, 21.

7 Miller, 22.

8 Miller, 24.

9 "Lofoten Islands Raid," *Combined Operations Command*, n.d. "The Lofoten Raid." *Lofoten War Museum*, n.d.

10 Miller, 29.

11 "British Commandos Raid Hitler's Europe," *Life*, January 26, 1942, 17–21.

12 Hugh Sebag-Montefiore, *Enigma: The Battle for the Code* (New York: John Wiley & Sons, Inc., 2000), 197–198.

13 "British Commandos Raid Hitler's Europe."

14 Christopher M. Bell, *Churchill and Sea Power* (Oxford: Oxford University Press, 2013), 214.

15 "Service in a Commando," *Commando Veterans Association*, n.d.

16 Michael J. King, "Rangers: Selected Combat Operations in World War II," *US Army Combined Arms Center*, June 1985, 1–11.

17 James Owen, *Commando: Winning WW2 Behind Enemy Lines* (London: Little, Brown Book Group, 2013), 132.

18 "Rangers Are Impressed by British And Canadians on Dieppe Foray," *New York Times*, August 22, 1942: 4.

19 Robert W. Black, *Rangers in World War II* (New York: Presidio Press, 1992), 35.

20 Julian Thompson, "The Dieppe Raid," *BBC History*, n.d.

21 Ibid.

22 Doug Schmidt, "New research suggests World War II raid on Dieppe may have been attempt to find Nazi Enigma machine," *Canada.com*, August 17 2012.

23 Susan Ratcliffe, *Concise Oxford Dictionary of Quotations* (Oxford: Oxford University Press, 2011), 101.

24 "Nazis Threaten to Shackle Britons As Reply to Alleged Dieppe Order," *New York Times*, September 3, 1942, 1.

25 Owen, 171.

26 "Convention Between the United States of America and Other Powers, Relating to Prisoners of War; July 27, 1929," *The Avalon Project*, n.d.

27 Raymond Daniell, "British Would End Reprisals," *New York Times*, October 18, 1942, E4.

28 "London Threatens to Tie Up Captives," *New York Times*, October 9, 1942, 1.

29 "Close Combat Without and With Weapons As Taught At SOE STS 103," *IndaBook*, n.d.

30 Ibid.

31 P. J. Philip, "Canada Chains 1,376 Nazis In Reprisal Against Berlin," *New York Times*, October 11, 1942, 1.

32 "All War Prisoners Face Nazi Threat," *New York Times*, October 16, 1942, 6.

33 "Britain Unshackles Captives, Nazis Talk," *New York Times*. December 12, 1942, 55.

34 Cornell University Law Library, *Donovan Nuremberg Trial Collection*, n.d.

35 Ibid.

36 Ibid.

37 Ibid.

38 Owen, 196. Cornell University Law Library.

39 NARA RG 153, Entry 143, Box 531, Case 16–116.

40 Cornell University Law Library.

Chapter 3: The OSS Operational Groups

1 Roosevelt, *War Report of the OSS*, 223.

2 The questionnaires are in NARA RG 226, Personnel Files.

3 Details about the recruiting and training of personnel for the first operational groups are at NARA RG 226, Entry 99, Boxes 33–34 and 45–46.

4 Albert Materazzi, "Italian-American OGs Attend Memorial Ceremony in Ameglia," *OSS Society Newspaper*, Summer 2004, 10.

5 See the OSS personnel file for Vincent J. Russo in NARA RG 226, Personnel Files, for an example.

6 David G. Boak, *OSS Red Group 2: A Fisherman Goes to War* (Bloomington: AuthorHouse, 2011), 55–57.

7 Ibid.

8 Roosevelt, *War Report of the OSS*, 225.

9 Roosevelt, *The Overseas Targets*, 145–146.

10 Roosevelt, *The Overseas Targets*, 128–129.

11 Roosevelt, *The Overseas Targets*, 124, and USAHEC, Donovan Papers.

12 NARA RG 226, Entry 99, Boxes 45–46.

13 "Close Combat Without and With Weapons As Taught At SOE STS 103."

14 Ibid.

15 Phil Mathews, "W. E. Fairbairn—The Legendary Instructor," *CQB Services*, 2007.

16 "Close Combat Without and With Weapons As Taught At SOE STS 103."

17 Ibid.

18 Ibid.

Chapter 4: Special Operations in the Western Mediterranean

1 Roosevelt, *The Overseas Targets*, 59–60. Laurent Preziosi, and Toussaint Griffi, *Première Mission en Corse Occupée avec le Sous-marin Casabianca (Décembre 1942–Mars 1943)* (Paris: Éditions L'Harmattan, 1988).

2 Patrick K O'Donnell, *Operatives, Spies, and Saboteurs: The Unknown Story of the Men and Women of World War II's OSS* (New York: Free Press, 2004), 144.

3 Franklin D. Roosevelt, "Fireside Chat 25: On the Fall of Mussolini (July 28, 1943)," *University of Virginia Miller Center,* July 28, 1943.

4 Carlo D'Este, *World War II in the Mediterranean, 1942–1945* (Chapel Hill: Algonquin Books of Chapel Hill, 1990), 57.

5 Frido von Senger und Etterlin, *Neither Fear Nor Hope* (Novato: Presidio Press, 1989), 150.

6 Senger, 148.

7 NARA RG 226, Entry 99, Boxes 45–46.

8 Roosevelt, The Overseas Targets, ix.

9 "Drive Begun Here for Polish Relief."

10 Max Corvo, *OSS in Italy, 1942–1945* (New York: Enigma Books, 2005), 88.

11 NARA RG 226, Entry 99, Box 39. Troy Files, Box 1, Folder 4.

12 Carlo D'Este, *Bitter Victory: The Battle for Sicily, 1943* (New York: HarperCollins, 1988), 431.

13 D'Este, *World War II in the Mediterranean, 1942–1945*, 78.

14 Ibid., 74.

15 Henry Hitch Adams, *Italy at War* (Chicago, IL: Time-Life Books, Inc., 1982), 159–161.

16 D'Este, *World War II in the Mediterranean, 1942–1945*, 82.

17 Adams, 159–161.

18 Ibid.

19 Corvo, 106.

20 John Steinbeck, *Once there was a war* (New York: Penguin Group, 2007), 176.

21 Steinbeck, 185.

22 John B Dwyer, *Seaborne Deception: The History of U.S. Navy Beach Jumpers* (New York: Praeger Publishers, 1992), 40.

23 Corvo, 108–109. Steinbeck, 186.

24 Steinbeck, 187.

25 Adams, 159–161.

26 Senger.

27 "Obolensky Headed US Chutists Whose Leap Sped Sardinia's Fall," *New York Times*, October 8, 1943, 4.

28 Jean Meegan, "Prince Serge Obolensky Wants to Be Called 'Colonel' Now," *Palm Beach Post*, October 25, 1945, 5.

29 NARA RG 226, Entry 99, Boxes 45–46.

30 Meegan.

31 "Obolensky Headed US Chutists Whose Leap Sped Sardinia's Fall."

32 Corvo, 51, 56, and 119. Roosevelt, *The Overseas Targets*, 61.

33 NARA RG 226, Entry 99, Boxes 45–46.

34 Miller, 144–146.

35 Jean-Louis Cremieux-Brilhac, *La France Libre* (Paris: Editions Gallimard, 2013), 859–860.

36 Cremieux-Brilhac, *La France Libre*, 859–860. "The Liberation of Corsica." *Chemins de Memoire*, n.d.

37 Senger, 164.

38 "The Liberation of Corsica."

39 NARA RG 226, Entry 99, Boxes 45–46.

39 Anthony Scariano, "Operations Carried out in Corsica and at Capraia and Gorgona during the Period of September 1943 to May 1944," *Gli Americani e la Guerra di Liberazione d'Italia: Office of Strategic Services (O.S.S.) e la Resistenza* (Venice: Instituto Veneziano per la Storia della Resistenza, 1994), 267–270.

40 Ibid.

41 "Handful od US Soldiers battled like 'Lions' in Corsican Conquest." *Stars and Stripes*, October 19, 1943.

42 Ibid.

43 Ibid.

44 Ibid.

45 Scariano.

Chapter 5: Rescuing Escaped Prisoners of War

1 Details about mission Simcol are in NARA RG 226, Entry 99, Box 45–46.

2 NARA, RG 389, World War II Prisoners of War Data File, 12/7/1941–11/19/1946).

3 Ibid.

Chapter 6: Operations from Corsica

1 Details about the OG operations from Corsica are in NARA RG 226, Entry 99, Box 45–46.

2 Roosevelt, *The Overseas Targets*, 78–79.

3 Ibid.

4 NARA RG 226, Entry 99, Boxes 45–46.

5 NARA RG 226 Di Scalfani OSS Personnel file.

6 "AFS Letters No. 33, January 1945," *American Field Service*, n.d.

7 Steinbeck, 60.

8 Ibid.

9 Richard Langworth, *Churchill by Himself: The Definitive Collection of Quotations* (New York: Perseus Books Group, 2008), 283.

10 NARA RG 226, Entry 99, Boxes 45–46.

11 Roosevelt, The Overseas Targets, 78.

Chapter 7: The Ill-Fated Ginny Mission

1 The story of the Ginny mission is reconstructed from documents in NARA RG 226, Entry 99, Boxes 45–46; Entry 146, Box 36 (Case 100); and RG 153, Entry 143, Boxes 530–531 (Case 16–116).

2 Aldo Icardi, *American Master Spy* (Pittsburgh: Stalwart Enterprises, Inc., 1954), 215.

3 USAHEC, Donovan Papers.

Chapter 8: Operational Groups in France

1 Cremieux-Brilhac, Jean-Louis. *La France Libre, Tome II* (Paris: Editions Gallimard, 2013), 1230–1231.

2 Roosevelt. *The Overseas Targets*, 197–198.

3 Ibid.

4 Cremieux-Brilhac, *La France Libre, Tome II*, 1235.

5 Roosevelt, *The Overseas Targets*, 198–199.

6 Ibid.

7 Cremieux-Brilhac, *La France Libre, Tome II*, 1235.

8 Roosevelt, The Overseas Targets, 199, 204.

9 "Operations in Southern France, " *OSS Operational Groups*, n.d.

10 Ibid.

11 "Brockhall Hall and Manor," *Waymarking*, July 22, 2008.

12 Ellsworth Johnson, "One Small Part," Office of Strategic Services Operational Groups, n.d.

13 Ibid.

14 William M. Henhoeffer, "If Donovan Were Here Today," *Studies in Intelligence*, Fall 1988, 10–119-1.

14 John W Shaver, *Office of the Strategic Services: Operational Groups in France during World War II* (Fort Leavenworth, Kansas: US Army Command and General Staff College, 1993), 59.

15 Ibid.

16 Meegan.

17 Johnson, Ellsworth.

18 John Mendelsohn, *Covert Warfare: Other OSS Teams* (New York: Garlans, 1989), 82.

19 Johnson, Ellsworth.

20 Ibid.

21 Johnson, Ellsworth. Shaver, 62–63.

Chapter 9: Americans in Vercors

1 DREX, La Division Recherche et Retour d'EXpérience, *La guérilla n'aura pas lieu . . . la bataille du Vercors 1940–1944* (Paris: Ministère de la Défénse, 2010), 20.

 2 "Jean-Pierre Levy (Movement "Franc-Tireur")," *Fondation de la Résistance*, n.d.

 3 DREX, 25.

 4 Paul Dreyfus, *Vercors, Citadelle de la Liberté* (Grenoble: Arthaud, 1969), 77.

 5 DREX, 31.

 6 DREX, 22.

 7 Ibid.

 8 Gilles Vergnon, *Le Vercors: histoire et mémoire d'un maquis* (Paris: Les Éditions de l'Atelier, 2002), 107, 121.

 9 "La Milice française," 70e Anniversaire de la Liberation de France, n.d.

10 Richard Juillet, "La "Saint-Barthélemy" grenobloise,"*Isère Magazine*, October 2013.

11 DREX, 33–34.

12 Ibid.

13 M. R. D. Foost, *SOE in France* (London: Routledge, 2004), 315.

14 DREX, 34.

15 Foost, 315–316.

16 Cremieux-Brilhac, *La France Libre, Tome II*, 1222, 1407.

17 H. R.Kedward, *In Search of the Maquis: Rural Resistance in Southern France 1942–1944* (Oxford: Oxford University Press, 1993), 175.

18 DREX, 37.

19 Cremieux-Brilhac, *La France Libre, Tome II*, 1227–1229.

20 Ibid.

21 Ibid.

22 Vergnon, 96.

23 DREX, 44.

24 DREX, 45.

25 DREX, 42.

26 John Houseman, "John Houseman's Diary—Mission Eucalyptus," *WW2 People's War*, n.d.

27 Ibid.

28 Ibid.

29 Vergnon, 93–94.

30 Nathan C. Hill, "Sowing Dragon's Teeth: OSS Operational Groups of World War II," *Military Review*, July–August 2013, 31–37.

31 Vergnon, 102.

32 DREX, 42.

33 Vergnon, 107.

34 DREX, 40.

35 Ibid.

36 Houseman.

37 DREX, 45–46.

38 Vergnon, 122.

39 DREX, 51.

40 Tim Lynch, *Silent Skies: Gliders at War 1939–1945* (Barnsley, South Yorkshire: Pen & Sword Military, 2008).

41 DREX, 46.

42 DREX, 51.

43 DREX, 47.

44 Ibid.

45 Roosevelt, *The Overseas Targets*, 195.

46 Hill.

47 "Histoire de la Grotte de la Luire," *Grotte de la Luire*, n.d.

48 Roosevelt, *The Overseas Targets*, 196.

49 "Andre E. Pecquet Awards and Citations," *MilitaryTimes Hall of Valor*, n.d.

50 Houseman.

51 Roosevelt, *The Overseas Targets*, 196. Hill.

52 DREX, 48.

53 DREX, 51.

54 Kedward: 180.

55 Vergnon, 111 (note 196).

Chapter 10: Mission Walla Walla in Italy

1 Roosevelt, *The Overseas Targets*, 109.

2 Santo Peli, *Storia della Resistenza in Italia* (Torino: Einaudi, 2006), 62–65.

3 "Azioni tedesche contro i civili in Toscana," *Regione Toscana*, December 28, 2012.

4 Daniele Rossi, "Resistenza: L' eccidio di Mommio," *Informati*, December 27, 2013.

5 Antonio Lanfaloni, *L'azione dello Stato Maggiore Generale per lo sviluppo del movimento di Liberazione* (Rome: Stato Maggiore del'Esercito Ufficio Storico, 1975), 97.

6 D'Este, *World War II in the Mediterranean, 1942–1945*, 180–182.

7 Roosevelt, *The Overseas Targets*, 110.

8 NARA RG 226, Entry 99, Boxes 45–46

9 Peli, 106.

10 Nuto Revelli, *La guerra dei poveri* (Rome: Einaudi, 2005), 261.

11 "Anton Ukmar," Associazione Nazionale Partigiani d'Italia, n.d.

12 "Fausto Cossu," Associazione Nazionale Partigiani d'Italia, n.d.

13 "Domenico Mezzadra ("Americano")," Associazione Nazionale Partigiani d'Italia, n.d.

14 Materazzi, Albert. "The Italian-American O.S.S. with the Italian Resistance: An Overview," *Gli Americani e la Guerra di Liberazione d'Italia*, 211–213.

15 "Divisione Giustizia e Libertà," Associazione Nazionale Partigiani d'Italia Comitato Provinciale di Piacenza, n.d.

16 Peli, 109.

Chapter 11: Mission Mangosteen-Chrysler

1 Richard J. H. Johnston, "Brother of Victim Made Long Inquiry," *New York Times*, August 16, 1951, 12.

2 "Figures Involved in Murder History," *New York Times*, August 16, 1951, 13.

3 Corvo, 204.

4 Icardi, 215.

5 "Alfredo Di Dio," Associazione Nazionale Partigiani d'Italia, n.d.

6 Peter Tompkins, *L'altra Resistenza* (Milano: Saggiatore, 2005), 281.

7 "Vincenzo "Cino" Moscatelli," Associazione Nazionale Partigiani d'Italia, n.d.

8 "La Repubblica della Val d'Ossola," Associazione Nazionale Partigiani d'Italia, n.d. NARA RG 226, Entry 99, Boxes 45–46.

9 Icardi, 18.

10 Icardi, 48.

11 Icardi, 51.

12 Tompkins, 288–290.

13 Ibid.

14 Corvo, 234.

15 Icardi, 207.

Chapter 12: Rescue Missions in the Balkans

1 "General James Harold Doolittle," *U.S. Air Force*, n.d.

2 "General Nathan F. Twining," *U.S. Air Force*, n.d.

3 "2641st Special Group," *The Fifteenth Air Force*, n.d.

4 "The Fifteenth Air Force," *The Fifteenth Air Force*, n.d.

5 Ronald H. Bailey, *Partisans and Guerrillas* (Alexandria, Virginia: Time-Life Books, Inc., 1978), 74.

6 Gregory A. Freeman, *Red Tails, The Tuskegee Airmen and Operation Halyard* (New York: New American Library, 2011), 122.

7 "Screen News Here and in Hollywood," *New York Times*, September 8, 1942, 26.

8 James MacDonald, "Satellite States Alarmed," *New York Times*, August 8, 1943, E5.

9 Richard M. Kelly, "The Halyard Mission," *Blue Book Magazine*, August 1946, 52–62.

10 Ibid.

11 Thomas K. Oliver, "Unintended Visit to Yugoslavia," *Black Hills Veterans Writing Group*, n.d.

12 Ibid.

13 Ibid.

14 Kelly.

15 Peter Lucas, *The OSS in World War II Albania* (Jefferson, North Carolina: McFarland & Company, Inc., 2007), 52–53.

16 Agnes Jensen Margerich, *Albanian Escape* (Lexington, Kentucky: Univesity Press of Kentucky, 1999), 202.

17 Margerich, 200.

18 Margerich, 208.

19 Kelly.

20 Arthur Jibilian, "Rescuer In Yugoslavia," *America in WWII*, April 2008.

21 Ibid.

22 Kelly.

23 Ibid.

24 Jibilian.

25 Kelly.

26 Bailey, 189.

27 Kelly.

28 Freeman, 11.

29 Kelly.

30 "OSS 'Underground Railway' Plan Saved U.S. Fliers in Axis Areas," *New York Times*, September 17, 1945, 5.

31 Kevin Morrow, "Rescue Behind Enemy Lines," *HistoryNet*, March 20, 2008.

Chapter 13: Mission Peedee-Roanoke

1 Peli, 114.

2 Roosevelt, *The Overseas Targets*, 113.

3 Peli, 113.

4 Roosevelt, *The Overseas Targets*, 109.

5 D'Este, *World War II in the Mediterranean, 1942–1945*, 110

6 Ibid., 181.

7 See Peedee and Roanoke mission reports at NARA RG 226, Entry 99, Boxes 45–46.

8 Claudia Nasini, "The OSS in the Italian Resistance: A Post Cold War Interpretation," *Eurostudium*, 2012, 46–82.

9 "Italo Pietra ("Edoardo")," Associazione Nazionale Partigiani d'Italia di Voghera, n.d.

10 Philip Francis, "O.G. Doctors: Snapshot of the Sixth Zone," *Gli Americani e la Guerra di Liberazione d'Italia*, 274–281.

11 Ibid.

12 Robert Hodges, "African-American 92nd Infantry Division Fought in Italy During World War II." *Historynet.com*, June 12, 2006.

13 Ulysses Lee, *United States Army in World War II: The Employment of Negro Troops* (Washington, D.C.: U.S. Government Printing Office, 2001), 579–581.

14 Lee, 586–587.

15 Thomas A. Popa, *Po Valley* (Washington, D.C.: US Army Center of Military History, n.d.), 16.

16 Lee, 586–587.

17 Paolo Emilio Taviani, *Breve Storia dell'Insurrezione di Genova* (Rome: Terzo Migliaio, 1960).

18 Lee, 587–588.

19 Roberto Raja, "I giorni della liberazione," *Cinquanta Mila Giorni*. n.d.

20 Ettore Botti, "Lo Scempio del Duce nel Giorno della Vergogna," *Cinquanta Mila Giorni*. September 20, 2001.

21 Italo Pietra ("Edoardo").

22 "Walter Audisio," Associazione Nazionale Partigiani d'Italia, n.d.

23 Botti.

24 Francis.

25 "La Sicherheits," Associazione Nazionale Partigiani d'Italia di Voghera, n.d.

26 Italo Pietra ("Edoardo").

27 Peli, 173.

28 Peli, 172.

29 Popa, 21–22.

30 NARA RG 153, Entry 143, Boxes 530–531, Case 16–116.

31 Popa, 23.

32 Senger, 303–304.

33 Senger, 308.

Chapter 14: OSS Investigations into War Crimes

1 Details about the OSS investigation into the fate of the Ginny mission (Case 100) are at NARA RG 226, Entry 146, Box 36, Case 100. See also Records of the Office of the Judge Advocate General at NARA RG 153, Entry 143, Boxes 530–531, Case 16–116.

2 Army Battle Casualties and Non-Death Reports during World War II, June 1, 1953.

3 Scariano.

4 "History of Cinecittà," *Rome File*. n.d.

5 John Oswald, "An Interrogator's Life," *WW2 People's War*, October 27, 2004.

6 Corvo, 233.

7 Icardi, 62.

8 Corvo, 265.

9 Icardi, 187.

10 "La Missione Americana Chrysler sul Lago d'Orta," *La Stampa*, March 29, 1950, 4.

11 Icardi, 188.

Chapter 15: Swift Justice for the Ginny Men

1 For details about the trial of Anton Dostler see Records of the Office of the Judge Advocate General at NARA RG 153, Entry 143, Boxes 530–531, Case 16–116.

2 Senger, 345.

3 Karel Margry, "The Dostler Case," *After the Battle, Number 94*, 1996, 1–19.

4 Senger, 345.

5 Stephen Stratford, "Falkenhorst Trial," *British Military & Criminal History 1900 to 1999*. n.d.

6 Richard Raiber, *Anatomy of Perjury: Field Marshal Albert Kesselring, Via Rassella, and the GINNY Mission* (Newark: University of Delaware Press, 2008), 164–190.

Chapter 16: No Justice for Major Holohan

1 Richard J. H. Johnston, "Brother of Victim Made Long Inquiry," *New York Times*, August 16, 1951, 12.

2 Icardi, 192–194.

3 Details of the Army CID investigations into the disapearance of Major Holohan are in NARA RG 60, Identifier 623168, Box 1.

4 "Italian Lieutenant Solved Killing, Turin Paper Said 18 Months Ago," *New York Times*, August 17, 1951, 5.

5 "Ripescata dal Lago d'Orta la Salma del Maggiore Holohan," *La Stampa*, June 17, 1950, 4. NARA RG 60, Identifier 623168, Box 1.

6 Icardi, 220.

7 "Text of Lo Dolce Confession in Holohan Murder, Signed Aug. 3, 1950," *New York Times*, August 17, 1951, 4.

8 Icardi, 220.

9 "Lo Dolce Disowns His 'Confession'," *New York Times*, August 18, 1951, 4.

10 "Story Suppressed Here, Says Editor," *New York Times*, August 17, 1951, 3.

11 "War Murder of US Major to Help Reds Laid to Aides," *New York Times*, August 16, 1951, 1.

12 "Murder Charges Scorned by Icardi," *New York Times*, August 19, 1951, 4.

13 "Lo Dolce Disowns His 'Confession'."

14 Ibid.

15 "Gen. Donovan Says Victim Had $14,000," *New York Times*, August 17, 1951, 5.

16 "Lo Dolce Disowns His 'Confession'."

17 "Warrants Issued in Holohan Case as Italy Prepares Extradition Plea," *New York Times*, August 28, 1951, 1.

18 "US Arrests Lo Dolce for Italy in '44 Death of OSS Major," *New York Times*, March 29, 1952: 1.

19 Donald R. Klenk and James M. Gabler, "A Collapse of International Extradition: The Lo Dolce Case," *Washington and Lee Law Review, Volume 12, Issue 2*, 1955, 213–222.

20 "Ruling on Lo Dolce Bars Extradition," *New York Times*, August 12, 1952, 1.

21 "Nemici in gabia gli imputati," *La Stampa*, October 20, 1953, 3. "Two at Trial Accuse Maj. Holohan's Aides," *New York Times*, October 20, 1953, 13. "Holohan Suspect Called US Agent," *New York Times*, October 21, 1953, 19.

22 "Nemici in gabia gli imputati."

23 "Il Processo Holohan alle Assise di Novara," *La Stampa*, October 20, 1953, 6.

24 "Udienza Movimentata Stamane al Processo Holohan," *La Stampa*, October 20–21, 1953, 4.

25 "Sfilata di Testi al Processo Holohan," *La Stampa*, October 22, 1953, 6.

26 "Ulitmi Testimoni al Processo Holohan," *La Stampa*, October 23, 1953, 4.

27 "Severa Inquisitoria al Processo Holohan," *La Stampa*, October 29, 1953, 5.

28 "Il Processo Holohan verso l'Epilogo," *La Stampa*, November 6, 1953, 4.

29 "La Difesa al Processo Holohan," *La Stampa*, November 1, 1953, 6.

30 "Sentenza al Processo Holohan," *La Stampa*, November 7, 1953, 6.

31 "Holohan Inquiry Opened in Capital," *New York Times*, December 20, 1951, 19.

32 Michael Stern, *No Innocence Abroad* (New York: Random House, 1952), 310.

33 "Inquiry Accuses Aides to Holohan," *New York Times*, July 26, 1953, 15.

34 *United States v. Icardi. No. 821–55*, United States District Court District of Columbia, April 19, 1956.

35 "House Group Finds Evidence Against 2 in Holohan Slaying," *Washington Post*, July 26, 1953, M2. "Inquiry Accuses Aides to Holohan."

36 "17 from Italy Help New Holohan Study," *New York Times*, August 7, 1955, 24.

37 Evan Thomas, *The Man to See* (New York: Simon & Schuster Inc., 1991), 80–81.

38 Ibid., 82.

39 Edward Bennett Williams, *One Man's Freedom* (New York: Atheneum, 1962), 31–34.

40 Ibid., 43.

41 Ibid., 47–48.

42 Ibid., 46–47.

43 Ibid.

44 "Holohan Slaying Called Red Coup," *New York Times*, April 18, 1956, 16.

45 Williams, 53.

46 Ibid., 54–55.

47 "Icardi and the Law," *New York Times*, April 22, 1956, 19.

48 United States v. Icardi.

49 Thomas, 90.

50 "Vincenzo "Cino" Moscatelli."

51 "A Holohan Witness Believed a Suicide," *New York Times*, June 6, 1965, 15.

52 Francesco Allegra, "Lo 007 della Resistenza," *La Stampa*, November 6, 1991, 37.

Epilogue

1 USAHEC, Donovan Papers.

2 Ibid.

3 Ibid.

4 Ibid.

5 Ibid.

6 Troy Papers, Box 1, Folder 4.

7 Richard Dunlop, *Donovan: America's Master Spy* (New York: Skyhorse Publishing, 2014), 468–469.

8 Ibid.

9 "NSC 10/2," NARA NSC Documents, June 18, 1948.

10 USAHEC, Donovan Papers.

11 Ibid.

12 "Remarks Delivered by CIA Director John Brennan at the OSS Society Awards Dinner," October 26, 2013.

13 Bruce Barcott, "Special Forces," *New York Times.*, May 14, 2009.

14 "Our Agency's Blueprint for the Future," March 6, 2015.

Bibliography

Archive Materials

The following records are at the National Archives and Records Administration (NARA) II, College Park, Maryland:

- Record Group (RG) 226, Records of the Office of Strategic Services 1940–1946
  - Entry 99 OSS History Office: Boxes 33–34 contain activity reports; Boxes 45–46 contain operational reports.
  - Entry 146 OSS War Crimes Investigations: Box 36 contains Case 100, Ginny Mission investigation.
  - Personnel Files, 1942–1945, National Archives Identifier: 1593270.
- Troy Papers: Background Papers for "Donovan and the CIA: A History of the Establishment of the Central Intelligence Agency," ca. 1967—1980.
- Record Group 153, Records of the Office of the Judge Advocate General.
- Entry 143, Boxes 530–531 contain Case 16–116, Anton Dostler's case and trial.
- Record Group 389: Records of the Office of the Provost Marshal General.
- World War II Prisoners of War Data File, 12/7/1941–11/19/1946.

- Record Group 60: General Records of the Department of Justice, 1790–2002.
  - Select Subject Files Relating to Investigations of Alleged Treasonable Utterances by Aldo Icardi (Identifier 623168).
- Record Group 273: Records of the National Security Council.

The following records are in the Manuscript Collection at the United States Army Heritage and Education Center (USAHEC), Ridgeway Hall, Carlisle, Pennsylvania:

- William J. Donovan Papers
- Mathew B. Ridgeway Papers

Books

Adams, Henry Hitch. *Italy at War*. Chicago, IL: Time-Life Books, Inc., 1982.

Bailey, Ronald H. *Partisans and Guerrillas*. Alexandria, VA: Time-Life Books, Inc., 1978.

Bell, Christopher M. *Churchill and Sea Power*. Oxford: Oxford University Press, 2013.

Black, Robert W. *Rangers in World War II*. New York: Presidio Press, 1992.

Boak, David G. *OSS Red Group 2: A Fisherman Goes to War*. Bloomington, IN: AuthorHouse, 2011.

Churchill, Winston S. *London to Ladysmith Via Pretoria*. London: Longman, Green, and Co., 1900.

Corvo, Max. *OSS in Italy, 1942–1945*. New York: Enigma Books, 2005.

Cremieux-Brilhac, Jean-Louis. *La France Libre*. Paris: Editions Gallimard, 2013.

———. *La France Libre, Tome II*. Paris: Gallimard, 2013.

D'Este, Carlo. *Bitter Victory: The Battle for Sicily, 1943*. New York: Harper-Collins, 1988.

———. *World War II in the Mediterranean, 1942–1945*. Chapel Hill: Algonquin Books of Chapel Hill, 1990.

DREX, Bureau Recherche de la Division Recherche et Retour d'Expérience. *La guérilla n'aura pas lieu... la bataille du Vercors 1940–1944*. Cahier de la Recherche Doctrinale. Paris: Ministère de la Défense, 2010.

Dreyfus, Paul. *Vercors, Citadelle de la Liberté*. Grenoble: Arthaud, 1969.

Dunlop, Richard. *Donovan: America's Master Spy*. New York: Skyhorse Publishing, 2014.

Dwyer, John B. *Seaborne Deception: The History of U.S. Navy Beach Jumpers*. New York: Praeger Publishers, 1992.

Foost, M. R. D. *SOE in France*. London: Routledge, 2004.

Freeman, Gregory A. *Red Tails, The Tuskegee Airmen and Operation Halyard*. New York: New American Library, 2011.

———. *The Forgoten 500: The Untold Story of the Men Who Risked All for the Greatest Rescue Mission of World War II*. New York: New American Library, 2007.

Gli Americani e la Guerra di Liberazione d'Italia: Office of Strategic Services (O.S.S.) e la Resistenza. Venice: Instituto Veneziano per la Storia della Resistenza, 1994.

Icardi, Aldo. *American Master Spy*. Pittsburgh, PA: Stalwart Enterprises, Inc., 1954.

Kedward, H. R. *In Search of the Maquis : Rural Resistance in Southern France 1942–1944*. Oxforfd: Oxford University Press, 1993.

Lanfaloni, Antonio. *L'azione dello Stato Maggiore Generale per lo sviluppo del movimento di Liberazione*. Rome: Stato Maggiore del'Esercito Ufficio Storico, 1975.

Langworth, Richard. *Churchill by Himself: The Definitive Collection of Quotations*. New York: Perseus Books Group, 2008.

Lee, Ulysses. *United States Army in World War II: The Employment of Negro Troops*. Washington, DC: U.S. Government Printing Office, 2001.

Lucas, Peter. *The OSS in World War II Albania*. Jefferson, North Carolina: McFarland & Company, Inc., 2007.

Lynch, Tim. *Silent Skies: Gliders at War 1939–1945*. Barnsley, South Yorkshire: Pen & Sword Military, 2008.

Margerich, Agnes Jensen. *Albanian Escape*. Lexington, Kentucky: Univesity Press of Kentucky, 1999.

Mendelsohn, John. *Covert Warfare: Other OSS Teams*. New York: Garlans, 1989.

Miller, Russell. *The Commandos*. Chicago, IL: Time-Life Books, Inc., 1981.

O'Donnell, Patrick K. *Operatives, Spies, and Saboteurs: The Unknown Story of the Men and Women of World War II's OSS*. New York: Free Press, 2004.

Owen, James. *Commando: Winning WW2 Behind Enemy Lines*. London: Little, Brown Book Group, 2013.

Peli, Santo. *Storia della Resistenza in Italia*. Torino: Einaudi, 2006.

Popa, Thomas A. *Po Valley*. Washington, DC: US Army Center of Military History, n.d.

Preziosi, Laurent and Toussaint Griffi. *Première Mission en Corse Occupée avec le Sous-marin Casabianca (Décembre 1942–Mars 1943)*. Paris: Éditions L'Harmattan, 1988.

Ratcliffe, Susan. *Concise Oxford Dictionary of Quotations*. Oxford: Oxford University Press, 2011.

Raiber, Richard. *Anatomy of Perjury: Field Marshal Albert Kesselring, Via Rassella, and the GINNY Mission*. Newark: University of Delaware Press, 2008.

Revelli, Nuto. *La guerra dei poveri*. Rome: Einaudi, 2005.

Roosevelt, Kermit. *War Report of the OSS*. New York: Walker and Company, 1976.

———. *The Overseas Targets: War Report of the OSS, Volume II*. New York: Walker and Company, 1976.

Sebag-Montefiore, Hugh. *Enigma: The Battle for the Code*. New York: John Wiley & Sons, Inc., 2000.

Senger und Etterlin, Frido von. *Neither Fear Nor Hope*. Novato, CA: Presidio Press, 1989.

Shaver, John W. *Office of the Strategic Services: Operational Groups in France during World War II*. Fort Leavenworth, Kansas: US Army Command and General Staff College, 1993.

Steinbeck, John. *Once there was a war*. New York: Penguin Group, 2007.

Stern, Michael. *No Innocence Abroad*. New York: Random House, 1952.

Taviani, Paolo Emilio. *Breve Storia dell'Insurrezione di Genova*. Rome: Terzo Migliaio, 1960.

The Bureau of Ships. *Know your PT Boat*. Washington, DC: Navy Department, 1945.

Thomas, Evan. *The Man to See*. New York: Simon & Schuster Inc., 1991.

Tompkins, Peter. *L'altra Resistenza*. Milano: Saggiatore, 2005.

Vergnon, Gilles. *Le Vercors: histoire et mémoire d'un maquis*. Paris: Les Éditions de l'Atelier, 2002.

Williams, Edward Bennett. *One Man's Freedom*. New York: Atheneum, 1962.

Williamson, Gordon. *German Special Forces of World War II*. Oxford: Osprey Publishing, 2009.

Articles in Newspapers, Magazines, Journals, and Online Sources

The articles from the *New York Times* and the *Washington Post* listed below are available in the ProQuest Historical Newspapers databases at http://search. proquest.com. I accessed the ProQuest databases courtesy of the Fairfax County, Virginia, Public Library.

The articles from the Turin daily *La Stampa* are available at the online historical archive of the newspaper at http://www.archiviolastampa.it.

For all other online resources, I have provided the URL and the date last accessed.

"17 from Italy Help New Holohan Study." *New York Times*. August 7, 1955: 24.

"2641st Special Group." n.d. *The Fifteenth Air Force*. http://www.15thaf. org/2641st_SG/2641st.html (accessed December 17, 2014).

"A Holohan Witness Believed a Suicide." *New York Times*. June 6, 1965: 15.

"Al Processo Holohan." *La Stampa*. November 6, 1953: 4.

"Alfredo Di Dio." n.d. *Associazione Nazionale Partigiani d'Italia*. http://www. anpi.it/donne-e-uomini/alfredo-di-dio (accessed January 19, 2015).

"All War Prisoners Face Nazi Threat." *New York Times*. October 16, 1942: 6.

Allegra, Francesco. "Lo 007 della Resistenza." *La Stampa*. November 6, 1991: 37.

"Andre E. Pecquet Awards and Citations." n.d. *MilitaryTimes Hall of Valor*. http://projects.militarytimes.com/citations-medals-awards/recipient. php?recipientid=22529 (accessed November 3, 2014).

"Anton Ukmar." n.d. *Associazione Nazionale Partigiani d'Italia*. http://www. anpi.it/donne-e-uomini/anton-ukmar (accessed November 5, 2014).

Army Battle Casualties and Non-Death Reports during World War II. June 1, 1953. http://www.ibiblio.org/hyperwar/USA/ref/Casualties/Casualties-Intro. html (accessed May 23, 2014).

"Azioni tedesche contro i civili in Toscana." December 28, 2012. *Regione Toscana*. http://www.regione.toscana.it/en/storiaememoriedel900/fonti/azioni-tedesche-contro-i-civili (accessed October 11, 2014).

"Bar Arrest for Italy." *New York Times*. February 8, 1952: 11.

Belkin, Lisa. "Lucy Monroe Dies; A Celebrated Singer Of National Anthem." October 16, 1987. *New York Times Archives*. http://www.nytimes.

com/1987/10/16/obituaries/lucy-monroe-dies-a-celebrated-sing-er-of-national-anthem.html (accessed September 2, 2014).

"Bids Convention Back Cabinet Appointees." *New York Times.* June 22, 1940: 10.

"Bill Robinson." n.d. *Biography.com.* http://www.biography.com/people/bill-bojangles-robinson-9460594 (accessed September 2, 2014).

Blosser, Charles. "Dostler Dies Before U.S. Firing Squad." *The Stars and Stripes Mediterranean* December 3, 1945: 1.

"Boers Traits and British Traits." *New York Times.* March 6, 1900. http://query.nytimes.com/mem/archive-free/pdf?res=9A0DE4DE1339E733A-25755C0A9659C946197D6CF (accessed September 12, 2014).

Botti, Ettore. "Lo Scempio del Duce nel Giorno della Vergogna." September 20, 2001. *Cinquanta Mila Giorni.* http://cinquantamila.corriere.it/story-TellerArticolo.php?storyId=4db01bec5c48f (accessed November 9, 2014).

"Britain Unshackles Captives, Nazis Talk." *New York Times.* December 12, 1942: 55.

"British Commandos Raid Hitler's Europe." *Life* January 26, 1942: 17–21.

"Brockhall Hall and Manor." July 22, 2008. *Waymarking.*

http://www.waymarking.com/waymarks/WM48PX_Brockhall_Hall_and_Manor_Brockhall_Estate_Northamptonshire_UK (accessed October 23, 2014).

Captain Robert J. Bulkley, Jr. *At Close Quarters: PT Boats in the United States Navy.* Washington, DC: Naval History Division, 1962. http://www.ibiblio.org/hyperwar/USN/CloseQuarters/PT-6.html (accessed June 13, 2014).

"Close Combat Without and With Weapons As Taught At SOE STS 103." n.d. *IndaBook.* http://www.indabook.org/preview/QNLQZZ2u1h5Lufx_RT-5d0xKVxFmUHW5aV9Chx8RcVU,/Close-Combat-Without-and-With-Weapons-As-Taught-At.html?query=Province-of-Manitoba-Map (accessed September 16, 2014).

"Col. Donovan Back, Has Seen 'A Lot'." *New York Times.* March 19, 1941: 9.

"Convention Between the United States of America and Other Powers, Relating to Prisoners of War; July 27, 1929." n.d. *The Avalon Project.* http://avalon.law.yale.edu/20th_century/geneva02.asp (accessed September 16, 2014).

"Cornell University Law Library." n.d. *Donovan Nuremberg Trial Collection.* http://ebooks.library.cornell.edu/n/nur/pdf/nur00701.pdf (accessed September 17, 2014).

Daniell, Raymond. "British Would End Reprisals." *New York Times*. October 18 ,1942: E4.

Darling, Arthur B. "Origins of Central Intelligence." *Studies in Intelligence*, Volume 8, Number 3 (1953).

Darnton, Byron. "Vast Throng Jams the Mall to Cheer Amercan Day Fete." *New York Times*. May 19, 1941: 1.

"Divisione Giustizia e Libertà." n.d. *Associazione Nazionale Partigiani d'Italia Comitato Provinciale di Piacenza*. http://www.partigiani-piacentini.net/divisione-giustizia-liberta/index.jspeldoc?IdC=1524&IdS=1541 (accessed November 6, 2014).

"Domenico Mezzadra ("Americano")." n.d. *Associazione Nazionale Partigiani d'Italia*. http://lombardia.anpi.it/voghera/biografie/mezzadra.htm (accessed November 5, 2014).

Donovan, William J. and Edgar Mowrer. "Germans Said to Spend Vast Sums Abroad to Pave Way for Conquest." *New York Times*. August 23, 1940: 5.

"Drive Begun Here for Polish Relief." *New York Times*. February 26, 1940: 2.

Dulles, Allen W. "William J. Donovan and the National Security." n.d. *CIA Center for the Study of Intelligence*. https://www.cia.gov/library/center-for-the-study-of-intelligence/kent-csi/vol3no3/html/v03i3a07p_0001.htm (accessed June 8, 2014).

"Fausto Cossu." n.d. *Associazione Nazionale Partigiani d'Italia*. http://www.anpi.it/donne-e-uomini/fausto-cossu (accessed November 5, 2014).

"Figures Involved in Murder History." *New York Times*. August 16, 1951: 13.

"Gen. Donovan Says Victim Had $14,000." *New York Times*. August 17, 1951: 5.

"General James Harold Doolittle." n.d. *U.S. Air Force*. http://www.af.mil/AboutUs/Biographies/Display/tabid/225/Article/107225/general-james-harold-doolittle.aspx (accessed December 16, 2014).

"General Joseph T. McNarney." n.d. *US Air Force Website*. http://www.af.mil/AboutUs/Biographies/Display/tabid/225/Article/106132/general-joseph-t-mcnarney.aspx (accessed September 2, 2014).

"General Nathan F. Twining." February 10, 1958. *U.S. Air Force*. http://www.af.mil/AboutUs/Biographies/Display/tabid/225/Article/105367/general-nathan-f-twining.aspx (accessed December 16, 2014).

"God Bless America." n.d. *Library of Congress*. http://www.loc.gov/exhibits/treasures/trm019.html (accessed September 2, 2014).

Hill, Nathan C. "Sowing Dragon's Teeth: OSS Operational Groups of World War II." *Military Review*. July-August 2013: 31–37.

"Histoire de la Grotte de la Luire." n.d. *Grotte de la Luire*. http://grottedelaluire.com/histoire (accessed November 3, 2014).

"History of Cinecittà." n.d. *Rome File*. http://www.romefile.com/culture/cinecitta.php (accessed November 23, 2014).

Hodges, Robert. "African American 92nd Infantry Division Fought in Italy During World War II.". *Historynet.com*. November 6, 2014. http://www.historynet.com/african-american-92nd-infantry-division-fought-in-italy-during-world-war-ii.htm (accessed June 12, 2006).

"Holohan Inquiry Opened in Capital." *New York Times*. December 20, 1951: 19.

"Holohan Slaying Called Red Coup." *New York Times*. April 18, 1956: 16.

"Holohan Suspect Called US Agent." *New York Times*. October 21, 1953: 19.

"Horne." July 11, 2007. *Naval Historical Center*. http://www.history.navy.mil/danfs/h8/horne.htm (accessed September 2, 2014).

"House Group Finds Evidence Against 2 in Holohan Slaying." *Washington Post* July 26, 1953: M2.

"House of Commons Debate, June 18, 1940." n.d. *Hansard 1803–2005*. http://hansard.millbanksystems.com/commons/1940/jun/18/war-situation (accessed July 16, 2014).

"House of Commons Debate, June 4, 1940." n.d. *Hansard 1803–2005*. http://hansard.millbanksystems.com/commons/1940/jun/04/war-situation#S5CV0361P0_19400604_HOC_231 (accessed July 16, 2014).

"House of Commons Debate, May 13, 1940." n.d. *Hansard 1803–2005*. http://hansard.millbanksystems.com/commons/1940/may/13/his-majestys-government-1 (accessed July 16, 2014).

Houseman, John. "John Houseman's Diary - Mission Eucalyptus." n.d. *WW2 People's War*. http://www.bbc.co.uk/history/ww2peopleswar/categories/c55673 (accessed October 31, 2014).

"Icardi and the Law." *New York Times*. April 22, 1956: 19.

"Il Drama della Chrysler sul Lago d'Orta." *La Stampa*. March 30, 1950: 4.

Il Piave. October 23, 2010. http://www.ilpiave.it/modules.php?name=News&file=article&sid=7528 (accessed May 23, 2014).

"Il Processo Holohan alle Assise di Novara." *La Stampa*. October 20, 1953: 6.

"Il Processo Holohan verso l'Epilogo." *La Stampa*. November 6, 1953: 4.

"Inquiry Accuses Aides to Holohan." *New York Times*. July 26, 1953: 15.

"Italian Lieutenant Solved Killing, Turin Paper Said 18 Months Ago." *New York Times*. August 17, 1951: 5.

"Italo Pietra ("Edoardo")." n.d. *Associazione Nazionale Partigiani d'Italia di Voghera*. http://lombardia.anpi.it/voghera/biografie/pietra.htm (accessed November 8, 2014).

"Jean-Pierre Levy (Movement "Franc-Tireur")." n.d. *Fondation de la Résistance*. http://www.fondationresistance.org/pages/rech_doc/?p=portraits&iIdPortrait=2 (accessed October 26, 2014).

Jibilian, Arthur. "Rescuer In Yugoslavia." April 2008. *America in WWII*. http://www.americainwwii.com/articles/rescuer-in-yugoslavia (accessed December 21, 2014).

Johnson, Ellsworth. "One Small Part." n.d. *Office of Strategic Services Operational Groups*. http://www.ossog.org/france/patrick.html (accessed October 24, 2014).

Johnston, Richard J. H. "Brother of Victim Made Long Inquiry." *New York Times*. August 16, 1951: 12.

Juillet, Richard. "La "Saint-Barthélemy" grenobloise." October 2013. *Isere Magazine*. http://www.isere-magazine.fr/culture/histoire/Pages/139-La-St-Barthelemy-iseroise/la-saint-barthelemy-grenobloise.aspx (accessed October 27, 2014).

Kelly, Richard M. "The Halyard Mission." *Blue Book Magazine*. August 1946: 52–62.

King, Dr. Michael J. "Rangers: Selected Combat Operations in World War II." June 1985. *US Army Combined Arms Center*. http://usacac.army.mil/cac2/cgsc/carl/download/csipubs/king.pdf (accessed September 14, 2014).

Klenk, Donald R. and James M. Gabler. "A Collapse of International Extradition: The Lo Dolce Case." *Washington and Lee Law Review, Volume 12, Issue 2* (1955): 213–222. http://scholarlycommons.law.wlu.edu/wlulr/vol12/iss2/4 (accessed January 4, 2015).

Krock, Arthur. "The War in Pictures." *New York Times*. October 8, 1941: 4.

"La Difesa al Processo Holohan." *La Stampa*. November 1, 1953: 6.

"La Milice française." n.d. *70e Anniversaire de la Liberation de France*. http://www.le70e.fr/en/repression/milice-francaise (accessed October 27, 2014).

"La Missione Americana Chrysler sul Lago d'Orta." *La Stampa*. March 29, 1950: 4.

"La Repubblica della Val d'Ossola." n.d. *Associazione Nazionale Partigiani d'Italia*. http://www.anpi.it/la-repubblica-della-val-dossola (accessed December 10, 2014).

"La Sicherheits." n.d. *Associazione Nazionale Partigiani d'Italia di Voghera*. http://lombardia.anpi.it/voghera/savini2/sicherheits.htm (accessed November 9, 2014).

"Lindbergh Joins in Wheeler Plea to U.S. to Shun War." *New York Times*. May 24, 1941: 1.

"Lo Dolce Disowns His 'Confession'." *New York Times*. August 18, 1951: 4.

"Lofoten Islands Raid." n.d. *Combined Operations Command*. http://www.combinedops.com/Lofoten_Islands_Raid.htm (accessed September 12, 2014).

"London Threatens to Tie Up Captives." *New York Times*. October 9, 1942: 1.

MacDonald, James. "Satellite States Alarmed." *New York Times*. August 8, 1943: E5.

Margry, Karel. "The Dostler Case." *After the Battle, Number 94* 1996: 1–19.

Materazzi, Albert. "Italian-American OGs Attend Memorial Ceremony in Ameglia," *OSS Society Newspaper*, Summer 2004, 10.

Mathews, Phil. "W. E. Fairbairn - The Legendary Instructor." 2007. *CQB Services*. http://www.cqbservices.com/?page_id=59 (accessed September 17, 2014).

Meegan, Jean. "Prince Serge Obolensky Wants to Be Called 'Colonel' Now." *The Palm Beach Post* October 25, 1945: 5.

Moorhead, Eleony. "The OSS and Operation TORCH: The Beginning of the Beginning." *Tempus: The Harvard College History Review, Vol. X, Issue 1, Summer 2009* (2009).

Morrow, Kevin. "Rescue Behind Enemy Lines." March 20, 2008. *HistoryNet*. http://www.historynet.com/rescue-behind-enemy-lines.htm (accessed December 25, 2014).

"Murder Charges Scorned by Icardi." *New York Times*. August 19, 1951: 4.

Nasini, Claudia. "The OSS in the Italian Resistance: A Post Cold War Interpretation." *Eurostudium* (2012): 46–82.

National Museum of the Pacific War, PT Boat Virtual Tour. n.d. http://www.pacificwarmuseum.org/your-visit/pt-boat-virtual-tour (accessed June 14, 2014).

NavSource Online: Motor Torpedo Boat Photo Archive, PT-203. n.d. http://www.navsource.org/archives/12/05203.htm (accessed June 13, 2014).

"Nazis Threaten to Shackle Britons As Reply to Alleged Dieppe Order." *New York Times*. September 3, 1942: 1.

"Nemici in gabia gli imputati." *La Stampa*. October 20, 1953: 3.

"Obolensky Headed US Chutists Whose Leap Sped Sardinia's Fall." *New York Times*. October 8, 1943: 4.

Oliver, Thomas K. "Unintended Visit to Yugoslavia." n.d. *Black Hills Veterans Writing Group*. http://www.battlestory.org/index.php?p=1_86_THOMAS-K-OLIVER-USAAF- (accessed December 20, 2014).

"Operation Archery." n.d. *Combined Operations Command*. http://www.combinedops.com/vaagso.htm (accessed September 13, 2014).

"OSS 'Underground Railway' Plan Saved U.S. Fliers in Axis Areas." *New York Times*. September 17, 1945: 5.

Oswald, John. "An Interrogator's Life." October 27, 2004. *WW2 People's War*. http://www.bbc.co.uk/history/ww2peopleswar/stories/61/a3189161. shtml (accessed November 23, 2014).

Philip, P. J. "Canada Chains 1,376 Nazis In Reprisal Against Berlin." *New York Times*. October 11, 1942: 1.

Pinck, Charles. "General Donovan's Glorious Amateurs." *The OSS Society Journal* Fall 2012: 14–15.

"POW camp Stalag VII A." October 10, 2013. *Moosburg Online*. http://www. moosburg.org/info/stalag/indeng.html (accessed January 15, 2015).

Raja, Roberto. "I giorni della liberazione." n.d. *Cinquanta Mila Giorni*. http:// cinquantamila.corriere.it/storyTellerThread.php?threadId=25aprile (accessed November 9, 2014).

"Rangers Are Impressed by British And Canadians on Dieppe Foray." *New York Times*. August 22, 1942.

"Ripescata dal Lago d'Orta la Salma del Maggiore Holohan." *La Stampa*. June 17, 1950: 4.

Roosevelt, Franklin D. "Executive Order Designating a Coordinator of Intelligence." The White House, July 11, 1941.

———. "Fireside Chat 25: On the Fall of Mussolini." July 28, 1943. *University of Virginia Miller Center*. http://millercenter.org/president/speeches/ speech-3331 (accessed September 24, 2014).

Rossi, Daniele. "Resistenza: L'Eccidio di Mommio." December 27, 2013. *Informati*. http://garfagnanacontr.blogspot.com/2013/12/resistenza-l-eccidio-di-mommio.html (accessed November 10, 2014).

"Ruling on Lo Dolce Bars Extradition." *New York Times*. August 12, 1952: 1.

Schmidt, Doug. "New research suggests World War II raid on Dieppe may have been attempt to find Nazi Enigma machine." August 17, 2012.

Canada.com. http://o.canada.com/news/new-research-suggests-world-war-ii-raid-on-dieppe-may-have-been-attempt-to-find-nazi-enigma-machine (accessed September 15, 2014).

"Sentenza al Processo Holohan." *La Stampa.* November 7, 1953: 6.

"Service in a Commando." n.d. *Commando Veterans Association.* http://www.commandoveterans.org/ServiceinaCommando (accessed September 14, 2014).

"Severa Inquisitoria al Processo Holohan." *La Stampa.* October 29, 1953: 5.

"Sfilata di Testi al Processo Holohan." *La Stampa.* October 22, 1953: 6.

"Story Suppressed Here, Says Editor." *New York Times.* August 17, 1951: 3.

"Text of Lo Dolce Confession in Holohan Murder, Signed Aug. 3, 1950." *New York Times.* August 17, 1951: 4.

"The Fifteenth Air Force." n.d. *The Fifteenth Air Force.* http://www.15thaf.org/index.htm (accessed December 17, 2014).

"The Liberation of Corsica." n.d. *Chemins de Memoire.* http://www.chemins-dememoire.gouv.fr/en/liberation-corsica-9-september-4-october-1943 (accessed October 5, 2014).

"The Lofoten Raid." n.d. *Lofoten War Museum.* http://lofotenkrigmus.no/e_lofotraid.htm (accessed September 12, 2014).

Thompson, Julian. "The Dieppe Raid." n.d. *BBC History.* http://www.bbc.co.uk/history/worldwars/wwtwo/dieppe_raid_01.shtml (accessed September 15, 2014).

Tompkins, Peter. "The OSS and Italian Partisans in World War II." April 14, 2007. *Center for the Study of Intelligence.* https://www.cia.gov/library/center-for-the-study-of-intelligence/csi-publications/csi-studies/studies/spring98/OSS.html (accessed November 6, 2014).

"Two at Trial Accuse Maj. Holohan's Aides." *New York Times.* October 20, 1953: 13.

"Udienza Movimentata Stamane al Processo Holohan." *La Stampa.* October 20, 1953: 4.

"Ulitmi Testimoni al Processo Holohan." *La Stampa.* October 23, 1953: 4.

United States Airforce. *General Joseph T. McNarney.* n.d. http://www.af.mil/AboutUs/Biographies/Display/tabid/225/Article/106132/general-joseph-t-mcnarney.aspx (accessed May 23, 2014).

United States Department of State, Office of the Historian. *American Isolationism in the 1930s.* n.d. https://history.state.gov/milestones/1937–1945/american-isolationism (accessed July 11, 2014).

United States v. Icardi. No. 821–55. United States District Court District of Columbia. April 19 1956. https://www.courtlistener.com/opinion/2349124/united-states-v-icardi (accessed January 9, 2015).

"US Arrests Lo Dolce for Italy in '44 Death of OSS Major." *New York Times.* March 29, 1952: 1.

Valentine, Elizabeth R. "Fact-Finder and Fighing Man." *New York Times.* May 4, 1941: SM8.

"Vincenzo 'Cino' Moscatelli." n.d. *Associazione Nazionale Partigiani d'Italia.* http://www.anpi.it/donne-e-uomini/vincenzo-cino-moscatelli (accessed January 21, 2015).

"Walter Audisio." n.d. *Associazione Nazionale Partigiani d'Italia.* http://www.anpi.it/donne-e-uomini/walter-audisio (accessed November 9, 2014).

"War Murder of US Major to Help Reds Laid to Aides." *New York Times.* August 16, 1951: 1.

"Warrants Issued in Holohan Case as Italy Prepares Extradition Plea." *New York Times.* August 28, 1951: 1.

Weaver, Warren, Jr. "Confession Fight Lost by Lo Dolce." *New York Times.* April 19, 1952: 5.

———. "Lo Dolce Decision Put Off by Judge." *New York Times.* July 2, 1952: 5.

Index